VMware vSAN 8.0 U1
Express Storage Architecture
Deep Dive

VMware vSAN 8.0 Update 1, Express Storage Architecture, Deep Dive

Copyright © 2023 by Cormac Hogan, Duncan Epping, and Pete Koehler.

International Standard Book Number: 9798388871923

Cover design by Aaron Epping (AaronEpping.nl).

Version: 1.0.3

About the authors

Cormac Hogan is a Chief Technologist in the Office of the CTO in the Cloud Infrastructure Business Group at VMware, focusing predominantly on Kubernetes platforms running on vSphere. Cormac has previously held roles in VMware's Technical Marketing, Integration Engineering and Support organizations. Cormac is the owner of CormacHogan.com, a blog site dedicated to storage, virtualization and container orchestration. He can be followed on Twitter @CormacJHogan.

Duncan Epping is a Chief Technologist working for VMware in the Office of CTO of the Cloud Infrastructure Business Group. Duncan is responsible for ensuring VMware's future innovations align with essential customer needs, translating customer problems to opportunities and functioning as the global lead evangelist for Cloud Infrastructure. Duncan is the owner of VMware Virtualization blog Yellow-Bricks.com, the host of the Unexplored Territory Podcast (UnexploredTerritory.tech), and the author of the "vSphere Clustering Deep Dive" book series. He can be followed on Twitter @DuncanYB.

Pete Koehler is a Staff Technical Marketing Architect working for VMware in the Cloud Infrastructure Business Group at VMware. With a primary focus on vSAN, much of Pete's experience in infrastructure design and optimization came from hands-on experience as a customer, consultant and later as an engineer for a VMware reseller and VMware partner. You can find all of Pete's latest content related to vSAN out on https://core.vmware.com/users/pete-koehler. He can be followed on Twitter @vmpete.

Acknowledgements

We would like to thank our VMware Management team for supporting us on this project. A special thanks goes out to our technical reviewer Jitender Rohilla, thanks for keeping us honest and for contributing to this book. We also would like to thank everyone for supporting us by buying this book, attending our sessions at VMUGs and VMware Explore, reading our blogs, and listening to our podcasts. We truly appreciate it.

Index

Preface

Welcome to the latest in our series of vSAN Deep Dive books. In this book, the focus is solely on the new vSAN Express Storage Architecture (ESA). The authors debated long and hard on how to approach this book. The crux of the debate was around whether or not we should continue to include the traditional vSAN architecture, now officially referred to as the Original Storage Architecture (OSA). Considering how many caveats and breakouts we would have to make to explain if something applies to the ESA, the OSA or both, we decided to forego the inclusion of references to the vSAN OSA. The deciding factor was based on the fact that the contents of the previous vSAN Deep Dive book, which was written for version 7.0U3, did not change significantly in the 8.0 release. Thus, we made an "executive decision" to focus on the Express Storage Architecture. We hope the title of the book reflects that. However, as you might expect, there are regular comparisons between ESA and OSA throughout the book, especially when there is a significant change in behavior.

Now, you might be wondering if the vSAN Express Storage Architecture is going to provide a completely different User Experience (UX). This is especially relevant if you are familiar with the Original Storage Architecture (OSA) and have been operating vSAN infrastructure for many years. The answer is a resounding NO. One of the guiding principles in the vSAN ESA design was to keep a similar if not identical user experience. Therefore, you will notice that many of the workflows that you already know from vSAN OSA will remain the same in vSAN ESA. But, of course, there are some significant changes to allow the vSAN ESA leverage the performance capabilities of the latest storage and networking technologies. Many of these enhancements to vSAN ESA are not visible via the User Interface (UI) but will be noticeable when workloads are deployed. The authors will be spending a significant amount of time explaining how the new vSAN ESA has been architected to benefit from these new device capabilities, while at the same time ensuring that these devices are used optimally to maximize durability and lifespan.

With that said, many of the traditional storage challenges outlined in previous vSAN Deep Dive books continue to be relevant today. Storage continues to be a pain point in many organizations. The reasons are still varied, ranging from the operational effort, or complexity, to performance problems, or even availability constraints. The software-defined datacenter, software-defined networking, and software-defined storage via vSAN all helped to alleviate many of these challenges for our customers. In this book, you will see how the next iteration of vSAN architecture continues to help customers to overcome the aforementioned storage challenges while leveraging some of the latest and greatest hardware functionality.

You, the reader

This book is targeted at IT professionals who are involved in the care and feeding of a VMware vSphere environment. Ideally, you have been working with VMware vSphere for some time and perhaps you have attended an authorized course in vSphere, such as the "Install, Configure, and Manage" class. This book is not a starters guide, it is a deep dive. However, there should be enough information in the book for administrators and architects of all levels.

Dedication

"The average person can only keep 7 (plus or minus 2)
items in their working memory"

"Miller's Law"

"In a matter of time, you're out in the open
You shall prove yourself in the bitter end
But for now, brace yourself"

"Hold on" by Gojira

Foreword

Welcome to the world of VMware vSAN and hyperconverged infrastructure (HCI)! Since the initial release of vSAN in 2014, we have made remarkable progress, and I am thrilled to introduce the next evolution in vSAN architecture. Our pioneering software-based storage solution has transformed data center modernization, enabling a new category of deploying infrastructure called HCI. Traditional purpose-built hardware and specialized appliances were no longer economically viable options for many of our customers, leading to the emergence of software-defined services built on standard x86 servers, significantly reducing operational overhead and cost of ownership.

Today, VMware HCI is the deployment model of choice for over 30,000 customers, hosting exabytes of data. Over the years, vSAN has continued to deliver new innovations, such as HCI Mesh, vSAN File Services, Data Persistence platform, and Cloud Native Storage control plane. Now, we stand at the precipice of yet another leap in the evolution of vSAN. With the emergence of NVMe-based flash devices and newer solid-state devices such as QLC flash, we saw this shift as an inflection point for the vSAN architecture, providing the opportunity to evolve the vSAN architecture with these new devices as the primary design point.

This new architecture, called vSAN Express Storage Architecture (vSAN ESA), offers a significant leap in terms of performance, scale, and enterprise features, providing the highest performance and flexibility required by IT admins and developers. With a brand new log-structured file system, including built-in snapshots, vSAN ESA provides the level of resiliency needed for the most demanding workloads. We believe that vSAN ESA can be a fundamental building block for your own multi-cloud infrastructure.

In this book, Cormac, Duncan, and Pete provide valuable insights and guidance on how to leverage these capabilities to get the most out of vSAN ESA. Their expertise will help you navigate this ever-evolving technology landscape, unlocking the full potential of vSAN for your organization. We hope you find this book informative and insightful, and we look forward to continuing to innovate and serve our customers in the years to come.

Vijay Ramachandran
VP, Product Leader, Storage
VMware
April 2023

01

Introduction to VMware vSAN

This chapter introduces you to the world of the software-defined datacenter, but with a focus on the storage aspect. The chapter covers the premise of the software-defined datacenter and then delves deeper to cover the concept of software-defined storage and associated solutions such as hyperconverged infrastructure (HCI).

Software-Defined Datacenter

Over 10 years ago, at VMware's annual conferencing event which was then called VMworld 2012, VMware's vision for the software-defined datacenter (SDDC) was introduced. The SDDC is VMware's architecture for the public and private clouds where all pillars of the datacenter—computing, storage, and networking (and the associated services)—are virtualized. Virtualizing datacenter components enables the IT team to be more flexible. If you lower the operational complexity and cost while increasing availability and agility, you will lower the time to market for new services.

To achieve all of that, virtualization of components by itself is not sufficient. The objective is to virtualization the complete infrastructure platform, end-to-end. The platform must be capable of being installed and configured in a fully automated fashion. More importantly, the platform should enable you to manage and monitor your infrastructure in a smart and less operationally intense manner. That is what the SDDC is all about! Raghu Raghuram (Chief Executive Officer, VMware) captured it in a single sentence: The essence of the software-defined datacenter is "abstract, pool, and automate."

Abstraction, pooling, and automation are all achieved by introducing an additional layer on top of the physical resources. This layer is usually referred to as a virtualization layer. Everyone reading this book should be familiar with the leading product for compute virtualization, VMware vSphere. By now, most people are probably also familiar with network virtualization, sometimes referred to as software-defined network (SDN) solutions. VMware offers a solution named NSX to virtualize networking and security functionality. NSX does for networking what vSphere does for compute. These layers do not just virtualize the physical resources but also allow you to abstract resources, pool them, and provide you with an API that enables you to automate all operational aspects.

Automation is not just about scripting, however. A significant part of the automation of virtual machine (VM) provisioning is achieved through policy-based management. Predefined policies allow you to provision VMs in a quick, easy, consistent, and repeatable manner. The resource characteristics specified on a resource pool or a vApp container exemplify a compute policy. These characteristics enable you to quantify resource policies for compute in terms of reservation, limit, and priority. Network policies can range from security and firewall settings to quality of service (QoS). Storage policies enable you to specify availability, performance, and recoverability characteristics.

This book examines the storage component of VMware's SDDC. More specifically, the book covers how a product called VMware vSAN (vSAN), fits into this vision. It should be noted, however, that with the release of vSAN version 8.0, there are now two distinct architectures for vSAN. There is the Original Storage Architecture (OSA) which has been the architecture used since the very first vSAN release. And then there is the newer architecture introduced with version 8.0 which is referred to as the Express Storage Architecture (ESA). This book will focus on the latter and introduce you to all aspects of vSAN ESA and how it utilizes newer hardware components with greater performance capabilities. Just like previous vSAN Deep Dive books, you will learn how vSAN ESA has been implemented and integrated within the vSphere platform. This book will teach you how to leverage its capabilities and will expand on the lower-level implementation details. Before going further, though, it is important to have a general understanding of where vSAN fits into the bigger software-defined storage picture.

Software-Defined Storage

Software-defined storage (SDS) is a term that has been used, and abused, by many vendors. Because software-defined storage is currently defined in so many different ways, consider the following quote from VMware:

> **"Software-Defined Storage is the automation and pooling of storage through a software control plane, and the ability to provide storage from industry-standard servers. This offers a significant simplification to the way storage is provisioned and managed, and also paves the way for storage on industry-standard servers at a fraction of the cost."**

A software-defined storage product is a solution that abstracts the hardware and allows you to easily pool all resources and provide them to the consumer using a user-friendly user interface (UI) and application programming interface (API). A software-defined storage solution allows you to both scale up and scale out, without increasing the operational effort.

Many industry experts feel that software-defined storage is about moving functionality from the traditional storage devices to the host. This trend was started by virtualized versions of storage solutions such as HP's StoreVirtual VSA, often referred to as virtual storage appliances. These evolved into solutions that were built to run on many different hardware platforms. An example of such a solution is Nexenta. These solutions were the start of a new era.

Hyperconverged/Server SAN Solutions

Over the past decade there have been many debates around what hyperconverged is versus a Server SAN solution. In our opinion, the big difference between these two is the level of integration with the platform it is running on, as well as the delivery model. When it comes to the delivery model there are two distinct flavors:

- Appliance based
- Software only

An appliance-based solution is one where the hardware (x86 server) and the software are sold and delivered as a single bundle. The appliance-based solutions often come preinstalled with a hypervisor and usually requires little to no effort to configure. A key factor is also a deep integration with the platform it sits on (or in) typically. This integration can range from providing storage APIs, to providing extensive data services, to being a solution that is fully embedded in the hypervisor.

In all of these cases, local storage devices across multiple hypervisors are aggregated into a large, shared pool by leveraging a virtual storage appliance or a kernel-based storage stack. In the early days of appliance-based solutions, a typical "hyperconverged appliance" would have been a 2U form factor with four hosts. However, hyper-convergence is not about a form factor in our opinion, and most vendors have moved on from this concept. Yes, some still offer this form factor, but they offer it alongside various other form factors like 1U, 2U, 1U two hosts, 2U two hosts, and even blade and composable infrastructure solutions.

But it is not about the form factor of the solution. It is about combining different components into a single solution. This solution needs to be easy to install, configure, manage, and monitor.

One might ask, "If these are generic x86 servers with hypervisors installed and a virtual storage appliance or a kernel-based storage stack, what are the benefits over a traditional storage system?" The benefits of a hyperconverged platform can be outlined as follows:

- Time to market is short. Typically, less than 1 hour to install and configure
- Ease of management and level of integration
- Ability to scale out and scale up, both capacity and performance
- Lower total costs of acquisition compared to traditional environments
- Lower upfront investment required. Start small and grow as needed

As mentioned, many of these solutions are sold as a single stock keeping unit (SKU), and typically a single point of contact for support is provided. This can make support discussions much easier.

It is worth noting that many of these appliance-based solutions are tied to hardware and specific configurations. The hardware used by (appliance-based) hyperconverged vendors is often not the same as the preferred hardware supplier you may already have as a customer. This can lead to operational challenges when it comes to updating/patching or even cabling and racking. In addition, a trust issue exists. Some people swear by server vendor X and would never want to touch any other brand, whereas others won't come close to server vendor X. Fortunately, most hyperconverged vendors these days offer the ability to buy their solution through different server hardware vendors. If that does not provide sufficient flexibility, then this is where the software-based storage solutions come into play.

Software-only storage solutions come in two flavors. The most common solution today amongst HCI vendors is the virtual storage appliance (VSA). VSA solutions are deployed as a virtual machine / virtual appliance on top of a hypervisor, which is itself installed on physical hardware. VSAs allow you to pool underlying physical resources into a shared storage device. The advantage of software-only solutions is that you can typically leverage existing hardware if it is on the appropriate hardware compatibility list (HCL). In most cases, the HCL is comparable to what the underlying hypervisor supports, except for key components like disk controllers and flash devices.

vSAN is also a software-only solution, but vSAN differs significantly from a VSA. vSAN sits in a different layer and is not an appliance-based solution. On top of that, vSAN is typically combined with hardware from a range of different vendors. Hence, VMware refers to vSAN as a hyperconverged infrastructure solution.

Introducing VMware vSAN

VMware's strategy for software-defined storage is to focus on a set of VMware initiatives related to local storage, shared storage, and storage/data services. In essence, VMware wants to make vSphere a platform for storage services.

Historically, storage was configured and deployed at the start of a project and was not changed during its life cycle. If there was a need to change some characteristics or features of a LUN or volume that were being leveraged by VMs, in many cases the original LUN or volume was deleted and a new volume with the required features or characteristics was created. This was a very intrusive, risky, and time-consuming operation due to the requirement to migrate workloads between LUNs or volumes, which may have taken weeks to coordinate.

This is one of the most significant advantages of software defined storage. With software-defined storage, VM storage requirements can be dynamically instantiated. There is no need to repurpose LUNs or volumes. It is true to say that virtual machine workloads and requirements can change over time. Now the underlying storage can be adapted to the workload at any time. vSAN aims to provide storage services and service-level agreement (SLA) automation through a software layer on the hosts that integrates with, abstracts, and pools the underlying hardware.

A key factor for software-defined storage is, in our opinion, storage policy-based management (SPBM). SPBM is a critical component of how VMware is implementing software-defined storage.

Using SPBM and vSphere APIs, the underlying storage technology surfaces an abstracted pool of storage capacity with various capabilities. This pool of storage is presented to vSphere administrators as a datastore that may be used for VM provisioning. The capabilities that are surfaced up to the vSphere administrator can relate to performance, availability, or storage services such as thin provisioning, compression, replication, and more. A vSphere administrator can then create a VM storage policy using a subset of the capabilities that are required by the application running in the VM. At VM provisioning time, the vSphere administrator selects a VM storage policy. SPBM then ensures that the VM is always instantiated on the appropriate underlying storage, based on the requirements placed in the VM storage policy. It also ensures that the VM is provisioned with the right amount of resources and the required services from the abstracted pool of storage resources.

Should the VM's workload, availability requirement, or I/O pattern change over time, it is simply a matter of applying a new VM storage policy that meets the new requirements. This new policy includes the requirements and characteristics that reflect the changed workload for that specific VM, or even a specific virtual disk of the VM. The new policy is seamlessly applied without any manual intervention with the underlying storage system from the administrator. This is in sharp contrast to many legacy storage systems, where a manual migration of VMs or virtual disks to a different datastore may be required. vSAN has been developed to seamlessly integrate with vSphere and the SPBM functionality it offers.

What is vSAN?

vSAN is a storage solution from VMware, released as a beta in 2013, made generally available to the public in March 2014, and reached version 8.0U1 in April of 2023. vSAN is fully integrated with vSphere. It is an object-based storage system that aims to simplify VM storage placement decisions for vSphere administrators by leveraging storage policy-based management. It fully supports, and is integrated with, core vSphere features such as vSphere High Availability (HA), vSphere Distributed Resource Scheduler (DRS), and vMotion. vSAN and vSphere go hand in hand as illustrated next.

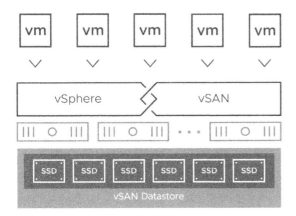

Figure 1: Simple overview of vSAN Cluster

vSAN's goal is to provide both resilience and scale-out storage functionality. It can also be thought of in the context of QoS in so far as VM storage policies can be created that define the level of performance and availability required on a per-VM, or even virtual disk, basis.

vSAN is a software-based distributed storage solution that is built directly into the hypervisor. As mentioned, vSAN is not a virtual appliance like many of the other solutions out there. vSAN can best be thought of as a kernel-based solution that is included with the hypervisor. Technically, however, this is not completely accurate because components critical for performance and responsiveness such as the data path and clustering are in the kernel, while other components that collectively can be considered part of the "control plane" are implemented as native user-space agents. Nevertheless, with vSAN, there is no need to install anything other than the software you are already familiar with: VMware vSphere.

vSAN is about simplicity, and when we say simplicity, we do mean simplicity. Want to try out vSAN? Within a few easy steps, you can have your environment up and running. Of course, one of the decisions that administrators need to make today is whether they wish to implement vSAN Original Storage Architecture (OSA) or vSAN Express Storage Architecture (ESA). Various recommendations and requirements to optimize your experience will be discussed in further detail in chapter 2.

Figure 2: Enabling vSAN

Now that you know it is easy to use and simple to configure, what are the benefits of a solution like vSAN? What are the key selling points?

- **Software-defined:** Use industry-standard hardware
- **Flexible:** Scale as needed and when needed, both scale-up and scale-out
- **Simple:** Easy to configure, manage and operate
- **Automated:** Per-VM or per-disk policy-based management
- **Hyperconverged:** Repeatable building-block

That sounds compelling, doesn't it? Where does vSAN fit you may ask, what are the use cases and are there situations where it doesn't fit today? Today the use cases are as follows:

- **Business critical apps:** Stable storage platform with all data services required to run business critical workloads, whether that is Microsoft Exchange, SQL, Oracle etc.
- **Virtual desktops:** Scale-out model using predictive and repeatable infrastructure blocks lowers costs and simplifies operations.
- **Test and dev:** Avoid acquisition of expensive storage (lowers *total cost of ownership* [TCO]), fast time to provision.
- **Cloud-Native Applications:** Provides the storage infrastructure needed for running your cloud-native apps and persisting your associated data.
- **Management or DMZ infrastructure:** Fully isolated resulting in increased security and no dependencies on the resources it is potentially managing.
- **Disaster recovery target:** Inexpensive disaster recovery solution, enabled through a feature like vSphere replication that allows you to replicate to any storage platform.
- **Remote office/branch office (ROBO):** With the ability to start with as little as two hosts, centrally managed, vSAN is the ideal fit for ROBO environments.
- **Stretched cluster:** Providing very high availability across remote sites for a wide range of potential workloads.

Now that you know what vSAN is and that it is ready for any type of workload, let's have a brief look at what was introduced in terms of functionality with each release.

- **vSAN 1.0: March 2014**
  Initial release
- **vSAN 6.0: March 2015**
  All-flash configurations
  64 host cluster scalability
  2x performance increase for hybrid configurations
  New snapshot mechanism
  Enhanced cloning mechanism
  Fault domain/rack awareness
- **vSAN 6.1: September 2015**
  Stretched clustering across a max of 5 ms RTT (milliseconds)
  2-node vSAN for remote office, branch office (ROBO) solutions
  vRealize Operations management pack
  vSphere replication—5 minutes RPO

Health monitoring
- **vSAN 6.2: March 2016**
RAID 5 and 6 over the network (erasure coding)
Space efficiency (deduplication and compression)
QoS–IOPS limits
Software checksums
IPv6 support
Performance monitoring
- **vSAN 6.5: November 2016**
vSAN iSCSI Service
vSAN 2-node Direct Connect
512e device support
Cloud-Native Application support
- **vSAN 6.6: April 2017**
Local Protection for Stretched Clusters
Removal of Multicast
ESXi Host Client (HTML-5) management and monitoring functionality
Enhanced rebalancing, repairs, and resyncs
Resync throttling
Maintenance Mode Pre-Check
Stretched Cluster Witness Replacement UI
vSAN Support Insight
vSAN Easy Install
vSAN Config Assist / Firmware Update
Enhanced Performance and Health Monitoring
- **vSAN 6.6.1: November 2017**
Update Manager Integration
Performance Diagnostics added to Cloud Analytics
Storage Device Serviceability
New Licensing for ROBO and VDI
- **vSAN 6.7: April 2018**
HTML-5 User Interface support
Native vRealize Operations dashboards in the HTML-5 client
Support for Microsoft WSFC using vSAN iSCSI
Fast Network Failovers
Optimization: Adaptive Resync
Optimization: Witness Traffic Separation for Stretched Clusters
Optimization: Preferred Site Override for Stretched Clusters
Optimization: Efficient Resync for Stretched Clusters
Optimization: Enhanced Diagnostic Partition
Optimization: Efficient Decommissioning
Optimization: Efficient and consistent storage policies
4K Native Device Support
FIPS 140-2 Level 1 validation

- **vSAN 6.7 U1: October 2018**
  Trim/Unmap
  Cluster Quickstart Wizard
  Mixed MTU Support
  Historical Capacity Reporting
  Additional vR Ops Dashboards
  Enhanced support experience
  Secondary FTT for Racks
- **vSAN 6.7 U3: August 2019**
  Cloud-Native Storage
  Native SCSI-3 PGR for Windows Server Failover Cluster (WSFC) support
  Improved Capacity Usage views (including block container volumes)
  Improved Resync insights – ability to see queued but not yet active resyncs
  Maintenance Mode/Data Migration pre-checks
  Online iSCSI LUN Resize
  Improved destage performance with LSOM enhancements
  Parallel resync operations
  vsantop command line tool for performance monitoring
- **vSAN 7.0: April 2020**
  Integrated Native File Services (NFS File Shares)
  Read-Write-Many Persistent Volumes via CSI-CNS and vSAN 7
  vSAN Memory performance metric now displayed
  Shared disks with multi-writer flag no longer need to be Easy Zero Thick on vSAN 7
  Support for larger 1PB Logical capacity when deduplication and compression enabled
  Objects immediately repaired when Witness Appliance replaced
  NVMe hot-plug support
- **vSAN 7.0 U1: October 2020**
  vSAN File Services now supports the SMB protocol
  vSAN File Services now supports Kerberos and Active Directory
  vSAN File Services Scale Increase from 8 to 32
  HCI Mesh introduced for mounting remote vSAN datastore
  A new Compression Only Data Service
  vSAN "Shared" Witness Appliance
  vSAN Data Persistence platform for cloud-native applications in vSphere with Tanzu
  Increased usable capacity with new capacity management features
- **vSAN 7.0 U2: March 2021**
  HCI Mesh now allows remote mounting of vSAN datastore from non-vSAN clusters
  HCI Mesh, vSAN datastores can support up to 128 remote host mounts
  vSAN Stretched Cluster now supports 20+20+1 configurations
  vSAN Stretched Cluster has deeper integrations with DRS for object sync and fail-back
  vSAN File Services now supported on vSAN Stretched Cluster and 2-node vSAN
  vSAN File Services Scale increase from 32 to 100 shares
  vSAN now supports vSphere Proactive HA
  vSAN supports the new vSphere Native Key Provider

vSAN over RDMA

Skyline Health Check History

- **vSAN 7.0 U3: October 2021**

Stretched cluster site/witness failure resiliency

Nested fault domains for two-node deployments

vSAN File Services - Access Based Enumeration

vSAN cluster shutdown and restart

Enhanced network monitoring and anomaly detection

vSAN health check correlation

VM I/O trip analyzer

Stretched Cluster support for vanilla Kubernetes

vSAN Data Persistence Platform now supports asynchronous installation and upgrades

CNS platform has improved performance, scale, and resiliency

- **vSAN 8.0: November 2022**

Launch of the vSAN Express Storage Architecture, and introducing Original Storage Architecture naming convention for traditional vSAN

vSAN ESA introduces a new Log Structured Filesystem (LFS) and a new Log Structured Object Manager (LSOM) for fast data ingestion and efficient metadata storage

vSAN ESA Adaptive RAID-5 mechanism

vSAN ESA leverages a single tier of NVME-based TLC (triple level cell) flash devices, removing the construct of disk groups and introducing the construct of storage pools

vSAN OSA support a much larger write buffer of 1.6TB

- **vSAN 8.0U1: April 2023**

vSAN ESA introduces support for HCI Mesh

vSAN OSA introduces support for HCI Mesh with a stretched cluster

vSAN ESA introduces support for Delta components for improved durability and resilience

A new dynamic default storage policy is introduced for the ESA

vSAN ESA introduces enhancements for streaming writes

PowerCLI support for vSAN ESA

Enhancements to the overall vSAN management experience, including higher resolution monitoring, network diagnostic enhancements and Skyline health remediation

VM I/O trip analyzer tasks may now be scheduled

Hopefully, that gives a quick overview of most of the capabilities introduced and available in each of the releases. Even though there are many items shown in each release, the list is still not complete. But all these features and capabilities do not mean that vSAN is complex to configure, manage, and monitor. Let's take a look from an administrator's perspective; what does vSAN look like?

What does vSAN look like to an administrator?

It was already mentioned that one of the design goals of vSAN ESA was to keep a consistent user experience to the one that the vSAN OSA offers. This is true for both the initial install experience as well as the day-2 management experience. When vSAN is enabled, storage devices across the vSphere cluster are aggregated into a single shared datastore. This datastore is then presented to all hosts that are part of the vSAN-enabled cluster. Just like any other storage solution used in virtualization environments, this datastore can be used as a destination for VMs and all associated components, such as virtual disks, swap files, and VM configuration files. When you deploy a new VM, you will see the familiar interface and a list of available datastores, including your newly created, vSAN-based datastore, as shown in the following screenshot.

Figure 3: Selecting vSAN as storage for VM configuration and disk files

This vSAN datastore is formed out of host local storage resources. Typically, all hosts within a vSAN-enabled cluster will contribute storage to this shared datastore. In the vSAN ESA, the local storage resource, i.e., the NVMe-based TLC (Triple Level Cell) device, is used as a performance cache and as a capacity device for storing data. This design, based on using local storage, means that as your vSphere cluster grows with the addition of new ESXi hosts, your datastore can automatically grow along with it. The NVMe devices in the newly added hosts will be claimed by vSAN and added to the vSAN datastore. vSAN is what is called a scale-out storage system (adding hosts to a cluster), but also allows scaling up (adding devices to a host).

Each host contributing storage capacity to the vSAN ESA cluster will require at least four NVMe TLC flash devices. At a minimum, vSAN ESA typically requires three hosts in a vSphere cluster to contribute storage. There is also a remote office/branch office (ROBO) solution that allows two hosts to be configured with a dedicated witness host. This ROBO configuration is discussed in chapter 8 later in the book. Returning to the three host configuration, we mentioned that typically all hosts in the cluster would contribute devices towards the vSAN datastore. This does not need to be the case, however. Other hosts within the same vSphere cluster, but which do not contribute storage, could leverage the resulting vSAN datastore without contributing storage resources to the cluster itself.

The diagram below shows a cluster that has four hosts, of which three (esxi-01, esxi-02, and esxi-03) contribute storage and a fourth (esxi-04) does not contribute but only consumes storage resources. Although it is technically possible to have a non-uniform cluster and have a host not contributing storage, VMware highly recommends creating a uniform cluster and having all hosts contribute storage for overall better utilization, performance, and availability. Most vSAN configurations are built with all hosts contributing storage resources to the vSAN datastore.

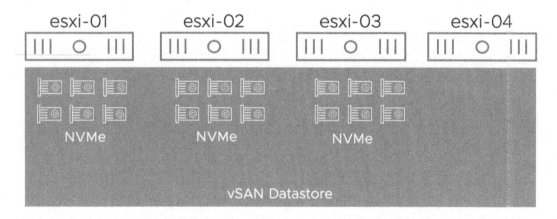

Figure 4: non-uniform vSAN cluster example

The boundary for vSAN in terms of both size and connectivity is a vSphere cluster. This means that vSAN supports single clusters/datastores of up to 64 hosts, but of course a single vCenter Server instance can manage many 64-host clusters. It is a common practice for most customers however to limit their clusters to around 24 hosts. This is for operational considerations such as lifecycle management, particularly the time it takes to update a full cluster. Each host can run a supported maximum of 200 VMs, up to a total of 6,400 VMs within a 64-host vSAN cluster. Whilst these numbers are accurate at the time of going to press, they may increase at some point in the future. As you can imagine with a storage system at this scale, performance and responsiveness are of the utmost importance. vSAN ESA is designed to take advantage of NVMe-based TLC flash devices to provide the experience users expect in today's world. Flash resources are used for all writes and reads by workloads to the vSAN datastore.

To ensure VMs can be deployed with certain characteristics, vSAN enables vSphere Administrators to set policies on a per-virtual disk or a per-VM basis. These policies help meet the defined service level objectives (SLOs) for workloads. These can be performance-related characteristics such as disk striping but can also be availability-related characteristics that ensure strategic replica placement of your VM's disks (and other important files) across racks or even locations.

If you have worked with VM storage policies in the past, you might now wonder whether all VMs stored on the same vSAN datastore will need to have the same VM storage policy assigned. The answer is no. vSAN allows you to have different policies for VMs provisioned to the same datastore. It even allows different policies to be placed on the different virtual disks belonging to the same VM.

As stated earlier, by leveraging policies, the level of resilience can be configured on a per-virtual disk granular level. How many hosts and disks a mirror copy will reside on depends on the selected policy. Because vSAN can use mirror copies (RAID-1) or erasure coding (RAID-5/6) defined by policy to provide resiliency, it does not require a host local RAID configuration (RAID stands for Redundant Array of Inexpensive Disks). In other words, hosts contributing to vSAN storage capacity should simply provide a set of NVMe-based TLC devices as part of a construct called a Storage Pool to vSAN. vSAN will take care of configuring protection levels for workloads in software; you as an administrator do not need to worry about doing this at the hardware level.

Whether you have defined a policy to tolerate a single host failure or a policy that will tolerate up to three hosts failing, vSAN will ensure that enough replicas of your storage objects are created. The following example illustrates how this is an important aspect of vSAN and one of the major differentiators between vSAN and most other virtual storage solutions out there.

In this example, we have configured a policy that can tolerate one failure and created a new virtual disk using that policy. We have chosen to go with failures to tolerate = 1, which in this case results in a RAID-1 configuration. To make things simple, we can assume that this means that vSAN will create two identical storage objects. Now there is a significant difference here for administrators who are familiar with the vSAN OSA. With the OSA, an additional witness component would also be created. The witness component allows vSAN OSA to determine which replica copy of the data is active and valid in the case of a failure. If you are familiar with clustering technologies, think of the witness component as a quorum object that will arbitrate ownership in the event of a failure. However, since we are now using a single-tiered storage architecture in vSAN ESA, some additional components get created when we build an object. Each object now gets a protected set of performance components (P-LEG) as well as capacity components (C-LEG) which match the storage policy. What that means and how this works will be explained in the chapters to come but suffice to say that there is no witness component created as part of the object on a standard vSAN ESA deployment as shown below.

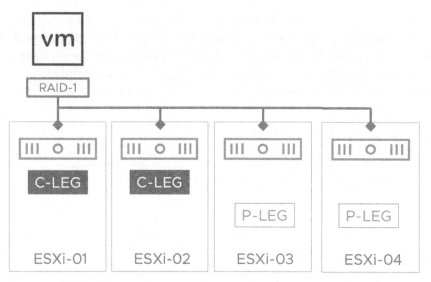

Figure 5: vSAN Failures to tolerate

The diagram shown here is a simplified example, and you may see a slightly different layout on your vSAN ESA, depending on the size of your cluster, the number of devices, the use of fault domains, the size of the object being created, or advanced capabilities like stretched clustering. The reason for this new object layout will be discussed in much greater detail in later chapters. There is no witness component associated with these objects since there are more than enough components to allow for ownership arbitration to take place in the event of a failure. This figure illustrates what it would look like at a high level for a VM with a virtual disk that can tolerate one failure. This could be the complete failure of a host, or even the failure of a NIC or a flash device. On the diagram above, the VM's compute resides on the first host and its virtual disk components reside across all hosts in the cluster. In this scenario, the vSAN network is used for storage I/O, allowing for the VM to freely move around the cluster without the need for storage components to be migrated along with the compute.

This might still sound complex, but vSAN masks away all the complexity as you will learn as you progress through the various chapters in this book.

Summary

To conclude, VMware vSAN is a market-leading, hypervisor-based distributed storage platform that enables the convergence of compute and storage resources, typically referred to as hyperconverged infrastructure. It enables you to define VM-level granular service level objectives through policy-based management. It allows you to control availability and performance in a way never seen before, simple, and efficient.

In the 8.0 release, vSAN introduces a new Express Storage Architecture for vSAN. While VMware continues to support the Original Storage Architecture (OSA) design of vSAN, the new ESA design is the focus of this book.

This chapter just scratched the surface. Now it's time to take it to the next level. Chapter 2 describes the requirements for installing and configuring vSAN.

02

vSAN Prerequisites and Requirements

Before delving into the installation and configuration of vSAN, let's begin by first of all discussing the requirements and the prerequisites. VMware vSphere is the foundation of every vSAN-based virtual infrastructure, whether it is the original storage architecture (OSA) or the express storage architecture (ESA).

VMware vSphere

vSAN was first officially released with VMware vSphere 5.5 U1 way back in 2014. Many additional versions of vSAN have since been released, the most recent release being vSphere 8.0U1 which was released in 2023. Each release of vSAN includes additional features. Since this book is focused on the new vSAN Express Storage Architecture (ESA), the ESA features will be discussed at various stages of this book. The different features included in each vSAN release are listed in Chapter 1, "Introduction to VMware vSAN."

VMware vSphere consists of two major components: the vCenter Server management tool and the ESXi hypervisor. To install and configure vSAN, both vCenter Server and ESXi are required.

VMware vCenter Server provides a centralized management platform for VMware vSphere environments. It is the solution used to provision new VMs, configure hosts, and perform many other operational tasks associated with managing a virtualized infrastructure. vSAN ESA has a requirement on vCenter Server 8.0. However, VMware strongly recommends using the latest version of vSphere where possible. vSAN is configured and monitored via the vSphere Client, a web-based client which allows administrators to access the vCenter Server. vSAN can also be fully configured and managed through the command-line interface (CLI) and the vSphere API for those wanting to automate some (or all) of the aspects of vSAN configuration, monitoring, or management. Although a single cluster can contain only one "local" vSAN datastore, a vCenter Server can manage multiple vSAN and compute clusters.

ESXi

VMware vSphere ESXi is an enterprise-grade virtualization hypervisor product that allows you to run multiple instances of an operating system in a fully isolated fashion on a single server. It is a bare-metal solution, meaning that it does not require a guest-OS and has an extremely thin footprint. ESXi is the foundation for the large majority of virtualized environments worldwide.

For standard datacenter deployments, vSAN ESA requires a minimum of three ESXi hosts (where each host has local storage and is contributing this storage to the vSAN datastore) to form a *supported* vSAN ESA cluster. A three-node configuration allows the cluster to meet the minimum availability requirements of tolerating at least one host failure. There is of course the option of deploying a 2-node vSAN ESA configuration along with a witness appliance, but this is aimed primarily are remote office/branch office type environments and not datacenters. There are some additional considerations around the use of a two-node vSAN ESA cluster which will be discussed in more detail in Chapter 8, "Two Host vSAN Cluster Use Case." The role of the witness appliance, and indeed the witness components will be discussed in detail later in this book, so don't worry about those for the moment.

As of vSAN ESA, which was released with vSAN version 8.0, a maximum of 64 ESXi hosts in a cluster continues to be supported.

From a CPU usage perspective, the important factor to keep in mind is that the ESXi CPU is now performing storage tasks, alongside virtualization tasks, when vSAN ESA is configured. As storage device density increases, the more VMs we may be able to provision to a vSAN ESA cluster. This in turn means increased CPU consumption as vSAN is running more and more workloads. All this needs to be considered when sizing a vSAN ESA cluster. One helpful fact is that the latest generations of CPUs are much more efficient when it comes to offloading certain operations, for example Advanced Encryption Standard – New Instructions (AES-NI) for encryption and Intel CRC32/CRC32C for checksum calculations which makes the processing extremely fast and efficient.

Each vSAN ESA ESXi host must be configured with at least 512GB per host to ensure that the workloads, vSAN and the hypervisor have sufficient resources to ensure an optimal user experience. vSAN does not consume all this memory, but it is required to implement the correct configuration.

One last point on memory – vSAN allocates 0.4% of memory per host, up to a maximum of 1GB, for its client cache. Client cache is a low latency host local read cache. This is an in-memory cache that caches the data of a VM on the same host where the VM is located. This local client-side cache will be discussed in further detail in the vSAN Architecture chapter.

Capacity devices

Unlike the vSAN OSA which supports two models (the all-flash model and the hybrid model), vSAN ESA supports a single all-NVMe tier only. This is possibly the most noticeable customer-facing difference when comparing the OSA with the ESA. Whilst the OSA has the concept of a caching tier and a capacity tier, the ESA is a single tier platform. The NVMe devices handle caching for performance, and also persist the data. To add some clarification, vSAN ESA does not dedicate some NVMe devices for caching and other for capacity; vSAN ESA utilizes a single tier architecture where all devices contribute toward performance and capacity.

The vSAN ESA hardware guidance gives some requirements around storage devices. These are listed here for completeness and are accurate at the time of going to press. However, these will likely change over time, so always check the official VMware documentation for the latest and greatest information.

- Only NVMe based TLC (Triple Level Cell) flash devices are supported.
- Devices must be for 'Mixed Use' .
- Devices must have a Write Endurance of Class D or higher - three full drive writes per day, over a five year period.
- A minimum of 15TB of capacity and 4 devices per vSAN ESA node is required.
- A maximum of 24 devices per vSAN ESA node.
- Each device must have a minimum capacity of 1.6TB.
- Devices must have a Performance of Class F or higher. At a minimum, this entails 100,000 writes per second.

ESXi boot considerations

When installing an ESXi host for vSAN-based infrastructure, various options are available regarding where to place the ESXi image. ESXi can be installed on a local magnetic disk or hard disk drive (HDD), USB flash drive, SD card or SATADOM devices. At the time of writing (vSAN 8.0U1), stateless booting of ESXi (auto-deploy) is not supported, as documented in the official vSAN Design Guide.

Historically, the preferred method of deploying ESXi was to a USB flash device or SD card. This provided the advantage of not consuming a persistent disk on the ESXi host for the boot image. However, there were some drawbacks to this approach, such as a lack of space for storing log files and vSAN trace files, as well as endurance considerations of the device itself. This led to VMware changing their guidance on using USB/SD cards as boot devices. Note that VMware continues to support USB/SD card as a boot device through vSphere 8.0 but recommends an additional persistent device to store the OSData partition. The OSData contains the VMTools and scratch areas. The scratch areas are critical regions which could incur considerable I/O, and in the past has led to 'burn-out' of the USB/SD card. This is why VMware no longer recommends their use. Further details regarding ESXi boot considerations can be found in VMware KB 85685 which is revised regularly.

The authors of this book also highly recommend using local persistent devices for the installation of ESXi. This will provide the ability to not only store log files and trace files locally, but it will also provide the added benefit that memory dumps can be stored persistently in the case of a host failure.

There are a large variety of devices supported for the installation of ESXi, and we have seen customers using solutions ranging from HDDs in a RAID-1 configuration, to an M.2 flash device or a SATADOM device. VMware has outlined in the aforementioned VMware KB article that it will no longer certify servers that carry SD/USB devices as boot devices.

VMware Hardware Compatibility Guide

Before installing and configuring ESXi, please validate that your configuration is on the official VMware compatibility guide for vSAN ESA, which you can find at the following website for ready node configurations https://vmwa.re/vsanesahcl or the following website if you want to validate individual components: https://vmwa.re/vsanesahclc. Please note, vSAN Skyline Health has a health finding which will validate your hardware configuration in combination with the firmware and drivers regularly. Supported configurations and combinations may change over time because of discovered issues or introduced enhancements.

vSAN has always had strict requirements around driver and firmware versions when it comes to server components. With all the various options, configuring the perfect vSAN host using a Do-It-Yourself (DIY) approach can be a complex exercise. But there is an alternative: vSAN ReadyNode Configurations. In fact, with the initial launch of vSAN ESA, the only option available to customers are vSAN ReadyNode configurations. The reason for this is simple. VMware wanted their customers to have the best possible experience with vSAN ESA. Any misconfiguration resulting in a poor performing vSAN ESA would reflect negatively on both the product and on VMware. Thus, the decision was made to release vSAN ESA with ReadyNodes only. A supported DIY approach may appear at a later date, but at present, customers need to select a ReadyNode if they wish to deploy an ESA configuration. Of course, it is possible to customize the configuration, but we will get to that later.

Another advantage is that the boot device concerns outlined previously should not be an issue for the vSAN ESA ReadyNodes. However, if and when a Do-It-Yourself (DIY) approach to building vSAN ESA nodes becomes available, customers will need to be diligent when ordering new server hardware. Customers will need to verify that the server is not using USB/SD for a boot device.

vSAN ReadyNode

ReadyNodes were always the preferred way of building a vSAN OSA configurations. In the case of vSAN ESA, it has already been highlighted that this is the only way to create a supported configuration at the time of going to press. Many vendors have already gone through the exercise of building vSAN ReadyNode configurations. These ReadyNodes consist of tested and certified hardware for the vSAN ESA. In the authors opinion, ReadyNodes provide an additional guarantee that the hardware components, along with the driver and firmware versions, have been validated for use with vSAN ESA. It is important to note that even with vSAN ESA ReadyNodes, the configurations can be modified and tweaked to use different hardware components, and your configuration will still be fully supported. Refer to VMware KB 90343 for supported configuration details and allowable changes. Further information is available in the compatibility guide which provides a list of supported ReadyNodes, as shown in the figure below. Note, at the time of writing the list of supported configurations was still limited, but new configurations, and vendors, are being added on a regular basis.

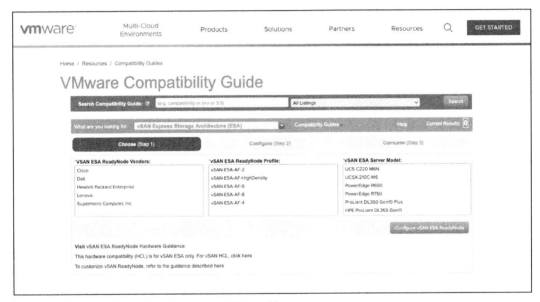

Figure 6: vSAN ESA ReadyNode compatibility guide

NVMe

NVM Express (NVMe) is a protocol that provides high-bandwidth and low-latency. It has focused on optimizing NAND-based flash storage devices. NVMe devices are most commonly connected with Peripheral Component Interconnect Express (PCIe) as the transport medium, although other connectors are available. NVMe devices have been supported by vSAN OSA since 2015 for both the caching tier and the capacity tier. NVMe provides various benefits to vSAN OSA, with performance and endurance being the most important characteristics. In recent years, NVMe devices have become more and more prevalent, as more and more customers have begun to adopt the technology.

vSAN ESA is an NVMe-only solution. Historically, many vSAN OSA customers leveraged SAS (Serial-Attached SCSI) and SATA (Serial Advanced Technology Attachment) based flash devices. NVMe based devices have many characteristics that makes them superior over SAS and SATA devices. NVMe can connect directly to the CPU, resulting in much lower latency when compared to devices that need to connect via a storage I/O controller. There is also a significant bus speed difference. SATA, originally introduced as a protocol for hard drives, could achieve a throughput of up 6Gbps. SAS was an improvement over SATA, being able to reach a throughput rate of up to 12Gbps. In comparison, NVMe can achieve up to 32Gbps. SAS also had a larger queue depth in comparison to SATA, being able to support up to 256 commands compared to a SAS queue depth of 32. By contrast, NVMe is able to support up the 64,000 commands per queue.

These impressive performance characteristics are some of the main reasons why NVMe based devices are the only devices supported on the vSAN ESA.

Storage Controllers

Storage Controllers are a significant consideration when configuring vSAN OSA. However, since vSAN ESA is an NVMe-only platform, and modern processors have implemented NVMe PCIe 3.0 directly on the CPU, there is no need for a host bus adapter or storage I/O controller. The NVMe flash devices are inserted directly onto the PCIe bus. As previously highlighted, this has the benefit of a much lower I/O latency. Removing the need for a storage controller also reduces another possible failure point, leading to decreased total cost of ownership (TCO) for vSAN ESA.

Storage Pools

The introduction of storage pools is possibly the most noticeable administrator-visible change when comparing the vSAN ESA with the vSAN OSA. The vSAN OSA architecture includes a caching tier and a capacity tier. To build a relationship between the capacity tier and its cache device, vSAN OSA has the concept of disk groups. Any I/O destined to the capacity tier of that disk group will have its I/O cached on the flash devices in the cache tier that are part of the same disk group.

With the vSAN OSA disk group feature, the failure domain is at the disk group level. Thus, certain device failures could impact the whole of a disk group. Device failures were also a consideration when certain space efficiency features such as deduplication and compression were enabled.

In essence, vSAN ESA removes the need for separate cache and capacity tiers. A new single tier storage pool architecture in the vSAN ESA means that each NVMe NAND flash device contributes to both performance and capacity. With this new architecture, the failure domain is much reduced. vSAN ESA now has improved availability in the event of a single device failure. A single device failure has no impact on the other devices in the same storage pool.

At most, a vSAN host can have one storage pool, each containing a minimum of 15TB worth of flash capacity, and a minimum of 4 devices, although this is dependent on the vSAN ReadyNode configuration. Some configurations may require more. The configuration of this is extremely simple, and we will go through the exact steps in chapter 3. Nevertheless, the below screenshot shows the section of the UI that is used to claim all available devices into storage pools in a single step. The warning about the lack of certification of the devices for vSAN ESA is expected in this case, since we are building the environment using nested, or virtual ESXi hosts. Thus, the devices are not compatible for an actual vSAN ESA deployment. However, it should allow you to appreciate the simplicity of the setup.

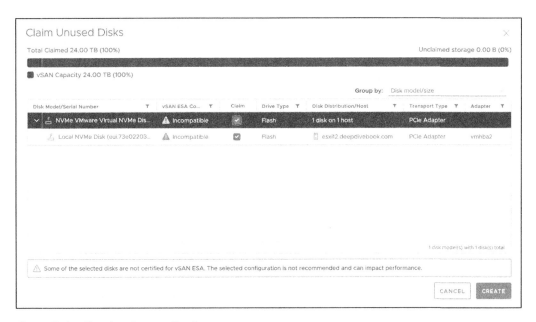

Figure 7: Configuring Storage Pools

Network Requirements

This section covers the requirements and prerequisites from a networking perspective for vSAN ESA. vSAN is a distributed storage solution and therefore heavily depends on the network for intra-host communication. Consistency and reliability are key. Therefore, it is critical that the network interconnect between the hosts is of a high quality and has no underlying issues. It is strongly recommended that the network health is monitored just as closely as the vSAN health.

Network Interface Cards

The vSAN ESA network requirements are determined by the specific class of ReadyNode. Each ESXi host that is participating in a vSAN ESA cluster must have at least one 25GbE network interface card (NIC). vSAN ESA ReadyNode profiles will contain 25Gb or 100Gb NICs. vSAN ESA AF6, and AF High Density nodes require 50Gbps of vSAN networking throughput, and ESA AF8 requires 100Gbps of networking throughput to deliver maximum performance. For redundancy, customers can configure a team of NICs on a per-host basis. We consider this a best practice, but it is not necessary to build a fully functional vSAN ESA cluster. However, while this approach may provide availability, it may not necessarily provide an increase in bandwidth, so the rule is not to rely on a teaming methodology to meet the bandwidth requirements.

You might ask why the network requirement is so high. These network requirements relate to the performance of the NVMe-based flash devices used in the vSAN ESA storage pools. Specifying such a high network requirement ensures that vSAN ESA is able to exploit the full performance capabilities of the storage devices.

Another advantage of the vSAN ReadyNode approach for the vSAN ESA configurations is that customers do not need to worry about validating the NIC model, its driver, and its firmware versions. This was a consideration with the DIY approach on the vSAN OSA and required customers to use the VMware Compatibility Guide – IO Devices section to verify that their NIC is indeed supported and at the correct versions. There were numerous vSAN OSA support issues caused by misbehaving networks cards, which are a critical component of distributed systems like vSAN. Again, if and when the DIY approach is added to vSAN ESA configurations, customers will need to take great care to ensure that the network device they choose is supported.

Supported Virtual Switch Types

vSAN ESA is supported on both VMware vSphere distributed switches (VDS) and VMware vSphere standard switches (VSS). There are some advantages to using a Distributed Switch that will be covered in Chapter 3, "vSAN Installation and Configuration." No other virtual switch types have been explicitly tested with vSAN. A license for the use of VDS is included with vSAN, irrespective of the vSphere edition used.

NSX Interoperability

NSX is VMware's network virtualization platform. Whilst it is possible to run both vSAN and NSX on the same physical infrastructure, VMware does not support running vSAN traffic on NSX, or as is stated more specifically in the vSAN Network Design Guide: "NSX-T does not support the configuration of the vSAN data network over an NSX-managed VXLAN or Geneve overlay."

VMware strongly recommends simplifying the network path of all VMkernel traffic (including vSAN-ESA traffic) as much as possible. The reason for this recommendation is that firewalls and IDS/IPS systems (Intrusion detection systems and intrusion prevention systems which constantly monitor the network) can inadvertently block this mission critical storage I/O. This could result in some substantial impacts on the performance or availability of data.

Layer 2 or Layer 3

vSAN ESA is supported over layer 2 (L2/switched) or layer 3 (L3/routed) networks. All vSAN ESA traffic is unicast. There has been no multicast vSAN traffic since vSAN OSA version 6.6.

VMkernel Network

On each ESXi host that wants to participate in a vSAN ESA cluster, a VMkernel port for vSAN communication must be created. The VMkernel port is labeled vSAN traffic and is used for intra-cluster node communication. It is also used for reads and writes when one of the ESXi hosts in the cluster runs a particular VM but the actual data blocks making up the VM components are located on a different ESXi host in the cluster. In this case, I/O will need to traverse the network configured between the hosts in the cluster. As depicted in the diagram below, VMkernel interface vmk2 is used for vSAN traffic by all the hosts in the vSAN cluster. The VM residing on the first host does all of its reads and writes leveraging the vSAN network as most of the components of that VM are stored elsewhere. After an initial glance at the diagram below, you may be wondering what the Perf Leg (Performance Leg) and Cap Leg (Capacity Leg) are used for. If you are familiar with the vSAN OSA, you may also be wondering what has happened to the witness component for this object. Rest assured all of this will be explained in the upcoming chapters. For the moment, it suffices to say that under the covers, certain parts of vSAN have been redesigned to address the single tier architecture, and to ensure vSAN optimally utilizes the new class of flash devices. Part of this involves a new layout of the objects that make up a virtual machine, represented by components in the Performance Leg and components in the Capacity Leg, as show below.

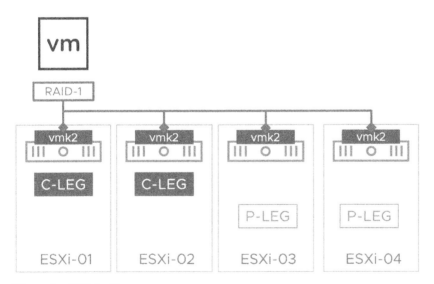

Figure 8: vSAN traffic

vSAN ESA Network Traffic

For inter-cluster host communication, vSAN uses a proprietary protocol called RDT, the Reliable Datagram Transport. VMware has not published a specification of the protocol. This is similar to the approach taken for other VMware products and features such as vMotion, Fault Tolerance, and vSphere Replication. The vSAN network may be used for two different traffic types.

- Clustering service (CMMDS): This traffic does metadata updates like object placement and statistics. These generate a very small percentage of overall network traffic.

- Storage traffic (e.g., reads, writes): This is most of the network traffic. All host to host communication within the cluster is unicast.

Jumbo Frames

Jumbo frames are supported on the vSAN network. We believe that every vSAN deployment is different, both from a server hardware perspective and from a network hardware perspective. Therefore, it is difficult to recommend for or against the use of jumbo frames. In addition, there is an operational impact in implementing jumbo frames on non-greenfield sites. When jumbo frames are not consistently configured end to end, network problems may occur.

Most of the improvements observed with jumbo frames relates to CPU usage. Data can fit in a smaller number of packets (sometimes into a single frame when the packet is 8KB or less in size) when jumbo frames are enabled, and thus no fragmentation/defragmentation operations are needed to send and receive these packets.

In an operationally mature environment where a consistent implementation can be guaranteed, the use of jumbo frames is left to the administrator's discretion.

NIC Teaming

Another potential way of optimizing network performance is teaming of NICs. NIC teaming in ESXi is transparent to vSAN. You can use any of the NIC teaming options available in vSphere on the vSAN network. For the most part, NIC teaming offers availability rather than any performance gain. The only drawback with NIC teaming is that it adds complexity to the networking configuration of vSAN. Chapter 3 covers the teaming configuration options, and their various parameters, in more detail.

NIC Teaming - Performance vs. Availability

There is no guarantee that NIC Teaming will give you a performance improvement. This is because most of the NIC teaming algorithms are not able to utilize the full bandwidth of multiple physical NICs at the same time. Various factors play a part, including the size of the vSAN cluster, the number of NICs, and the number of different IP addresses used. In our testing, Link Aggregation Control Protocol (LACP) offers the best chance of balancing vSAN traffic across multiple vSAN networks using Link Aggregation Groups (LAG). Thus, if performance is your key goal, then LACP is the best option for network configuration. This comes with the downside of added complexity as you will also need to make configuration changes on the physical network switch. If availability is your key goal, then any of the other supported NIC teaming policies should suffice. Be aware that VMware does not support multiple VMkernel adapters (vmknics) on the same subnet for either vSphere or vSAN. See VMware KB 2010877 for further details.

Network I/O Control

Although it is a requirement to use NICs that provide 25GbE minimum for vSAN ESA, there is no requirement to solely dedicate these cards to the vSAN network. NICs can be shared with other traffic types. However, you should consider using Network I/O Control (NIOC) to ensure that the vSAN traffic is guaranteed a certain amount of bandwidth over the network in the case where contention for bandwidth of the network arises. This is especially true if a NIC is shared with (for instance) vMotion traffic, which is infamous for utilizing all available bandwidth when possible. NIOC requires the creation of a distributed switch because NIOC is not available with standard switches. Luckily, the distributed switch is included with the vSAN license.

Having said that, high-performance environments with dedicated interfaces for uniform traffic types have gained in popularity. vSAN ESA and tier 1 applications can benefit from not having to rely on NIOC and from not sharing bandwidth with other traffic types. This is once again at the discretion of the customer, and it is not possible to make a recommendation. In many cases, it becomes a cost vs performance conversation, although dedicated NICs for specific traffic types could also make troubleshooting easier by being able to monitor and isolate certain traffic types via the physical switch ports. Chapter 3 provides various examples of how NIOC can be configured for the various types of network configurations.

Firewall Ports

When you are enabling vSAN ESA, several ESXi firewall ports are automatically opened (both ingoing and outgoing) on each ESXi host that participates in the vSAN cluster. The ports are used for inter-cluster host communication and communication with the storage provider on the ESXi hosts. The table below provides a list of the most used vSAN-specific network ports. Most of the traffic in a vSAN cluster (98% or more) will be RDT traffic on port 2233. More extensive details can be found in VMware KB 52959.

NAME	PORT	PROTOCOL
CMMDS	12345, 23451, 12321	UDP
RDT	2233	TCP
VSANVP/SPBM	8080	TCP
Health	443	TCP
Witness Host	2233	TCP
Witness Host	12321	UDP
iSCSI clients	3260	TCP
KMS Server	Vendor specific	Vendor specific

Table 1: ESXi ports and protocols Opened by vSAN

vSAN Stretched Cluster

vSAN stretched cluster allows VMs to be deployed across sites in different datacenters, and if one site or datacenter fails, VMs can be restarted on the surviving site, utilizing vSphere High

Availability (HA). There are several items to consider for vSAN Stretched Cluster configurations, including latency and bandwidth requirements, not only between the datacenter sites but also to the witness site. These will be covered in greater detail in the vSAN Stretched Cluster section, later in this book (Chapter 7), but we will list some of the basic guidelines here for your convenience:

- Maximum 5ms Round Trip Time (RTT) latency between data sites (requirement)
- RTT between data sites and the witness site depends on the number of hosts
  - Less than 200 ms latency RTT for up to 10 hosts per site
  - Less than 100 ms latency RTT for 11-15 hosts per site
- 25Gbps between data sites for vSAN ESA
- 2Mbps per 1000 vSAN components from data sites to witness site

vSAN 2-Node Remote Office/Branch Office (ROBO)

In much the same way as there are specific network requirements for vSAN stretched cluster, there are also network requirements around latency and bandwidth for 2-node ROBO deployments. For 2-node configurations the following general guidelines apply:

- Maximum 500ms RTT between 2-node/ROBO location and central witness (requirement)
- 2Mbps per 1000 vSAN components from 2-node/ROBO location to central witness

VMware vSAN ESA supports back-to-back cabling of the network between the 2-nodes at a remote office/branch office. This provides the added benefit that at a relatively low cost, 25GbE can be introduced in a 2-node configuration without the need for a 25GbE physical switch infrastructure.

vSAN Fault Domains

The concept of fault domains has been mentioned a few times now. Throughout the book, various vSAN topologies which leverage fault domains will be discussed. These will include vSAN stretched cluster deployments, 2-node vSAN deployments and what might be termed "rack awareness" deployments. In each case, fault domains simply represent a way of grouping one, but usually multiple, ESXi hosts together so that they act as a destination for a capacity leg and performance leg of an object.

All ESXi hosts continue to participate in the vSAN cluster, but now rather than having the fault domain set to a single host, you can set a fault domain to be a group of hosts. An example could be to group hosts in a vSAN cluster by rack, giving what is termed "rack awareness". This means that components of a capacity leg or performance leg object can be placed on ESXi hosts across different racks in the datacenter. vSAN will continue to place objects and components to meet the policy requirements so that in the case of a failure, only a subset of the object is impacted. However, now if there is a complete rack failure, or even in the case of a stretched cluster, a complete site failure, the workloads remain online and available. This behaviour, and use of fault domains, will become much clearer as we delve into the inner workings of vSAN stretched clusters in chapter 7 and vSAN 2-node configurations in chapter 8.

vSAN ESA Requirements

Before enabling vSAN ESA, it is highly recommended that the vSphere administrator validate that the environment meets all the prerequisites and requirements. To enhance resilience, this list also includes recommendations from an infrastructure perspective:

- Minimum of three ESXi hosts for standard datacenter deployments of vSAN ESA. Minimum of two ESXi hosts and a witness host for the smallest deployment, for example, remote office/branch office.
- Minimum memory per ESXi host is 512GB.
- VMware vCenter Server. Recommended is 8.0U1 at the time of writing, but the latest is preferred. vCenter Server version needs to be equal to, or newer than, the ESXi version. Remember that vCenter Server contains a great deal of management and monitoring functionality for vSAN ESA.
- At least 15TB worth of NVMe TLC flash capacity for the storage pool, and a minimum of 4 devices, with a maximum of 24 devices.
- One boot device to install ESXi. Boot device should meet the requirements outlined in VMware KB article 85685.
- Dedicated network port for vSAN – VMkernel interface. A dual 25GbE configuration is preferred, but a single 25GbE is also supported. Higher density vSAN ESA ReadyNodes will require higher bandwidth NICs, up to 100GbE. The NIC does not need to be dedicated to vSAN traffic, but can be shared with other traffic types, such as management traffic, vMotion traffic, etc. Network I/O Control can be used to ensure fairness.

Summary

Although configuring vSAN takes a couple of clicks, it is important to take the time to ensure that all requirements are met and to ensure that all prerequisites are in place. A stable storage platform starts at the foundation, which is of course the infrastructure on which it is enabled. Before moving on to Chapter 3, you should run through the requirements above.

We have also discussed additional recommendations, which are not requirements for a fully functional vSAN ESA, but which might be desirable from a production standpoint such as networking redundancy, jumbo frames, and Network IO Control.

03

vSAN Installation and Configuration

This chapter describes in detail the installation and configuration process, as well as all initial preparation steps that you might need to consider before proceeding with a vSAN cluster deployment. You will find information on how to correctly set up network and storage devices, as well as some helpful tips and tricks on how to deploy the most optimal vSAN configuration.

Cluster Quickstart

In the early versions of vSAN, there were various steps and workflows involved to get a vSAN cluster fully configured. These steps involved adding ESXi hosts to a vCenter Server instance. Next, administrators would normally configure these hosts manually, unless of course, you had fully automated the installation and configuration. Manual configuration, for the most part, means setting up all the required VMkernel interfaces (vSAN, Management, and vMotion networks) and vSwitch port groups (or distributed port groups for that matter). After the configuration of the network, a cluster could be created, and the hosts could be added to a cluster to enable vSphere services such as vSphere HA, vSphere DRS, and of course vSAN.

Although not overly complicated, it would require the administrator to go from one UI workflow to the other, some of which were in a completely different section of the vSphere Client. In later releases of vSphere, a dedicated UI was developed for the creation of a vSAN cluster. This workflow, named the Cluster Quickstart wizard, combines all the different workflows and steps needed to form a vSAN cluster into a single workflow.

Cluster Quickstart Wizard

When creating a vSAN cluster in a greenfield deployment the steps that you need to go through are all part of the Cluster Quickstart wizard. When vCenter Server has been deployed the first thing you will need to do is create a cluster. When you create a cluster, you have the option to enable vSphere HA, vSphere DRS, and vSAN. When the cluster is created, the vSphere Client will automatically continue with the Cluster Quickstart workflow, regardless of whether vSAN is enabled or not.

Let's look at this process a bit more in-depth. The first step in the vSphere Client UI is to create a cluster. You can do this by right-clicking in the vSphere Client on the virtual datacenter object. Next you select "New Cluster". You provide the cluster with a name, and then select the cluster services you would like to have enabled. In our case, this will be vSphere HA, vSphere DRS, and vSAN ESA.

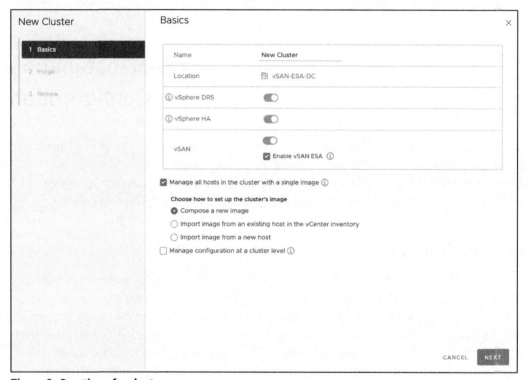

Figure 9: Creation of a cluster

After you have clicked "Next" and "Finish" you are taken to the section in the UI called Cluster Quickstart. The next step will be to click "ADD", and add hosts into your newly created vSAN cluster.

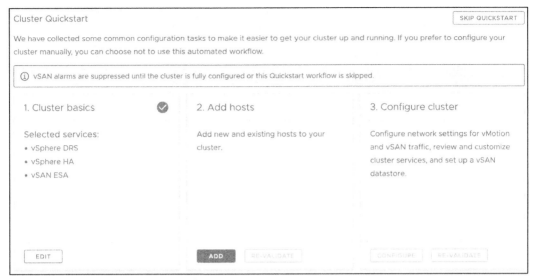

Figure 10: Cluster Quickstart wizard

In our case, we add twelve existing hosts to Cluster. These hosts are already part of the vCenter Server inventory. Before the hosts are added to the cluster, a host summary is provided with relevant information. For instance, it is highlighted if any of the hosts that you are adding have powered-on VMs.

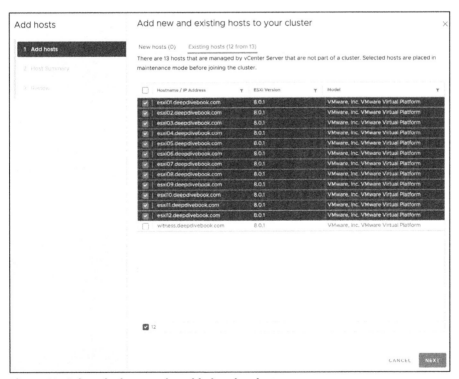

Figure 11: Select the hosts to be added to the cluster

When you finish the "Add hosts" workflow, the hosts will be added to the cluster and all cluster services will be configured. What is useful to know is that the hosts are added to the cluster in "maintenance mode". This is to prevent any workloads from using a host which may not be fully configured yet. Another feature as part of this workflow is the fact that after adding the host to the cluster the hosts are validated against various Skyline Health findings. This is to ensure that the hosts are healthy and compatible with the VMware compatibility guide. If an NVMe device is not certified, for instance, then this will be called out. Unsupported driver and firmware versions are also highlighted. This allows the administrator to install the correct driver, or firmware, before enabling vSAN and deploying workloads. Note that in the next screenshot you will notice some of the Skyline Health findings have failed. This is the result of running our lab in a virtual environment. In your (production) environment, all checks should pass.

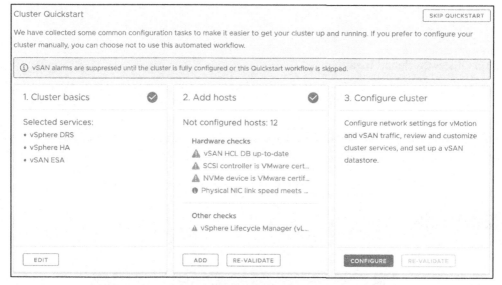

Figure 12: Health validation during cluster creation

After verifying the health of the hosts, and potentially correcting issues, the last step can be taken. In this final step, required networking settings for vMotion and vSAN traffic will be configured, as well as clustering services.

The Quickstart wizard assumes that a distributed switch is used. It will configure the distributed switch as recommended by the *VMware Validated Designs* (VVD). You can, if preferred, configure the network settings after this workflow has been completed. We would, however, recommend doing it as part of the workflow. As mentioned in previous chapters, vSAN includes the vSphere Distributed Switch feature irrespective of the vSphere Edition being used.

In our case, we are going to add two physical adapters to the distributed switch as shown in the next screenshot.

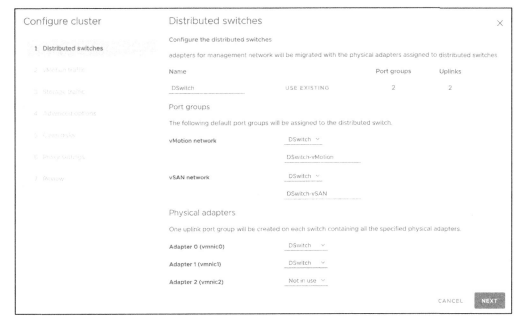

Figure 13: Configuration of the Distributed Switch

After the configuration of the distributed switch, the VMkernel interfaces for both vMotion and vSAN traffic will need to be configured. The interface allows you to specify static IP addresses or use DHCP. Note that in a single window you can provide all the needed IP details for all hosts in the cluster.

Configure cluster	vMotion traffic		
	Specify the IP addresses for the vMotion traffic		
1 Distributed switches			
	Distributed switch	DSwitch	
2 vMotion traffic	Distributed port group name	DSwitch-VMOTION	
3 Storage traffic	✓ Use VLAN	0	
4 Advanced options	Protocol	IPv4	
5 Claim disks	IPv4 Configuration		
6 Create fault domains	IP type	DHCP ✓ Static IPs	
7 Ready to complete	Each host is configured automatically based on the input below. Empty default gateway might result in a segmented network.		
	10.160.136.119	IPv4	Subnet Mask	Default gateway
	10.160.142.216	IPv4	Subnet Mask	Default gateway
	10.160.144.122	IPv4	Subnet Mask	Default gateway
	10.160.148.37	IPv4	Subnet Mask	Default gateway
	10.160.151.155	IPv4	Subnet Mask	Default gateway

Figure 14: Configuration of the VMkernel interfaces

Next, it is possible to configure various advanced configuration aspects of vSphere HA and vSphere DRS. Configuration options continue with advanced vSAN functionality like Data-At-Rest and In-Transit encryption, Fault Domains, Stretched Clusters, etc. We will discuss each of these features and their functionality in later chapters.

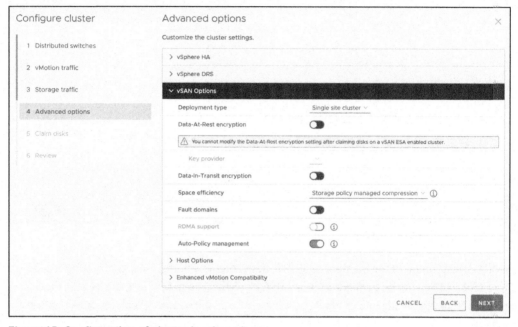

Figure 15: Configuration of cluster level services

In the next step, all the host local NVMe devices that need to be part of the vSAN Datastore can be claimed. Note that vSAN will group the devices based on their model, and that all devices will become part of what is now called a storage pool. Note that in the screenshot the devices appear as incompatible. This is once again due to the fact that our devices are virtual devices. In your environment they should be physical devices and always show up as compatible!

Figure 16: Claim vSAN devices

After claiming disks and enabling services, there is now the ability to configure either fault domains or configure a stretched cluster. If you are unfamiliar with these concepts, do not worry. They will be covered in detail in upcoming chapters. However, if you are configuring a stretched cluster then two additional steps are presented, namely the selection of the witness host and claiming the disks of the witness host. The function of the witness components and witness host will also be covered in greater detail in the architecture chapter. For the moment it is enough to understand that it plays a role in the configuration of stretched clusters.

Another configuration option at this point is to configure fault domains. This is a configuration option when you wish to deploy a single vSAN cluster across three racks, for example. In that case, you would create three fault domains and then add the ESXi hosts from the different racks to each fault domain according to the physical placement of the host, i.e., hosts in the same rack are placed in the same fault domain. Fault domains and how they work is something we will discuss in-depth at a later time. For now, it is sufficient to know that these can be configured from the same Quickstart workflow end-to-end, but they can also be configured afterwards. We will show later in the book how you can configure Fault Domains when the cluster has fully formed, especially for vSAN stretched cluster and 2-node configurations.

This completes the configuration of the cluster with a summary of all settings that have been configured. Note that if anything is misconfigured, you can step back through the wizard and make the required changes.

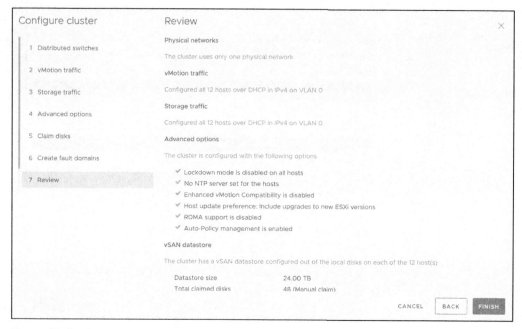

Figure 17: Summary

Now when you click finish the cluster will be fully configured end-to-end. This will, depending on which services are enabled, take several minutes.

After the configuration of the hosts has been completed, each of them will be taken out of maintenance mode and will be ready to host workloads. Of course, there are a couple of other things to consider when it comes to installing and configuring a vSAN infrastructure end to end. Let's look at those next.

Networking

Network connectivity is the heart of any vSAN cluster. vSAN cluster hosts use the network for virtual machine (VM) I/O to disk, but also use the network to communicate their state with one another. As previously mentioned, vSAN ESA requires 25Gbps networking at a minimum. However, for higher density configurations, higher bandwidth is required. The vSAN ESA AF6 ReadyNode has a requirement for 50Gbps and the vSAN ESA AF8 ReadyNode requires 100Gbps. Consistent and correct network configuration is key to a successful vSAN deployment.

As mentioned in the previous chapter, VMware vSphere provides two different types of virtual switches, both of which are fully supported with vSAN. These are the vSphere Distributed Switch (VDS) and the VMware Virtual Standard Switch (VSS). Although the authors recommend using the vSphere Distributed Switch (VDS), it is fully supported to use the VMware Virtual Standard Switch (VSS). Note that when using the Cluster Quickstart wizard, the vSphere Distributed Switch is chosen by default. A VDS provides administrators with the ability to enable a feature called Network I/O Control (NIOC). This allows administrators to prioritize traffic streams when the environment is under contention. Before we dive into NIOC, let's discuss some of the basic aspects of vSAN networking, and some of the design decisions around it.

VMkernel Network for vSAN

All ESXi hosts participating in a vSAN network need to communicate with one another. As such, a vSAN cluster will not successfully form until a vSAN VMkernel port is available on the ESXi hosts participating in the vSAN cluster. The vSphere administrator can create a vSAN VMkernel port manually on each ESXi host in the cluster before the vSAN cluster forms, or alternatively can have the VMkernel ports created as part of the Cluster Quickstart wizard.

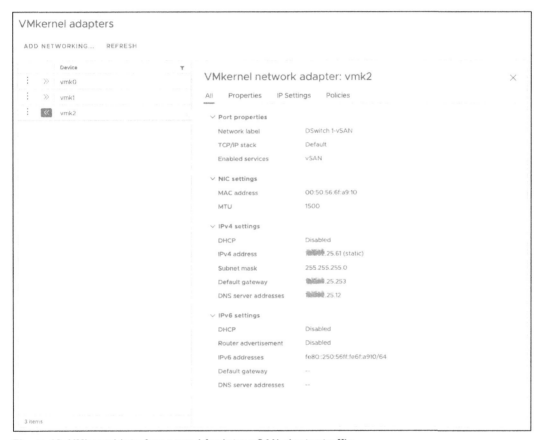

Figure 18: VMkernel interfaces used for intra-vSAN cluster traffic

Without a VMkernel network for vSAN, the cluster will not form successfully. If communication is not possible between the ESXi hosts in the vSAN cluster, only one ESXi host will join the vSAN cluster. Other ESXi hosts will not be able to join. This will still result in a single vSAN datastore, but each host can only see itself as part of that datastore. A warning message will display when there are communication difficulties between ESXi hosts in the cluster. If the cluster is created before the VMkernel ports are created, a warning message is also displayed regarding communication difficulties between the ESXi hosts. Once the VMkernel ports are created and communication is established, the cluster will form successfully.

VSS vSAN Network Configuration

With a VSS, creating a port group for vSAN network traffic is straightforward. By virtue of installing an ESXi host, a VSS is automatically created to carry ESXi network management traffic and VM traffic. Administrators can use an already-existing standard switch and its associated uplinks to external networks to create a new VMkernel port for vSAN traffic. Alternatively, administrators may choose to create a new standard switch for the vSAN network traffic VMkernel port by selecting unused uplinks for the new standard switch. Of course, the steps to create a VMkernel interface will have to be repeated for every ESXi host in the vSAN cluster. Each time vSAN is scaled out and a new host gets added to the cluster, administrators must ensure that the VSS configuration is identical on the new host. This leads to additional operational overhead and unnecessary complexity. This is the big advantage of the vSphere Distributed Switch.

VDS vSAN Network Configuration

In the case of a VDS, distributed portgroups become available to all hosts sharing the switch automatically. A distributed port group can be used to carry the vSAN traffic. Once the distributed port group is created, VMkernel interfaces on the individual ESXi hosts can then be created to use that distributed port group. This ensures that all VMkernel interfaces across the different ESXi hosts have the same characteristics, e.g., port binding, port allocation, VLAN ID, security settings, traffic shaping as well as teaming and failover settings.

Although the official VMware documentation makes no distinction regarding which versions of Distributed Switch you should be using, the authors recommend using the latest version of the Distributed Switch with vSAN. Note that all ESXi hosts attaching to this Distributed Switch must be running the same version of ESXi when a given Distributed Switch version has been selected. Preferably, the version of the selected Distributed Switch should be the same as the ESXi/vSphere version. Earlier versions of ESXi are not able to utilize newer versions of the Distributed Switch when added to the cluster. Since vSAN ESA was launched with vSphere 8.0, the recommendation is to choose a Distributed Switch version which is compatible with ESXi 8.0 or later.

One of the steps when creating a Distributed Switch is to select whether Network I/O Control is enabled or disabled. We recommend leaving this at the default option of enabled. Later, we discuss the value of NIOC in a vSAN environment.

Port Group Port Allocations

One important consideration with the creation of port groups is the port allocation settings and the number of ports associated with the port group. Note that the default number of ports is eight and that the allocation setting is elastic by default. This means that when all ports are assigned, a new set of eight ports is created. A port group with an allocation type of elastic can automatically increase the number of ports as more devices are allocated. With the port binding set to static, a port is assigned to the VMkernel port when it connects to the distributed port group. If you plan to have a 16-host or larger vSAN cluster, you could consider configuring a greater number of ports for the port group instead of the default of eight. This means that in times of maintenance and outages, the ports always stay available for the host until it is ready to rejoin the cluster, and it means that the switch doesn't incur any overhead by having to delete and re-add the ports.

When creating a distributed switch and distributed port groups, there are a lot of additional options to choose from, such as port binding type. These options are well documented in the official VMware vSphere documentation, and although we discussed port allocation in a little detail here, most of the settings are beyond the scope of this book. Readers who are unfamiliar with these options can find explanations for each of the advanced portgroup settings in the official VMware vSphere documentation. However, you can simply leave these Distributed Switch and port groups at the default settings and vSAN will deploy just fine with those settings.

TCP/IP Stack

One thing we would like to discuss is the TCP/IP stack. The authors often get questions about this. The common question is whether vSAN can use a custom TCP/IP stack, or does vSAN have its own TCP/IP stack? Neither is the case, unfortunately. At the time of writing, vSAN only supports the use of the default TCP/IP stack for the vSAN network. The TCP/IP provisioning stack can only be used for Provisioning traffic and the vMotion TCP/IP stack can only be used for vMotion traffic. You will not be able to select these stacks for vSAN traffic. Options for configuring different network stacks may be found in official VMware documentation and are beyond the scope of this book. Suffice to say that different network stacks can be configured on the ESXi host and can have unique properties such as specific default gateways associated with each network stack. However, these different network stacks are not available to vSAN.

In normal vSAN configurations, not having a custom TCP/IP stack is not an issue. However, when a stretched cluster is implemented additional network configuration steps may need to be considered for each of the hosts in the cluster. This is also a consideration in the case of an L3 (routed network) implementation for the vSAN network. There is of course the ability to override the default gateway when creating the vSAN VMkernel interface and the administrator chooses to use static IP settings in the Add Networking wizard. An alternative to using the "override default gateway" option would be to configure static routes using the CLI. We will talk about these network considerations and configuration in more detail, and how ESXi hosts in a stretched vSAN cluster can communicate over L3 networks in Chapter 7.

IPv4 and IPv6

Other decisions that need to be made when manually configuring the vSAN network stack is whether to use of IPv4 or IPv6, and of course whether to use of DHCP or static IP addresses. VMware vSAN supports both the use of IPv4 and IPv6, so the choice is up to the administrator as an administrator or the network administrator.

Note: While vSAN supports IPv4 or IPv6 for the vSAN network, vSAN File Services currently only supports IPv4. At the time of going to press, vSAN ESA did not support the vSAN File Service. It is currently only available with vSAN OSA. However, it is only a matter of time before vSAN File Service is also supported on vSAN ESA, so it is an important infrastructure consideration. If you do want to use vSAN File Service on vSAN ESA when it becomes available, it is the author's understanding that administrators will need still require IPv4 networking to implement it.

When it comes to the allocation of IP addresses we prefer statically assigned. Although DHCP is fully supported it will make troubleshooting more complex. One definite recommendation around the use of DHCP-allocated IP addresses is to make sure that the range of IP addresses is reserved for vSAN use on the DHCP server. This will prevent other devices from consuming them should a host be offline for an extended period.

Network Configuration Issues

If the vSAN VMkernel is not properly configured, a warning will be displayed in the Skyline Health section on the monitor tab of your vSAN cluster object. If you click the warning for the particular tests that have failed, further details related to the network status of all hosts in the cluster will display. In this scenario none of the hosts in a twelve-host cluster are correctly configured, leading to network connectivity issues as expected. You can also see all hosts in the cluster are in their own partition.

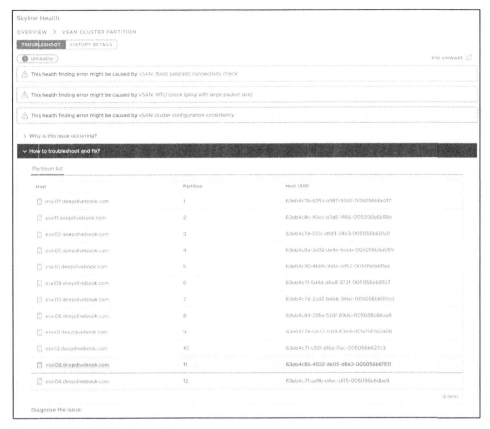

Figure 19: Health Check warning

The Disk Management section of the UI also shows the network partition groups. This issue is also displayed in the Disk Management section of the UI, as lack of network connectivity will impact vSAN capacity. Once the networking issue is addressed, the network partition issue is resolved and all hosts appear in the same network partition group, Group 1, as show next.

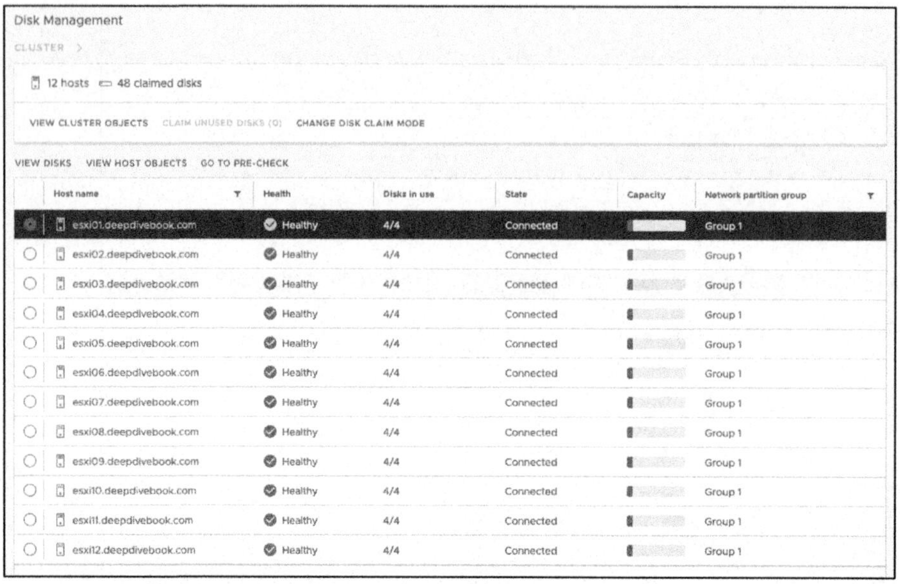

Figure 20: Disk Management

Network I/O Control Configuration Example

As previously mentioned, Network I/O Control (NIOC) can be used to guarantee bandwidth for vSAN cluster communication and I/O. NIOC is available only on VDS, not on the standard switch, VSS. Indeed, for non-vSAN deployments, VDS is only available with some of the higher vSphere editions. However, as mentioned earlier, vSAN includes VDS irrespective of the vSphere edition used.

If you are using an earlier version of a Distributed Switch which is earlier than your vSphere version, although not explicitly called out in the vSphere documentation, the authors recommend upgrading to the most recent version of the Distributed Switch (8.0 or later) if you plan to use it with vSAN ESA.

Network I/O Control

VMware does not require dedicated NICs for vSAN traffic, but dedicated interfaces have become common in high-performance environments. However, to offset the cost of purchasing high speed NICs, NIOC may be used to ensure fairness of bandwidth to the different traffic types sharing the same adapter. NIOC has a traffic type called *vSAN traffic,* and thus provides QoS on vSAN traffic. Although this QoS configuration might not be necessary for most vSAN cluster environments, it is a good feature to have available if vSAN traffic appears to be impacted by other traffic types sharing the same network interface card.

An example of a traffic type that could impact vSAN is *vMotion*. By its very nature, vMotion traffic is "bursty" and might claim the full available bandwidth on a NIC port, impacting other traffic types sharing the NIC, including vSAN traffic. Leveraging NIOC in those situations will avoid a self-imposed *denial-of-service* (DoS) attack which might be observed during a maintenance mode operation for instance, where many VMs are migrated concurrently.

Setting up NIOC is quite straightforward, and once configured it will guarantee a certain bandwidth for the vSAN traffic between all hosts. NIOC is enabled by default when a VDS is created. If the feature was disabled during the initial creation of the Distributed Switch, it may be enabled once again by editing the Distributed Switch properties via the vSphere Client. To begin with, use the vSphere Client to select the VDS in the network section. From there, select the VDS and navigate to the configure tab and select the resource allocation view. This displays the NIOC configuration options.

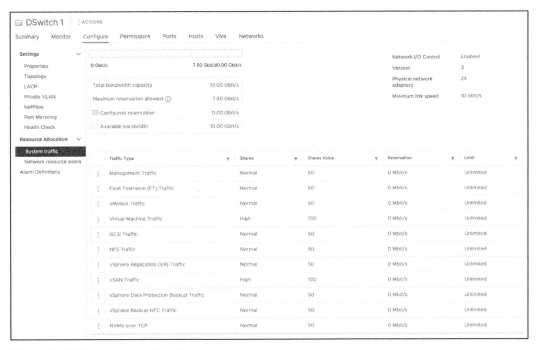

Figure 21: NIOC resource allocation

To change the resource allocation for the vSAN traffic in NIOC, simply click on the three vertical dots next to the vSAN traffic type and select Edit. The next screenshot shows the modifiable configuration options for each traffic stream.

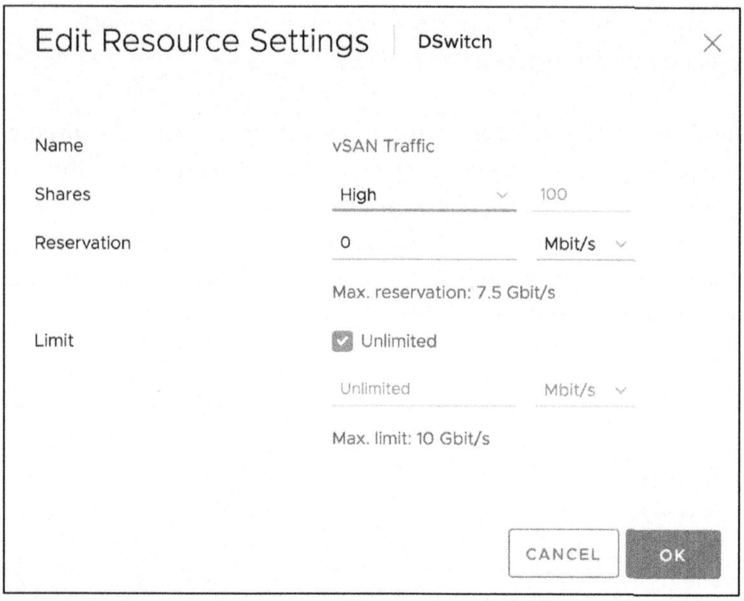

Edit Resource Settings | DSwitch | X

Name	vSAN Traffic	
Shares	High ∨	100
Reservation	0	Mbit/s ∨
	Max. reservation: 7.5 Gbit/s	
Limit	☑ Unlimited	
	Unlimited	Mbit/s ∨
	Max. limit: 10 Gbit/s	

CANCEL   OK

Figure 22: NIOC configuration

By default, the limit is set to unlimited, physical adapter shares are set to 100 (High), and there is no reservation. The unlimited value means that vSAN network traffic is allowed to consume all the network bandwidth when there is no congestion. We do not recommend setting a limit on the vSAN traffic. The reason for this is because a limit is a "hard" setting. In other words, if a 10Gbps limit is configured on vSAN traffic, the traffic will be limited even when additional bandwidth is available. Therefore, you should not use limits because of this behavior.

With a reservation, you can configure the minimum bandwidth that needs to be available for a particular traffic stream. This must not exceed 75% of available bandwidth. The reason for not using reservations is because unused reserved bandwidth cannot be allocated to other traffic like, for instance, VM traffic. We recommend leaving this at the default setting and instead using the shares mechanism.

With the share mechanism, if network contention arises, the shares setting will be used by NIOC for traffic management. These shares are compared with the share values assigned to other traffic types to determine which traffic type gets priority. You can use shares to "artificially limit" your traffic types based on actual resource usage and demand.

With vSAN deployments, VMware is recommending a 25GbE network infrastructure at a minimum. In these deployments, two 25GbE network ports are usually used and are connected to two physical 25GbE capable switches to provide availability. The various types of traffic will need to share this network capacity, and this is where NIOC can prove invaluable.

Design Considerations: Distributed Switch and Network I/O Control

To provide QoS and performance predictability, vSAN and NIOC should go hand in hand. Before discussing the configuration options, the following types of networks are being considered:

- Management Network
- vMotion Network
- vSAN Network
- VM Network

This design consideration assumes 25GbE redundant networking links and a redundant switch pair for availability. Two scenarios will be described. These scenarios are based on the type of network switch used:

1. Redundant 25GbE switch setup *without* "link aggregation" capability
2. Redundant 25GbE switch setup *with* "link aggregation" capability

Note: Link aggregation (IEEE 802.3ad) allows users to use more than one connection between network devices. It combines multiple physical connections into one logical connection and provides a level of redundancy and bandwidth improvement.

In both configurations, recommended practice dictates that you create the following port groups and VMkernel interfaces:

- 1 × Management VMkernel interface
- 1 × vMotion VMkernel interface
- 1 × vSAN VMkernel interface
- 1 × VM port group

To simplify the configuration, you should have a single vSAN and vMotion VMkernel interface per host.

To ensure traffic types are separated on different physical ports, we will leverage standard Distributed Switch capabilities. We will also show how to use shares to avoid noisy neighbor scenarios.

Scenario 1: Redundant 25GbE Switch Without "Link Aggregation" Capability

In this configuration, two individual 25GbE uplinks are available. It is recommended to separate traffic and designate a single 25GbE uplink to vSAN for simplicity reasons. We often are asked how much bandwidth each traffic type requires; we recommend monitoring current bandwidth consumption and making design decisions based on facts. However, for this exercise, we will make assumptions based on our experience and commonly used configurations by our customers.

The recommended minimum amount of bandwidth to dynamically keep available per traffic type is as follows:

- **Management VMkernel interface**: 5 GbE
- **vMotion VMkernel interface**: 10 GbE
- **VM Port Group**: 10 GbE
- **vSAN VMkernel interface**: 25 GbE

Again, it is important to highlight that these are not applicable if there is no contention for network resources. These bandwidth throttling mechanisms only kick-in when there is network contention.

Note that various traffic types will share the same uplink. The management network, VM network, and vMotion network traffic are configured to share uplink 1, and vSAN traffic is configured to use uplink 2. With the network configuration done this way, sufficient bandwidth exists for all the various types of traffic when the vSAN cluster is in a normal operating state.

To make sure that no single traffic type can impact other traffic types during times of contention, NIOC is configured, and the shares mechanism is deployed. When defining traffic type network shares, this scenario works under the assumption that there is only one physical port available and that all traffic types share that same physical port for this exercise.

This scenario also considers a worst-case scenario approach. This will guarantee performance even when a failure has occurred. By taking this approach, we can ensure that vSAN always has 50% of the bandwidth at its disposal while leaving the remaining traffic types with sufficient bandwidth to avoid a potential self-inflicted Denial of Service (DoS).

The following table outlines the recommendations for configuring shares for the different traffic types. Note that in the table we have only outlined the most used traffic types. In our scenario, we have divided the total amount of shares across the different traffic types based on the expected minimum bandwidth requirements per traffic type.

TRAFFIC TYPE	SHARES	LIMIT
Management VMkernel Interface	20	N/A
vMotion VMkernel Interface	40	N/A
VM Port Group	40	N/A
vSAN VMkernel Interface	100	N/A

Table 2: Recommended share configuration per traffic type

Explicit Failover Order

When selecting the uplinks used for the various types of traffic, you should separate traffic types to provide predictability and avoid noisy neighbor scenarios. The configuration listed in the next table is our recommendation.

TRAFFIC TYPE	EXPLICIT FAILOVER ORDER
Management VMkernel Interface	Uplink 1 active/Uplink 2 standby
vMotion VMkernel Interface	Uplink 1 active/Uplink 2 standby
VM Port Group	Uplink 1 active/Uplink 2 standby
vSAN VMkernel Interface	Uplink 2 active/Uplink 1 standby

Table 3: Recommended explicit failover order per traffic type

Setting an explicit failover order in the teaming and failover section of the port groups is recommended for predictability. The explicit failover order always uses the highest-order uplink from the list of active adapters that passes failover detection criteria.

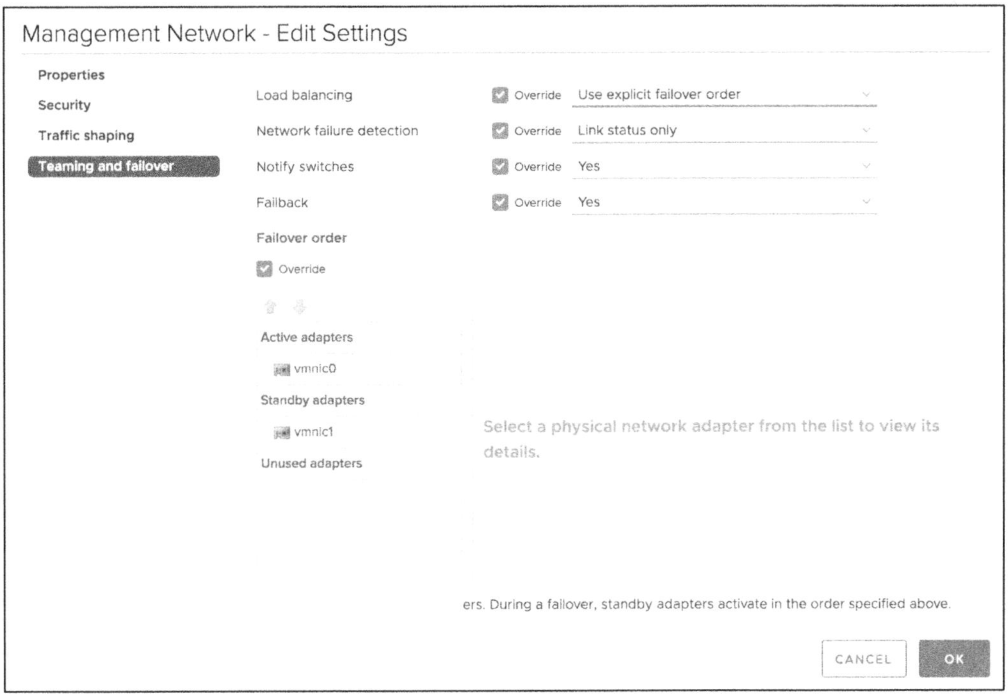

Figure 23: Using Explicit Failover Order

Separating traffic types allows for optimal storage performance while also providing sufficient bandwidth for the vMotion and VM traffic. This could also be achieved by using the *load-based teaming* (LBT) mechanism. However, the LBT load balancing period is 30 seconds, potentially causing a short period of contention when "bursty" traffic share the same uplinks. Also note that when troubleshooting network issues, it might be difficult to keep track of the relationship between the physical NIC port and VMkernel interface when using LBT.

While this configuration provides a level of availability, it doesn't offer any sort of balancing for the vSAN traffic. It Is either using one uplink or the other uplink. Thus, one disadvantage of this approach is that the vSAN traffic will never be able to use more than the bandwidth of a single NIC port. In the next section, we will discuss a network configuration that provides availability as well as load-balancing across uplinks, allowing vSAN to consume available bandwidth on multiple uplinks.

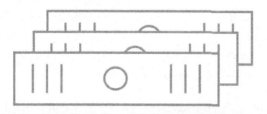

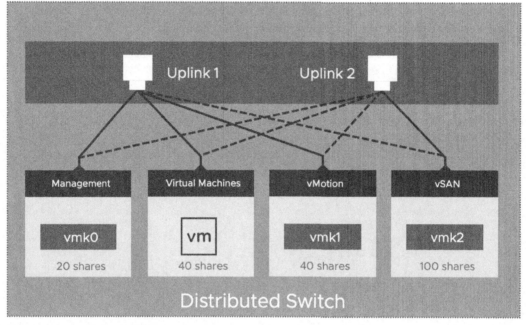

Figure 24: Using Explicit Failover Order

Scenario 2: Redundant 25 GbE Switch with Link Aggregation Capability

In this next scenario, there are two 25 GbE uplinks set up in a teamed configuration (often referred to as EtherChannel or Link Aggregation - LAG). Because of the physical switch capabilities, the configuration of the virtual layer will be extremely simple. We will consider the previous recommended minimum bandwidth requirements for the design:

- **Management Network interface**: 5 GbE
- **vMotion VMkernel interface**: 10 GbE
- **VM Port Group**: 10 GbE
- **vSAN VMkernel interface**: 25 GbE

When the physical uplinks are teamed (link aggregation), the Distributed Switch load-balancing mechanism is required to be configured with one of the following configuration options:

- IP-Hash
- Link Aggregation Control Protocol (LACP)

IP-Hash is a load-balancing option available to VMkernel interfaces that are connected to multiple uplinks on an ESXi host. An uplink is chosen based on a hash of the source and destination IP addresses of each packet. For non-IP packets, whatever is located at those IP address offsets in the packet is used to compute the hash. Again, this may not work well with vSAN since there may be only a single vSAN IP address per host.

LACP allows you to connect ESXi hosts to physical switches by employing dynamic link aggregation. LAGs (link aggregation groups) are created on the Distributed Switch to aggregate the bandwidth of the physical NICs on the ESXi hosts that are in turn connected to LACP port channels.

The official vSphere networking guide has much more detail on IP-hash and LACP support and should be referenced for additional details. Also, the vSAN Network Design documentation discusses LACP extensively. (https://vmwa.re/vsannetwork)

> **Although IP-Hash and LACP aggregate physical NICs (and/or ports), the algorithm used selects which physical NIC port to use for a particular data stream. A data stream with the same source and destination address will, as a result, only use a single physical NIC port and thus not use the aggregate bandwidth.**

It is recommended to configure all port groups and VMkernel interfaces to use either LACP or IP-Hash depending on the type of physical switch being used:

- Management VMkernel interface = LACP/IP-Hash
- vMotion VMkernel interface = LACP/IP-Hash
- VM Port Group = LACP/IP-Hash
- vSAN VMkernel interface = LACP/IP-Hash

Because various traffic types will share the same uplinks, you also want to make sure that no traffic type can affect other types of traffic during times of contention. For that, the NIOC shared mechanism is once again used.

Working under the same assumptions as before that there is only one physical port available and that all traffic types share the same physical port, we once again take a worst-case scenario approach into consideration. This approach will guarantee performance even in a failure scenario. By taking this approach, we can ensure that vSAN always has 50% of the bandwidth at its disposal while giving the other network traffic types sufficient bandwidth to avoid a potential self-inflicted DoS situation arising.

When both uplinks are available, this will equate to 25GbE for vSAN traffic. When only one uplink is available (due to NIC failure or maintenance reasons), the bandwidth is also cut in half, giving a 12.5GbE bandwidth. Once more, this is only applicable in times of network contention. During normal operations, the network is given as much bandwidth as it wants. Table 2 in the previous example outlines the recommendations for configuring shares for the traffic types.

The next diagram depicts this configuration scenario.

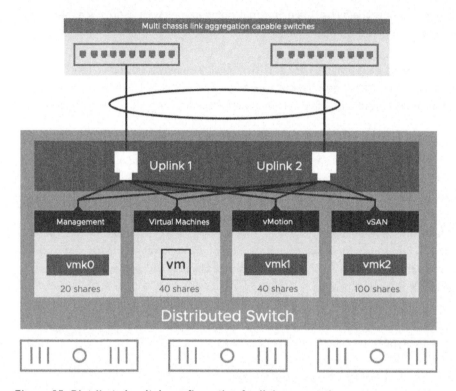

Figure 25: Distributed switch configuration for link aggregation

Either of the scenarios discussed here should provide an optimal network configuration for your vSAN cluster. However, once again we do want to highlight that whilst all these configurations provide availability, the one that we have found to provide the best load-balancing across uplinks, and thus the best-aggregated performance is the LACP configuration. This has to be weighed up against the added complexity of configuring Link Aggregation on the physical switch.

vSAN over RDMA

vSAN OSA began supporting Remote Direct Memory Access (RDMA) with release 7.0 U2. vSAN ESA also supports RDMA. RDMA is an alternative network communication protocol to TCP. The advantages of RDMA are that it typically lowers CPU utilization and has lower I/O latency. There are a number of requirements before RDMA can be enabled on a vSAN deployment. The Network Interface Cards must be RDMA capable, listed on the VMware Hardware Compatibility Guide and must be the same NIC on all vSAN hosts in the cluster. If for some reason one of the hosts cannot use RDMA, the entire vSAN cluster will switch back to communicating over TCP. RDMA over Converged Ethernet (RoCE) is the network protocol which allows RDMA over an ethernet network. To enable RDMA support on a vSAN cluster, the hosts must support RoCE v2.

Note that vSAN clusters which use RDMA are limited to 32 hosts. Also note that vSAN hosts which use RDMA cannot implement LACP or IP-hash-based NIC teaming as discussed in the previous sections. However, vSAN hosts using RDMA do support NIC failover. The vSAN cluster must also use RDMA over Layer 2. Using RDMA over Layer 3 is not supported.

RDMA makes extensive use of the DCB, the Data Center Bridging protocol. VMware recommends that the network interface cards that support RDMA are configured with DCBx mode set to IEEE. It also requires that the network switches are configured to use DCB with Priority Flow Control. vSAN traffic must be configured as lossless and have a priority level of 3.

vSphere High Availability

vSphere *High Availability* (HA) is fully supported on a vSAN cluster to provide additional availability to VMs deployed in the cluster; however, several significant changes have been made to vSphere HA to ensure correct interoperability with vSAN. These changes are important to understand as they will impact the way you configure vSphere HA.

vSphere HA Communication Network

In non-vSAN deployments, communication of vSphere HA agents takes place over the management network. In a vSAN environment, vSphere HA agents communicate over the vSAN network. The reasoning behind this is that in the event of a network failure we want vSphere HA and vSAN to be part of the same network partition. This avoids possible conflicts when vSphere HA and vSAN observe different partitions when a failure occurs, with different partitions holding subsets of the storage components and objects. As such vSAN always needs to be configured before vSphere HA is enabled. If vSAN is configured after vSphere HA is configured, then a warning will inform you to temporarily disable HA first before continuing with the configuration of vSAN.

> **vSAN always needs to be configured before vSphere HA is enabled. If vSphere HA is already enabled, it needs to be disabled temporarily!**

vSphere HA in vSAN environments, by default, continues to use the management network's default gateway for isolation detection. We suspect that most vSAN environments will have the management network and the vSAN network sharing the same physical infrastructure, but logically separate them using VLANs. If the vSAN and management networks are on a different physical or logical network, it is required to change the default vSphere HA isolation address from the management network to the vSAN network. The reason for this is that in the event of a vSAN network issue that leads to a host being isolated from a vSAN perspective, vSphere HA won't take any action. This is because the isolation response IP address is set on the management network, implying that it might still be possible to ping the isolated host.

By default, the isolation address is the default gateway of the management network as previously mentioned. VMware's recommendation when using vSphere HA with vSAN is to use an IP address on the vSAN network as an isolation address. To prevent vSphere HA from using the default gateway, and to use an IP address on the vSAN network, the following settings must be changed in the advanced options for vSphere HA.

- das.usedefaultisolationaddress=false
- das.isolationaddress0=<IP address on vSAN network>

In some cases, there may not be a suitable isolation address on the vSAN network. However, most network switches can create a so-called Switch Virtual Interface. Discuss this with your network administrator as this may be a viable alternative. We have seen customers who configured the isolation address to use one, or multiple, IP addresses of their vSAN VMkernel interfaces. This however is not recommended. In a scenario where the host is isolated, and it is the IP address of that host which is used as the isolation address, it will be impossible to declare the host isolated as the host will always be able to ping its own interface.

vSphere HA Heartbeat Datastores

Another noticeable difference with vSphere HA on vSAN is that the vSAN datastore cannot be used for datastore heartbeats. These heartbeats play a significant role in determining VM ownership in the event of a vSphere HA cluster partition with traditional Storage Area Networks (SAN) or Network Attached Storage (NAS) datastores. vSphere HA does not use the vSAN datastore for heart-beating and won't let a user designate it as a heartbeat datastore. If no heartbeat datastores can be configured, vSphere HA will display a warning. This warning can be disabled by configuring the following advanced setting.

- das.ignoreInsufficientHbDatastore = true

Note: If ESXi hosts participating in a vSAN cluster also have access to shared storage, either VMFS (Virtual Machine File System) or NFS (Network File System), these traditional datastores may be used for vSphere HA heartbeats.

vSphere HA Admission Control

There is another consideration to discuss regarding vSphere HA and vSAN interoperability. When configuring vSphere HA, one of the decisions that should be made is about admission control. Admission control ensures that vSphere HA has sufficient resources at its disposal to restart VMs after a failure, e.g., an ESXi host has failed, and the CPU and memory resources on that failed host are no longer available to run virtual machine workloads. vSphere HA does this by setting aside resources which can be used when a failure has occurred.

vSAN has a mechanism which automatically sets aside storage capacity resources. This is to ensure that objects which are impacted by a failure can be rebuilt. This functionality is called "Host rebuild reserve" and can be enabled under the Reservation and Alerts configuration options for vSAN on the Configure > vSAN > Services view in the vSphere client. Although it provides similar functionality as vSphere HA Admission Control does, it is not the same. If a failure occurs, vSAN will try to use the reserved capacity on the remaining nodes in the cluster to bring the VMs to a compliant state by rebuilding any missing or failed components. The next screenshot shows our environment where we have both Host rebuild reserve, as well as Operations reserve enabled. These reserves will be discussed in greater detail in chapter 6, vSAN Operations.

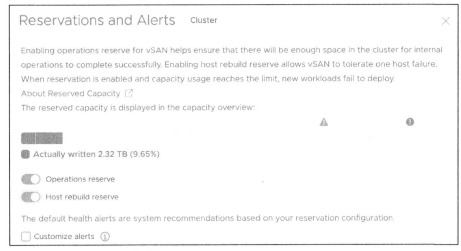

Figure 26: vSAN Host rebuild reserve

vSphere HA Isolation Response

When a host isolation event occurs in a vSAN cluster with vSphere HA enabled, vSphere HA will apply the configured isolation response. With vSphere HA, you can select a number of different types of responses to an isolation event to specify what action to take on virtual machines that are on the isolated host:

- Disabled (Default)
- Power off and restart VMs (vSAN Recommended)
- Shut down and restart VMs

The recommendation is to have vSphere HA automatically power off the VMs running on that host when a host isolation event occurs. Therefore, the "isolation response" should be set to "**power off and restart VMs**" and not the default setting that is "Disabled".

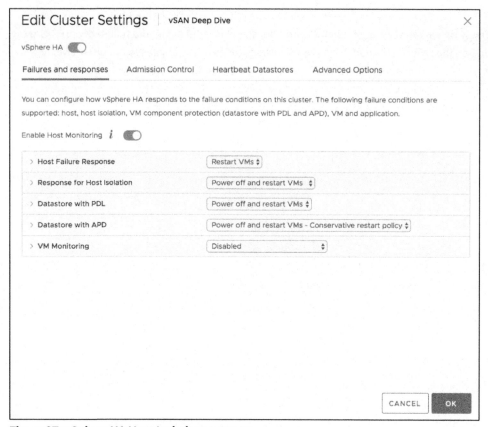

Figure 27: vSphere HA Host Isolation response

Note that "Power off and restart VMs" is like pulling the power cable from a physical host. The VM process is killed. *This is not a clean shutdown!* In the case of an isolation event, however, it is unlikely that vSAN can write to the disks on the isolated host and, as such, powering off is recommended. If the ESXi host is partitioned, it is also unlikely that any VM on the isolated host will be able to access a quorum of components of the storage object.

The question then remains, would it be beneficial to configure heartbeat datastores when available in a vSAN environment. The following table describes the different failure scenarios we have tested with a logically separated vSAN and Management network, with and without the availability of heartbeat datastores and a correctly and incorrectly configured isolation address.

ISOLATION ADDRESS	DATASTORE HEARTBEATS	OBSERVED BEHAVIOR
IP on vSAN Network	Not configured	The isolated host cannot ping the isolation address, isolation is declared, VMs killed and VMs restarted
IP on Management Network	Not configured	Can ping the isolation address, isolation is not declared, yet rest of the cluster restarts the VMs even though they are still running on the isolated hosts
IP on vSAN Network	Configured	The isolated host cannot ping the isolation address, isolation is declared, VMs killed and VMs restarted
IP on Management Network	Configured	VMs are not powered-off and not restarted as the "isolated host" can still ping the management network and the datastore heartbeat mechanism is used to inform the master about the state. The master knows HA network is not working, but the VMs are not powered off.

Table 4: Recommended share configuration per traffic type

Key Takeaways

- Always use an isolation address that is in the same network as vSAN when the management network and the vSAN network is logically or physically separated. By doing so, during an isolation, the isolation is validated using the vSAN VMkernel interface.
- Always set the isolation response to power-off, this would avoid the scenario of a duplicate MAC address or IP address on the network when VMs are restarted when you have a single network being isolated for a specific host.
- Last but not least, if you have traditional storage, then you can enable heartbeat datastores. It doesn't add much in terms of availability, but still, it will allow vSphere HA to communicate state through the datastore.

Proactive HA support

Proactive HA is a feature which monitors the state of a host and enables vSphere to decide on whether to proactively migrate VMs from a degraded host before it has a complete failure.

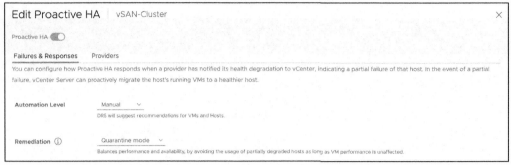

Figure 28: Configure Proactive HA

When Proactive HA is configured, vSphere client plugins from server vendors are required to configure it. These plugins are known as Providers. vSAN will now consider the state of a host when placing data and will also proactively move data from a host when a host is degraded.

If your server vendor of choice supports Proactive HA, we would recommend considering enabling it with the automation level set to "Automated" and the remediation level set to "Mixed mode". In the case of "Mixed mode" Proactive HA will decide, based on the type of failure that has occurred, whether to place the host into maintenance mode or to place it into quarantine mode. This "Mixed mode" balances performance with availability. It only uses partially or moderately degraded hosts for data placement if virtual machine workloads performance is at risk by not doing so.

vSphere HA VM Component Protection (VMCP)

In a traditional SAN and NAS environment it is possible to configure a response to an *all paths down* (APD) scenario *and permanent device loss* (PDL) scenario within HA. This capability is part of a feature called VM Component Protection (VMCP) and if vSphere HA detects a datastore accessibility issue, it can automatically begin failing over virtual machines to a host that can still access the datastore.

At the time of writing this is not supported for vSAN and as such a response to APD and/or PDL does not have to be configured for vSphere HA in a vSAN only cluster. However, it can be configured when traditional datastores are available in your environment, or when you are leveraging vSAN HCI Mesh to mount remote vSAN datastores. HCI Mesh will be discussed in greater detail in later chapters of the book.

Now that we know what has changed for vSphere HA, let's take a look at some core constructs of vSAN.

Storage Pool

The vSAN ESA removes the concept of disk groups and negates the need for administrator to consider sizing and compatibility of the different caching and capacity tiers. In its place, vSAN ESA introduces the construct called "storage pool." This storage pool contains all storage devices on a host that are used to provide storage resources to vSAN. At the time of going to press, the only support storage devices for vSAN ESA are NVMe. All devices in a storage pool contribute to both capacity and performance. Note that there can only be one storage pool per host, and this storage pool contributes to a single vSAN datastore per cluster.

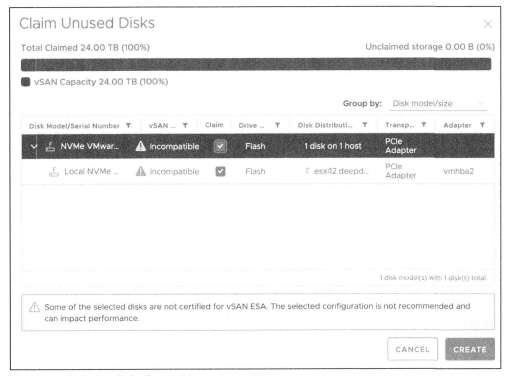

Figure 29: Claiming disks for vSAN

After the storage pools have been created on each host, the vSAN datastore is created. This vSAN datastore can now be used for the deployment of VMs or other types of vSAN objects like iSCSI volumes, CNS Container Volumes, etc.

vSAN Datastore Properties

The raw size of a vSAN datastore is governed by the number of storage pool devices per ESXi host and the number of ESXi hosts in the vSAN cluster. Since vSAN ESA now uses a single tier for both performance and capacity, storage devices use a new, modified object format to store data in an object in two legs. These legs are known as the performance leg, and the capacity leg. These constructs will be covered in much greater detail in the architecture section but suffice to say that these legs are used by components from the same object. This enables vSAN to deliver both performance and capacity all from the same tier.

Let's now look at the raw capacity of the datastore. Raw capacity is measured by simply adding the capacity of all of the NVMe devices in each storage pool in each host in the vSphere/vSAN cluster. Now we know how to calculate how much raw capacity available. But how do we know much effective capacity we will have? This calculation needs to include the overheads one might observe when enabling vSAN ESA. Thus, effective capacity depends on various factors. One aspect is whether the data compression feature is enabled. It is enabled by default, but in vSAN ESA, it is configurable on a per object basis. Therefore, this space efficiency feature plays a big factor in the effective capacity. We will discuss space efficiency features in more detail in Chapter 4.

But it is not just compression that can provide space-saving on the vSAN datastore or can change the amount of available effective capacity. There is also the number of replica copies configured if the VM is using a RAID-1 policy. This is enabled through the policy-based management framework. Conversely, you may decide to use erasure coding policies such as RAID-5 and RAID-6 which include one or more parity components depending on the configuration chosen.

Similarly, all objects on vSAN ESA are thin provisioned by default. Thus, if an 8TB VMDK is requested, but only 4TB is written, then the overhead of the replica copies mentioned previously is only 4TB as well. Replica overheads only apply to the capacity used, not the capacity provisioned.

On top of that, there's also the ability to reserve capacity for vSAN maintenance operations and rebuild operations after host failures. Enabling these reservation options will directly impact how many VMs can be deployed on the datastore.

From an overhead perspective, there are two areas that should be considered. These are the vSAN Log-Structured File System (LFS) overheads for an object, and the global metadata. Both will be discussed in detail in chapter 4 when the architecture of the vSAN ESA is reviewed. At present, it is enough to understand that the LFS helps deliver the high performance associated with the vSAN ESA, while the global metadata helps vSAN ESA store large amounts of data in a very space-efficient and scalable manner. The vSAN LFS overheads for an object will consume an additional 13% of the total raw capacity of a cluster, whilst global metadata will typically consume 10% of the total raw capacity of a cluster.

Once the storage pools are created, vSAN is configured and the vSAN datastore is formed. At this point, a number of datastore capabilities are surfaced up into vCenter Server. These capabilities will be used to create the appropriate VM storage policies for VMs, and their associated virtual machine disk (VMDK) storage objects deployed on the vSAN datastore. Before deploying VMs, however, you first need to understand how to create appropriate VM storage policies that meet the requirements of the application running in the VM.

VM storage policies and vSAN capabilities will be discussed in greater detail later in Chapter 5, "VM Storage Policies and VM Provisioning," but at present it is enough to know that these capabilities form the VM policy requirements. These allow a vSphere administrator to specify requirements based on performance, availability, and data services when it comes to VM provisioning. Chapter 5 discusses VM storage policies in the context of vSAN and how to correctly deploy a VM using vSAN capabilities.

Summary

If everything is configured and working as designed, vSAN can be configured in just a few clicks. However, it is vitally important that the infrastructure is ready in advance. Identifying appropriate performance and capacity characteristics of the NVMe devices and verifying that your networking is configured to provide the best availability and performance are all tasks that must be configured and designed up front.

Now the vSAN cluster is up and running, let's look at some of the architectural components of vSAN in the next chapter.

04

Architectural Details

This chapter examines some of the underlying architectural details of vSAN as implemented in the Express Storage Architecture (ESA). While the vSAN ESA is significantly different from the Original Storage Architecture (OSA), it shares many of the architectural details found in the OSA. In a distributed storage solution like vSAN, concepts around data availability and resilience have not changed, but hardware has, and the ESA was designed to exploit the full capabilities of today's hardware.

This chapter covers concepts of data storage, resilience, and availability in the vSAN ESA. These concepts introduce terminology and a model of storage that is different from traditional three-tier architectures. Although most vSphere administrators will never see many of these low-level constructs, it will be useful to understand the various aspects of vSAN to help in your design, operation, and optimization of the platform in your environment.

Before examining some of the lower-level details, here is one concept that we need to discuss first as it is the core of vSAN: distributed RAID (Redundant Array of Inexpensive Disks).

Distributed RAID

vSAN stores data in a resilient way by distributing data across multiple hosts in a vSAN cluster. It achieves this by using many types of distributed RAID schemes. In the case of vSAN, these data placement schemes use the network to distribute data across hosts in a resilient way. As the name suggests, it means that a vSAN cluster can withstand the failure of one or more ESXi hosts (or physical components in that host, such as a storage device, or network interface card) while ensuring that the VM and the data it serves remains available.

vSAN allows administrators to define resilience in a granular way. VM resilience settings are defined on a per-VM or per-VMDK basis using storage policies. This unique ability comes from how vSAN defines and uses a relatively small boundary of data, known as objects, which will be discussed in more detail in this chapter.

Assigning levels of resilience through storage policies applies to all object types in vSAN, including iSCSI LUNs, and persistent volumes for cloud-native services. To simplify comprehension, we will often use a VM or objects that comprise a VM such as a virtual disk for the examples used in this book.

Storage policies allow the administrator to define how many hosts or device failures an object can tolerate for the hosts that the object resides on while remaining available. If you choose not to set an availability requirement in the storage policy by setting the number of *failures to tolerate* equal to zero, a host or storage device failure can impact an object's availability. More detailed information on policy settings will be discussed in chapter 5.

Early versions of vSAN only used RAID-1 (synchronous mirroring) as a way to provide data resilience across hosts. vSAN would synchronously mirror an object's data to one or more locations, or hosts. The number of copies (replicas) of an object depended on the *number of failures to tolerate* requirement in the storage policy assigned. The ability to select a higher level of failures to tolerate depended on the available resources in the cluster, such as the number of hosts, and storage devices. Depending on the VM storage policy, you could have up to three replica objects of a VM's disk (VMDK) object across a vSAN cluster for availability, assuming there were enough hosts in the cluster to accommodate this. By default, vSAN always deploys VMs with *failures to tolerate* equal to 1, meaning that when new VM objects are deployed that are not using a user-defined storage policy, the data will be stored in a resilient way.

vSAN also uses other RAID types: RAID-5 and RAID-6. These are commonly referred to as erasure coding. Erasure coding is a method of storing data resiliently by fragmenting data across some physical boundary in a manner that maintains access to the data in the event of a fragment or fragments becoming unavailable. In vSAN, erasure codes stripe the data with parity across hosts. Unlike a RAID-1 mirror where there are two or more copies of the data, an object using erasure coding will have the data and parity fragments spread across the hosts storing the object to provide this resilience. Data and parity fragments reside within each of the components that comprise an object. There is no dedicated parity component.

RAID-5/6 erasure coding allows for data to be stored resiliently in a much more space-efficient way than data stored resiliently using RAID-1. How much better will depend on the *failures to tolerate* setting chosen. The erasure code used by vSAN is embedded into the *failures to tolerate* setting in the storage policy, stated as "1 failure – RAID-5 (Erasure Coding)" and "2 failures – RAID-6 (Erasure Coding)" respectively.

Since the vSAN ESA only supports all-flash configurations, both RAID-5 and RAID-6 can be used if there are a sufficient number of hosts in the cluster to support the desired configuration. In the OSA, a RAID-5 erasure code would spread the object data and parity in a 3+1 (data+parity) configuration across a minimum of 4 hosts, thus requiring a minimum cluster size of 4 hosts. The ESA uses a new adaptive erasure coding scheme that will use one of two RAID-5 schemes depending on the size of the cluster. For ESA clusters with 6 or more hosts, an object using RAID-5 will distribute the object data with parity in a 4+1 (data+parity) configuration across 5 hosts. For ESA clusters with fewer than 6 hosts, an object using RAID-5 will distribute the object data with parity in a 2+1 (data+parity) configuration across 3 hosts. This offers guaranteed levels of space efficiency for data stored on vSAN clusters with a very small number of hosts. The following diagram shows an example of a RAID-5 object using a 4+1 configuration. Not shown in this diagram is the 6th ESXi host in the vSAN cluster, which is a requirement for RAID-5 in ESA.

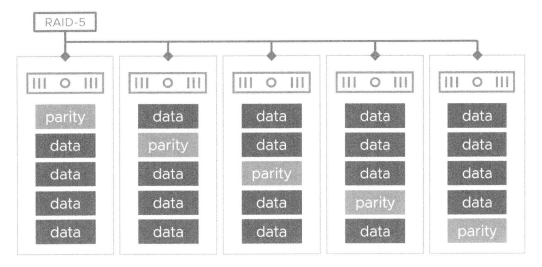

Figure 30: RAID-5 using distributed parity in vSAN

Since a RAID-5 object will include a single parity fragment for every stripe written, it can tolerate only one host failure. A RAID-6 object will include two parity fragments for every stripe written and can tolerate two host failures. As shown in the next diagram, an object using RAID-6 will distribute data across a minimum of 6 hosts.

An object using RAID-5 can tolerate only one host failure since it stores one parity segment for every stripe written. An object using RAID-6 is designed to tolerate two host failures. It will distribute the object data with parity across 6 hosts.

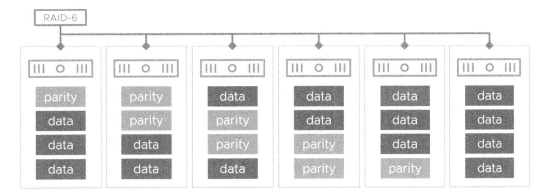

Figure 31: RAID-6 deployment with distributed parity

The capacity savings can be understood with the following simplified comparison. If a VMDK stores 100GB of data, and *failures to tolerate* is set to 1 using RAID-1, a total of 200GB of capacity would be consumed on the vSAN datastore. If *failures to tolerate* is set to 2 using RAID-1, a total of 300GB of capacity would be consumed on the datastore. With RAID-5, depending on the size of the cluster, a total of 125GB (4+1) or 150GB (2+1) would be consumed to tolerate one failure. With RAID-6, a total of 150GB (4+2) would be consumed to tolerate two failures.

While RAID-5/6 stores data in a resilient and space-efficient manner, it did have some performance trade-offs when using the OSA. For performance-sensitive workloads, customers could use storage policies based on RAID-1 mirroring to ensure optimal performance. The design of the ESA eliminates this consideration, as it will deliver efficient RAID-5 and RAID-6 erasure coding with performance as fast or faster than RAID-1 mirroring. This can simplify the use and management of storage policies, where RAID-5/6 can be used in all conditions except for site-level resilience in a stretched cluster, and host-level resilience in 2-node clusters.

Objects and Components

Now that we have explained how VMs are protected, it is important to understand the concept that the vSAN datastore is an *object storage system* and that VMs are now made up of a few different storage objects. This is a different concept for vSphere administrators as traditionally a VM has been made up of a set of files on a LUN or volume.

We have not spoken in detail about objects and components so far, so before we go into detail about the various types of objects, let's start with the definition and concepts of an object and component on vSAN.

Objects are the main unit of storage on vSAN. They are a logical boundary of data that instead of representing an entire clustered file system like VMFS, represent a much smaller unit of storage, such as a VMDK supporting a VM. This is an ideal approach for a distributed storage system like vSAN that must account for temporary or sustained failure conditions in hosts or devices across a cluster and scale out easily when adding more hosts. It eliminates the complexity of trying to maintain a classic, monolithic file system across a distributed architecture, and provides better availability, simplified scalability, and more granular management of the VMs and data stored.

An *object* is an individual storage block device, compatible with SCSI semantics that resides on the vSAN datastore. It may be created on-demand and at any size, though some object sizes are limited. For example, VMDKs follow the vSphere capacity limitation of 62TB. In vSAN, the objects that make up a virtual machine are VMDKs, the VM home namespace, and when the VM is powered on, a VM swap object is also created. A namespace object can be thought of as a directory-like object, where files can be stored. When using the vSAN OSA, snapshots are treated as their own object. In the ESA, snapshots exist within the properties of an existing object.

In case a failure has occurred, you may also see a special object called a durability component.

This component is used by vSAN to temporarily store new writes and is very similar to a regular VMDK component, but we will discuss this in more depth at a later stage.

Other object types include iSCSI targets and LUNs, and a performance stats object used for storing vSAN performance metrics. iSCSI targets are like VM home namespaces, and iSCSI LUNs and file shares are like VMDKs. The performance stats database is also akin to a namespace object. vSAN will also use objects for storing infrastructure-supporting files on a vSAN datastore. For example, if a directory is created to store ISO files or content libraries, this will create a namespace object. vSAN 8.0 U1 and newer will also use namespace objects to store trace files to help with troubleshooting.

Each object in vSAN uses its own RAID tree that translates the requirements set in the assigned policy into a layout of data on physical devices across the hosts in a cluster. It is the RAID tree that spreads the data across hosts in a structured, resilient way. A storage policy is what defines the layout of the object.

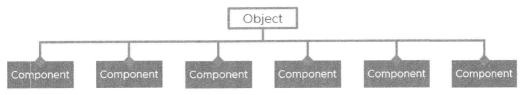

Figure 32: Simplified RAID tree in vSAN

To make an object resilient, vSAN breaks objects into smaller chunks of data and ensures copies of that data are placed on different hosts across a cluster. A *component* is a term used to represent this smaller piece of data. Components are the leaves of an object's RAID tree. They are an implementation detail of vSAN's object structure and do not need you to perform management tasks at a component level.

The vSAN ESA uses a slightly different data structure than what is found in the OSA. Objects are still comprised of components, but the RAID tree of an object in the ESA is a concatenation of two parts: A *performance leg* and a *capacity leg*.

The components in the performance leg of a RAID tree are used for vSAN's new log-structured file system (vSAN LFS). These components are used to temporarily ingest new writes, hold recently accessed metadata, and prepare the data and metadata for a fully aligned, full-stripe write to the capacity leg. Components that make up the performance leg of a resilient object are always in a two-way or a 3-way mirror, depending on the *failures to tolerate* setting defined in the assigned storage policy. When an object uses a RAID-5 or RAID-6 erasure code, these mirrored components in the performance leg of an object will always reside on the same hosts that store the object's capacity leg components.

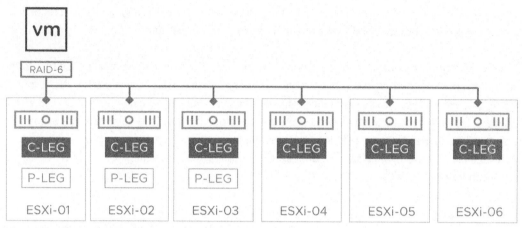

Figure 33: Concatenated RAID trees used in the vSAN ESA

The RAID tree that makes up the components in the capacity leg is very similar to what is found in the OSA. These capacity leg components of an object are distributed across hosts in accordance with the resilience settings used in the assigned storage policy.

A VM in a cluster running the vSAN ESA can have four different types of objects residing in its datastore. Keep in mind that each VM may have multiples of some of these objects associated with it:

- The VM home or "namespace directory"
- A swap object (when the VM is powered on)
- Virtual disks/VMDKs
- Snapshot memory (each is a unique object) optionally created for snapshots

Unlike the vSAN OSA, the ESA does not store VM snapshot delta disks as their own unique object. In the ESA, snapshots exist within the properties of an existing object.

Of the object types listed, the VM home namespace may need a little further explanation. Every VM gets its unique home namespace object. In the vSAN ESA, all VM files, excluding VMDKs, memory (snapshots), durability component, and swap, reside in this *VM home namespace* object on the vSAN datastore. The typical files found in the VM home namespace are the ".vmx", the ".log" files, ".vmdk" descriptor files, snapshot deltas descriptors files, and everything else one would expect to find in a VM home directory.

Each storage object is deployed on vSAN as a RAID tree, and each leaf of the tree is said to be a component. For example, if a VMDK is configured to tolerate a single failure by selecting a RAID-1 policy, a mirror of the VMDK object would be created with a set of replica components on one host and another set of components on another host in the vSAN cluster.

In this RAID-1 configuration, vSAN must use another component in this object to give us quorum in the event of failure or split-brain/cluster partition scenarios. In the vSAN OSA, one or more dedicated witness components are used for each RAID-1 object. This witness component only stores metadata and does not store any data belonging to a VM. When RAID-1 is used in the ESA, a dedicated witness component is no longer used, unless it is for site-level resilience in a stretched cluster or host-level resilience in a 2-node cluster. The vSAN ESA will place one of the performance leg components on a third host to provide this quorum functionality.

Unlike the OSA, the ESA does not create a dedicated object for snapshot delta disks. A VM's snapshots in the ESA will contain these snapshots within the object. As changed data accumulates with these snapshots, vSAN will create additional components within the object as necessary.

Component Limits

Components serve as a flexible way for vSAN to distribute an object across hosts in a resilient way, but a vSAN host does have hard limits on the number of components that can reside on a single host.

- **Maximum number of components per host limit for vSAN ESA: 27,000**

You might notice that the component limit per host for the ESA is three times the limit of the OSA. This is because the modified data structure of objects residing in an ESA cluster will typically use more components than the same objects running on an OSA cluster.

Components per host include components from powered-off VMs, unregistered VMs, and templates. vSAN distributes components across the various hosts in the cluster and will always try to achieve an even distribution of components for balance. However, some hosts may have more components than others, which is why VMware recommends, as a best practice, that hosts participating in a vSAN cluster be similarly or identically configured. Components are a significant sizing consideration when designing and deploying vSAN clusters. If hosts participating in a vSAN cluster are uniformly configured, vSAN will try to evenly distribute components across all storage devices in the hosts that are claimed by vSAN.

The vSphere Client enables administrators to interrogate objects and components of a VM. The next screenshot provides an example of one such layout. The VM has a single hard disk. From the list of object components, you can see that the performance leg for the object (Hard disk 1) is mirrored across three different hosts to provide FTT=2, the same as the RAID-6 in the capacity leg for the object. This is visible in the "hosts" column, which shows the host location of the components.

Figure 34: Physical disk placement of objects related to a VM

Virtual Machine Storage Objects

As stated earlier, the four storage objects are VM home namespace, VM Swap, VMDK, and snapshot memory as illustrated in the diagram below.

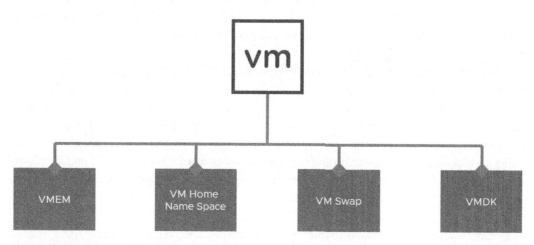

Figure 35: VM storage objects

We will now look at how characteristics defined in the VM storage policy impact these storage objects.

Namespace Object

Virtual machines use the namespace object as their VM home and use it to store all of the virtual machine files that are not dedicated objects in their own right. So, for example, this includes, but is not limited to, the following:

- The ".vmx", ".vmdk" (the descriptor portion), and ".log" files that the VMX uses.
- Digest files for *content-based read cache* (CBRC) for VMware Horizon View. This feature is referred to as the View Storage Accelerator. *Virtual desktop infrastructure* (VDI) is a significant use case for vSAN.
- vSphere Replication and Site Recovery Manager files.
- Guest customization files.
- Files created by other solutions.

These VM home namespace objects are not shared between VMs; there is one per VM. vSAN uses VMFS as the file system within the namespace object to store all the files of the VM. This is a fully fleshed VMFS that includes cluster capabilities to support all the solutions that require locks on VMFS (e.g., vMotion, vSphere HA). This appears as an auto-mounted subdirectory when you examine the ESXi hosts' file systems.

The VM home namespace uses a variant of the storage policy applied to the VM. Since the VM home namespace object has unique responsibilities, it will only inherit a subset of storage policy rules assigned to the VM. It will honor the VM's assigned *failures to tolerate* setting and RAID type but ignores other rules that may not be ideal for the object type. For example, it will ignore the *number of disk stripes per object* rule, using the default value of 1, as using any other value would serve little purpose for the object type. It will also ignore any special object space reservations, assuming the default value of 0. This ensures that the VM home namespace object remains thin provisioned, maintaining as much free capacity as possible for other objects. However, as files within the VM home namespace grow over time, logs, etc., the VM home namespace will grow accordingly.

One other important note is that if the option force provisioning is set in the policy, the VM home namespace object also inherits that, meaning that a VM will be deployed even if the full complement of resources is not available. You will learn more about this in the next chapter when policies are covered in detail. However, suffice it to say that a VM home namespace could be deployed as a RAID-0 rather than a RAID-1 if there are not enough resources in the cluster.

Note that the namespace object has other uses other than the VM's home namespace. The iSCSI on vSAN feature uses the namespace object for the iSCSI target and is used to track iSCSI LUNs available through this target. The vSAN Performance stats database is also held in the namespace object. vSAN 8.0 U1 will use a new namespace object to centrally store trace files to improve diagnostics for technical support issues. And finally, any files that might be uploaded to the vSAN datastore, such as ISO images, will be stored in a namespace object as well.

Virtual Machine Swap Object

The vSAN ESA treats a VM swap object in a similar way to recent releases of vSAN using the OSA. The VM swap object inherits the *failures to tolerate* setting in the VM's assigned storage policy, meaning that the swap object can be configured using RAID-1, RAID-5, or RAID-6. Similar to the VM home namespace object, the Virtual Machine Swap Object will ignore the *number of disk stripes per object* rule, using the default value of 1. The object will also assume the default value of 0 for its object space reservations, making it a thin provisioned object.

VMDKs

As you have just read, VM home namespace and VM swap have their own default policies when a VM is deployed and do not adhere to all of the capabilities set in the policy. Therefore, it is only the VMDK objects that obey all the capabilities that are set in the VM storage policies. Each VMDK object will have their own RAID tree configuration with its components distributed across hosts to satisfy the requirements in resilience prescribed by the storage policy.

Note that full clones, linked clones, and instant clones all create VMDK objects on the vSAN datastore. To determine what type of VMDK a disk object is, the VMDK descriptor file in the VM Home Namespace object can be referenced.

Witnesses and Replicas

vSAN uses components and depending on the circumstances, one or more special witness components to help determine the availability of an object in the event of failure or split-brain/cluster partition scenarios. Each component is assigned one or more votes to determine quorum. Historically, in the vSAN OSA, these object witness components were most visibly on display in objects assigned a RAID-1 configuration, as they are a part of the object's RAID-1 tree. RAID-5 and RAID-6 configurations did not use dedicated witness components, as quorum could be determined by the components making up a RAID-5 or RAID-6 object.

Witness components contain only metadata, meaning they do not store any VM-specific data. Typically, around 16 MB in size, the witness component contains the minimal information necessary to understand the characteristics of the object, such as the layout of the object's RAID tree, and act as a tiebreaker in the event of a failure or partitioning of the hosts used to store the object. While witness components are small, they do contribute to the overall count of components residing on a host.

The vSAN ESA has greatly reduced the times that it uses a dedicated witness component. Since all components in the performance leg and capacity leg are assigned votes to determine object quorum, in most RAID-1 configurations, the vSAN ESA will place one of the performance leg components on another host to provide the same functionality as a dedicated witness component. Dedicated witness components are still used for site-level resilience in a stretched cluster, and host-level resilience in a 2-node cluster.

To understand this more clearly, let's look at a simple example of an object assigned a *failures to tolerate* of 1, using RAID-1 mirroring. The RAID tree will be comprised of a performance leg, concatenated with a capacity leg. The capacity leg will be comprised of two replicas, each consisting of components that represent the full copy of data within that object. The components from one replica will reside on a different host than the components from the other replica. With the OSA, vSAN would use a witness component on a third host to differentiate between a network partition and a host failure. But with the vSAN ESA, one of the two performance leg components resides on a third host. Since performance leg components and capacity leg components all help determine availability, one of the performance leg components residing on a third host accomplishes the same result as a dedicated witness component.

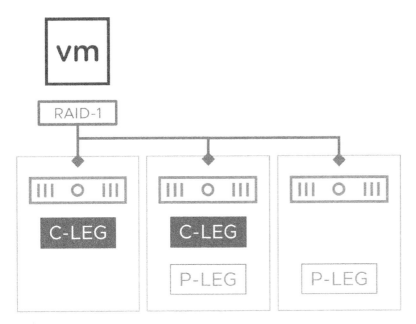

Figure 36: RAID-1 mirroring without using dedicated witness components

For an object in vSAN to be available, two conditions must be met.
- For a RAID-1 configuration, at least one full replica needs to be intact for the object to be available. For a RAID-0 configuration, all stripes need to be intact. For RAID-5 configurations, four out of five (or two out of 3) RAID-5 components must be intact for the object to be available, and for RAID-6, four out of the six RAID-6 components must be intact.
- The second rule is that there must be more than 50% of all votes associated with components available.

When determining object availability in the ESA, all performance leg components and capacity leg components contribute to a vote count. For RAID-5 and RAID-6, the performance leg components of an object typically will reside on the same hosts as the capacity leg components for an object.

When using RAID-1, one of the performance leg components will reside on a host that does not contain the capacity leg components. This provides a sort of "witness" functionality to help determine quorum when using RAID-1. In the preceding example, if the capacity leg components of an object replica and a performance leg component comprise of more than 50% of the votes, or the capacity leg of both object replicas are available, and at least one performance leg component is available, the object will remain accessible. This ensures that only one part of a partitioned cluster can ever access an object in the event of a network partition.

While some concepts such as object availability, component placement and component voting can be complex, this is a task that is entirely the responsibility of vSAN, and not the administrator.

Performance Stats DB Object

vSAN provides a performance service for monitoring vSAN, both from a VM (front-end) perspective, vSAN (back-end) perspective, and iSCSI perspective. This service aggregates performance information from all the ESXi hosts in the cluster and stores the metrics in a stats database (statsDB) on the vSAN datastore. As previously mentioned, the object in which the statsDB is stored is also a namespace object. Therefore, the use of namespace objects is not limited to VMs, although this is the most common use. Administrators can choose bespoke policies for the Performance Stats object when enabling the Performance Service. The screenshot below demonstrates how the storage policy can be customized for the Performance Service.

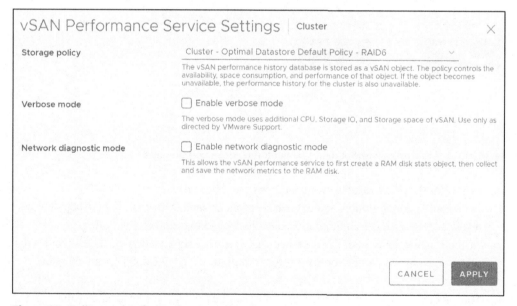

Figure 37: Policy setting for Performance Service

Note that when using the vSAN ESA, the performance service can no longer be disabled via the UI. You can however delete and create the vSAN performance database through rvc (and the APIs). Rvc, short for Ruby vSphere Console, is a command line tool that is available on vCenter Server and can be used to query and interact with vSAN. We will demonstrate how this works in chapter 7 and chapter 10.

Object Layout

The idea of a datastore distributed across hosts is a new concept to many, and as a result, it is not uncommon to hear questions about how objects and their components are dispersed across hosts. vSAN takes care of object placement to meet the *failure to tolerate* requirements and while an administrator should not worry about these placement decisions, we understand that with a solution unfamiliar to you, there may be a desire to have a better understanding of the physical placement of components and objects. The vSphere user interface enables administrators to easily interrogate the layout of a VM object and see where each component that makes up a storage object resides.

> **vSAN will never let components of different replicas (mirrors) share the same host for availability purposes.**

The vSphere Client provides the most convenient way to view objects such as VMDKs, VM home namespace, and VM swap objects. Navigate to the vSAN cluster, then the Monitor tab, then vSAN followed by Virtual Objects, select either the VM or an individual object, and then click View Placement Details. The default view will display the physical disk placement of the object components grouped by the object. The physical disk placement of the objects will be listed there. One can also group components belonging to a VM on a per-host basis, as shown in the screenshot.

Figure 38: Components grouped by host placement

vSAN Object Formats

An object format refers to the hierarchical data structure of an object and its components. Occasionally an update in vSAN will include an enhancement that in order to realize the benefit of the improvement, the format of some or all objects must be updated. For example, vSAN 7 U1 reduced the amount of free capacity required for transient activities, simply through an update of vSAN, and the upgrading of the object format. Object formats should not be confused with on-disk formats, which are discussed later in this chapter.

vSAN makes an object format upgrade easy to identify and remediate. Skyline Health for vSAN includes a *vSAN object format health* finding that will be triggered when an upgrade is available. Clicking on the *Change Object Format* in the triggered health finding will perform the upgrade. Depending on the type of update, it may change the object format on a small subset of objects, or all the objects in the vSAN cluster.

Objects do remain available throughout the upgrade process, but the upgrade process can generate a fair amount of resynchronization traffic and use additional space temporarily as a result of reconstructing components of an object to a new structure. To ensure sufficient resources remain for VM activities, the vSAN ESA will use adaptive resynchronization techniques on each host and over each host uplink to ensure the fair prioritization of VM traffic over resynchronization traffic.

vSAN Software Components

This section outlines some of the software components that make up the distributed software layer. Much of this information will not be of particular use to vSphere administrators on a day-to-day basis. All this complexity is hidden away in how VMware has implemented the installation, configuration, and management of vSAN. However, we do want to highlight some of the major components behind the scenes for you because you may see messages occasionally related to these components appearing in the vSphere UI and the VMkernel logs. We want to provide you with some background on what the function is of these components, which may help in troubleshooting scenarios.

The vSAN architecture consists of four major components, as illustrated in the diagram below and described in more depth in the sections that follow.

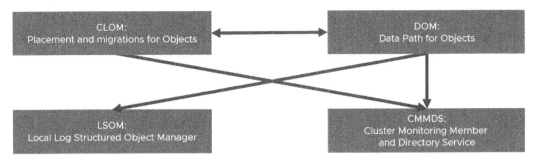

Figure 39: vSAN software components

While the vSAN ESA introduces significant changes in the data path, it shares many architectural traits found in the vSAN OSA. The following will highlight some of those key similarities and differences.

Component Management

The vSAN local log-structured object manager (LSOM) works at the physical disk level. It is the lowest layer of vSAN and interacts directly with the pluggable Storage Architecture (PSA) found in vSphere. It is responsible for persisting data it receives from upper layers of vSAN to storage devices on a vSAN host. LSOM does not communicate with other hosts, relying on the upper layers of vSAN for those tasks.

LSOM has been heavily revamped in the vSAN ESA. It is no longer responsible for tasks like I/O caching, data compression, and checksum verifications as found in the OSA, and is more focused on processing uniform, large I/Os in parallel from the upper layers of vSAN dedicated to processing variable I/O sizes. It achieves this through a new block engine, which is an I/O processor that interacts with the vSAN layers above it. LSOM also now writes data using uniform, large I/O sizes. This makes LSOM more efficient, as its metadata only needs to remember large blocks. It also aligns well with the characteristics of various types of NVMe flash devices.

Storing large amounts of data quickly involves much more than just a highly parallel I/O engine. It must be able to store the data in a referenceable way. The vSAN ESA uses a new key-value store known as SplinterDB. Developed by the VMware Research Group in collaboration with the vSAN product team, and debuting as open source in 2022, this transactional metadata store was specifically designed to exploit the capabilities of high-performing NVMe-based devices. At up to 7 times faster than other leading key-value stores, SplinterDB uses write-optimized data structures to minimize the number of times the data must be written for data and metadata updates. This keeps I/O and CPU amplification low, helping not only performance but improving scalability by allowing the system to write and read vast amounts of data to keep up with increasing densities of capacity devices.

These architectural changes in LSOM, paired with the use of NVMe devices, allow the vSAN ESA to do away with the construct of disk groups. This makes the ESA simpler to administer and reduces the failure domain, or maintenance domain, down to a discrete storage device instead of a full disk group with vSAN OSA.

Data Paths for Objects

The *distributed object manager* (DOM) provides distributed data access paths to objects built from local (LSOM) components. The DOM is responsible for the creation of reliable, fault-tolerant storage objects from local components across multiple ESXi hosts in the vSAN cluster. It does this by implementing distributed RAID types for objects.

DOM is also responsible for handling different types of failures such as I/O failing from a device and being unable to contact a host. In the event of an unexpected host failure, during recovery DOM must resynchronize all the components that make up every object. Components publish a *bytesToSync* value periodically to show the progress of a synchronization operation. This can be monitored via the vSphere Client UI when recovery operations are taking place.

In the vSAN ESA, DOM takes on several new responsibilities abdicated by LSOM. Sitting at the top of the vSAN stack, it is now responsible for data compression, data encryption, calculating checksums, and committing writes and metadata to a new log-structured file system.

Object Ownership and Interaction

The distributed object manager (DOM) has multiple layers that are responsible for their own unique tasks. It is this layered approach of DOM that allows it to work efficiently across conditions and topologies.

The DOM client represents the highest layer of the stack in the vSAN ESA. It interfaces with the vSCSI layer of ESXi, where reads and writes for a VMDK originate. The DOM client interacts with the DOM owner, below it. For every storage object in the cluster, vSAN elects an owner for the object. The DOM owner can be considered the storage head responsible for coordinating (internally within vSAN) who can perform I/O to the object. As the arbiter of object access, the DOM owner is the entity that ensures consistent data on the distributed object by performing a transaction for every operation that modifies the data/metadata of the object.

The DOM client to DOM owner relationship is analogous to the concept of an NFS client to NFS server, where only certain clients can communicate successfully with the server. In this case, the DOM client acts similarly to an NFS client, and the DOM owner acts similarly to an NFS server, where the DOM owner determines which clients can perform I/O to the owner, and which clients cannot. The DOM client in the ESA has several new responsibilities, including compressing data, encrypting data, and performing checksums. All of these will be discussed in more detail later in this chapter.

A new element of DOM introduced in the vSAN ESA is the new log-structured file system. Known as the vSAN LFS, it is a part of the DOM owner and is responsible for ingesting incoming I/Os, coalescing them into larger I/Os, packaging them with metadata, and committing them to a persistent durable log in a log-like fashion. This data is written to the components living on the **performance leg** of a concatenated RAID tree. As these I/Os accumulate in a log, vSAN will write the data segments in the durable log as a highly efficient, fully aligned, full stripe write to the **capacity leg** of an object, while the metadata is compacted and stored in a metadata log. This frees up the durable log for new incoming I/Os. Full-stripe writes are a critical step to improving the efficiency of writing data. This helps vSAN avoid the costly CPU and I/O amplification associated with read-modify-write sequences often found with writing data using erasure codes.

Note that the references to a "log-structured file system" do not refer in any way to a traditional file system such as NTFS, ext4, etc. This common industry term refers to a method of how data and metadata are persisted in the storage subsystem in an appended, log-like way, and is one of the keys behind the ability of the vSAN ESA to deliver high performance while using space-efficient erasure coding.

The use of log-structured file systems is not new. Mendel Rosenblum, the co-founder of VMware, is cited as the first to implement a log-structured file system in 1992. vSAN's implementation is novel in several ways. Each object has its own LFS, which contrasts with a more monolithic approach found elsewhere. The vSAN LFS also uses discrete durable logs for both initial data handling, and metadata. The metadata log allows vSAN to accumulate metadata in a highly compact way, then write it efficiently in a structured manner. The vSAN LFS has mechanisms in place to retain metadata using multiple data tree structures known as B-Trees. vSAN's unique design also allows for portions of the respective B-trees to live in the part of its concatenated RAID tree where it makes the most sense.

The final part of object ownership is the concept of a component manager. The component manager can be thought of as the network front end of LSOM (in other words, how a storage object in vSAN can be accessed). An object owner communicates to the component manager to find the leaves on the RAID tree that contain the components of the storage object. Typically, only one client is accessing the object. However, in the case of a vMotion operation, multiple clients may be accessing the same object as the DOM object is being moved between hosts.

In most cases, the DOM client and DOM owner co-reside on the same node in the vSAN cluster but may temporarily reside on another host during a routine activity like a vMotion event. When using HCI Mesh, which allows for the mounting of remote vSAN datastores from other vSAN clusters, as well as traditional vSphere clusters, the DOM client and DOM owner will reside on different hosts in different clusters. This is a good example of this agility is with vSAN's layered DOM model. We will discuss HCI Mesh in detail in chapter 6 covering vSAN operations.

Placement and Migration for Objects

The *cluster level object manager* (CLOM) is responsible for ensuring that an object has a configuration that matches its policy (i.e., the requested stripe width is implemented or that there are enough mirrors/replicas in place to meet the availability requirement of the VM). Effectively, CLOM takes the policy assigned to an object and applies a variety of heuristics to find a configuration in the current cluster that will meet that policy. It does this while also load-balancing the resource utilization across all the nodes in the vSAN cluster.

DOM then applies a configuration as dictated by CLOM. CLOM distributes components across the various ESXi hosts in the cluster. CLOM strives to achieve a balance of data across hosts, but it is not unusual for some hosts to have a modest difference in component counts and capacity used.

Each node in a vSAN cluster runs an instance of *CLOM, called clomd*. Each instance of CLOM is responsible for the configurations and policy compliance of the objects owned by the DOM on the ESXi host where it runs. Therefore, it needs to communicate with *cluster monitoring, membership, and directory service* (CMMDS) to be aware of ownership transitions.

CLOM only communicates with entities on the node where it runs. It does not use the network.

Cluster Monitoring, Membership, and Directory Services

The purpose of *cluster monitoring, membership, and directory services* (CMMDS) is to discover, establish, and maintain a cluster of networked node members. It manages the physical cluster resources inventory of items such as hosts, devices, and networks and stores object metadata information such as policies, distributed RAID configuration, and so on in an in-memory database. The object metadata is always also persisted on disk. It is also responsible for the detection of failures in nodes and network paths.

Other software components browse the directory and subscribe to updates to learn of changes in cluster topology and object configuration. For instance, DOM can use the content of the directory to determine which nodes are storing which components of an object, and the paths by which those nodes are reachable.

CMMDS is used to elect "owners" for objects. The owner of an object will manage which clients can do I/O to a particular object, as discussed earlier.

Host Roles

When a vSAN cluster is formed, you may notice through *esxcli* commands that each ESXi host in a vSAN cluster has a particular role. These roles are for the vSAN clustering service *only*. The clustering service (CMMDS) is responsible for maintaining an updated directory of storage devices and objects that resides on each ESXi host in the vSAN cluster. This has nothing to do with managing objects in the cluster or doing I/O to an object by the way; this is simply to allow nodes in the cluster to keep track of one another. The **clustering service** is based on a master (with a backup) and agents, where all nodes send updates to the master and the master then redistributes them to the agents.

Roles are applied during a cluster discovery, at which time the ESXi hosts participating in the vSAN cluster elect the master. A vSphere administrator has no control over which role a cluster member takes.

A common question is why a backup role is needed. The reason for this is that if the ESXi host that is currently in the master role suffers a catastrophic failure and there is no backup, all ESXi hosts must reconcile their entire view of the directory with the newly elected master. This would mean that all the nodes in the cluster might be sending all their directory contents from their respective view of the cluster to the new master. Having a backup negates the requirement to send all of this information over the network, and thus speeds up the process of electing a new master node.

In the case of vSAN stretched clusters, which allow nodes in a vSAN cluster to be geographically dispersed across different sites, the master node will reside on one site while the backup node will reside on the other site.

An important point to make is that, to a user or even a vSphere administrator, the ESXi node that is elected to the role of a master has no special features or other visible differences. Because the master is automatically elected, even on failures, and given that the node has no user-visible difference in abilities, doing operations (create VM, clone VM, delete VM, etc.) on a master node versus any other node makes no difference.

Reliable Datagram Transport

The *reliable datagram transport* (RDT) is the communication mechanism within vSAN. It is a purpose-built low-overhead protocol that offers quick establishment and tear down of communication sessions between ESXi hosts.

When using traditional ethernet for host-to-host connectivity, RDT will use Transmission Control Protocol (TCP) for the transport layer. When using networking that supports RDMA over Converged Ethernet (specifically, RoCE v2), it will use RDMA for the transport layer.

When an operation needs to be performed on a vSAN object, DOM uses RDT to talk to the owner of the vSAN object. Because the RDT promises reliable delivery, users of the RDT can rely on it to retry requests after a path or node failure, which may result in a change of object ownership and hence a new path to the owner of the object. RDT creates and tears down TCP connections (sockets) on demand.

RDT is built on top of the vSAN clustering service. The CMMDS uses heartbeats to determine the link state. If a link failure is detected, RDT will drop connections on the path and choose a different healthy path where possible. Thus, CMMDS and RDT are responsible for handling path failures and timeouts.

RDT is also used in HCI Mesh topologies to establish communication and the mounting of a remote vSAN datastore to another vSAN cluster, or a vSphere cluster. The efficiency and customization of RDT make it the ideal protocol for other vSAN clusters or vSphere clusters to use when mounting a remote datastore. Even though vSAN iSCSI services and vSAN File Service storage services exist (in the OSA at this time), they are built for other purposes and do not allow you to mount a remote datastore.

On-Disk Formats and Disk Format Changes (DFC)

Before looking at the various I/O-related flows, let's discuss the on-disk formats used by vSAN, their role with the vSAN OSA, and the ESA.

The on-disk format refers to a thin underlying layer that helps vSAN store data and metadata on its capacity devices. Known as vSANFS, this substrate has played a key part in VMware's ability to introduce new capabilities in vSAN over its past and current releases of the vSAN OSA, and now, the ESA.

Typically, a new release of vSAN includes a new on-disk format version. When an in-place upgrade of vSAN is completed, Skyline Health for vSAN will recognize the on-disk format version used on the storage devices against the version of vSAN installed. If there is an upgrade available for the on-disk format, it will alert the administrator, and provide an easy way to upgrade the format, by simply clicking on the button *Upgrade On-Disk Format*.

On-Disk Formats in the vSAN OSA

After an in-place upgrade of the vSAN OSA was completed, many of these on-disk format upgrades for the vSAN OSA consisted of simple metadata updates, while others occasionally required a rolling evacuation of disks and disk groups followed by an upgrade, then proceeding to the next disk or disk group until completed.

For the OSA, the on-disk format occasionally needed to be changed in non-upgrade scenarios, such as enabling or disabling a cluster-based data service like deduplication and compression, or data-at-rest encryption. This is sometimes known as a "disk format change" or DFC. In these cases, it proceeds with a rolling upgrade, where it will evacuate a disk or disk group, perform the upgrade, then proceed with the next disk or disk group until completed.

On-Disk Formats in the vSAN ESA

After an in-place upgrade of vSAN ESA is completed (e.g., vSAN 8.0 to vSAN 8.0 U1), the upgrade process for a new on-disk format in the ESA will be very similar to that of the OSA. With vSAN 8.0 the on-disk format version is 17.0. After the upgrade to vSAN 8.0 U1 and the on-disk format upgrade, the version is 18.0. Since the ESA eliminates the concept of disk groups, all on-disk format upgrades or changes will occur on the discrete storage devices, instead of treating multiple devices as a logical unit. Making a change to a smaller unit of resources tends to lessen the impact on an environment.

In the ESA, a DFC may occur less often for non-upgrade scenarios. For example, compression is no longer a cluster-based service and can be enabled or disabled using a storage policy without needing a DFC. Data-at-rest encryption does use a different on-disk format, as low-level LSOM metadata is encrypted. However, at the time of this writing, data-at-rest encryption in the ESA can only be enabled at the time of the initial cluster configuration, thus a DFC on an existing cluster for this service would not occur.

Note that the vSAN OSA also used a proprietary on-disk format for devices assigned as the caching device in each disk group. Since the ESA no longer uses devices dedicated to caching, all storage devices contributing resources to vSAN will use the same on-disk format.

In chapter 10 we will demonstrate the output of various commandline tools, including vdq. For now, it is good to know that the on-disk format can be discovered using "vdq -sH -d <device id>". For example:

```
vdq -sH -d naa.55cd2e4150afff35
```

vSAN I/O Flow

The vSAN ESA processes and stores data in a significantly different way than what is found in the vSAN OSA. This section will discuss the flow of I/O in the vSAN ESA on both read and write operations from an application within a guest OS when a VM is deployed on a datastore. Other processes that manipulate or verify the data will be discussed, including data compression, encryption, and checksum verification.

For our examples, we will be using a storage policy with the number of *failures to tolerate* is set to 2, using RAID-6. Since the ESA can store data using erasure coding as fast, if not faster than RAID-1, RAID-5 and RAID-6 will be the most common way that data is stored on a standard vSAN ESA cluster.

Before we begin, let's understand the role of caching, and how it is implemented differently in the ESA than in the OSA.

Data Caching and Buffering Concepts

Data caching is a common way for systems to quickly retrieve frequently accessed data. Data buffering is the term used to describe how new data is committed temporarily, *buffering* its initial impact so that it can be saved more quickly. Both caching and buffering aim to improve levels of performance, efficiency, and consistency. It is why you will find these techniques used throughout most hardware and solutions, including CPUs, device controllers, network interface cards, network switches, and storage systems.

Data caching and buffering can be implemented in dramatically different ways. The OSA and ESA take very different approaches to caching and buffering, as described in more detail below.

Data Caching and Buffering in the vSAN OSA

The vSAN OSA used a very distinct tiering model for caching and buffering. In this model, some storage devices are dedicated as a cache and/or write buffer, while other storage devices are dedicated for the purpose of providing storage capacity. In the OSA, vSAN uses these devices to flow reads and writes through. It uses multiple algorithms to determine what data should be cached, and when new writes and their respective metadata landing in the write buffer should be destaged. Much of the vSAN OSA's caching and buffering occurred in LSOM, the lowest layer of the vSAN stack. This approach is the reason why the OSA is generally described as a two-tier architecture, even when configurations are comprised of all-flash devices.

It was a fitting model for the era of hardware that the vSAN OSA typically used, such as spinning disks, and much lower-performing flash devices using SATA and SAS interfaces. The architecture did introduce some challenges as the capabilities of new hardware advanced. Disk groups, the unit of storage resources that provided this caching and capacity tiers, were the mechanism through which all I/O was funneled. However, this model limited the ability for vSAN to take advantage of newer, faster devices. An architecture that used a clear line of demarcation between a caching tier and a capacity tier also limited flexibility based on the needs of the workloads, and in some cases amplified I/O, consuming CPU and network resources. Dedicating several storage devices for caching and buffering meant fewer storage devices available to store the data. Customers were sometimes uncertain as to how much caching and buffering they should have for their specific workloads.

Data Caching and Buffering in the vSAN ESA

The design of the vSAN ESA is based on the use of high-performance solid-state NVMe devices paired with high-performance networking. Designing a new architecture includes more than just an assumption of fast hardware. For example, different types of NVMe devices have their own unique characteristics and preferred approaches to writing data. With this knowledge, VMware could design a storage stack that better represented the capabilities of the hardware and ensure that the design of the software stack could scale to the performance potential of those devices.

As a result, the vSAN ESA was designed with the utmost levels of flexibility in its architecture to accommodate the attributes of these emerging technologies. In vSAN 8.0, and vSAN 8.0 U1, the ESA uses a single-tier architecture, where all storage devices assigned for use by vSAN contribute to capacity and performance.

This single tier does not mean there is an absence of caching and buffering mechanisms in the

ESA. They simply exist in different forms, and in different locations throughout the storage stack to better align with the capabilities of the hardware. Here are some examples.

To ingest writes quickly, the object's RAID tree that consists of a performance leg and a capacity leg will coalesce smaller I/Os in memory and write them to a small durable log residing in a two-way or three-way mirror across hosts to the components on the performance leg. This, paired with its log-structured approach, where it always writes data and metadata in an appended form, provides a similar outcome as a circular buffer, absorbing the write I/Os to persistent storage quickly so that the write acknowledgement can be sent to the guest VM as fast as possible to keep latency low. But unlike the OSA, where it strived to keep as much hot data in a buffer as possible, this durable log only keeps segments of data long enough to commit an efficient, full-stripe write to the capacity leg. Thus, it is more accurate to describe it as an efficient pipeline for writing data quickly versus a classic buffer.

For recently updated metadata, the vSAN LFS, our log-structured file system in the ESA, uses in-memory caching for each object consisting of many types of frequently accessed metadata pages residing in the object's metadata tree structures, known as B-Trees. Storing this mapping metadata in memory allows for subsequent I/O, snapshotting activities, and garbage collection tasks to perform faster, as it reduces the need to perform numerous I/O requests to the metadata structures on the storage devices.

For less recently updated metadata, the vSAN LFS also uses a dedicated metadata log. This resides in the performance leg components of an object and holds segment metadata in a log-like appending form. It is also highly compacted so that large amounts of metadata pages can be persisted to disk then written to B-Trees efficiently, coalescing those metadata page updates into fewer transactions.

An object's B-Trees will reside in the performance leg components of an object, but if they can no longer fit in the performance leg, it will use a technique called log-structured leaf pages to take some of the B-Tree and place it on the capacity leg. This allows the less recently accessed leaf pages at the bottom of the B-Tree to live on the capacity leg, while all of the small, recently used index pages will live in the performance leg.

Lower in the stack, SplinterDB, the key-value store that is a part of LSOM in the vSAN ESA, contains a relatively small in-memory cache. While SplinterDB is an on-disk key-value store, it uses a small amount of in-memory cache to hold metadata pages recently accessed or created, reducing I/O activity to the devices.

The vSAN ESA also uses the DOM client cache as found in the vSAN OSA. This small cache, which is no greater than 1GB per host, serves as a low latency host-based read cache for VMs and their respective DOM clients they are interfacing with.

Anatomy of a vSAN Read on the vSAN ESA

Compared to the tasks involved in writing data resiliently, efficiently, and fast, the objective of a read operation may appear to be simpler but is equally important as writing data. The goal of the storage system is to know *where* to read the data from, retrieve the data requested, and ensure the integrity of the data retrieved.

For our example, the storage policy assigns a level of *failures to tolerate* of 2 using RAID-6. We will also assume incoming I/O is aligned, and that checksum verifications and data compression are enabled since they are both enabled by default in the ESA. Checksums, compression, and encryption will be covered in more detail later in this chapter.

At a high level, when a VM issues a read operation, the DOM client for that VM will intercept the request and check the DOM client cache. If the block is in cache, it will be fetched and returned to the guest, completing the read request. If not, the cluster service (CMMDS) is consulted to determine the DOM owner of the object, and using the block, determines which component will service the request. The fetched read I/O has its checksum validated and is returned to the guest VM.

However, the DOM client must also be aware of how data is processed through the vSAN LFS. There is a possibility that a read request must fetch data from multiple locations. The diagram below depicts the flow of a read operation in the vSAN ESA.

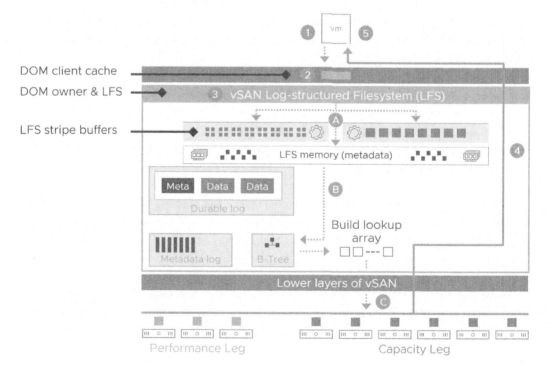

Figure 40: vSAN I/O flow: Read Operation in the vSAN ESA

In this example, a guest OS will issue a read request. The DOM client for the object will check the DOM client cache for any recently used blocks and satisfy the read operation if it resides there. If not, the DOM owner for the object will be consulted. The object's LFS in-memory stripe buffer, sometimes referred to as a bank, will also be checked for data payload. If the requested data does not exist in the stripe buffers, a B-Tree lookup will be performed to build a collection (known as an array) of physical addresses from in-memory metadata, as well as potentially on-disk metadata to issue a multi-read operation to the portions of the requested data payload it is interested in. This multi-read operation will return the payload to the DOM client and will be received by the guest OS.

Even a simple example of a read request demonstrates the importance of the efficient and scalable structures that store the metadata to help know where to read the data from. It is one of many reasons why the ESA is designed the way we describe it in this chapter.

Anatomy of a vSAN Write on the vSAN ESA

Writing data resiliently, efficiently, and quickly tends to be more complex than reading data. Let's step through a basic example of how data is written to a VM running on the vSAN ESA.

When a new VM is deployed, the cluster-level object manager (CLOM) will determine where to place the object components based on the requirements of the assigned storage policy. The VM may or may not reside on one of the ESXi hosts that the object components reside.

For our example, the storage policy assigns a level of *failures to tolerate* of 2 using RAID-6, as shown in the diagram below. We will also assume incoming I/O is aligned, and that checksum verifications and data compression are enabled since they are both enabled by default in the ESA. As noted earlier, checksums, compression, and encryption will be covered in more detail later in this chapter.

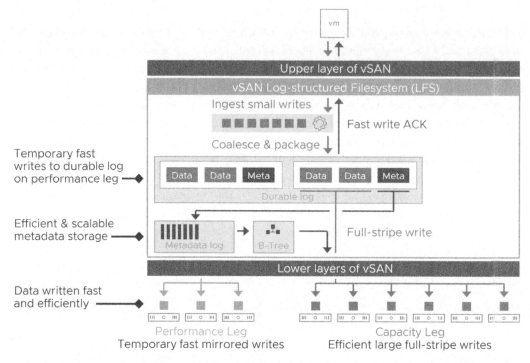

Figure 41: vSAN I/O flow: Write using default write path

In this example, when an application within a VM issues a write operation, the DOM client receives this write operation from the guest. In most cases, the DOM client is now responsible for compression, encryption (if enabled), and checksum operations, so it will perform these steps in that order. Note that if the guest VM is sending unaligned I/Os, the ESA will behave a bit differently. It will checksum the data at the DOM client but leave it uncompressed (and unencrypted if encryption is enabled). The checksum is then verified by the vSAN LFS, then will proceed with a full 4KB block read. The new partial block is then patched into the block, where it is compressed and a checksum calculated using the vSAN LFS, not the DOM client.

Next, the DOM client will send one or more write operations to the vSAN LFS, which is part of the DOM owner of the object. The write I/Os will enter into an in-memory stripe buffer, also known as a bank. This 512KB bank where the I/O will be coalesced with other I/Os and packaged with metadata. This metadata helps vSAN determine where the data is stored through logical to physical maps and tracks the consumption of data used by the LFS. The data and metadata will be flushed to a durable log. vSAN will trigger the write to the durable log within microseconds if it were a single I/O with no subsequent I/Os. This durable log is where data and metadata will be written resiliently to storage media, using the mirrored components on the performance leg. As soon as the write is persisted to the durable log, the write acknowledgement will be sent back to the VM, which completes the write operation as seen by the guest VM. While the VM interprets this write operation as complete, vSAN performs additional steps to ensure that the data and metadata are written efficiently and can be quickly accessed and updated.

Note that even though the metadata is persisted to on-disk logs, its purpose is to store those accumulated metadata pages to disk in the event they have to be reconstructed from failure. The ESA in vSAN will strive to keep this metadata in memory for fast operations.

As the I/O segments (data and packaged metadata) accumulate in the durable log, vSAN will determine when to take the next step. The objective of the durable log is to persist new writes and updates in a log-like fashion, holding just enough to pipeline the data to the next series of steps. It does not hold a large number of I/Os, and is frequently truncated to make room for new incoming I/O.

The next step consists of taking an I/O segment and committing the data portion of that segment to a fully aligned, full-stripe write to the RAID-6 components that comprise the capacity leg of the object's RAID tree. The DOM owner is responsible for calculating the parity and writing the full-stripe write to the respective hosts. The write operation from the DOM owner sends 128KB I/Os to each of the six hosts, which all have a combination of data and parity in them.

Only the data payload with its parity is written to these components in this step. The metadata packaged with that data is stripped out, compacted, and written to a metadata log. Think of this as a durable log for metadata only. This metadata log serves as a fast and efficient way for vSAN to accumulate this metadata that can be used to reconstruct the metadata in the event of a failure. It resides on the components that comprise the performance leg of the object. These metadata pages are eventually coalesced and written to B-Trees and truncated from the metadata log. The B-Trees are self-balancing data tree structures that retain information about the data. In some cases, the B-Trees may not necessarily fit within the performance leg components of the RAID tree. This is where vSAN uses a concept known as log-structured leaf pages, where it can strategically place some less frequently used pages on the capacity leg side of the object's RAID tree.

A common theme in the ESA's write path is to combine many I/Os worth of work into a single I/O, using I/O sizes that are very efficient for modern flash devices to process. This applies to data (coalescing I/Os before writing them to the durable log) and metadata (accumulating metadata pages in memory and in a dedicated log) before writing them to a B-Tree. This helps produce more efficient updates by allowing metadata to be repeatedly updated before it is written to the respective B-Trees.

But what if a VM's workload is generating large I/Os? The ESA in vSAN helps accommodate these scenarios.

Adaptive Write Paths

The vSAN ESA was designed to store data with a minimal amount of effort using space-efficient erasure codes. It achieves this in part by always writing data as full-stripe writes across a set of hosts. But writing a full stripe of data requires a minimum amount of data to make a full stripe possible. This is why the ESA's default write path coalesces data, writes it quickly in a mirrored fashion to a durable log, then eventually writes it as a full-stripe write its associated parity. This allows it to ingest, for example, many small 8KB blocks of data and coalesce them to form a large I/O that can satisfy the minimum data needed to complete a full-stripe write. This eliminates the need to perform read-modify-write steps used to update data and parity fragments that can be found with other erasure coding techniques, reducing CPU and I/O amplification dramatically.

But guest VMs can issue write operations using a wide variety of I/O sizes. These can be between 4KB and 1MB in size and will often be a wide distribution of these I/O sizes that changes by the second. If larger write operations are being issued, this changes the optimal way that data can be written. The ESA uses an adaptive write path in 8.0 U1, where it dynamically determines the best approach for writing data.

If vSAN detects incoming I/O that meets certain criteria, the data payload itself will bypass the usual step of being written to the durable log in a two-way or three-way mirror (depending on the assigned storage policy). vSAN will create the metadata for those larger I/Os and commit their metadata to the log on the performance leg and write the data payload itself as a RAID-6 stripe on the capacity leg of the RAID tree. The write acknowledgment is sent back to the guest VM when the metadata is written to the log, and the data payload is written with parity to the hosts storing the object. This bypass of the data payload landing in the durable log reduces effort, as only the metadata is being written to the three-way mirror on the performance leg. The result is higher throughput on workloads using these larger I/O sizes.

Which I/Os are eligible for the large I/O write path will be based on the conditions of incoming I/O. If vSAN detects a single I/O that exceeds the 512KB size of the in-memory stripe buffer, it will use this large I/O write path. If a combination of smaller I/Os in flight, or in flight and residing within the stripe buffer exceed the size of the stripe buffer, it will use this write path. These are time-dependent decisions, and if vSAN does not detect the conditions promptly (microseconds), it will fall back to using the default write path.

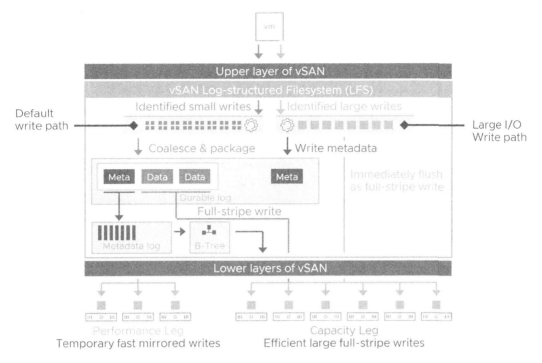

Figure 42: vSAN I/O flow: Write using large I/O write path

Data Compression

Erasure coding offers guaranteed levels of space savings when storing data resiliently. Data compression is a method to look for opportunities to compress data, reducing its impact on processing and storage.

As a refresher, the vSAN OSA offered compression as a cluster-based service, meaning that it is off or on for the entire cluster. It was performed low in the vSAN stack, on each host where an object stored its components. This meant that not only were more hosts responsible for compressing the data of an object but that the network traffic transmitted to these other object components was in an uncompressed state. And lastly, compression in the OSA would evaluate data on a 4KB block size but would only reduce it to less than or equal to 2KB if it were possible, otherwise, it would skip any compression efforts.

Aside from its use of the LZ4 compression mechanism, compression in the ESA bears little resemblance to the implementation in the OSA. The vSAN ESA offers data compression that now can be controlled by a storage policy and is enabled by default. Compression in the ESA occurs at the top of the vSAN stack, as data is being received at the DOM client from the guest VM. This offers several advantages. It is performed once from the DOM client, meaning that all processing of that data on the same host, or other hosts holding the object remains compressed. This reduces the amount of data processed inside of the hosts and transmitted across the network. Performance testing by VMware has demonstrated network throughput in some cases exceeded the wire-speed of the network as a result of this new approach.

When a guest VM issues a write, the DOM client will receive these writes, evaluate each 4KB of data, and compress at the granularity of a 512 byte sector size. With 8 sectors in a 4KB block, this means it may compress the 8 sectors down to 7, 6, 5, or all the way down to the potential of a single 512 byte sector if the data can be compressed that much. The vSAN ESA will perform checksums on each sector. When compression is complete and the block is sent to the DOM owner, the per-sector checksums will be converted to a single 4KB checksum. In subsequent reads requests, decompression is typically performed at the DOM client.

For unaligned write operations issued by the guest, the DOM client will still checksum the data but will defer the compression steps to the vSAN LFS and DOM owner, where it will take some steps to make it aligned and proceed with the compression task.

Note that while compression can be enabled or disabled using storage policies, the changing of this policy will not retroactively change the data at rest. It will only affect new incoming writes, and as a result, may not show the potential compression the data can achieve until all data has been written to once, under the desired setting.

Should the storage policy setting ever be configured to disable compression? In most cases, no. Some applications do exist that write their data entirely in a compressed state. In these cases, it might make sense to use a different storage policy and save vSAN from the effort of attempting to compress data that is already compressed.

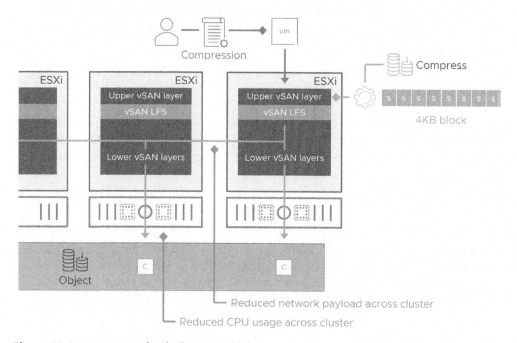

Figure 43: Data compression in the vSAN ESA

Data Integrity through Checksum

Checksum verification is a process that verifies that any written data is the same at the source and the destination of the data. The primary objective of a checksum is to verify the integrity of the data with minimal overhead. It is an integral part of both read and write operations within a storage system and is enabled by default in the vSAN ESA.

Just as with data compression and encryption, the vSAN ESA moves the checksum processes up higher in the stack to improve efficiency and help account for additional data integrity needs in the vSAN LFS.

The ESA uses the almost-ubiquitous cyclic redundancy check (CRC-32C) (Castognoli) error-detecting code as found in the OSA. It is a high-performing algorithm that can take advantage of special CPU instructions on Intel processors.

When a guest VM issues a write, the DOM client will receive the write and proceed to perform compression, encryption, and checksum in that order. If the I/O exceeds 64KB in size, it first will break them into 64KB I/O chunks for checksum processing. While the ingested I/O may be up to 64KB in size, the checksum is performed at a 4KB level of granularity. As these I/Os traverse into the vSAN LFS on the object's DOM owner, the data payload and its checksum are placed in the durable log and the stripe buffer. As the stripe buffer is full, it is flushed to the durable log, and the logical map is updated, including the existing checksums for all 4KB blocks residing in the stripe buffer. These checksums will persist in the metadata portion of the in the durable log.

The ESA also uses special functions to calculate a checksum for a larger block using the checksums from the smaller blocks. This prevents the need to calculate a large checksum from scratch. The ESA uses this technique for compressed data as well as larger data payload segments living in the durable log, and the respective 128KB I/Os comprising the full stripe write to the capacity leg.

When a VM issues a read request, the DOM client will simply verify the checksum when the read request is returned from the DOM owner, followed by decrypting (if enabled) and decompressing the data at the DOM client. The metadata structure in the vSAN LFS will be used to verify the checksum. If a checksum verification results in a mismatch, the requested data can be automatically rebuilt from the erasure code or mirrored data.

As a result, the ESA can perform checksums throughout the stack but do so in a manner that eliminates repetitive steps. For example, the ESA writes its data payload as efficient full-stripe writes. Not only does this eliminate the read-modify-write steps of a discrete block in a fragment of a partial stripe write, but it also eliminates the checksum verification of that step.

Much like the vSAN OSA, the ESA checksum functionality also includes a data scrubber mechanism, which validates the data and checksums up to 36 times per year. This will protect your vSAN environment for instance against data corruption because of bit rot. This number is defined through the advanced setting called *VSAN.ObjectScrubsPerYearBase*.

Figure 44: Scrub advanced setting

Administrators can configure checksum to be enabled or disabled on a per vSAN object basis if they so wish. This feature should only be disabled if an application can provide its own checksumming functionality, for example, in the case of Hadoop HDFS. We would recommend leaving it at the default setting of enabled for the vast majority of vSAN workloads. Such a policy setting is shown below.

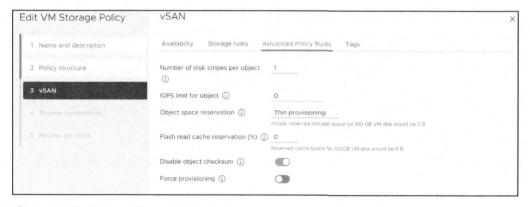

Figure 45: Checksum policy setting

vSAN Encryption

The vSAN ESA provided data-at-rest and data-in-transit encryption. This is a cluster-based feature that as the name implies, allows for the encryption of all vSAN data stored, and transmitted. The encryption feature is hardware agnostic and does not require any special encryption devices such as self-encrypting drives (SEDs). The encryption cipher used is the Advanced Encryption Standard XTS-AES 256.

Much like data compression and checksums, vSAN encryption has been also moved to near the top of the vSAN stack. This has several advantages. Much like compression, encryption is performed once from the DOM client as the write occurs. All other hosts participating in the resilient storage of that data receive and store this encrypted data. The architecture found in the vSAN ESA eliminates the encrypt, decrypt, re-encrypt process found when using data-at-rest encryption on the OSA where data must be encrypted as it enters the cache tier, decrypted as it leaves the cache tier and encrypted once more as it enters the capacity tier. This reduces CPU and I/O amplification significantly.

The I/O flow of encrypted traffic is very similar to what is described in the data compression and checksum sections discussed earlier. When enabled, encryption simply occurs after the data is compressed, but before the checksums are calculated.

If the vSAN ESA encrypts all its vSAN traffic across the network, why does the vSAN data-in-transit feature still exist? Although the data-at-rest encryption feature in the ESA transmits all data encrypted, any cloned write operations would use the same hash. To ensure the highest levels of security, the data-in-transit encryption feature will guarantee no encrypted packet transmitted across the network is the same.

Data-at-rest encryption on the ESA manages the Disk Encryption Key (DEK) differently than what is found in the OSA. In the ESA, the DEK is used across the cluster, instead of individual storage devices. This allows each host in the cluster to decrypt the objects owned by other hosts. vCenter Server will send a wrapped DEK to each host in the cluster, where the vSAN management daemon on each host will unwrap it with the Key Encryption Key (KEK). The vSAN management daemon on each host will notify other parts of the stack which DEK is used, and the unwrapped DEK will be inserted in the host key cache where vSAN can look it up.

The implementation of vSAN Encryption in the ESA includes some noteworthy caveats. At this time, it can only be enabled upon the initial configuration of an ESA cluster. It cannot be enabled or disabled once the cluster is configured. The cluster must be recreated if this type of change is desired. And finally, a deep rekey procedure is not supported at this time.

vSAN Encryption vs vSphere VM Encryption

One common question is why we have vSAN Encryption mechanisms as well as a per-VM encryption mechanism available in vSphere? Historically, VM encryption did not lend itself well to deduplication or compression found in the vSAN OSA, since it would negate some of the benefits of those space efficiency techniques.

The vSAN ESA currently does not use deduplication. While this does alleviate some of the concern on running encryption on top of encryption, it can still impact compression and use resources unnecessarily for no significant benefit. The general guidance would be to choose one or the other, but not both.

Encryption Key Providers

If you plan to use vSAN encryption, or even the VM encryption mechanism for that matter, please be aware that VMware does not provide a full *key manager server* (KMS). However, starting with vSAN 7.0 U2 there is the option to use the Native Key Provider which is included with vCenter

Server. You may wonder why anyone would want to use a 3rd party vendor when a native key provider is included. The Native Key Provider does not provide the same functionality as a key management server. For instance, the Native Key Provider can only be used for vSphere and vSAN at the time of writing. Also, the Native Key Provider does not have support for the Key Management Interop Protocol (KMIP), and it also doesn't come with the resiliency or availability features a full KMS typically comes with. If those previously mentioned features are required, we recommend selecting a KMS from one of our supported partners. Details of supported KMS partners can be found on the official VMware vSAN compatibility website.

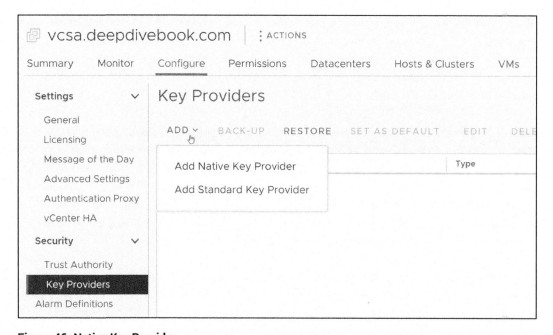

Figure 46: Native Key Provider

The KMS solution provides the *key encryption key* (KEK) and *data encryption keys* (DEK). The KEK is used to encrypt the DEKs. The DEK does the on-disk encryption. The DEKs created by the KMS are transferred to vSAN **hosts** using the *key management interoperability protocol* (KMIP). You might think that if the keys are stored on the host, isn't this somewhat insecure? This is the reason why the KEK is used to encrypt the DEKs, i.e., the keys are themselves encrypted. Unless you have access to the KEK, you cannot decrypt the DEK, and thus you cannot decrypt the data on disk. The vSAN ESA uses a different approach in its placement and management of the DEK. Since encryption in the ESA occurs high in the vSAN stack, the DEK is used across the cluster, instead of the discrete hosts, as found in the OSA. This allows each host in the cluster to decrypt the objects owned by other hosts. The managing vCenter Server will send the wrapped DEK to each host in the cluster, where the vSAN management daemon on each host will unwrap it by the KEK. The vSAN Management daemon on each host will notify other parts oof the vSAN stack which DEK is used, and the unwrapped DEK will be inserted in the host key cache for use by the host.

Prior to vSAN 7 U3, it was highly advised to store a KMS on a cluster that it is not encrypting. This helped avoid a circular dependency if there was a failure of the KMS. While this approach can still be used, a more practical approach was introduced in vSAN 7 U3, where the use of Trusted Platform Module (TPM) chips can be used to persist the keys safely and securely to each vSAN host to ensure availability of keys if the key provider is inaccessible. These modules will work with external KMS solutions, as well as the vSphere Native Key Provider. TPM 2.0 chips are an affordable component to your vSphere hosts that make the key management and distribution process much more robust. The authors recommend that TPMs are a part of any new vSphere host introduced into an environment.

The vSAN encryption feature relies heavily on *Advanced Encryption Standard Native Instruction* (*AESNI*). This is available on all modern CPUs. There are also health findings which ensure that the KMS is still accessible and that all the hosts in the vSAN cluster support AESNI.

Although outside the scope of this book, if ever vCenter Server needs to be replaced when vSAN Encryption is enabled we like to refer to VMware KB 76306 and KB 2151610. (https://kb.vmware.com/s/article/76306 and https://kb.vmware.com/s/article/2151610).

In the case of a KMS replacement, VMware KB 76479 includes the process for vSAN. (https://kb.vmware.com/s/article/76479)

Data Locality

A question that usually comes now is this: What about data locality? Is cache (for instance) kept local to the VM? Do the VM cache and the VMDK storage object need to travel with the VM each time vSphere *distributed resource scheduler* (DRS) migrates a VM due to a compute imbalance?

In general, the answer is no – vSAN is designed to treat the cluster as a first-class citizen. VMs and their respective objects with no data locality. There are some exceptions which we will come to shortly. However, vSAN has been designed with core vSphere features in mind. In other words, one should be able to do vMotion and/or enable DRS without worrying about a decrease in performance when a VM is migrated to a new host. Similarly, we did not want to have every vMotion operation turn into a Storage vMotion operation and move all of its data every time that you move a VM's compute. This is especially true when you consider the fact that by default vSphere DRS runs once every 60 seconds at a minimum which can result in VMs being migrated to a different host every 60 seconds. Benefits of data locality typically only benefited read operations, as writes must be written resiliently across hosts. For these reasons, vSAN may deploy a VM's compute and a VM's storage on completely different hosts in the cluster.

But vSAN employs smart caching and buffering techniques throughout the storage stack. These are detailed in the vSAN I/O Flow section of this chapter It is also aware of optimal data paths when processing data. This is particularly applicable to vSAN stretched clusters, and topologies using HCI Mesh. See those sections of this chapter for more details.

Content Based Read Cache

If there is a specific requirement to provide an additional form of data locality, however, it is good to know that vSAN integrates with *content based read cache* (CBRC), mostly seen when used as an in-memory read cache for VMware Horizon View. This can be enabled without the need to make any changes to your vSAN configuration. Note that CBRC does not need a specific object or component created on the vSAN datastore; the CBRC digests are stored in the VM home namespace object.

Data Locality in vSAN Stretched Clusters

We mentioned that there are some caveats to this treatment of data locality. One such caveat arises when considering a vSAN stretched cluster deployment. vSAN stretched clusters allow hosts in a vSAN cluster to be deployed at different, geographically dispersed sites. In a vSAN stretched cluster, one mirror of the data is located at site 1 and the other mirror is located at site 2. vSAN stretched cluster supports RAID-1 protection across sites. Should it be a requirement, administrators can implement a *secondary failure to tolerate* setting at each site if they wish.

When an object is assigned a *failures to tolerate* of 1 using a RAID-1 mirror, vSAN implements a sort of round-robin policy when it comes to reading from mirrors. This would not be suitable for vSAN stretched clusters as 50% of the reads would need to traverse the link to the remote site. Since VMware supports latency of up to 5ms between the sites, this would hurt the performance of the VM.

Rather than continuing to read in a round-robin, block offset fashion, vSAN now has the intelligence to determine which site a VM is running in a stretched cluster configuration and change its read algorithm to do 100% of the reads from the mirror/replica at the local site. This means that there are no reads requested across the link during steady-state operations. It also means that all the caching is performed on the local site, or even on the local host using the in-memory cache. This avoids incurring any additional latency, as reads do not have to traverse the inter-site link.

Note that this is **not read locality** on a per-host basis. It is **read locality on a per VM and per-site basis**. On the same site, the VM's compute could be on any of the ESXi hosts while its local data object could be on any other ESXi host within the site.

Data Locality in Shared Nothing Applications

vSAN continues to expand on the use cases and applications that it can support. One of the application types that is gaining momentum on vSAN is what might be termed next-gen applications, and a common next-gen application is Hadoop/Big-Data. We have worked closely with some of the leading Hadoop partners on creating reference architecture for running Hadoop on vSAN. One of the initial requirements was to have data locality – in other words, a VM's compute and storage should run on the same host. We should caveat that this is an optional requirement. However, if the application has built-in replication and its service is provided by multiple VMs, administrators need to ensure the data of the VMs are placed on different hosts. If two replica copies ended up on the same host, and if that host suffered a failure, then this would render the application inaccessible.

For example, with an application like *Hadoop distributed file system* (HDFS) which has a built-in replication factor, we can provision HDFS with several VMs, and with vSAN data locality and DRS anti-affinity rules, we can ensure that each VMs compute and storage are placed on different vSAN nodes. Thus, a failure of a single node would not impact the availability of the application's data, since it is being replicated to other VMs which also have host affinity and data locality. In this case, we would not need vSAN to protect the VMs as the application has built-in protection, so the VMs could be deployed with a *failures to tolerate* of zero.

Note that this feature was only available under special request at the time of writing and may introduce additional operational considerations.

In this particular use case described above, an interesting option reveals itself with the capabilities of the vSAN ESA. We've described how the ESA can store data using space-efficient erasure coding that is as fast, or faster than RAID-1 mirroring. In clusters with 6 or more hosts, assigning a policy of a level of *failures to tolerate* of 1 using RAID-5 would consume just 25% of additional capacity for resilience, yet be just as fast, if not faster. The use of the ESA's data compression would likely reduce this capacity consumption even more. This configuration would avoid the need to request approval from VMware and would be consistent with other application deployments.

Recovery to Regain Levels of Compliance

The resilience of an object is prescribed by its assigned storage policies. Objects can fall out of compliance with the prescribed storage policy for a few reasons. Two of the most common reasons are planned maintenance events such as entering a host into maintenance mode, and unplanned events such as a host outage.

Depending on the type of event, vSAN will take immediate action or wait for some period of time before it starts the resync process. This is called the CLOM repair delay timer and it is 60 minutes by default. This timer may be used in planned events such as entering a host into maintenance mode using the *Ensure accessibility* option, and unplanned events such as a host or network failure.

The distinction here is if vSAN knows what has happened. For example, when a host fails, vSAN typically does not know why this happened, or even what has happened exactly. Is it a host failure, a network failure, or is it transient or permanent? It may be something as simple as a reboot of the host in question. Should this occur, the affected components are said to be in an *"absent"* state and the repair delay timer starts counting. If a device such as a NVMe-based flash device reports a permanent error, it is marked as *"degraded"* and it is re-protected immediately by vSAN (replacement components are built and synchronized).

When an unplanned failure has been detected, vSAN will determine which objects had components on the failed device. These failing components will then get marked as either *degraded* or *absent*, but I/O flow is renewed instantaneously to the remaining components in the object.

The vSAN ESA adopts the concept of durability components found in the OSA. Durability components increase the availability of the very latest written data to objects impacted by a degraded event. In the OSA, when a component is marked *absent*, a durability component will be created to ensure we still maintain the specified level of *failures to tolerate* for newly written data. The benefit to this approach is that if a second host fails in a *failures to tolerate* equal to 1 scenario, one can still recover the very latest writes from the first failed host, as we can merge the data with the first failed host with the data contained in the durability component.

At the time of this writing, the support of durability components in the ESA is limited to vSAN 8.0 U1. It is only available for objects using RAID-5 or RAID-6 erasure coding, and only used in non-failure events, such as entering a host into maintenance mode using the *Ensure accessibility* option.

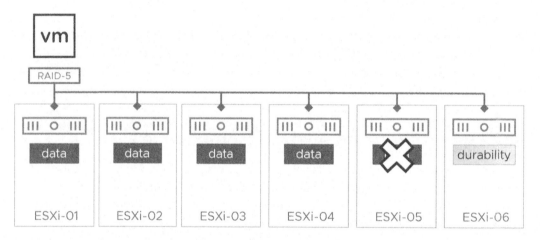

Figure 47: Durability component in a RAID-5 configuration

Let's use a simple example in a cluster running the ESA, where one of the hosts storing an object has been entered into maintenance mode using the *Ensure Accessibility* option. As soon as vSAN recognizes the component is absent, a timer of 60 minutes will start. In this scenario, the component is marked absent, and a durability component is created immediately on another available host.

If the absent component comes back within 60 minutes, vSAN will update the component in the stripe with its appropriate data and parity fragments. It will strive to use the updated data in the durability component as the source of the resynchronization, as it can be a much faster process than a rebuild of the stripe from calculated data and parity across the other hosts holding the stripe.

If the host and its component do not come back within 60 minutes, it will rebuild a new component on a new host using data and parity calculations from the other available hosts storing the object. It may or may not use the durability component in this effort. Whether the reason for the non-compliance was planned, or unplanned, the methods vSAN uses to regain levels of prescribed compliance are the same as what is described above.

In the latest version of vSAN, the Object repair timer advanced parameter is now available in the vSphere Client. As shown below, this can be found under Cluster > Configure > vSAN > Services > Advanced options.

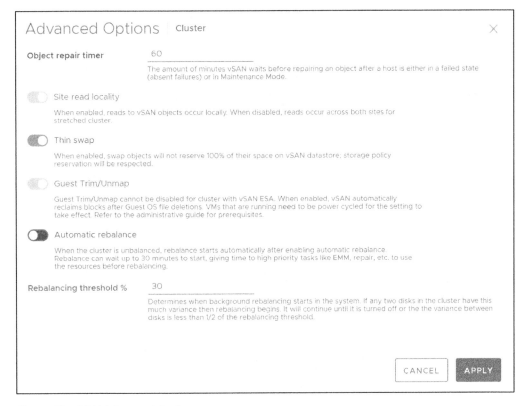

Figure 48: vSAN Advanced Options

Caution should be exercised in reducing the value of the Object repair timer from its default. If it is set to a value that is too low, and you do a simple maintenance task such as rebooting a host, you may find that vSAN starts rebuilding new components before the host has completed its reboot cycle. This adds unnecessary overhead to vSAN and could have an impact on the overall performance of the cluster.

As mentioned, in some scenarios vSAN responds to a failure immediately. In some cases, the storage device itself will be able to indicate what has happened and will essentially inform vSAN that it is unlikely that the device will return within a reasonable amount of time. vSAN will then respond by marking all impacted components as *"degraded,"* and take immediate action on a rebuild. For objects using a RAID-1 mirror, it will create a new replica. For objects using erasure coding, it will build a new component on another available host by using the data and parity information from the other hosts holding the stripe. This scenario does not use durability components.

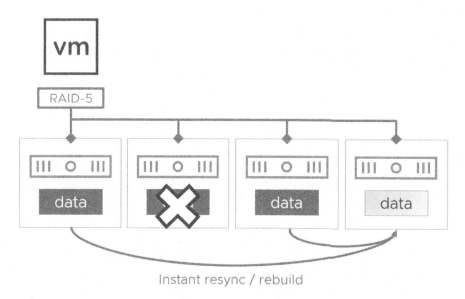

Instant resync / rebuild

Figure 49: Disk failure with immediate recovery with a RAID-5 (2+1) configuration

Before it creates the additional components to regain the level of prescribed resilience, vSAN will validate if there are sufficient capacity resources available.

If recovery occurs before the 60 minutes have elapsed or before the creation of the replica has been completed, vSAN will decide which method will be faster to complete. It may choose to continue to create new components to regain that level of compliance, or simply update the components that came back online.

Regaining compliance also applies to changes in assigned storage policies. A user might change an object's policy, where the current configuration does not conform to the newly prescribed policy. In this case, a reconfiguration must be performed and applied to the object.

A reconfiguration of an object can be a resource-intensive task because it may involve redistributing the entire data structure of an object in a new way. This can occur as the result of manual policy changes, or automatically for objects assigned an adaptive RAID-5 storage policy, where a change in the cluster size may initiate a different RAID-5 configuration. To ensure that regular VM I/O is not impacted by reconfiguration tasks, vSAN can throttle these resynchronizations in ways to minimize the impact on the performance of VMs. In the vSAN ESA, during times of contention in either the hardware stack (less likely in the ESA), or the network, vSAN may automatically throttle any resync I/O down to 20% of available bandwidth, giving VM I/O most of the available resource bandwidth. When there is no contention in the hardware stack or network, then resync traffic can consume all the available bandwidth.

Degraded Device Handling (DDH)

Much like the original storage architecture in vSAN, the ESA uses a feature called *degraded device handling* (DDH). The driving factor behind such a feature is to deal with storage devices that are demonstrating erratic or unexpected behavior. Storage devices that are imminently failing tend to show these characteristics for a period of time prior to a permanent failure. This mechanism allows vSAN to monitor the device's performance behaviors over time and mark it accordingly if it demonstrates inconsistent behavior.

One method that DDH uses to detect impending failures is observing latency patterns of read and write and write operations from the device. But detecting issues on latency thresholds requires levels of sophistication to prevent false positives that would mark its condition incorrectly. For example, perhaps a spike in latency was a result of a large burst of writes, which is not unusual behavior. To counter false positives, DDH will select non-contiguous intervals to better represent a pattern of degrading performance.

Another challenge is determining a proper threshold for poor latency. Today's NVMe-based flash devices can deliver much lower levels of latency than flash devices of the past, as well as spinning disk. DDH has evolved to accommodate the device types found in the ESA.

If a sustained period of high latency is observed, then vSAN will unmount the device. As a result, the components on the device that is unmounted will be marked as a permanent error and the components will be rebuilt elsewhere in the cluster. What this means is that the performance of the virtual machines can be consistent and will not be impacted by this one misbehaving device.

DDH will also make regular attempts to remount devices marked under permanent error. This will only succeed if the condition that caused the initial failure is no longer present. If successful, the physical device does not need to be replaced, although the components must be resynced. If unsuccessful, the device continues to be marked as a permanent error. This will be visible in the vSphere UI under Disk Management.

If the object is assigned a storage policy that uses a RAID-1 mirror, the feature checks to see whether there are any available replicas available before unmounting. If this is the last available replica, DDH will not unmount it but will continue to make it available since it is the last available replica. Unmounting it in this case would result in complete object unavailability. For objects assigned a storage policy that uses a RAID-5 or RAID-6 erasure code, vSAN can easily calculate the value from the device in question by using the data fragments in the remainder of the stripe.

vSAN Storage Services

vSAN is mostly known as a platform that provides block storage capacity for VMs running on top of vSphere. But vSAN offers data services to provide storage in other ways. This includes the vSAN iSCSI Target Service, vSAN File Services, and the ability to mount remote datastores through HCI Mesh. Let's look at what these services are, and how they apply to the vSAN ESA.

iSCSI Targets and LUNs

Using the vSAN iSCSI Target Service, vSAN can create iSCSI targets and LUNs using vSAN objects and present the LUNs to external iSCSI initiators. When enabled, vSAN will create an iSCSI Target namespace object to help store metadata about the configurations and connections. Just like most other objects, an administrator can choose a storage policy setting for this object that best suits their environment. In the next image, we can see where the storage policy for the iSCSI Target home object can be selected.

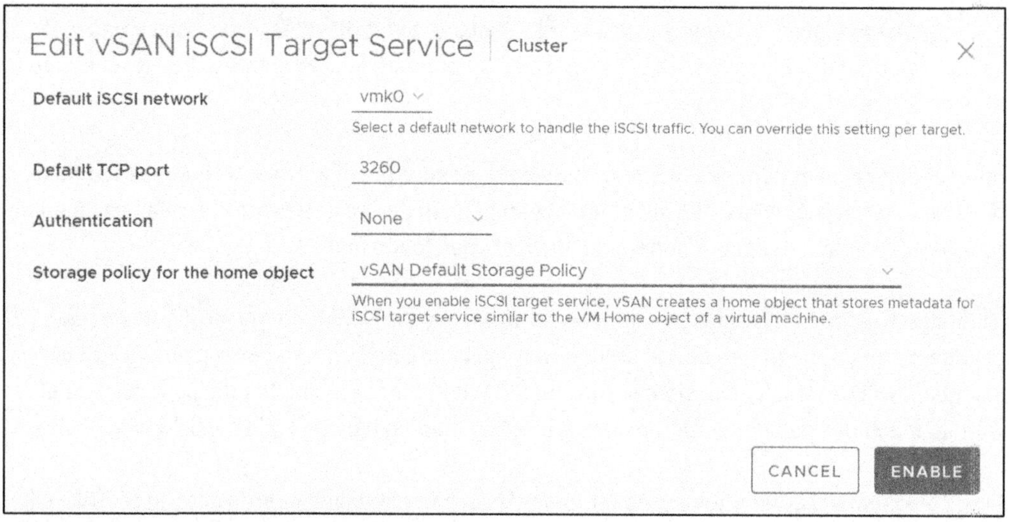

Figure 50: Policy setting for iSCSI Target

As you proceed to create iSCSI Targets and iSCSI LUNs on vSAN, these can be assigned their own different policy as well.

With the iSCSI implementation on vSAN, there is the concept of a Target I/O owner for vSAN iSCSI. The Target I/O owner (or just I/O owner) is responsible for coordinating who can do I/O to an object and is basically what an iSCSI initiator connects to, i.e., whoever wants to consume the storage, most likely a virtual machine elsewhere in the datacenter. The I/O owner may be on a completely different vSAN node/host to the actual iSCSI LUN backed by a vSAN VMDK object. This is not a problem for vSAN deployments, as this can be considered akin to a VM's compute residing on one vSAN host and the VM's storage residing on a completely different vSAN host. This 'non-locality' feature of vSAN allows us to do operations like maintenance mode, vMotion, capacity balancing, and so on without impacting the performance of the VM. The same is true for the vSAN iSCSI implementation - the I/O owner should be able to move to a different host, and even the iSCSI LUNs should be able to migrate to different hosts while not impacting our iSCSI availability or performance. This enables the vSAN iSCSI implementation to be unaffected by operations such as maintenance mode, balancing tasks, and of course any failures in the cluster.

With iSCSI LUNs on a vSAN stretched cluster, a scenario could arise where the I/O owner is residing on one site in the stretched cluster, while the actual vSAN object backing the iSCSI LUN could be on the other site. In that case, all the traffic between the iSCSI initiator and the iSCSI target would have to traverse the inter-site link. But remember that this is already true for writes since write data is written to both sites anyway in a vSAN stretched cluster (RAID-1). When it comes to read workloads, we do have the ability to read data from the local site for both iSCSI and VM workloads, and not traverse the inter-site link. This means that it doesn't matter which site has the I/O owner resides.

But there is one caveat when it comes to supporting iSCSI on vSAN stretched clusters. The key issue is the location of the iSCSI initiator. If the initiator is somewhere on site A, and the target I/O owner is on site B, then, in this case, the iSCSI traffic (as well as any vSAN traffic) would need to **traverse the inter-site link**. In a nutshell, such a configuration could end up adding an additional inter-site trip for iSCSI traffic. For this reason, the vSAN ESA supports the ability to specify site affinity when creating an iSCSI Target as shown in the screenshot below.

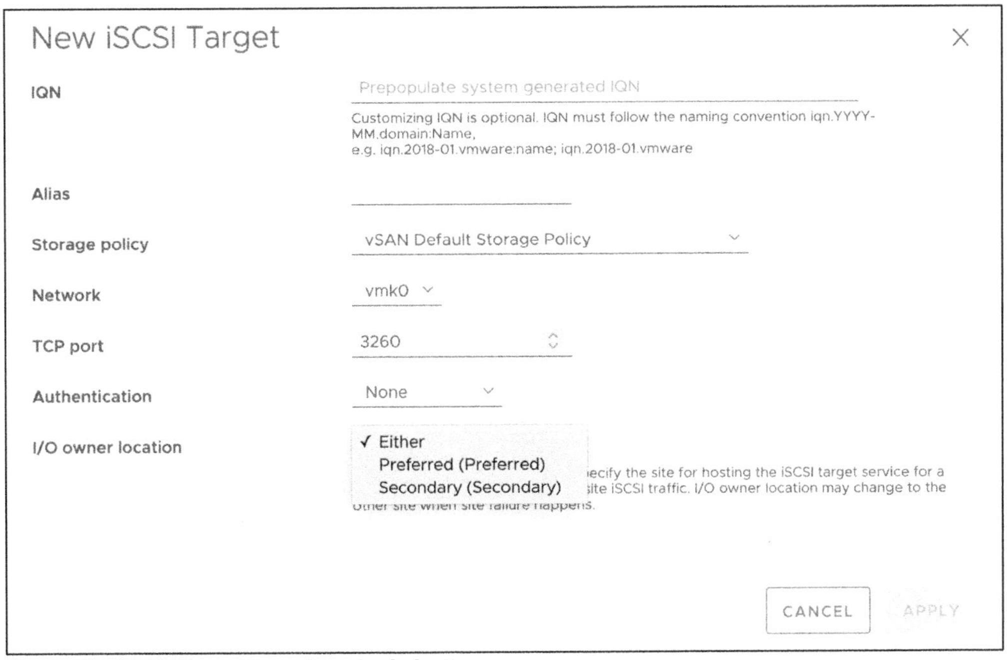

New iSCSI Target   ✕

IQN	Prepopulate system generated IQN
	Customizing IQN is optional. IQN must follow the naming convention iqn.YYYY-MM.domain:Name, e.g. iqn.2018-01.vmware:name; iqn.2018-01.vmware
Alias	
Storage policy	vSAN Default Storage Policy ⌄
Network	vmk0 ⌄
TCP port	3260 ⌄
Authentication	None ⌄
I/O owner location	✓ Either
	Preferred (Preferred) ...ecify the site for hosting the iSCSI target service for a
	Secondary (Secondary) site iSCSI traffic. I/O owner location may change to the
	Other site when site failure happens.

CANCEL   APPLY

Figure 51: iSCSI Target in a stretched cluster

vSAN File Service

The native file services capability introduced in version 7 of vSAN is not supported in vSAN 8.0 or vSAN 8.0 U1 when using the ESA. If you are interested in using vSAN File Services immediately, you can continue to use this capability found in the vSAN OSA. Enhancements continue to be introduced with the vSAN file services, up to and including vSAN 8.0 U1.

vSAN HCI Mesh

HCI Mesh allows a vSAN cluster's datastore to be remotely mounted by another cluster. The cluster mounting the vSAN datastore can either be another vSAN cluster, or a vSphere cluster. Beginning in vSAN 8.0 U1, the vSAN ESA supports HCI Mesh.

Note that the introduction of vSAN 8.0 U1 introduced two new enhancements to HCI Mesh, including support of HCI Mesh in stretched cluster configurations, and connecting to remote vSAN datastores when using multiple vCenter Server instances. These two features are not available when using the ESA in vSAN 8.0 U1.

You may ask yourself, why would you want to do this? It could be that you are running out of disk space on your local vSAN datastore, or maybe you do not have any local storage or SAN-attached even. HCI Mesh enables you to run VM instances in one cluster while having the objects associated with that VM stored remotely. Of course, it means that an administrator will need to mount the remote datastore, and the decision will need to be made to use that remote datastore from a storage point of view. But when this has been done you can even move the VM between clusters by simply doing a compute-only vMotion. One thing to note is that we use RDT, vSAN's native protocol for communication between the two clusters. The datastore is not exposed through NFS or iSCSI.

As mentioned earlier in this chapter, the way we have implemented this is by separating certain processes that normally would run on a single host. In this case, we are referring to the DOM components, specifically the DOM Client and the DOM Owner. On top of that, a CMMDS Client has been developed, which connects to CMMDS directly. The relationship between the various processes is shown in the diagram below.

Figure 52: vSAN HCI Mesh components

When HCI Mesh, or Datastore Sharing as it is called in the vSphere Client, is enabled on a cluster that does not have vSAN enabled, the DOM Client and the CMMDS client are loaded on each host of the cluster. The DOM Client and the CMMDS Client then connect with the DOM Owner and CMMDS to provide the ability to provision workloads on the remote datastore. Note that a remote datastore can only be mounted when the "Server Cluster" is managed by the same vCenter Server instance as the "Client Cluster". There are various operational considerations, but we will discuss these in chapter 6 where we are discussing various operational aspects of vSAN.

The data path of the ESA as described in this chapter remains largely the same when using HCI Mesh. The layered approach to the vSAN storage stack allows for the respective data processing to be extended logically when communicating across clusters. One difference when using HCI Mesh is when data-at-rest encryption is enabled on the ESA. Instead of the encryption processes occurring at the highest layer in the stack (the DOM client), encryption processes will occur at the DOM owner, which will reside in the "Server Cluster" side of the two clusters. This is transparent to the administrator and does not change operations in any way.

One thing we do want to bring up is vSphere HA. From an architectural perspective, the implementation of vSAN with HCI Mesh is different, it also means that there's an additional consideration when it comes to availability. To ensure VMs are protected by vSphere HA in the situation anything happens between a "client" host and the "server" cluster, it is recommended to enable the APD response. This is very straightforward. You simply go to the HA cluster settings and set the "Datastore with APD" setting to either "Power off and restart VMs – Conservative" or "Power off and restart VMs – Aggressive". The difference between conservative and aggressive is that with conservative HA will only kill the VMs when it knows for sure the VMs can be restarted. With aggressive, it will also kill the VMs on a host impacted by an APD while it isn't sure it can restart the VMs. VMware recommends using the "Conservative Restart Policy".

Summary

The growing prevalence of high-performing storage devices and fast networking allowed the Engineering teams working on vSAN to rethink how data could be processed and stored. The vSAN ESA uses a new architecture to process and store data faster and more efficiently than ever before while retaining the easy of management found in past versions. This way, customers can continue to use techniques like VM Storage Policies to define an outcome of desired resilience and other capabilities and let vSAN take care of the rest.

In the next chapter, we will look at VM Storage Policies, and how to use them to make your VMs resilient to failures in vSAN.

05

VM Storage Policies and VM Provisioning

VM storage policies and storage policy-based management (SPBM) build on earlier vSphere functionality which tried to match the storage requirements of a VM to a particular vSphere datastore. This was known as profile driven storage in earlier versions of vSphere, and all VMs residing on the same datastore inherited the capabilities of the datastore. With vSAN, the storage quality of service no longer resides with the datastore; instead, it resides with the VM and is enforced by a VM storage policy associated with the VM and its VMDKs. Once the policy is pushed down to the storage layer, in this case, vSAN, the underlying storage is then responsible for creating and placing components for the VM to meet the requirements configured in the policy.

Introducing Storage Policy-Based Management in a vSAN Environment

vSAN leverages a policy-based approach for VM deployment, using a method called *storage policy-based management* (SPBM). All VMs deployed to a vSAN datastore must use a VM storage policy, and if one is not specified at deployment time, a default one that is associated with the datastore is assigned to the VM automatically. The VM storage policy may contain one or more vSAN capabilities. This chapter will describe the vSAN ESA capabilities and how the components for each object that makes up a VM are distributed according to the capabilities configured in the VM's policy.

After the vSAN ESA cluster has been configured and the vSAN datastore has been created, vSAN presents a set of capabilities to vCenter Server. These capabilities are surfaced by the *vSphere APIs for Storage Awareness* (VASA) storage provider (more on this shortly) when the vSAN cluster is successfully configured. These capabilities are used to set the availability, capacity, and performance policies on a per-VM (and per-VMDK) basis when that VM is deployed on the vSAN datastore.

Through SPBM, administrators create a policy defining the storage requirements for the VM, and this policy is pushed out to the storage, which in turn instantiates per-VM (and per-VMDK) storage for virtual machines. In vSphere 6.0, VMware introduced *Virtual Volumes* (vVols). SPBM for VMs using vVols is very similar to SPBM for VMs deployed on vSAN. In other words, administrators no longer need to carve up LUNs or volumes for virtual machine storage. Instead, the underlying storage infrastructure instantiates virtual machine storage based on the contents of the policy. Similarly, with the arrival of the Kubernetes platform, and the ability to run Kubernetes clusters on top of vSphere infrastructure, persistent volumes created in Kubernetes and backed by VMDKs can also leverage SPBM. Each persistent volume can, using Kubernetes Storage Classes which map to a vSphere storage policy, be instantiated with its own set of storage capabilities. The ability to use vSAN as a platform for modern, containerized applications will be discussed in detail in chapter 9.

Suffice to say that what we have now with SPBM is a mechanism whereby we can specify the requirements of the VM, and the associated VMDKs. These requirements are then used to create a policy. This policy is then sent to the storage layer (in the case of vVols, this is a SAN or *network-attached storage* (NAS) storage array) asking it to build a storage object for this VM that meets these policy requirements. In fact, both vVols based or a vSAN based VM can have multiple policies associated with it, and different policies for different VMDKs.

By way of explaining capabilities and policies, capabilities are what the underlying storage can provide by way of availability, performance, and efficiency. These capabilities are visible in vCenter Server. The capabilities are then used to create a VM storage policy (or just policy for short). A policy may contain one or more capabilities, and these capabilities reflect the requirements of your VM or application running in a VM.

Deploying VMs on a vSAN datastore is very different from previous approaches in vSphere. With traditional storage, an administrator presents a shared LUN or volume to a group of ESXi hosts. In the case of block storage, an administrator would then be required to partition, format, and build a VMFS datastore for storing VM files. Care had to be taken to ensure that any shared LUN was uniformly presented from the array to all ESXi hosts. Similarly, administrators had to ensure that the path policies were set identically for that LUN on all ESXi hosts. This resulted in operational complexity and overhead. In the case of *network-attached storage* (NAS), a *network file system* (NFS) volume is mounted to the ESXi hosts, and once again a VM is created on the datastore. There is no way from the ESXi host to specify, for example, a RAID-0 stripe width for a VM, nor is there any way to specify a RAID-1 replica for the VM. VMs simply inherited the capabilities of the underlying LUN or share that was presented to the ESXi hosts as a datastore.

In the case of vSAN (and vVols), the approach to deploying VMs is quite different. Consideration must be given to the availability, performance, and efficiency factors of the application running in the VM. Based on these requirements, an appropriate VM storage policy must be created and associated with the VM during deployment. However, it is possible to change the policy after the VM has been deployed, on-the-fly. This will be discussed shortly.

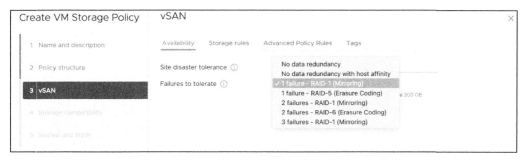

Figure 53: Standard vSAN capabilities

vSAN features include the ability to implement various storage configurations, for example, administrators can create RAID-5 and RAID-6 configurations for virtual machine objects deployed on vSAN ESA. Of course, there are also RAID-0 and RAID-1 configurations available, but they are less commonly used with vSAN ESA and we will explore why later in this chapter. With RAID-5 and RAID-6, administrators can deploy VMs that are able to tolerate one or two failures, but the amount of space consumed on the vSAN datastore is much less than a RAID-1 configuration.

There is also an additional policy rule for software checksum. Checksum is enabled by default, but it can be disabled through policy on a per VM basis if an administrator wishes to disable it. Another capability relates to quality of service and provides the ability to limit the number of *input/output operations per second* (IOPS) for a particular object. We can also specify how VMs, which are part of a stretched cluster, should be protected within a site. For this RAID-1, RAID-5, or RAID-6 can be used. This is an additional level of protection within a site that works alongside the cross-site protection. A similar configuration is also available for 2-node vSAN configurations. Since all vSAN ReadyNodes for ESA use at least 4 storage devices, a 2-node cluster using ESA will be able to support the secondary level of resilience capability as found with the OSA. It is more economical however, as it achieves this without the use of disk groups.

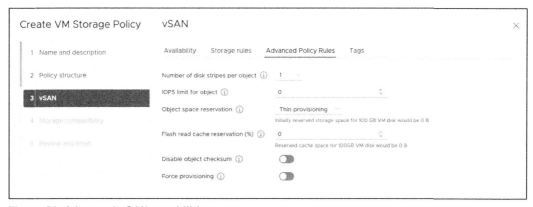

Figure 54: Advanced vSAN capabilities

You can select the capabilities when a VM storage policy is created. Note that certain capabilities apply to hybrid vSAN OSA configurations (e.g., flash read cache reservation), while other capabilities apply to all-flash vSAN OSA & ESA configurations only (e.g., RAID-5 and/or RAID-6). In the case of vSAN ESA, setting a "Flash read cache reservation", for instance, would make the policy incompatible with the vSAN Datastore.

VM storage policies are essential in vSAN deployments because they define how a VM is deployed on a vSAN datastore. Using VM storage policies, you can define the capabilities that can provide the number of VMDK RAID-0 stripe components or the number of RAID-1 mirror copies of a VMDK. Let's now revisit erasure coding before learning how to configure them via policies. We have already learned that if an administrator desires a VM to tolerate one failure but does not want to consume as much capacity as a RAID-1 mirror, a RAID-5 configuration can be used. If this configuration was implemented with RAID-1, the amount of capacity consumed would be 200% the size of the VMDK due to having two copies of the data. If this is implemented with RAID-5 with vSAN OSA, the amount of capacity consumed would be 133% the size of the VM, the extra 33% accounting for the single parity segment since RAID-5 is implemented on vSAN as 3 data segments and 1 parity segment. RAID-5 requires a minimum of four hosts in an all-flash vSAN cluster and will implement a distributed parity mechanism across the storage of all four hosts.

However, starting with vSAN ESA we now have a new adaptive RAID-5 mechanism, which either uses an extra 25% or 50%, depending on the size of the cluster. In a cluster with 5 hosts, or less, a RAID-5 configuration would lead to a 2+1 configuration. Meaning, 2 data segments and 1 parity segment. This leads to a total amount of capacity consumed of 150% of the size of the VM. In a cluster with 6 hosts, or more, a RAID-5 configuration would lead to a 4+1 configuration. Meaning, 4 data segments and 1 parity segment. This would lead to a total amount of capacity consumed of 125% of the VM.

Similarly, if an administrator desires a VM to tolerate two failures using a RAID-1 mirroring configuration, there will need to be three copies of the VMDK, meaning the amount of capacity consumed would be 300% the size of the VMDK. When using a RAID-6 implementation instead of RAID-1, a double parity is implemented, which is also distributed across all the hosts. By this, we mean 4 data segments and 2 parity segments. For RAID-6, there must be a minimum of six hosts in a vSAN cluster. RAID-6 also allows a VM to tolerate two failures, but only consumes capacity equivalent to 150% the size of the VMDK, the overhead of the two parity segments. When using the vSAN ESA with RAID-6 , a recommended minimum cluster size of 7 or more hosts would ensure that a spare fault domain would be available upon failure. This will simplify administration, and likely increase the effective resilience setting for most vSAN workloads while not inhibiting performance in any way.

The sections that follow will highlight where you should use these capabilities when creating a VM storage policy and when to tune these values to something other than the default. Remember that a VM storage policy can contain one or more capabilities.

Note: Some significant changes were made to how the layout of vSAN objects was implemented in vSAN 7.0 U1. A concerted effort was made to address the requirement of keeping 25-30% of what was termed slack space on the vSAN datastore. This was a considerable overhead but was necessary due to the way vSAN implemented its recovery and resyncing mechanism. Data that was being rebuilt or resynchronized used this slack space as a staging area. The slack space needed to be this large since vSAN would attempt to rebuild as many missing or failed components as possible, so if a complete host failed, vSAN needed space to stage the rebuild of all components on this host. In vSAN 7.0 U1, a new approach was envisioned. This revolved around negating the need to build whole replicas or mirrors. The decision was made to implement large objects greater than 255GB in size in a different way than objects smaller than 255GB. Therefore, instead of implementing a top of tree RAID-1 (mirror) with 2 x RAID-0 branches, vSAN implemented a top of tree RAID-0 (concatenation) with each of the underlying components mirrored in a RAID-1 configuration. Now when rebuild operations are required, for example when a policy change is requested, vSAN can work on each component on the concatenation as a distinct item, working on a much smaller chunk of data. Previously vSAN had to set aside slack space for the whole of the mirror. This is all preamble to some of the examples shown later, when vSAN objects with the same policy will get a different layout depending on their size.

As an administrator, you can decide which of these capabilities can be added to the policy, but this is of course dependent on the requirements of your VM. For example, what performance and availability requirements does the VM have?

The capabilities for "vSAN" storage datastore specific rules are as follows:

Availability
- Site disaster tolerance
  - None – standard cluster **(default)**
  - Host mirroring – 2 node cluster
  - Site mirroring - stretched cluster
  - None – keep data on preferred (stretched cluster)
  - None – keep data on non-preferred (stretched cluster)
  - None – stretched cluster
- Failures to tolerate
  - No data redundancy
  - No data redundancy with host affinity
  - 1 failure – RAID-1 (Mirroring) **(default)**
  - 1 failure – RAID-5 (Erasure Coding)
  - 2 failures – RAID-1 (Mirroring)
  - 2 failures – RAID-6 (Erasure Coding)
  - 3 failures – RAID-1 (Mirroring)

Storage rules
- Encryption Services
  - Data-At-Rest encryption
  - No encryption
  - No preference **(default)**
- Space Efficiency
  - Deduplication and compression
  - Compression only

- No space efficiency
- No preference **(default)**
- Storage tier
  - All flash
  - Hybrid
  - No preference **(default)**

Advanced Policy Rules
- Number of disk stripes per object (**default** value of 1)
- IOPS limit for an object (**default** value of 0 meaning unlimited)
- Object space reservation
  - Thin provisioning **(default)**
  - 25% reservation
  - 50% reservation
  - 75% reservation
  - Thick provisioning
- Flash read cache reservation (hybrid vSAN only) (**default** value of 0 meaning none)
- Disable object checksum (**default** off)
- Force provisioning (**default** off)

Storage rules

Whilst we have already seen what the Availability and Advanced Policy rules looked like in the vSphere UI, we have not yet seen the Storage rules. The next screenshot displays what the Storage rules look like.

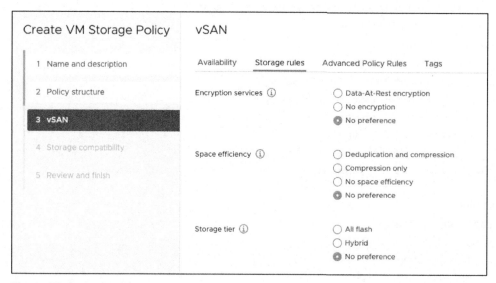

Figure 55: Storage rules

These configuration settings were originally intended to be related to HCI-Mesh (Datastore

Sharing), where a vSphere cluster can consume storage from both a local vSAN datastore as well as multiple remote vSAN datastores. Datastore Sharing is discussed in greater detail in the Operations chapter later in the book. However, in an all-flash configuration, which vSAN ESA is, you will need to select the correct storage tier. On top of that, there is another exception with the Storage Rules, as it can also be used to disable the use of "compression" with vSAN ESA on a per VM basis through policy. If "no preference" or "compression only is selected under "Space efficiency" then compression is essentially enabled on the associated VMs. If "No space efficiency" is selected then vSAN ESA compression is disabled for the VMs associated with this policy, as shown in the next screenshot.

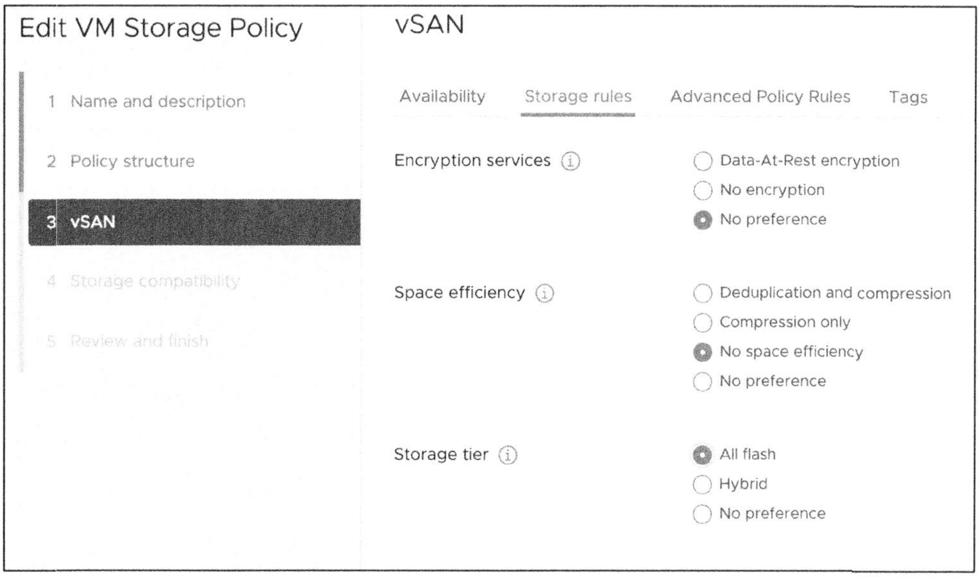

Figure 56: Disabling vSAN ESA Compression

One thing we do want to emphasize is what happens when you disable, or enable, vSAN ESA Compression. As mentioned, compression is enabled by default, and can be disabled by configuring the Storage Rules accordingly, i.e., "no space efficiency". Changing an existing VM from "compression enabled" to "compression disabled", or the other way around for that matter, does not trigger a recreation of the components of the VM and does not change the currently stored data in any shape or form. In other words, if compression is enabled and you have stored a total amount of compressed capacity of 40GB, then the total amount of compressed capacity after changing the policy on that object to "compression disabled" is still 40GB. Only new writes are stored as requested in policy, meaning that new writes will not be compressed when compression is disabled in policy.

Now you may ask yourself, do I really need to use these Storage Rules? Storage Rules are extremely useful, as mentioned, when you are using Datastore Sharing capabilities. Especially in larger environments where a variety of different data services are (or can be) enabled on each individual datastore. It could be that the local datastore has deduplication or compression enabled, or that a remote datastore is from a hybrid vSAN but the local datastore is a vSAN ESA all-NVMe based cluster. By using some of the settings in this configuration screen, an administrator can create policies that will place VMs with the same availability policy, and the selected data services, on either the local vSAN datastore or one of the remote datastores, depending on these settings. By default, these are all left at "No preference" meaning that none of these capabilities are considered when provisioning a VM in an HCI-Mesh environment.

The sections that follow describe the vSAN capabilities in detail.

Failures to tolerate

In this section, we are going to discuss *Failures to tolerate*, specifically **RAID-1**. In the next section, we will describe RAID-5 and RAID-6. *Failures to tolerate* is often short-handed to FTT and this shorthand is used quite extensively in this book. The maximum value for FTT is 3. This is available if RAID-1 is used. The maximum for FTT is 2 when using erasure coding assuming RAID-6 is used. We will examine these limits in more detail shortly.

The *Failures to tolerate* capability sets a requirement on the vSAN storage object (e.g., VM) to tolerate at least *n number of failures in the cluster.* This is the number of concurrent hosts, networks, or storage device failures that may occur in the cluster and still ensure the availability (accessibility) of the object. When failures to tolerate is set to *RAID-1* the VM's storage objects are mirrored; however, the mirroring is done across different ESXi hosts, as shown below. In the diagram "C-LEG" and "P-LEG" respectively refer to the "Capacity Leg" and the "Performance Leg", which are described in-depth in chapter 4.

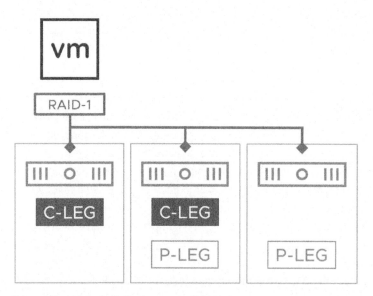

Figure 57: RAID-1 - Failures to tolerate

When this capability is set to a value of *n*, it specifies that the vSAN configuration must contain at least *n*+1 replica copies of the data; this also implies that there are 2*n*+1 hosts in the cluster.

With vSAN ESA there's a big difference in terms of how RAID-1 is implemented compared to vSAN OSA. With vSAN OSA witness components were used to ensure that the VM remained available even when there were as many as *failures to tolerate* concurrent failures in the vSAN cluster. The witness objects would provide a quorum when failures occurred in the cluster. With vSAN ESA this is no longer the case. As we have two different types of objects, namely the "performance leg" and the "capacity leg", it is possible to determine the owner of the object by placing components of both the performance leg and the capacity leg across the hosts and by using the existing voting mechanism. We will go through various examples in this chapter to demonstrate how the voting mechanism and the smart placement of components help determine who has retained ownership during certain failure scenarios.

One aspect worth noting is that any disk failure on a single host is treated as a "failure" for this metric (although multiple disk failures on the same host are also treated as a single host failure). Therefore, the VM may not persist (remain accessible) if there is a disk failure on host A and a complete host failure of host B when the number of failures to tolerate is set to one.

As mentioned earlier, the above diagram shows the layout when the object that is created on the vSAN datastore is less than 255GB in size. We will look at the larger size layout shortly.

The following table is true if the capability called *number of disk objects to stripe* is set to 1 and RAID-1 is used as the *Failures to tolerate* setting, which is the default.

NUMBER OF FAILURES TO TOLERATE	REPLICAS	MINIMUM NUMBER OF ESXI HOSTS
0	1	1
1	2	3
2	3	5
3	4	7

Table 5: Hosts required to meet the number of failures to tolerate requirement for RAID-1

If no policy is chosen when a VM is deployed, the default policy associated with the vSAN datastore is chosen. What that policy looks like depends on which policy was selected as the default policy for the vSAN datastore. Starting with vSAN 8.0 U1 ESA it is also possible to have vSAN provide recommendations about the configuration of your storage policy. This functionality can be enabled during the creation of the vSAN cluster or can be enabled after the vSAN cluster has been created as shown in the screenshot below.

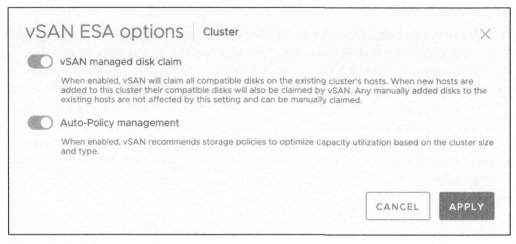

Figure 58: Enabling auto-policy management

Although we will come back to this at a later stage, we do already want to point out that there is a vSAN Optimal Datastore Default Policy Configuration health finding available under Skyline Health in the monitoring section of vSAN. This section will provide insights in both the current configuration, as well as the suggested configuration for your default policy. The suggested configuration is, as expected, based on the size of your vSAN ESA cluster.

When a new policy is created however, the default value of number of *failures to tolerate* is still 1 failure – RAID-1 (Mirroring).

Recommended Practice for Failures to Tolerate

The recommended practice for *Failures to tolerate* is 1 with RAID-5 or 2 with RAID-6. With vSAN OSA the recommendation was RAID-1 Mirroring, but as described in chapter 4, with vSAN ESA RAID-5 and RAID-6 perform similar to RAID-1, and as such it makes sense to take advantage of the lower capacity overhead of RAID-5 or RAID-6. Whether you should set Failures to tolerate to a value of 1 or 2 is entirely up to you. If you a sufficient number of hosts, and are not concerned about the additionally required capacity, then RAID-6 will provide extra protection against failures and can be a great choice. Either way, "Erasure coding", is preferred for all VMs deployed on vSAN ESA.

vSAN has multiple management workflows to warn/protect against accidental decommissioning of hosts that could result in vSAN being unable to meet the number of *failures to tolerate* policy of given VMs. This includes a noncompliant state being shown in the VM summary tab for the VM Storage Policy.

Then the question arises: What is the minimal number of hosts for a vSAN cluster? If we omit the 2-node configuration (more typically seen in remote office-branch office type deployments) for the moment, customers would for the most part require three ESXi hosts to deploy vSAN. However, what about scenarios where you need to do maintenance or upgrades and want to maintain the same level of availability during maintenance hours?

To comply with a policy of *failures to tolerate* = 1 using RAID-1 or RAID-5, you need three hosts at a minimum. RAID-1 will use mirroring for protection while RAID-5, in a 2+1 configuration, will use parity for protection. With RAID-1, even if one host fails, you can still access your data, because with components (votes) spread across three hosts, you will still have more than 50% of your components (votes) available. But what happens if, rather than a failure, you place one of those hosts in maintenance mode?

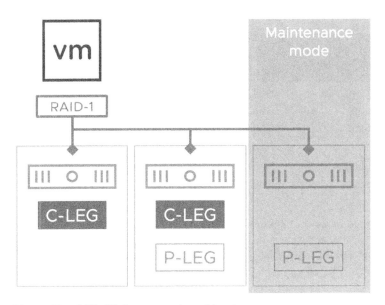

Figure 59: vSAN: Minimum number of hosts

Placing a host into maintenance mode will place all components on this host in an absent state. This host can no longer contribute capacity to the vSAN datastore when in maintenance mode. Similarly, it will not be possible to provision new VMs with an FTT=1 when one node is in maintenance mode (unless you force provision the VM or deploy a VM with an FTT=0). If both remaining hosts keep functioning as expected, all VMs will continue to run. However, if another host fails or needs to be placed into maintenance mode, you have a challenge. At this point, the remaining host will have less than 50% of the components of your VM. As a result, VMs cannot be restarted (nor do any I/O), and this is the reason you will see many people recommending a minimum of four hosts within a cluster, or the minimum your desired "Failures to tolerate" recommends plus one. Meaning that if you use RAID-6, which requires six hosts, the recommendation is to have seven hosts within your cluster to accommodate for maintenance mode or failure scenarios. Note, this is a general recommendation and not a product requirement, cluster sizes ultimately should be determined based on the workload, budget, service level agreement, and operational expectations.

RAID-5 and RAID-6

In this section, we are going to discuss *Failures to tolerate* implemented through RAID-5 and RAID-

6. Which should, as mentioned, be the default selected policy option for almost all vSAN ESA implementations.

Using the Site disaster tolerance set to "None – standard cluster", the table below explains the type of configuration that will be provisioned and the minimum number of ESXi hosts required. This table will help you determine which policy you can use based on the number of ESXi hosts within your cluster. Note that although the minimum number of ESXi hosts may be similar for some configurations, the capacity overhead will be different.

FAILURES TO TOLERATE	OBJECT CONFIGURATION	MINIMUM NUMBER OF ESXI HOSTS	CAPACITY OF VM SIZE
No data redundancy	RAID-0	1	100%
1 failure, RAID-1 (Mirroring)	RAID-1	3	200%
1 failure, RAID-5 (Erasure Coding, 2+1)	RAID-5	3	150%
1 failure, RAID-5 (Erasure Coding, 4+1)	RAID-5	6	125%
2 failures, RAID-6 (Erasure Coding, 4+2)	RAID-6	6	150%
2 failures, RAID-1 (Mirroring)	RAID-1	5	300%
3 failures, RAID-1 (Mirroring)	RAID-1	7	400%

Table 6: Object configuration when number of failures to tolerate and failure tolerance method set

As can be seen from the table, when RAID-5/6 is selected, the maximum number of failures that can be tolerated is 2. RAID-1 allows up to 3 failures to be tolerated in the cluster, using 4 copies of the data.

One might ask why RAID-5/6 is not less performing than RAID-1 any longer with vSAN ESA, as it used to be less performing with vSAN OSA. The reason lies in how vSAN ESA leverages the durable log, implemented in the performance leg, to coalesce data and create full-stripe writes to the performance leg, as explained in chapter 4.

One thing to note is that when there is a failure of some component in the RAID-5 and RAID-6 objects, and data needs to be determined using parity, then there will be a form of I/O amplification compared to RAID-1. Meaning that in failure scenarios, or maintenance mode situations, the performance of RAID-5/6 compared to RAID-1 may be different. However, these are what we would consider special situations. We do not recommend making the decision for your default policy based on that situation but rather base it on when your vSAN is running steady-state and is functioning normally.

Traditionally, even though RAID-5/6 consumed less capacity, it did require more hosts than the RAID-1 approach. When using RAID-1, the rule is that to tolerate n failures, there must be a minimum of $2n+1$ hosts for the mirrors/replicas and witness components. Therefore, to tolerate one failure, there must be at least three hosts. To tolerate two failures, there must be at least five hosts. For those wondering why we need five hosts, we need to ensure that in the case of a network partition scenario we need to determine who owns the data, which will be the partition that has the most votes. To do so we need an odd number of components, and because of this requirement, we need an odd number of hosts. To tolerate three failures, there must be seven hosts in the cluster. All of the hosts must be contributing storage to the vSAN datastore.

Starting with vSAN ESA and the newly introduced Adaptive RAID-5 mechanism, RAID-5 now requires a minimum of three hosts to tolerate one failure and with RAID-6 six hosts are needed to tolerate two failures, even though less space is consumed on each host. The following diagram shows an example of a RAID-5 configuration for the capacity leg, deployed across 3 hosts with a distributed parity in a 2+1 (data+parity) configuration.

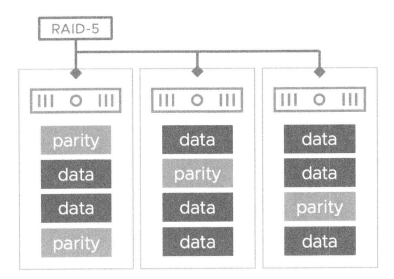

Figure 60: RAID-5 configuration

Why did we call out "capacity leg" specifically for the above diagram? Well, as mentioned before, the selected data placement scheme (Mirroring or Erasure Coding) only applies to the capacity leg. The performance leg of the object is always created as a RAID-1 configuration. The number of components of the performance leg is however still determined by the Failures to tolerate applied to the VM. Meaning that if you have a RAID-5 configuration your performance leg will consist of a RAID-1 configuration with two components (two-way mirror). If you have a RAID-6 configuration, the performance leg will exist of a RAID-1 configuration with three components (three-way mirror).

With vSAN OSA "Number of disk stripes per object" was always a debate. Should you, or should you not use this setting in policy. If you used it, what was the direct impact on performance and data placement? With vSAN ESA and with vSAN OSA 7.0 U1 component layout and placement has changed significantly. (https://core.vmware.com/blog/stripe-width-improvements-vsan-7-u1) Let's discuss in more depth.

Number of Disk Stripes Per Object

This capability defines the number of physical disks across which each replica of a storage object (e.g., VMDK) is striped. Number of disk stripes per object is often short-handed to stripe width or even SW.

When RAID-1 is used, this policy setting can be considered in the context of a RAID-0 configuration on each RAID-1 mirror/replica where I/O traverses several physical disks. When RAID-5/6 is used, each segment of the RAID-5 or RAID-6 stripe may also be configured as a RAID-0 stripe. The next screenshot shows a vSAN ESA object when both RAID-0 and RAID-1 capabilities are used. As demonstrated, the configuration becomes rather complex with even the most basic policy settings.

Type	Component State	Host	Fault Domain	Disk
∨ ⊂ Hard disk 1 (Concatenation)				
∨ RAID 1				
∨ RAID 0				
Component	✅ Active	esxi07.deepdive...		Local NVMe Disk (eui.137290ff840657700...
Component	✅ Active	esxi12.deepdive...		529f8ef9-bcb6-6ee9-6835-3718303b7716
Component	✅ Active	esxi04.deepdive...		525bbc8d-5698-886c-b31e-1fd82a61794f
∨ RAID 0				
Component	✅ Active	esxi02.deepdive...		5226810c-d4fd-d380-5d2e-167e8e8d588f
Component	✅ Active	esxi05.deepdive...		52d86cba-306a-2d88-e8ab-9f217805d5e9
Component	✅ Active	esxi06.deepdive...		52e5e11b-da26-f252-d543-f1b6172ea74b
∨ RAID 1				
∨ RAID 0				
Component	✅ Active	esxi02.deepdive...		Local NVMe Disk (eui.9500d68cb453e39a...
Component	✅ Active	esxi04.deepdive...		Local NVMe Disk (eui.7c0c8f785a592ff50...
Component	✅ Active	esxi11.deepdiveb...		Local NVMe Disk (eui.7fd9f12c9a70b55f0...
∨ RAID 0				
Component	✅ Active	esxi12.deepdive...		Local NVMe Disk (eui.73e02203ac63dca8...
Component	✅ Active	esxi01.deepdive...		Local NVMe Disk (eui.57dbcecd67f371b80...
Component	✅ Active	esxi10.deepdive...		Local NVMe Disk (eui.4c10459df34aa9140...

Figure 61: RAID-1 configuration with stripes

The "Number of disk stripes per object" storage policy rule has limited relevance in vSAN's new architecture, as a result of how the ESA is optimized for NVMe-based storage devices. This is because performance has been improved in the ESA, as explained in the architecture chapter. On top of that, vSAN ESA can exploit the full capabilities of these NVMe devices without the need to split the data into smaller chunks and disperse them across more devices - which was at times needed with vSAN OSA to achieve the desired performance.

While we recommend leaving the stripe width policy rule at its default value of 1, you may be curious as to what happens if the value is increased on a VM running in a cluster using the ESA. The stripe width setting in a vSAN cluster using the ESA will behave in a very similar way to a cluster using the OSA. How it splits the components will depend on whether the components are for the capacity leg or performance leg of an object and the selected RAID configuration (RAID-1,

RAID-5, RAID-6).

The capacity leg and performance leg of an object are new constructs in the object data structure for vSAN ESA and helps it deliver high levels of performance while using space-efficient erasure coding. As shown in in the previous screenshot, increasing the value to 3 will split the performance leg and capacity leg component components.

However, when using a stripe width setting of 2, the object components that comprise the RAID-6 erasure code will **not be changed**. If the stripe width setting was high enough (to 12), it would eventually increase the number of components in the RAID-6 stripe. This aligns with the changes introduced in vSAN 7.0 U1, where the stripe width values affect an erasure code differently than a RAID-1 mirror. (https://core.vmware.com/blog/stripe-width-improvements-vsan-7-u1)

Given that the new data structure and Log Structured Object Manager allow vSAN to deliver near device-level performance of NVMe devices, increasing the stripe width value does little more than create more data components, and complicate placement decisions for vSAN. Increasing the stripe width is not recommended as a mitigation step when troubleshooting vSAN performance with vSAN ESA. If it is no longer relevant for vSAN ESA, then why does the policy rule still exist? Storage policies and the rules that make up a storage policy are a construct of vCenter Server. A given vCenter Server instance may be responsible for many vSAN clusters, some of which may be running vSAN OSA, while others may be configured for vSAN ESA. Keeping these policy rules available across all cluster types helps maintain the compatibility of different cluster types and conditions across environments within the same vCenter Server instance.

RAID-0 used when no Striping is specified in the Policy

Those who have been looking at the vSphere Client regularly, where you can see the placement of components, may have noticed that vSAN appears to create a multi-component RAID-0 for your VM even when you did not explicitly ask it to. Or perhaps you have requested a stripe width of two in your policy and then observed what appears to be a stripe width of three (or more) being created. vSAN will split objects as it sees fit when there are space constraints. This is not striping per se, since components can end up on the same physical capacity device, which in many ways can be thought of as a concatenation. We can refer to it as chunking.

vSAN will use this chunking method on certain occasions. When an object is larger than any single chunk of free space. Essentially, vSAN hides the fact that even when there is a low amount of free capacity on a single device, administrators can still create very large VMs. Therefore, it is not uncommon to see objects split into multiple components, even when no stripe width is specified in the VM storage policy. vSAN will use this chunking method when an object is larger than the available free space on any capacity device.

There is another occasion where this chunking may occur. By default, an object will also be split if its size is greater than 255 GB (the maximum component size). An object might appear to be made up of multiple 255 GB RAID-0 chunks even though striping may not have been a policy requirement. It can be split even before it reaches 255 GB when free disk space makes vSAN think that there is a benefit in doing so. Note that just because there is a standard split at 255 GB, it doesn't mean all new chunks will go onto different capacity devices. In fact, since this is not striping per se, multiple chunks may be placed on the same physical capacity device. It may, or may not, depending on overall balance and free capacity.

Stripe Width Maximum

In vSAN, the maximum stripe width that can be defined in a policy is 12. This can be striping across storage devices in the same host, or across storage devices, in different hosts, as mentioned earlier. I'm going to add a caveat here that, since vSAN 7.0U1, certain limits have been placed on striping for both large objects as well as RAID-5 and RAID-6 objects. The description that follows applied to vSAN versions prior to 7.0U1, as well as to objects that are 255GB or less in size.

> **Remember that when you specify a stripe width there has to be at least a stripe width (SW) × (FTT+1) number of capacity devices before vSAN can satisfy the policy requirement.**

The larger the number of FTT and SW, the more complex the placement of object and associated components will become. The number of disk stripes per object setting in the VM storage policy means stripe across "at least" this number of storage devices per mirror. vSAN may, when it sees fit, use additional stripes.

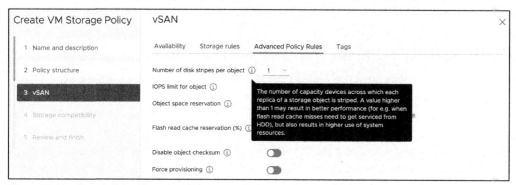

Figure 62: Number of disk stripes per object

Stripe Width Configuration Error

You may ask yourself what happens if a vSphere administrator requests the vSAN cluster to meet a stripe width policy setting that is not available or achievable, typically due to a lack of resources. During the creation of the policy, vSAN will verify if there is a datastore that is compatible with the capabilities specified in the policy. As shown in the screenshot below, where we have requested FTT=3 and SW=12, no datastore is shown as compatible with the defined policy.

Figure 63: No compatible datastore

If you would forcefully try to deploy a VM using this policy, then the creation of the VM will fail. This is demonstrated in the screenshot below.

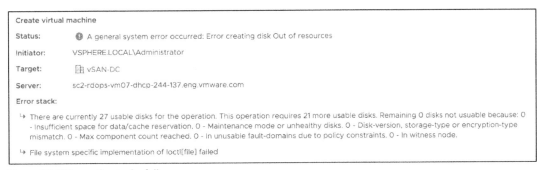

Figure 64: VM creation tasks fails

What this error message is telling us is that vSAN needs 48 disks (4 copies of the data by a stripe width of 12) to implement this policy. There are currently only 27 disks available in the cluster, so 21 more are needed to create such a policy.

We have discussed stripe width probably more than needed at this point, considering the recommendation is for vSAN ESA to not use this policy setting. There are, however, various policy capabilities that we will need to discuss and explore.

In order to be able to describe the various scenarios and capabilities, we have deployed a twelve node vSAN cluster, as demonstrated in the next screenshot.

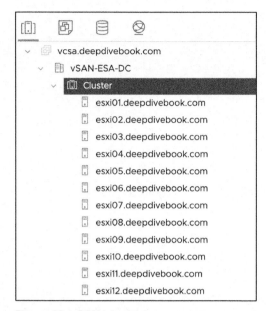

Figure 65: vSAN lab cluster

We will use this lab to demonstrate the different policy configurations and the impact on the layout of the objects. Before we do, let's discuss a few of the options first which are less common to be configured within policy, which is why they can be found under "Advanced Policy Rules".

IOPS Limit for Object

IOPS limit for object is a Quality of Service (QoS) capability introduced with vSAN 6.2. This allows administrators to ensure that an object, such as a VMDK, does not generate more than a predefined number of I/O operations per second. This is a great way of ensuring that a "noisy neighbor" virtual machine does not impact other virtual machine components on the same host by consuming more than its fair share of resources.

By default, vSAN uses a normalized I/O size of 32 KB as a base. **This means that a 64 KB I/O will therefore represent two I/O operations in the QoS calculation**. I/Os that are less than or equal to 32 KB will be considered single I/O operations. For example, 2 × 4 KB I/Os are considered two distinct I/Os. It should also be noted that both read and write IOPS are regarded as equivalent. Neither cache hit rate nor sequential I/O is considered. If the IOPS limit threshold is passed, the I/O is throttled back to bring the IOPS value back under the threshold. The default value for this capability is 0, meaning that there is no IOPS limit threshold and VMs can consume as many IOPS as they want, subject to available resources.

We do not see this capability used too often by vSAN customers. Only a small number of Service Providers use this to limit their customer's workloads.

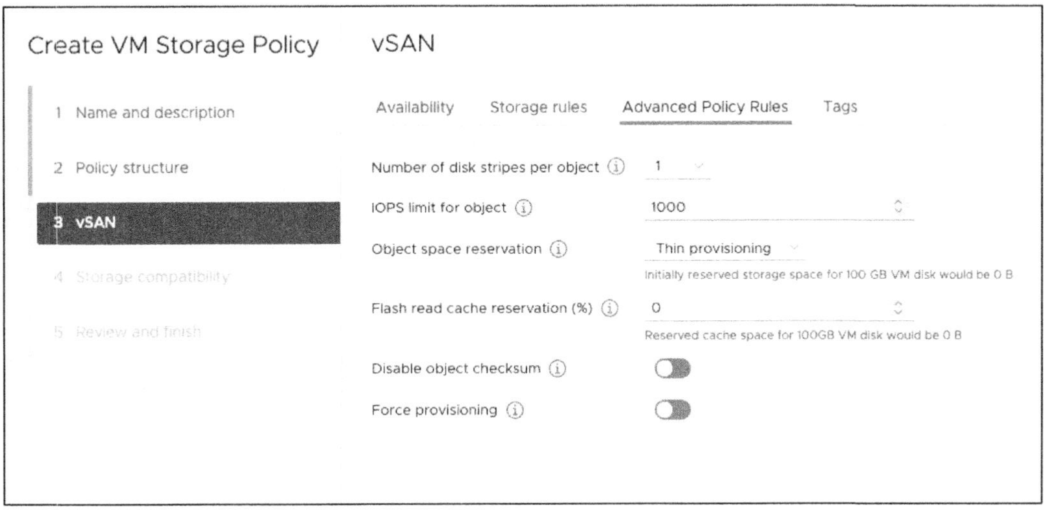

Figure 66: IOPS Limit of 1000

Flash Read Cache Reservation

This capability applies to hybrid vSAN OSA configurations only. It is the amount of flash capacity reserved on the cache tier device as read cache for the storage object. It is specified as a percentage of the logical size of the storage object (i.e., VMDK). This is specified as a percentage value (%), with up to four decimal places. This fine granular unit size is needed so that administrators can express sub 1% units. Take the example of a 1 TB VMDK. If you limited the read cache reservation to 1% increments, this would mean cache reservations in increments of 10 GB, which in most cases is far too much for a single VM.

Note, this policy setting **should not** be used with vSAN ESA.

Object Space Reservation

By default, all objects deployed on vSAN are thin provisioned. This means that no space is reserved at VM provisioning time but rather space is consumed as the VM uses storage. The object space reservation is the amount of space to reserve specified as a percentage of the total object address space.

This is a property used for specifying a thick provisioned storage object. If object space reservation is set to Thick provisioning (or 100% in the vSphere Client), all of the storage capacity requirements of the VM are reserved upfront. This will be *lazy zeroed thick* (LZT) format and not *eager zeroed thick* (EZT). The difference between LZT and EZT is that EZT virtual disks are zeroed out at creation time; LZT virtual disks are zeroed out at first write time.

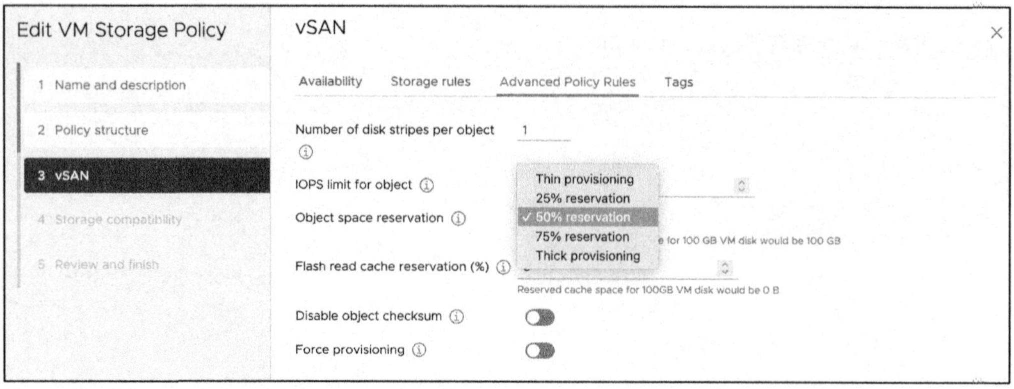

Figure 67: Object space reservation

Force Provisioning

If the force provisioning parameter is enabled, any object that has this setting in its policy will be provisioned even if the requirements specified in the VM storage policy cannot be satisfied by the vSAN datastore. The VM will be shown as noncompliant in the VM summary tab and relevant VM storage policy views in the vSphere client. If there is not enough space in the cluster to satisfy the reservation requirements of at least one replica, however, the provisioning will fail even if force provisioning is turned on. When additional resources become available in the cluster, vSAN will bring this object to a compliant state.

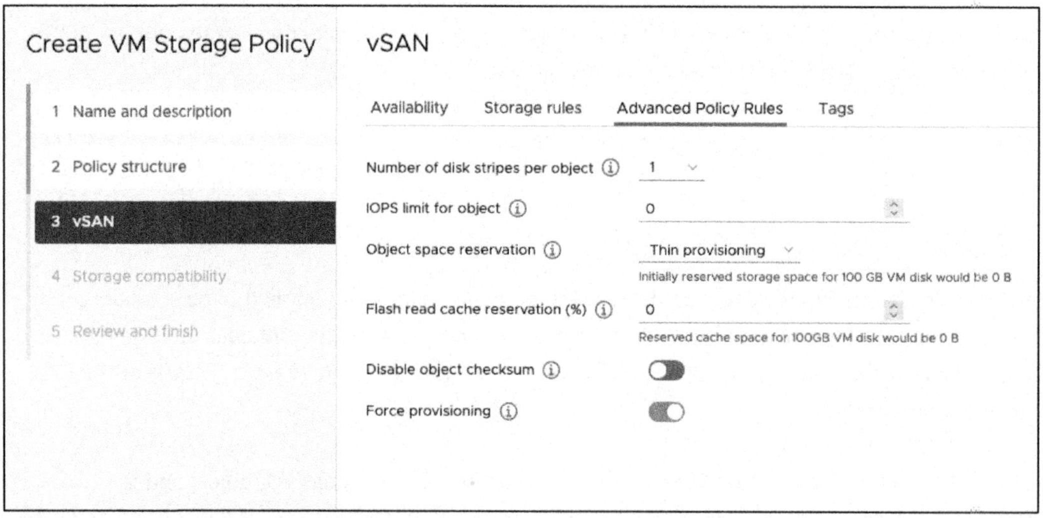

Figure 68: Force provisioning enabled

One thing that might not be well understood regarding *force provisioning* is that if a policy cannot be met, it attempts a much simpler placement with requirements that reduce *failures to tolerate* to 0. This means vSAN will attempt to create an object with just a single copy of data. Any *Object space reservation* policy setting is still honored. Therefore, there is no gradual reduction in capabilities as vSAN tries to find a placement for an object. For example, if the policy contains *failures to tolerate* = 2, vSAN won't attempt an object placement using *failures to tolerate* = 1. Instead, it immediately looks to implement *failures to tolerate* = 0.

Caution should be exercised if this policy setting is implemented. Since this allows VMs to be provisioned with no protection, it can lead to scenarios where VMs and data are at risk.

Administrators who use this option to *force provision* virtual machines need to be aware that although virtual machine objects may be provisioned with only one replica copy (perhaps due to lack of space), once additional resources become available in the cluster, vSAN may immediately consume these resources to try to satisfy the policy settings of virtual machines. Thus, administrators may see the additional space from newly added capacity devices very quickly consumed if there are objects that are force provisioned on the cluster.

In the past, the use case for setting *force provision* was when a vSAN management cluster needed to be bootstrapped. In this scenario, you would start with a single vSAN node that would host the vCenter Server, which was then used to configure a larger vSAN cluster. vCenter Server would be deployed initially with *failures to tolerate = 0* but once additional nodes were added to the cluster, it would get reconfigured with *failures to tolerate = 1*.

Another use case is the situation where a cluster is under maintenance or a failure has occurred, but there is still a need to provision new virtual machines.

> **Remember that this parameter should be used only when needed and as an exception. When used by default, this could easily lead to scenarios where VMs, and all data associated with them, are at risk due to provisioning with no FTT. Use with caution!**

Disable Object Checksum

This feature, which is enabled by default, is looking for data corruption (bit rot), and if found, automatically corrects it. Checksum is validated on the complete I/O path, which means that when writing data, the checksum is calculated and automatically stored. Upon a read, the checksum of the data is validated, and if there is a mismatch the data is repaired. vSAN also includes a checksum scrubber mechanism. This mechanism is configured to check all data on the vSAN datastore. Note that the scrubber runs in the background and only when there is limited I/O, to avoid a performance impact on the workload.

In some rare cases, you may desire to disable checksums completely. The reason for this could be performance, although the overhead is negligible, and most customers prefer data integrity over a minimal performance increase. In certain cases, the application, especially if it is a newer next-gen or cloud-native application, may already provide a checksum mechanism, or the workload does not require a checksum. If that is the case, then checksums can be disabled through the "disable object checksum" capability. There has already been some discussion around disabling object checksum in the 'Data Integrity through Checksum' topic in chapter 4. You may find it useful to review that section of the book when trying to decide if checksumming should be disabled on a workload.

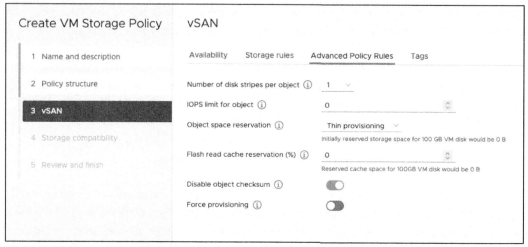

Figure 69: Object checksum disabled

> **We do not recommend disabling Object Checksum. This feature was introduced as a direct request by customers and partners who have workloads that have their own checksum mechanism. Even if that is the case, we would still not recommend disabling Object Checksum. Use at your own risk!**

That completes the vSAN advanced policy capabilities overview. All above-mentioned capabilities can be specified within a policy. There is however more to a virtual machine as explained in earlier chapters. Let's now look at those special objects and let's examine which policy capabilities are inherited and which are not.

VM Home Namespace

The VM home namespace on vSAN is a *255 GB thin object* by default. A namespace is a per-VM object. As you could imagine, if policy settings were allocated to the VM home namespace, such as proportional capacity and flash read cache reservation, much of the magnetic disk and flash resources could be wasted. To that end, the VM home namespace has its own special policy, as follows:

- Number of disk stripes per object: 1
- Failures to tolerate: <as-per-policy>
    - This includes RAID-1, RAID-5, and RAID-6 configurations
- Flash read cache reservation: 0% (Not used with ESA.)
- Force provisioning: Off
- Object space reservation: thin
- Checksum disabled: <as-per-policy>

- IOPS limit for object: <as-per-policy>

To validate our learnings, we deployed a VM, and for this virtual machine, disk stripes were configured to 3, failures to tolerate to 1 with RAID-1. We used "rvc" to inspect the VM, we will discuss rvc in more detail in chapter 10 of the book, for now it suffices to know that rvc is a commandline tool available on vCenter Server that enables you to inspect vSAN objects in-depth. As shown in the screenshot below, the ".vmx" file has a different policy configuration than the ".vmdk" file. Where the ".vmx" represents the VM Home object, and the ".vmdk" file the virtual disk attached to the VM.

```
[vSAN-ESA-DS] 5e64ef63-ac26-f6a4-ece9-005056b600ad/R1-SW3.vmx
  DOM Object: 5e64ef63-ac26-f6a4-ece9-005056b600ad (v18, owner: esxi03.deepdivebook.com, proxy owner: None, policy: stripeWidth = 1, cacheReservation = 0, proportional
Capacity = [0, 100], hostFailuresToTolerate = 1, forceProvisioning = 0, spbmProfileId = e3d6c319-aedf-4392-9b44-f381bc13f89e, spbmProfileGenerationNumber = 0, replicaPre
ference = Performance, iopsLimit = 0, checksumDisabled = 0, CSN = 1, spbmProfileName = R1-SW3)
    Concatenation
      RAID_1
        Component: 5e64ef63-eeff-b3a6-a385-005056b600ad (state: ACTIVE (5), host: esxi12.deepdivebook.com, capacity: 526e5f52-f970-db3a-539e-ac319d59a5bf, cache: ,
                                                         votes: 3, usage: 0.0 GB, proxy component: false)
        Component: 5e64ef63-dcbc-b7a6-aaa8-005056b600ad (state: ACTIVE (5), host: esxi03.deepdivebook.com, capacity: 5239b96a-ce47-0179-ef8b-a4bf518075ff, cache: ,
                                                         votes: 2, usage: 0.0 GB, proxy component: false)
      RAID_1
        RAID_0
          Component: 5e64ef63-b652-baa6-1f33-005056b600ad (state: ACTIVE (5), host: esxi09.deepdivebook.com, capacity: 52de7d36-7c9a-a39a-e59b-451adea643d3, cache: ,
                                                           votes: 1, usage: 0.0 GB, proxy component: false)
          Component: 5e64ef63-765c-hba6-5442-005056b600ad (state: ACTIVE (5), host: esxi09.deepdivebook.com, capacity: 52079f38-3845-d466-c8e7-95ee2f17d164, cache: ,
                                                           votes: 1, usage: 0.0 GB, proxy component: false)
          Component: 5e64ef63-a23a-bca6-eba6-005056b600ad (state: ACTIVE (5), host: esxi08.deepdivebook.com, capacity: 52edf46a-0423-8cce-0a76-33e6d1c58aaa, cache: ,
                                                           votes: 2, usage: 0.0 OB, proxy component: false)
        RAID_0
          Component: 5e64ef63-6219-bda6-db95-005056b600ad (state: ACTIVE (5), host: esxi06.deepdivebook.com, capacity: 52fe9834-baf1-28a9-81d6-b927dda59f57, cache: ,
                                                           votes: 2, usage: 0.0 GB, proxy component: false)
          Component: 5e64ef63-8cf6-bda6-ef5c-005056b600ad (state: ACTIVE (5), host: esxi01.deepdivebook.com, capacity: 52f752c3-b96a-ab7b-7a2c-8403ac43d8a9, cache: ,
                                                           votes: 2, usage: 0.0 GB, proxy component: false)
          Component: 5e64ef63-20ca-bea6-2181-005056b600ad (state: ACTIVE (5), host: esxi11.deepdivebook.com, capacity: 52ad687d-30f4-8cc2-5261-6a6116943920, cache: ,
                                                           votes: 2, usage: 0.0 GB, proxy component: false)

[vSAN-ESA-DS] 5e64ef63-ac26-f6a4-ece9-005056b600ad/R1-SW3.vmdk
  DOM Object: 5f64ef63-04b7-d514-88a1-005056b600ad (v18, owner: esxi03.deepdivebook.com, proxy owner: None, policy: stripeWidth = 3, cacheReservation = 0, proportional
Capacity = 0, hostFailuresToTolerate = 1, forceProvisioning = 0, spbmProfileId = e3d6c319-aedf-4392-9b44-f381bc13f89e, spbmProfileGenerationNumber = 0, replicaPreference
= Performance, iopsLimit = 0, checksumDisabled = 0, CSN = 1, spbmProfileName = R1-SW3)
    Concatenation
      RAID_1
        RAID_0
          Component: 5f64ef63-486a-2d16-3c0f-005056b600ad (state: ACTIVE (5), host: esxi06.deepdivebook.com, capacity: 52bb6e68-37b7-4cf6-eecf-aaf67604c244, cache: ,
                                                           votes: 2, usage: 0.0 GB, proxy component: false)
          Component: 5f64ef63-9026-3116-d169-005056b600ad (state: ACTIVE (5), host: esxi11.deepdivebook.com, capacity: 526bfb7e-1974-e5d3-779b-acbe21b67c81, cache: ,
                                                           votes: 2, usage: 0.0 GB, proxy component: false)
          Component: 5f64ef63-a887-3216-8855-005056b600ad (state: ACTIVE (5), host: esxi01.deepdivebook.com, capacity: 52f752c3-b96a-ab7b-7a2c-8403ac43d8aa, cache: ,
                                                           votes: 2, usage: 0.0 GB, proxy component: false)
        RAID_0
          Component: 5f64ef63-52e6-3316-b094-005056b600ad (state: ACTIVE (5), host: esxi08.deepdivebook.com, capacity: 526eff5d-ae2d-8fec-7c53-39ea6c43e1d8, cache: ,
                                                           votes: 1, usage: 0.0 GB, proxy component: false)
          Component: 5f64ef63-da4b-3516-2ce2-005056b600ad (state: ACTIVE (5), host: esxi09.deepdivebook.com, capacity: 52de7d36-7c9a-a39a-e59b-451adea643d4, cache: ,
                                                           votes: 1, usage: 0.0 GB, proxy component: false)
          Component: 5f64ef63-eca4-3616-dfe5-005056b600ad (state: ACTIVE (5), host: esxi07.deepdivebook.com, capacity: 5249c5f0-d39b-4437-432c-e5fe7a38ba18, cache: ,
                                                           votes: 1, usage: 0.0 GB, proxy component: false)
      RAID_1
        RAID_0
          Component: 5f64ef63-823b-3816-ccaa-005056b600ad (state: ACTIVE (5), host: esxi12.deepdivebook.com, capacity: 526e5f52-f970-db3a-539e-ac319d59a5be, cache: ,
                                                           votes: 2, usage: 0.0 GB, proxy component: false)
          Component: 5f64ef63-0098-3916-1468-005056b600ad (state: ACTIVE (5), host: esxi07.deepdivebook.com, capacity: 523789e4-82f5-37d1-75a9-4d370da10fff, cache: ,
                                                           votes: 1, usage: 0.0 GB, proxy component: false)
          Component: 5f64ef63-e4ba-3a16-8d1d-005056b600ad (state: ACTIVE (5), host: esxi08.deepdivebook.com, capacity: 52edf46a-0423-8cce-0a76-33e6d1c58aaa, cache: ,
                                                           votes: 1, usage: 0.0 GB, proxy component: false)
        RAID_0
          Component: 5f64ef63-10f7-3b16-da2e-005056b600ad (state: ACTIVE (5), host: esxi09.deepdivebook.com, capacity: 52064afe-5a33-0e6a-c90d-28ab1d011345, cache: ,
                                                           votes: 1, usage: 0.0 GB, proxy component: false)
          Component: 5f64ef63-1627-3d16-9c18-005056b600ad (state: ACTIVE (5), host: esxi03.deepdivebook.com, capacity: 522f3385-d5c7-bfb6-70de-66a799b95d22, cache: ,
                                                           votes: 2, usage: 0.0 GB, proxy component: false)
          Component: 5f64ef63-886a-3e16-00ce-005056b600ad (state: ACTIVE (5), host: esxi06.deepdivebook.com, capacity: 52bb6e68-37b7-4cf6-eecf-aaf67604c243, cache: ,
                                                           votes: 1, usage: 0.0 GB, proxy component: false)
```

Figure 70: VM Home components and SW=3

We started out this section by stating that the VM home namespace is a 255GB thin object by default. Starting with vSAN 8.0 U1 it is possible to change the size of the VM home namespace. You may wonder why anyone would want to do this? Well, the VM home namespace is not only used for the VM log files or the VMs .vmx file, but it is also used when you create folder on a vSAN datastore and upload ISOs to it. Another example of when a VM home namespace is used is Content Library. You can imagine that in these scenarios 255GB may not be sufficient.

If needed, you can increase the size of the VM home namespace through PowerCLI. We will describe how to do this in chapter 10, command line tools.

VM Swap Revisited

The VM Swap object is only created when the VM is powered on and is deleted when the VM is powered off. The VM swap follows much the same conventions as the VM home namespace. It has the same default policy as the VM home namespace. VM swap is thin provisioned by default. This was done to avoid relatively high amounts of capacity needlessly being reserved for swap space.

This behavior, if desired, can be disabled in the advanced options view of the vSAN Service section on your cluster. To disable this behavior, simply toggle the switch to the left.

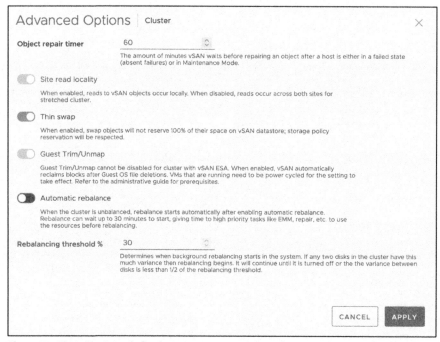

Figure 71: Changing Swap behavior

> **We recommend validating if memory is overcommitted or not and how much spare capacity is available on vSAN. Free capacity needs to be available for swap when a VM wants to consume it. If new blocks can't be allocated, the VM will fail!**

VM swap, like VM Home Namespace, follows the FTT specified by the administrator in the VMs policy. This is to ensure that the swap file has the same availability characteristics as the VM itself.

- Number of disk stripes per object: 1
- Number of failures to tolerate: <as-per-policy>
- Flash read cache reservation: 0% (Not used with ESA.)
- Force provisioning: On

- Object space reservation: 0% (thin)
- Failure tolerance method: <as-per-policy>
- Checksum disabled: <as-per-policy>
- IOPS limit for object: <as-per-policy>

There is one additional point concerning swap, and that is that it has force provisioning set to on. This means that if some of the policy requirements cannot be met, such as *failures to tolerate*, VM swap is still created.

Snapshot Changes

With vSAN ESA snapshots have also been implemented differently, as described in chapter 04. The big change, to briefly summarize, is the fact that "delta disks" no longer exist. With vSAN ESA all I/O is done to the existing objects, and changes are tracked in a new metadata structure. When creating a snapshot however, one caveat will have to called out, and that is the memory snapshot. If "Include virtual machine's memory" was selected during the snapshot creation process, then a so called ".vmem" file is created. This ".vmem" file contains the content of the memory of the VM and will always inherit the policy associated with the base disk as shown in the output of rvc of a VM with a RAID-5 policy associated.

```
[vSAN-ESA-DS] 6f4def63-348c-4ec9-71ca-005056b61931/R5-VM-Snapshot1.vmem
    DOM Object: 316cef63-5edd-b220-36d3-005056b61931 (v18, owner: esxi08.deepdivebook.com, proxy owner: None, policy: stripeWidth = 1, cacheReservation = 0, proportional
Capacity = 100, hostFailuresToTolerate = 1, forceProvisioning = 1, spbmProfileId = 4b97756b-3c50-481a-a105-d6a7b1507f9a, spbmProfileGenerationNumber = 0, storageType = A
llflash, replicaPreference = Capacity, CSN = 1, spbmProfileName = vSAN ESA Default Policy - RAID5)
    Concatenation
      RAID_1
        Component: 316cef63-5a9c-2122-bcbb-005056b61931 (state: ACTIVE (5), host: esxi05.deepdivebook.com, capacity: 5231bb3f-d58b-aaee-910c-934beb0b7529, cache: ,
                                                          votes: 2, usage: 0.1 GB, proxy component: false)
        Component: 316cef63-22d1-2322-ba41-005056b61931 (state: ACTIVE (5), host: esxi08.deepdivebook.com, capacity: 526eff5d-ae2d-8fec-7c53-39ea6c43e1d8, cache: ,
                                                          votes: 2, usage: 0.1 GB, proxy component: false)
      RAID_5
        Component: 316cef63-7032-2522-4744-005056b61931 (state: ACTIVE (5), host: esxi10.deepdivebook.com, capacity: 520b26d9-cf7e-c2d1-cfc8-8ada684144c4, cache: ,
                                                          votes: 2, usage: 1.0 GB, proxy component: false)
        Component: 316cef63-02ab-2622-6fa9-005056b61931 (state: ACTIVE (5), host: esxi04.deepdivebook.com, capacity: 52017b23-ff0e-7474-ef6a-d0181a5485f7, cache: ,
                                                          votes: 2, usage: 1.0 GB, proxy component: false)
        Component: 316cef63-6216-2822-d4b7-005056b61931 (state: ACTIVE (5), host: esxi11.deepdivebook.com, capacity: 52d111ac-ba75-9504-3673-fd0f623dc9c8, cache: ,
                                                          votes: 2, usage: 1.0 GB, proxy component: false)
        Component: 316cef63-dc60-2922-6a00-005056b61931 (state: ACTIVE (5), host: esxi09.deepdivebook.com, capacity: 52079f38-3845-d466-c8e7-95ee2f17d164, cache: ,
                                                          votes: 2, usage: 1.0 GB, proxy component: false)
        Component: 316cef63-6c95-2a22-806c-005056b61931 (state: ACTIVE (5), host: esxi05.deepdivebook.com, capacity: 52456125-85e4-193f-5995-d3eeb8fec714, cache: ,
                                                          votes: 1, usage: 1.0 GB, proxy component: false)
```

Figure 72: Snapshot and .vmem file

Now we have discussed all policy capabilities and the impact they have on a VM (and associated objects), let's have a look at the component which surfaces up the capabilities to vCenter Server before we start exploring all different policy configurations.

VASA Vendor Provider

As part of the vSAN cluster creation step, each ESXi host has a vSAN storage provider registered with vCenter Server. This uses the *vSphere APIs for Storage Awareness* (VASA) to surface the vSAN capabilities to vCenter Server. The capabilities can then be used to create VM storage policies for the VMs deployed on the vSAN datastore. If you are familiar with VASA and have used it with traditional storage environments, you'll find this functionality familiar; however, with traditional storage environments that leverage VASA, some configuration work needs to be done to add the storage provider for that storage. In the context of vSAN, a vSphere administrator does not need to worry about registering these; these are automatically registered when a vSAN cluster is created.

An Introduction to VASA

VASA enables storage vendors to publish the capabilities of their storage to vCenter Server, which in turn can display these capabilities in the vSphere Client. VASA may also provide information about storage health status, configuration info, capacity, thin provisioning info, and so on. VASA enables VMware to have an end-to-end story regarding storage. Traditionally, this enabled storage arrays to inform the VASA storage provider of capabilities. Then the storage provider informed vCenter Server to allow users to see storage array capabilities from the vSphere Client. Through VM storage policies, these storage capabilities are used in the vSphere Client to assist administrators in choosing the right storage in terms of space, performance, and *service level agreement* (SLA) requirements. This is true for both traditional storage arrays and vSAN.

With vSAN and vVols, the administrator defines the capabilities that they want to have for VM storage through a VM storage policy. This policy information is then pushed down to the storage layer, informing it of the requirements you have for storage. VASA will then inform the administrator whether the underlying storage (e.g., vSAN) can meet these requirements, effectively communicating compliance information on a per-storage object basis. VASA functionality is working in a bidirectional mode. Early versions of VASA for traditional storage arrays would only surface up capabilities. Today with vSAN, it not only surfaces up capabilities, but also verifies whether a VM's storage requirements are being met based on the contents of the policy.

Storage Providers

The next screenshot illustrates an example of what the storage provider section looks like. When a vSAN cluster is created, the VASA storage provider from every ESXi host in the cluster is registered to the vCenter Server. In an environment where the vCenter Server is managing multiple vSAN clusters (in the following example, there are 12 hosts across multiple clusters in total), the VASA vSAN storage provider configuration would look like this. Note that there's a long list of IOFILTER Providers, one per host. These providers are needed for features like Storage IO Control and VM Encryption, or any of the 3rd party IO Filters you may have installed. IO Filters are essentially storage services that are decoupled from your storage system. They may provide storage agnostic replication services, or host local flash caching for instance.

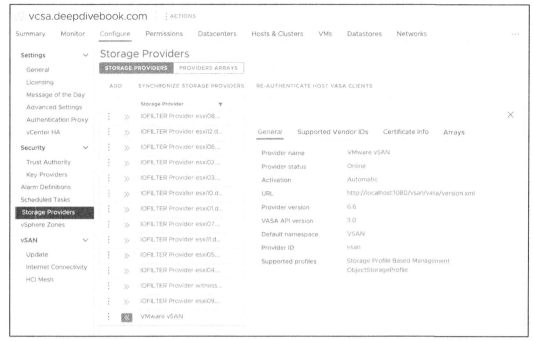

Figure 73: vSAN Storage Provider

You can always check the status of the storage providers by navigating in the vSphere Client to the vCenter Server inventory item, selecting the Configure tab, and then the Storage Providers view. The vSAN provider should always be online. Note that the vSAN storage provider is listed as "internally managed" and you will only see one listed. Internally managed means that all operational aspects are automatically handled by vSAN. In early versions of vSphere, you were able to view all hosts registered with the vSAN Storage Provider, but this is no longer the case.

vSAN Storage Providers: Highly Available

The vSAN storage provider is high availability. Should one ESXi host fail, another ESXi host in the cluster can take over the presentation of these vSAN capabilities. In other words, should the storage provider that is currently online go offline or fail for whatever reason (most likely because of a host failure), one of the standby providers on another ESXi host will be promoted to online.

There is very little work that a vSphere administrator needs to do with storage providers to create a vSAN cluster. This is simply for your own reference. However, if you do run into a situation where the vSAN capabilities are not surfacing up in the VM storage policies section, it is worth visiting this part of the configuration and verifying that the storage provider is online. If the storage provider is not online, you will not discover any vSAN capabilities when trying to build a VM storage policy. At this point, as a troubleshooting step, you could consider doing a resync of the storage providers by clicking on the Synchronize Storage Providers in the Storage Provider screen.

Figure 74: Synchronize storage provider

The VASA storage providers do not play any role in the data path for vSAN. If storage providers fail, this has no impact on VMs running on the vSAN datastore. The impact of not having a storage provider is a lack of visibility into the underlying capabilities, so you will not be able to create new storage policies. However, already running VMs and policies are unaffected.

Now that we have discussed both VASA and all vSAN policy capabilities, let's have a look at various examples of VMs provisioned with a specific capability enabled.

Assigning a VM Storage Policy during VM Provisioning

The assignment of a VM storage policy is done during the VM provisioning. At the point where the vSphere administrator must select a destination datastore, the appropriate policy is selected from the drop-down menu of available VM storage policies. The datastores are then separated into compatible and incompatible datastores, allowing the vSphere administrator to make the appropriate and correct choice for VM placement. Most environments will have a single datastore available, i.e., vSAN. In some environments you may have multiple datastores.

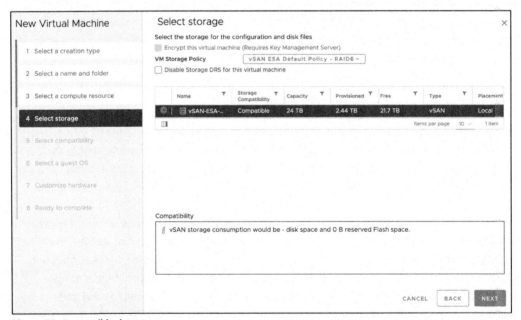

Figure 75: Compatible datastore

In early versions of vSphere and vSAN, this matching of datastores did not necessarily mean that the datastore would meet the requirements in the VM storage policy. It was a little confusing because what it meant was that the datastore understood the set of requirements placed in the policy because they were vSAN requirements. But it did not mean that it could successfully provision the storage object on the vSAN datastore. Thus, it was difficult to know if a VM with a specific policy could be provisioned until you tried to provision it with the policy. Then it would either fail or succeed.

In the currents versions of vSAN, the VM is now validated to check if it can be provisioned with the specified capabilities in the policy. In the screenshot above we have a policy with *failures to tolerate* set to 2 with Erasure Coding. As shown, the vSAN cluster is capable of matching those requirements, and as such, the datastore is listed as compatible and the VM can be successfully provisioned.

Virtual Machine Provisioning

You have previously learned about the various vSAN capabilities that you can add to a VM storage policy. This policy can then be used by objects (VMs, etc.) deployed on a vSAN datastore. This section covers how to create the appropriate VM storage policy using these capabilities. It also discusses the layout of these VM storage objects as they are deployed on the vSAN ESA datastore. Hopefully, this will give you a better understanding of the inner workings of vSAN ESA.

Before we dive into it, we do want to point out again that VMware, and the authors, recommend using Erasure Coding as your default. With vSAN ESA RAID-5 delivers the same, or even better, performance as RAID-1, but from a required capacity perspective, it comes at a much lower cost.

Policy Setting: Failures to Tolerate = 1, RAID-1

Let's begin by creating a very simple VM storage policy. Then we can examine what will happen if a VM is deployed to a vSAN datastore using this policy. Let's create the first policy to have a single capability setting of number of *failures to tolerate* set to 1. We are going to use RAID-1 mirroring to implement failures to tolerate initially. Later, we shall look at RAID-5 and RAID-6 configurations for the VM objects which offer different protection mechanisms. But before we get to that, it is important to understand that this policy *of failures to tolerate* = 1 means that any VMs deployed on the vSAN datastore with this policy will be configured with an additional mirror copy (replica) of the data. This means that if there is a single failure in the vSAN cluster, a full complement of the vSAN storage objects is still available. Let's see this in action, but before we do, let's visualize the expected results as shown in the next figure.

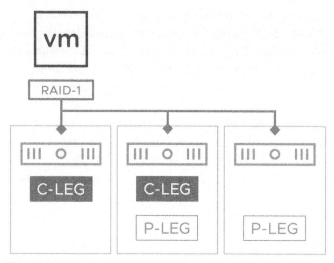

Figure 76: Failures to tolerate = 1

In this vSAN environment, there are twelve ESXi hosts. This is an all-NVMe configuration, and vSAN ESA has been enabled, and vSAN networking has been configured and the ESXi hosts have formed a vSAN datastore. To this datastore, we will deploy a new VM.

We will keep this first VM storage policy simple, with just a single capability, *failures to tolerate* set to 1.

To begin, go to the Policies and Profiles section in the navigation bar on the left-hand side of the vSphere Client, and click the VM Storage Policies icon. Next click on CREATE. This will open the Create VM Storage Policy screen, as shown below. Make sure to provide the new policy with a proper name. In this scenario, we will name the policy **FTT=1 – RAID 1**.

Create VM Storage Policy	Name and description	✕
1 Name and description	vCenter Server:	VCSA.DEEPDIVEBOOK.COM ⌄
2 Policy structure		
3 Storage compatibility	Name:	FTT=1 – RAID 1
4 Review and finish	Description:	

Figure 77: Create a new VM Storage Policy

The next screen displays information about the policy structure. This includes host-based services, vSAN rule sets, vSANDirect rule sets, and tag-based placement. The host-based services are I/O filters, in most environments limited to vSphere features called Storage I/O Control and VM Encryption. Note however that there are also 3rd party I/O filters, these can also be included in a policy. vSANDirect rules are like tag rules and are used to identify devices that are consumed by vSANDirect for the vSAN Data Persistence platform, which will be discussed in further detail when we discuss vSAN as a platform for modern applications in chapter 9. Tag-based placement rules are typically used in scenarios where VMs need to be deployed on datastores that are not represented by a storage provider or to differentiate between multiple datastores that offer the same capabilities, e.g., an HCI-Mesh environment, or when placement of VMs should be determined by specific categories that those VMs, or VM owners, belong to.

This was described on VMware's VirtualBlocks blog by Jason Massae as follows:

> "Many are familiar with SPBM policies when used with vSAN or VVols as they have some incredible features and functionalities. But another valuable SPBM use is with Tags and Categories. By using tags, we can create high-level generic policies or very custom and detailed policies. With tag based SPBM, you can create your own specific categories and tags based on almost anything you can envision. Performance levels or tiers, disk configurations, locations, OS type, departments, and disk types such as SAS, SATA or SSD are just a few examples. The categories and tags you can create are almost limitless!"

Select the option 'Enable rules for "vSAN" storage' as shown below.

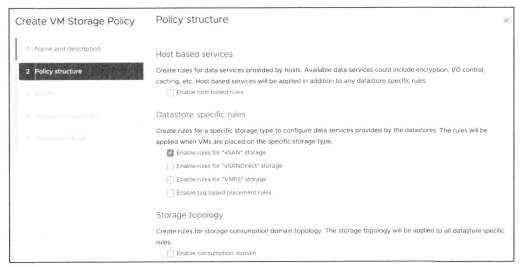

Figure 78: Enable rules for vSAN storage

On the next screen, we can begin to add requirements for vSAN. For our first policy, the capability that we want to configure is *Failures to tolerate*, and we will set this to *1 failure – RAID-1 (Mirroring)*, as shown below. Leave the Site disaster tolerance setting at the default of "None – standard cluster".

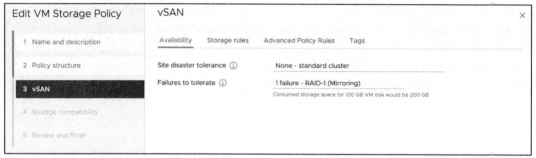

Figure 79: Failures to tolerate = 1 failure

Note that below the *Failures to tolerate* setting it now displays what the impact is on consumed storage space. It uses a 100 GB VM disk as an example, and as shown in the screenshot above, this policy setting results in 200 GB consumed. This of course is assuming that 100% of the capacity of the virtual disk is used, as vSAN disks are provision thin by default. This gives administrators a good idea of how much space will be consumed depending on the requirements placed in the policy.

Clicking Next moves the wizard onto the storage compatibility view, and at this point, all vSAN datastores managed by the vCenter Server should be displayed as compatible, as below. This means that the contents of the VM storage policy (i.e., the capabilities) are understood and the requirements **can be met** by the vSAN datastore.

Figure 80: Storage compatibility

Similarly, if the INCOMPATIBLE view is selected, we should see datastores that are not compatible with the policy.

Click Next and review your policy and click Finish to create it. Congratulations! You have created your first VM storage policy. We will now go ahead and deploy a new VM using this policy. The process for deploying a new VM is the same as before. The only difference is at the storage-selection step, here the created policy will need to be selected, as shown below. Any datastores available to the VM will be displayed, and their associated storage compatibility is also shown. In the example here, the vSAN datastore is shown as Compatible but an NFS v3 datastore would be shown as Incompatible since it cannot implement the required VM storage policy. Selecting the vSAN datastore will populate the Compatibility check window with details about whether the checks were successful or not.

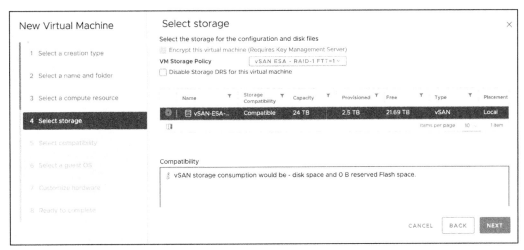

Figure 81: Select vSAN Storage Policy

Note that if no policy is selected the vSAN default storage policy will be applied. This policy is selected for all new VMs deployed on vSAN by default. The capabilities for the default policy are in our environment based on the size of the environment as we have Auto-Policy Management enabled. This means that with a 12 host vSAN ESA cluster the default results in FTT=2 – RAID-6. However, we have selected a policy during the VM deployment, 'RAID-1 FTT=1', so the Auto-Policy Management will not be used in this case.

Once the VM has been deployed, we can check the layout of the VM's objects. Navigate to the VM and then click Monitor > vSAN > Physical disk placement, as shown below. From here, we can see the layout of the VM's storage objects such as the VM home, VM Swap (if the virtual machine is powered on), and VM disk files (VMDKs).

Type	Component State	Host
⌄ ▭ Hard disk 1 (Concatenation)		
⌄ RAID 1		
Component	✓ Active	▯ esxi09.deepdive…
Component	✓ Active	▯ esxi11.deepdiveb…
⌄ RAID 1		
⌄ RAID 0		
Component	✓ Active	▯ esxi11.deepdiveb…
Component	✓ Active	▯ esxi03.deepdive…
Component	✓ Active	▯ esxi07.deepdive…
⌄ RAID 0		
Component	✓ Active	▯ esxi10.deepdive…
Component	✓ Active	▯ esxi05.deepdive…
Component	✓ Active	▯ esxi04.deepdive…

Figure 82: Physical disk placement

As you can see, there is a RAID-1 (mirror) configuration around all components, for both the performance leg (the top RAID-1 configuration), as well as the capacity leg (the bottom RAID-1 configuration).

There are two components making up the RAID-1 mirrored storage object for Hard disk 1 for the performance leg, one on the host esxi09 and the other on the host esxi11. These are the mirror replicas of the data temporarily stored in the performance leg. There are six components making up the RAID-1 mirror for the capacity leg of Hard disk 1. Here we have six components as the RAID-1 configuration is concatenated.

As mentioned earlier, with vSAN ESA witness objects are no longer used for regular clusters. We will only see witness objects when a Stretched Cluster or a 2-Node configuration is created. The quorum mechanism in this case solely relies on the voting mechanism and the placement of the components. The vote count is not visible in the UI unfortunately, but it can be examined using the command-line tool rvc, and the Ruby vSphere Console command vsan.vm_object_info. Next you can see a condensed version of this output which will give you an idea of how votes work.

```
[vSAN-ESA-DS] 9e4cf363-c820-01c5-e740-005056b69337/R1.vmdk
   DOM Object: 9f4cf363-4ad9-e132-d7a2-005056b69337
     Concatenation
       RAID_1
         Component: 9f4cf363-38f4-1034-07f2-005056b69337 (state: ACTIVE (5),
         host: esxi09.deepdivebook.com,
         votes: 3, usage: 0.0 GB, proxy component: false)
         Component: 9f4cf363-f88f-1434-c7c9-005056b69337 (state: ACTIVE (5),
         host: esxi11.deepdivebook.com,
         votes: 1, usage: 0.0 GB, proxy component: false)
       RAID_1
         RAID_0
           Component: 9f4cf363-1c18-1634-6728-005056b69337 (state: ACTIVE (5),
           host: esxi11.deepdivebook.com,
           votes: 1, usage: 0.0 GB, proxy component: false)
           Component: 9f4cf363-148d-1734-44af-005056b69337 (state: ACTIVE (5),
           host: esxi03.deepdivebook.com,
           votes: 2, usage: 0.0 GB, proxy component: false)
           Component: 9f4cf363-be0c-1934-97ba-005056b69337 (state: ACTIVE (5),
           host: esxi07.deepdivebook.com
           votes: 2, usage: 0.0 GB, proxy component: false)
         RAID_0
           Component: 9f4cf363-4e6b-1a34-9f2d-005056b69337 (state: ACTIVE (5),
           host: esxi10.deepdivebook.com,
           votes: 2, usage: 0.0 GB, proxy component: false)
           Component: 9f4cf363-92b1-1b34-5c3d-005056b69337 (state: ACTIVE (5),
           host: esxi05.deepdivebook.com,
           votes: 2, usage: 0.0 GB, proxy component: false)
           Component: 9f4cf363-68e5-1c34-576d-005056b69337 (state: ACTIVE (5),
           host: esxi04.deepdivebook.com,
           votes: 2, usage: 0.0 GB, proxy component: false)
```

As shown above, the RAID-1 configuration for the capacity leg has two RAID-0 configurations underneath and the RAID-1 configuration for the performance leg has no RAID-0 configurations underneath. A variety of vote counts is used, in this example ranging from 1 up to 3. This is to ensure that when a host is isolated it can't achieve majority by itself and potentially cause data corruption. There is one component with three votes, and there are two components with one vote. Note that the components which have one vote are located on the same host.

Policy Setting: RAID-5

Let us now look at a policy where we leverage erasure coding, more commonly referred to as RAID-5 or RAID-6. The big advantage of leveraging erasure coding over mirroring is that it requires less disk capacity to protect against a single failure (FTT=1). For a 100 GB VMDK, a 4+1 configurations only consumes 125GB, which is 25% above the actual size of the VMDK, whereas a 2+1 configuration consumed 150GB, which is 50% above the actual size of the VMDK. The additionally consumed disk capacity is used for parity.

Previously when we created a policy to protect against a single failure using RAID-1, because of the mirror copies, an additional 100% of capacity was consumed. In the event of a data component failure in a RAID-5 configuration, a single component's data can be reconstructed using the remaining data components along with the parity component.

When an Erasure Coding policy is created, administrators need to be aware that these are only available on All-Flash vSAN configurations. When failures to tolerate is set to RAID-5 or RAID-6 Erasure Coding, a warning is displayed to highlight this requirement. While you will not encounter this situation with vSAN ESA, you may encounter it when using a remotely mounted vSAN OSA datastore with HCI-Mesh. If that vSAN OSA datastore is a hybrid configuration, then you will not be able to use erasure-coding.

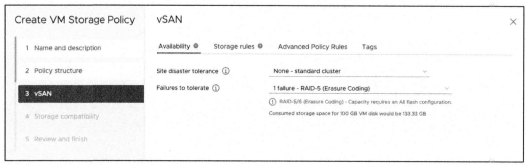

Figure 83: Erasure Coding warning in Availability

Note that a warning has also been added to Storage rules. If we examine the Storage rules, we can see why.

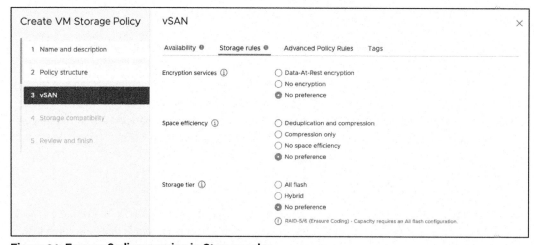

Figure 84: Erasure Coding warning in Storage rules

The warning is against the storage tier. This, if you recall, is a section primarily used for HCI-Mesh. Since we can remotely mount vSAN datastores to this vSphere cluster, which, if vSAN OSA, are both hybrid and all-flash, this setting will prevent a RAID-5 policy from showing remote vSAN OSA datastore as compatible, if they are not an All-flash vSAN configuration. Thus, even if you do not plan to use HCI-Mesh, the Storage tier needs to be set to All-flash for Erasure Coding policies. This step should also be done for vSAN ESA specifically! This will toggle the warning message.

After creating the RAID-5 FTT=1 policy, deploy a VM with it. The physical disk placement can be examined as before, and we should now observe a RAID-5 layout across five disks and five hosts. The below screenshot shows the physical disk placement view, and as described, we see a RAID-5 configuration for the objects, each having 5 components. This is a so-called 4+1 configuration, meaning 4 data and 1 parity segment. Note, that this only applies to the capacity leg. The performance leg leverages RAID-1.

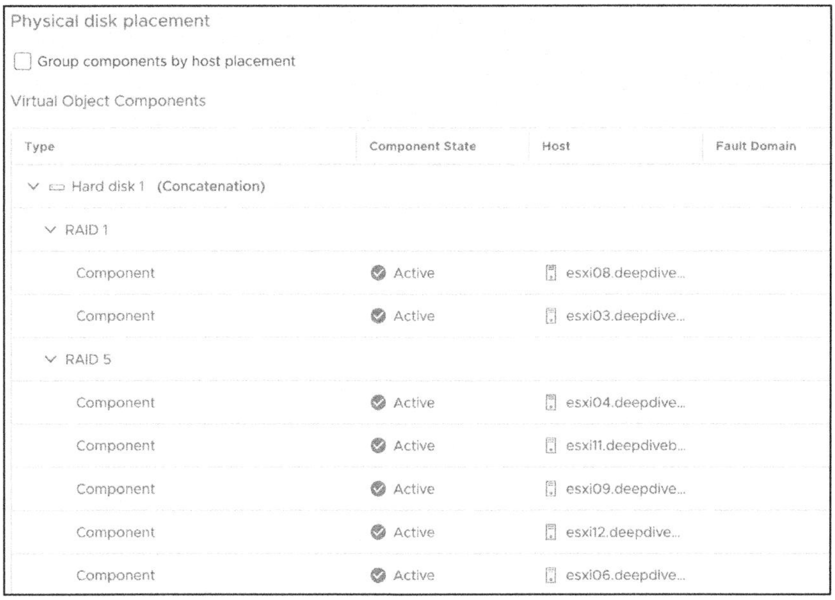

Type	Component State	Host	Fault Domain
∨ ⊏⊐ Hard disk 1 (Concatenation)			
∨ RAID 1			
Component	Active	esxi08.deepdive…	
Component	Active	esxi03.deepdive…	
∨ RAID 5			
Component	Active	esxi04.deepdive…	
Component	Active	esxi11.deepdiveb…	
Component	Active	esxi09.deepdive…	
Component	Active	esxi12.deepdive…	
Component	Active	esxi06.deepdive…	

Figure 85: Physical placement 4+1 RAID-5

Note that the VM home namespace and VM Swap objects also inherit the RAID-5 configuration.

As also mentioned in the RAID-1 example, votes are used as a quorum mechanism with vSAN ESA. The vote count can be examined using the command-line tool rvc, and the command vsan.vm_object_info. Next you can see a condensed version of this output for RAID-5.

```
[vSAN-ESA-DS] d959f363-c2ad-e0a9-5847-005056b69337/R5.vmdk
  DOM Object: da59f363-cc7c-d21c-d383-005056b69337
    Concatenation
      RAID_1
        Component: da59f363-34f8-011e-0ac3-005056b69337 (state: ACTIVE (5),
        host: esxi08.deepdivebook.com
        votes: 1, usage: 0.0 GB, proxy component: false)
        Component: da59f363-b014-041e-bae7-005056b69337 (state: ACTIVE (5),
        host: esxi03.deepdivebook.com,
        votes: 1, usage: 0.0 GB, proxy component: false)
      RAID_5
        Component: da59f363-3465-051e-0797-005056b69337 (state: ACTIVE (5),
        host: esxi04.deepdivebook.com,
        votes: 1, usage: 0.0 GB, proxy component: false)
        Component: da59f363-14b7-061e-8750-005056b69337 (state: ACTIVE (5),
```

```
host: esxi11.deepdivebook.com,
votes: 1, usage: 0.0 GB, proxy component: false)
Component: da59f363-c0e3-071e-4fe4-005056b69337 (state: ACTIVE (5),
host: esxi09.deepdivebook.com,
votes: 1, usage: 0.0 GB, proxy component: false)
Component: da59f363-c076-081e-f8ff-005056b69337 (state: ACTIVE (5),
host: esxi12.deepdivebook.com,
votes: 1, usage: 0.0 GB, proxy component: false)
Component: da59f363-f23a-091e-c020-005056b69337 (state: ACTIVE (5),
host: esxi06.deepdivebook.com,
votes: 1, usage: 0.0 GB, proxy component: false)
```

Note that in this scenario each component only has a single vote, but that each component is also placed on a different host within the cluster. So, depending on how components are distributed, and what kind of RAID configuration is used, the vote count will differ.

One thing we have not discussed in this chapter yet, but has been discussed in chapter 4, is the Adaptive RAID-5 mechanism which was introduced in vSAN 8.0 U1. Considering that this mechanism introduces a relatively big architectural difference, let's briefly discuss it again. Depending on the size of the cluster, and depending on availability of hosts, the RAID-5 configuration is either 4+1 or 2+1. In order to use a 4+1 RAID-5 configuration at minimum 6 hosts are required. In our situation we deployed a twelve node cluster, which is why we see the above configuration. If for whatever reason our cluster would have 7 hosts failing, vSAN ESA would after 24 hours automatically resync this 4+1 RAID-5 configuration to a 2+1 configuration. Of course, if additional hosts would be introduced or failed hosts would be recovered, vSAN ESA would resync the 2+1 configuration to a 4+1 configuration, assuming the minimum host count for 4+1 RAID-5 would be met.

This concept does not only apply to VMs which are already provisioned, but also applies during the provisioning process. If we place seven hosts into maintenance mode and provision a new RAID-5 VM then the VM would be configured with a 2+1 RAID-5 configuration, as demonstrated in the next screenshot.

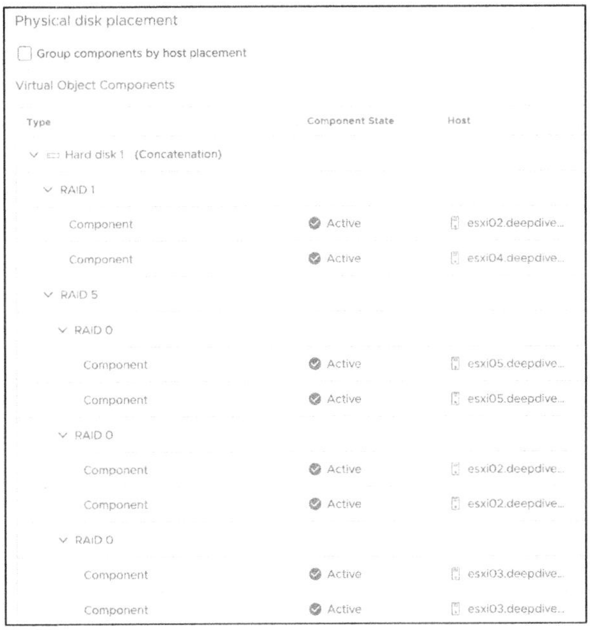

Figure 86: Physical placement 2+1 RAID-5

Of course, when we take the seven hosts out of maintenance mode, the 4+1 RAID-5 configuration would be recreated after 24 hours. Note, at the time of writing there's no mechanism available to force this recreation/resync from happening manually.

That then leads to the final question, is it possible to change the 24 hour time window? It is possible, however, if you want to change this time window then you will need to configure an advanced setting on each host of the cluster, and please note that at the time of writing VMware has not provided a support statement around modifying this advanced setting. We would also like to point out that lowering the default of 86400 seconds (24 hours) can have a significant impact on resync traffic. As a result, we recommend leaving the host level advanced setting "/VSAN/ClomRaidECReconfigureDelaySec" unchanged.

Policy Setting: RAID-6

Besides RAID-5, the option to tolerate two failures in a capacity-efficient manner is also available via erasure coding and is called RAID-6. To configure a RAID-6 object, select *2 failures – RAID-6* for the *Failures to tolerate* policy setting. Note the storage consumption model. For a 100 GB VMDK, this only consumes 150 GB, which is 50% above the actual size of the VMDK. The additional 50 GB is used by the two parity blocks of the RAID-6 object, 25GB each in the 100 GB VMDK example. Previously when we created a policy for RAID-1 objects with failures to tolerate set to 2, because of the mirror copies, an additional 200% of capacity was consumed. This means that a 100 GB VMDK required 300 GB of disk capacity at the backend. RAID-6 consumes half that amount of capacity to provide the same level of availability.

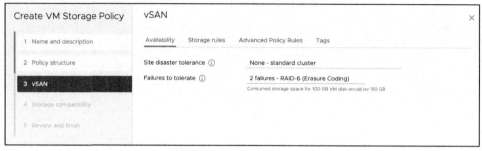

Figure 87: Failures to tolerate = 2, RAID-6

When a VM is deployed with this policy, the physical disk placement can be examined as before, and as demonstrated in the screenshot above, a RAID-6 layout is observed across six hosts for the capacity leg of the object. For the performance leg of the object, you will notice that a RAID-1 layout has been created, but across 3 hosts. This is to ensure that it is possible to tolerate two failures for both the capacity leg, as well as the performance leg.

Physical disk placement		
☐ Group components by host placement		
Virtual Object Components		
Type	**Component State**	**Host**
∨ 💾 Hard disk 1 (Concatenation)		
∨ RAID 1		
Component	✅ Active	🖥 esxi03.deepdive…
Component	✅ Active	🖥 esxi01.deepdive…
Component	✅ Active	🖥 esxi10.deepdive…
∨ RAID 6		
Component	✅ Active	🖥 esxi06.deepdive…
Component	✅ Active	🖥 esxi07.deepdive…
Component	✅ Active	🖥 esxi09.deepdive…
Component	✅ Active	🖥 esxi11.deepdiveb…
Component	✅ Active	🖥 esxi08.deepdive…
Component	✅ Active	🖥 esxi01.deepdive…

Figure 88: Physical placement RAID-6

Note that again the VM Swap and VM home namespace objects also inherit the RAID-6 configuration.

Default Policy

As mentioned earlier, vSAN has a default policy. This means that if no policy is chosen for a VM deployed on the vSAN datastore, a default policy that is automatically associated with the vSAN datastore is used. What this policy looks like will depend on a few things. First, and foremost, whether Auto-Policy Management is enabled or not, and secondly, what the size of the cluster is.

Figure 89: Auto-policy management

If Auto-Policy Management is disabled, then default policy contains the following capabilities:

- Number of failures to tolerate = 1
- Number of disk stripes per object = 1
- Object space reservation = Thin Provisioning
- Force provisioning = disabled
- Checksum = enabled
- IOPS Limit = 0 (unlimited)
- Compression = enabled

Note that this default policy for the vSAN datastore, called the vSAN default storage policy, can be edited. If you wish to change the default policy, you can simply edit the capability values of the policy from the vSphere Client by selecting the policy and clicking Edit Settings.

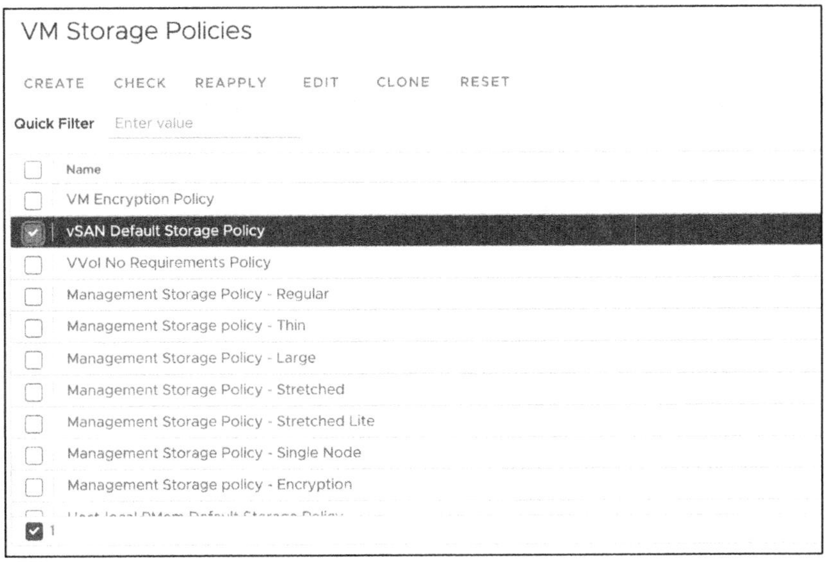

Figure 90: Default vSAN policy

An alternative to editing the default policy is to create a new policy with the desired capabilities and associate this new policy with the vSAN datastore. This would be the preferred way of changing the default policy inherited by VMs that are deployed on the vSAN datastore.

If you are managing multiple vSAN deployments with a single vCenter Server, different default policies can be associated with different vSAN datastores. Therefore, if you have a "test-and-dev" cluster and a "production" cluster, there can be different default policies associated with the different vSAN datastores. To change the default policy of the vSAN datastore you need to go to the Storage view in the vSphere Client and select the vSAN datastore then click Configure > General followed by clicking Edit on Default Storage Policy. Now you can simply associate a different policy with the datastore you selected as demonstrated in the screenshot below.

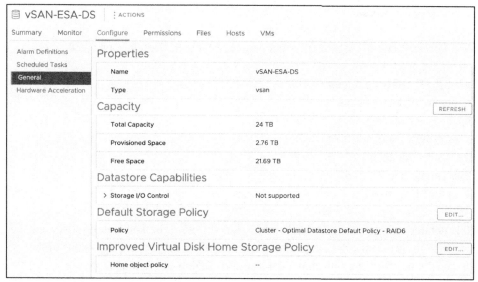

Figure 91: Change default vSAN policy

Hopefully, what stands out in the above screenshot is that the "Default Storage Policy" is not "vSAN Default Storage Policy" but rather "Cluster – Optimal Datastore Default Policy – RAID6". This policy is created by vSAN when the vSAN ESA Cluster was created and Auto-policy Management was enabled. Based on the configuration of the cluster, and whether "Host Rebuild Reserve" is used, this functionality will determine what the optimal policy should be. Let's list the different policy configurations proposed, based on the various potential cluster sizes.

- Standard Cluster (without Host Rebuild Reserve)
    - 3 hosts: FTT=1 using RAID-1
    - 4 hosts: FTT=1 using RAID-5 (2+1)
    - 5 hosts: FTT=1 using RAID-5 (2+1)
    - 6 hosts or more: FTT=2 using RAID-6 (4+2)
- Standard Cluster (with Host Rebuild Reserve)
    - 3 hosts: not supported with 3 hosts!
    - 4 hosts: FTT=1 using RAID-1

- 5 hosts: FTT=1 using RAID-5 (2+1)
  - 6 hosts: FTT=1 using RAID-5 (4+1)
  - 6 hosts or more: FTT=2 using RAID-6 (4+2)
- Stretched Cluster
  - 3 hosts in each location: Site Mirroring and Secondary FTT=1 using RAID-1
  - 4 hosts in each location : Site Mirroring and Secondary FTT=1 using RAID-5 (2+1)
  - 5 hosts in each location : Site Mirroring and Secondary FTT=1 using RAID-5 (2+1)
  - 6 hosts in each location or more: Site Mirroring and Secondary FTT=2 using RAID-6 (4+2)
- 2-Node Cluster
  - 2 hosts: Host level mirroring using RAID-1

Now that we know what the default policy will be for a certain cluster configuration, what happens if the cluster configuration changes?

If the cluster configuration changes, let's say the size of the cluster is increased from a 3-host configuration to a 6-host configuration, then after 24 hours Skyline Health will recommend changing the cluster specific policy from FTT=1 using RAID-1 to FTT=2 using RAID-6. Do note that this is, at the time of writing, a recommendation which is made, and this recommendation is not automatically applied.

Failure Scenarios

Failure scenarios are often a hot topic of discussion when it comes to vSAN. What should one configure, and how do we expect vSAN to respond? This section runs through some simple scenarios to demonstrate what you can expect of vSAN in certain situations when it comes to data availability. We will run through some of the more complex scenarios in the Stretched Cluster section of the book.

The following examples use a six-host vSAN cluster and use an FTT=1 configuration. We will examine both RAID-1 and RAID-5 and discuss the behavior in the event of a host failure. You should understand that the examples shown here are for illustrative purposes only. These are simply to explain some of the decisions that vSAN *might* make when it comes to object placement. vSAN may choose any configuration if it satisfies the customer requirements.

Example 1: Failures to Tolerate = 1, RAID-1

In this first example, failures to tolerate is set to 1 and RAID-1 Mirroring is used. Therefore, there is no striping per se, simply a single instance of the object. However, the requirements are that we must tolerate a single disk or host failure, so we must instantiate a replica (a RAID-1 mirror of the component). A split-brain could be when ESXi-01 and ESXi-3 continue to operate, but no longer communicate with each another. Whichever combination of the hosts (ESXi-01 and ESXi02, or ESXi03 and ESXi-02) has the highest number of votes retains access to data in that scenario. Where with vSAN OSA the witness component was used in combination with the voting mechanism, vSAN ESA depends on the performance leg and the capacity leg, combined with smart placement of those components and voting to help determine who owns the data. Data placement in these configurations may look like the one displayed in the next diagram.

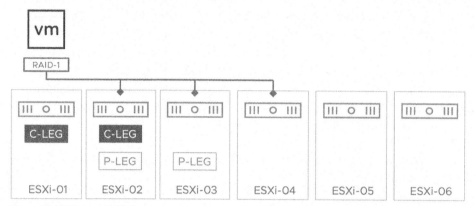

Figure 92: FTT = 1 – RAID-1

The data remains accessible in the event of a host or disk failure. If ESXi-02 has a failure, ESXi-01 and ESXi-03 continue to provide access to the data as a quorum continues to exist. However, if ESXi-02 and ESXi-03 both suffer failures, there is no longer a quorum, so data becomes inaccessible. Note that in this scenario the VM is running (from a compute perspective) on ESXi-01, while the components of the objects are stored on ESXi-01, 02, and 03. The VM can run on any host in the cluster, and vSphere DRS is free to migrate it anywhere when deemed necessary. If the VM runs on a host that fails, then vSphere HA will (when configured properly) automatically restart the impact VM(s).

Example 2: Failures to Tolerate = 1 and RAID-5

In this example, the failures to tolerate is set to 1, and RAID-5 is used instead of mirroring. In this example the minimum number of hosts needed is 3, and as we have a five host cluster we will see a 2+1 RAID-5 configuration deployed in the case of the capacity leg, as demonstrated in the next diagram. The performance leg will be configured as RAID-1 with 2 components.

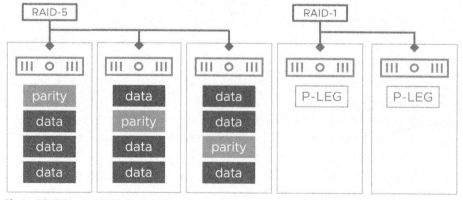

Figure 93: FTT = 1 – RAID-5

One thing to point out is that when it is desired to have the ability to resync data after a failure, an additional host will need to be part of the cluster. For a RAID-5 configured object, this means that the number of hosts required depends on the RAID-5 configuration used plus one. In other words, in the case of a 2+1 configuration, which requires 3 hosts at minimum, you would require 4 hosts to provide the ability to resync data after a failure to bring back the impact objects to policy compliance. When a single host fails in the example above, the VM will be able to access its disk. And by leveraging parity blocks, vSAN will be able to reconstruct the missing data on one of the other hosts within the cluster. In this example it would mean that if the first host has failed, data would be resynced to a capacity leg in one of the hosts which is currently also storing the performance leg.

Changing VM Storage Policy On-the-Fly

Being able to change a VM storage policy on-the-fly is a useful aspect of vSAN, or Storage Policy Based Management (SPBM) in general. This example explains the concept of how a VM storage policy can be changed on-the-fly, and how it changes the layout of a VM without impacting the application or the guest operating system running in the VM.

Consider the following scenario. A vSphere administrator has deployed a VM on a vSAN ESA cluster with a RAID-1 VM storage policy assigned. The layout of the VM would roughly look as follows.

Physical disk placement				
☐ Group components by host placement				
Virtual Object Components				
Type	Component State	Host	Fault Domain	Disk
∨ ▭ Hard disk 1 (Concatenation)				
∨ RAID 1				
Component	✅ Active	🖥 esxi04.deepdive...		🔗 Local NVMe Disk (eui.
Component	✅ Active	🖥 esxi12.deepdive...		52a9b7bc-f318-0ee9-193!
∨ RAID 1				
∨ RAID 0				
Component	✅ Active	🖥 esxi10.deepdive...		🔗 Local NVMe Disk (eui.
Component	✅ Active	🖥 esxi01.deepdive...		🔗 Local NVMe Disk (eui.
Component	✅ Active	🖥 esxi09.deepdive...		🔗 Local NVMe Disk (eui.
∨ RAID 0				
Component	✅ Active	🖥 esxi06.deepdive...		🔗 Local NVMe Disk (eui.
Component	✅ Active	🖥 esxi04.deepdive...		🔗 Local NVMe Disk (eui.
Component	✅ Active	🖥 esxi11.deepdiveb...		🔗 Local NVMe Disk (eui.
▯		16 vSAN components on 10 hosts	|< <	1 / 2 > >|

Figure 94: vSAN Default policy data layout

After some time, the vSphere administrator starts to notice that the VM is consuming a relatively large amount of disk capacity, and realizes that the VM is not using their standard vSAN ESA storage policy, which is configured with RAID-5.

On vSAN, the vSphere administrator has two options to address this. The first option is to simply modify the VM storage policy currently associated with the VM and change the RAID level from RAID-1 to RAID-5; however, this would change the storage layout of all the other VMs using this same policy simultaneously. Not just for a single cluster, but potentially for all clusters being managed by the same vCenter Server and running VMs using the same policy. This is because policies are defined on a vCenter Server level. This change could lead to a huge amount of rebuild traffic and is not our recommended approach as it is difficult to manage and estimate the impact.

We recommend creating a brand-new policy or selecting an existing policy with the correct capabilities enabled. This policy can then be attached to only that given VM (and, of course, to its VMDKs). Once the new policy is associated with the VM, vSAN takes care of changing the underlying VM storage layout required to meet the new policy, *while the VM is still running* without the loss of any failure protection. It does this by creating a new VM and resynchronizing the data from source to destination in the format associated to the destination object, RAID-5 in this situation.

After making the change the new components reflecting the new configuration (e.g., a RAID-5) will enter a state of reconfiguring. This will temporarily build out additional replicas or components, in addition to keeping the original replicas/components, so additional space will be needed on the vSAN datastore to accommodate this on-the-fly change. When the new replicas or components are ready and the configuration is completed, the original replicas/components are discarded.

> **One should keep in mind that making a change like this could lead to rebuilds and generate resync traffic on the vSAN network. For that reason, policy changes should be considered a maintenance task and kept to a minimum during production hours.**

Note that not all policy changes require the creation of new replicas or components. For example, adding an IOPS limit, or reducing the number of failures to tolerate with RAID-1, or reducing space reservation does not require this. However, in many cases, policy changes will trigger the creation of new replicas or components or potentially even trigger a full rebuild of the object. (Table 7, which we shall see shortly, describes which policy setting triggers a rebuild.) Therefore, caution should be used when changing storage policies on the fly, especially if the change may impact many virtual machines. Significant improvements have been made over the years to ensure that rebuild network traffic does not negatively impact VM network traffic, but our advice is to treat large policy changes as a maintenance task, and to implement those changes out of normal production hours.

Your VM storage objects will now reflect the changes in the vSphere Client, for example, a RAID-5 configuration, as shown below.

Figure 95: vSAN data layout after change of policy

Compare this to the tasks you may have to perform on many traditional storage arrays to achieve this. It would involve, at the very least, the following:

- The migration of VMs from the original datastore.
- The decommissioning of said LUN/volume.
- The creation of a new LUN with the new storage requirements (different RAID level).
- Possibly the reformatting of the LUN with VMFS in the case of block storage.
- Finally, you must migrate your VMs back to the new datastore.

In the case of vSAN, after the new storage replicas or components have been created and synchronized, the older storage replicas and/or components will be automatically removed. Note that vSAN is capable of striping across devices, and hosts when required, as mentioned before. It should also be noted that vSAN can create the new replicas or components without the need to move any data between hosts; in many cases, the new components can be instantiated on the same storage on the same host.

You can see the configuration changes taking place in the vSphere UI during this process. Select the vSAN cluster object in the vCenter Server inventory, then select monitor, vSAN, and finally "resyncing objects" in the menu. This will display all objects and components that are currently resyncing/rebuilding. The screenshot below shows the resyncing dashboard view with a resync in progress for a VM where we manually changed the policy from RAID-5 to RAID-6. Note, in this case it was a relatively small VM, and only a single VM, so the resyncing could literally be finished in seconds. In the case of multiple or relatively larger VMs, it could take minutes, or hours to complete.

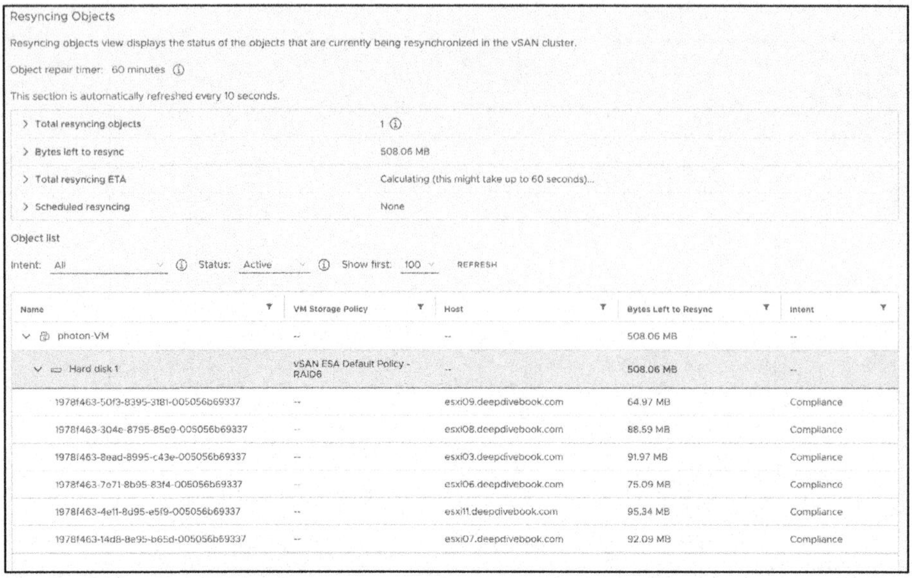

Figure 96: Resync/rebuild activity

The big question which then remains is when exactly is a full rebuild needed when changing a policy and when will vSAN simply create extra components? As you can imagine, a full rebuild of many virtual machines can have an impact on required storage capacity, and potentially also on performance. The following table outlines when a full rebuild is required and when it is not required.

POLICY CHANGE	REBUILD REQUIRED?	COMMENTS
Increasing/decreasing FTT without changing RAID type	Potentially	When increasing, resync occurs, when decreasing a delete occurs of 1 leg.
Changing the RAID type used	Yes	Also applies when going from RAID-5 to RAID-6 or back.
Increasing/decreasing stripe width	Potentially	Depending on the stripe width and the current striping applied.
Enabling/disabling Compression	No	Only newly stored data is stored differently.
Changing object space reservation	Potentially	OSR may not always initiate a resynchronization when increasing the value, but may, depending on the fullness of the storage devices.
Changing read cache reservation	Not Applicable	Applies to hybrid only.
Enabling/disabling checksum	No	

Table 7: Impact of policy changes

Summary

This completes the coverage of VM storage policy creation and VM deployments on the vSAN datastore. What you will have noticed is that there are a few behaviors with VM storage policies that might not be intuitive, such as the default policy settings when Auto-Policy Management is enabled, and that some virtual storage objects implement only some of the policy settings. We are hoping though that this chapter provided you with sufficient confidence to create, apply and edit VM storage policies.

06

vSAN Operations

This chapter covers the common procedures and tasks when monitoring and maintaining a vSAN deployment. It also provides some generic workflows and examples related to day-to-day management often referred to as day-2 management. While many aspects of management, monitoring, and maintenance of a vSAN cluster are the same regardless of the architecture (Express Storage Architecture versus Original Storage Architecture), some management tasks have changed with the ESA.

Recent versions of vSAN have also introduced significant improvements in the built-in tools that play a part in the day-to-day operations of vSAN clusters. This chapter will highlight some of those changes.

Skyline Health

We will begin this chapter with a look at what has become the most valuable tool in an administrator's arsenal for monitoring vSAN. Skyline Health, formerly known as vSAN health check, is embedded into both vCenter Server and ESXi and is automatically available without any administrative actions required. Skyline Health for vSAN immediately provides a complete overview of the current health of a vSAN cluster.

Skyline Health consists of two parts: A sophisticated health test engine, and new to vSAN 8.0 U1, a cluster scoring and remediation dashboard. These will be described in more detail below.

Skyline Health Engine

The Skyline Health Engine is comprised of dozens of integrated tests to help ensure that a vSAN cluster is configured to serve as a robust platform. It will provide a list of findings as a result of continuously monitoring the environment. It will report on these "health findings" (renamed from "health checks" in vSphere and vSAN 8.0 U1) for both successful tests, and failed tests. For the latter, it will help alert administrators when there is an identified configuration issue, such as a device not certified on the VMware Compatibility Guide (VCG) for vSAN. It will also alert an administrator if there is perhaps a degraded state of health of object data, such as a VM or VMs.

The Skyline Health engine is unique in its ability to understand the priority and severity of health findings in an unhealthy state, the relationships between health findings, and the history of the health findings. It is the combination of this intelligence that helps to not only understand the state of the cluster, but which identified issues should be addressed first.

Skyline Health Dashboard

The Skyline Health Dashboard in vSAN is new to both architectures in vSAN 8.0 U1. It replaces the previous user interface that enumerated a long list of health findings in general categories. While a listing of health findings can be a simple way to show discrete health findings, it lacked a way to convey the priority and importance of identified health issues. The dashboard displays the current cluster health score, the history of the cluster health score, and the status of the current health findings, as shown in the image below.

Figure 97: Skyline Health dashboard in vSAN

All tests are run at regular intervals, but a test can be initiated at any time by the administrator by clicking on the *Retest* button near the top of the dashboard.

To better understand the information portrayed in the Skyline Health dashboard, we first should look at how Skyline Health achieves this idea of priority and severity of health issues in a cluster.

Weighted Health Findings

The health findings used by Skyline Health for vSAN cover a wide range of cluster and host configuration settings, device compatibility, cluster capacity, and data availability states that are within the domain of management. While it may not be able to catch an issue out of its domain of management such as a misconfigured network switch, it is an invaluable tool for troubleshooting vSAN issues, quickly leading administrators to the root cause of an issue. Administrators should always refer to the Skyline health tests to ensure that vSAN is completely healthy before introducing a cluster into production, as well as embarking on any management, lifecycle, or maintenance tasks.

New to vSAN 8.0 U1, and a key part of its new functionality is the implementation of a multifactorial weighting mechanism for each health finding. This proportional "weight" for each health finding is based on a predefined category and priority of each finding.

Each health finding is associated with one of four categories: *Availability, Performance, Capacity Utilization,* and *Efficiency and Compliance*. The categories align with common responsibilities for an administrator and have a "weight" to rank them proportionally to each other. For example, triggered health findings that fall into the *Availability* category will have a much higher impact on the score than triggered health findings in the *Efficiency and Compliance* category.

Next, each health issue will have a weighted value to give it a rank within its associated category. This priority factor will help weigh them proportional to other health findings in the same category. It is the combination of these category factors and priority factors that will provide a *calculated score impact*, as shown in the image below.

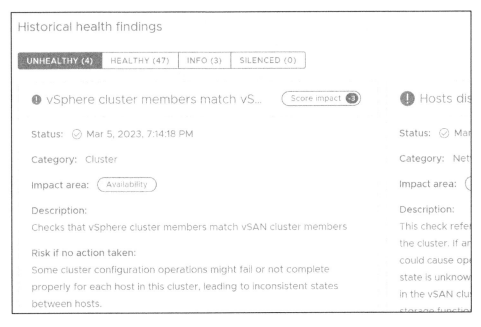

Figure 98: A health finding in an "unhealthy" state and its associated impact score

The resulting impact scores for each discrete unhealthy finding serve two purposes. It helps provide a single cluster score prominently on the dashboard, where the calculated impact score of each unhealthy finding is deducted from the theoretically perfect cluster score of 100. It also provides the ability to prioritize unhealthy findings to fix issues more quickly and effectively.

Note that many of the Skyline Health findings in a cluster will only display themselves if they are relevant to the configuration of a cluster. For example, vSAN data encryption configuration health findings will not be visible if data encryption is not configured in a cluster. Health findings for a given topology, such as stretched clusters, will only show when the topology is in use.

Cluster Health Score and Health Score Trend

The various weights of triggered health findings allow Skyline Health to project a score of health for the cluster. It will present a cluster score from 0 to 100, with 100 being a perfectly healthy cluster based on the conditions of the health findings. The health findings in an unhealthy state will have their weighted score deducted from the value of 100 to give a total cluster score. Cluster scores between 81-100 mean that the cluster is healthy enough that no immediate attention is required. A score of 61 – 80 means that some aspect of the cluster is in a degraded state, and that attention is suggested. A cluster score of 0 – 60 falls into an unhealthy state, and attention is required.

The weighting and calculation of impact scores have been designed in such a way as to ensure that the score is impacted sufficiently based on the type of condition it finds. For example, any triggered health findings regarding the "Availability" category will always reduce the total cluster health score enough to move it into the "Unhealthy - Attention required" range.

The health score history is presented adjacent to the current cluster health score, providing a history for the past 24 hours. Note that the top of the Y-axis of the graph will always show 100, but the bottom of the Y-axis graph will be relative to the lowest score for the period viewed. For clusters with a very healthy, high score, any small change can give the impression that the change in health was significant, where it actually may have just moved a point or two.

Clicking on the "View Details" button on the "Health score trend" area of the dashboard will expand the cluster score history view. This provides the ability to click anywhere on the cluster score history to see the specific healthy and unhealthy findings that resulted in the score for the time selected. An example of this is shown in the image below.

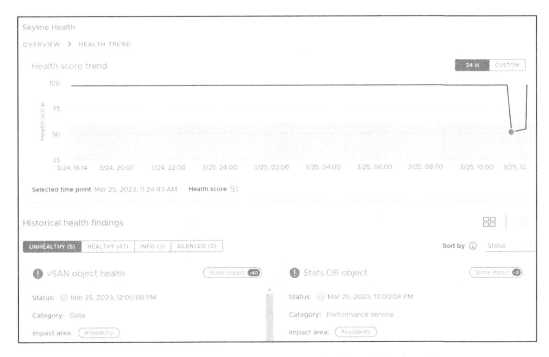

Figure 99: Health score trend with associated health findings for the period selected

A single value representing the health of a cluster provides another benefit to administrators. Knowing that the triggered health findings vary in their proportional weight to each other, an administrator can judge the health of a cluster not by the number of unhealthy findings, but by the severity or importance of the unhealthy findings. This is a much more accurate way to diagnose the state of the cluster.

Health Alerting and Remediation

The Skyline Health dashboard provides a health findings area. The objective of this area is to direct the administrator to the most important issue first – unhealthy checks appear in the order of their importance. The default view will sort by the triggered findings that have the most impact and are identified by vSAN as a root cause of any secondary, symptomatic issue.

All health findings will be grouped into one of four categories: Unhealthy, Healthy, Info, and Silenced. Note that silenced alerts still contribute to the impact of a cluster health score. For all healthy and silenced alerts, a "View Current Result" button will be provided to give more details on the test. Each health finding will have an "Ask VMware" link that will link the test to a VMware KB article which provides details about the nature of the test, what it means when it fails, and how to remediate the issue.

For all current, unhealthy findings, the "View Current Result" button is replaced with the "Troubleshoot" button. This may present a direct way to remediate the issue automatically or present one or more manual methods to remediate the issue.

Figure 100: Current unhealthy findings in Skyline Health

When looking at unhealthy findings stored in the health history, the "Troubleshoot" button will be replaced with "View History Details." Clicking on this button will show the history of this specific health finding and may look similar to the image below.

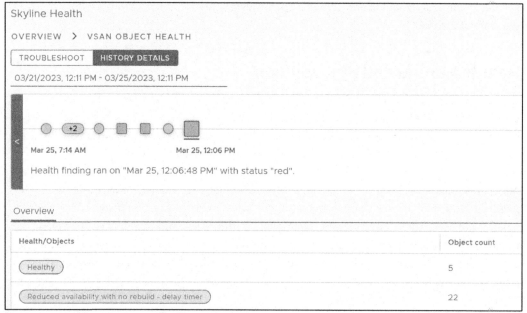

Figure 101: Health history of a specific health finding

When a group of alerts is condensed, it will present a bubble with a number indicating the number of health conditions. An administrator can click on that bubble with a number, and it will expand the period to show the timeline of those health findings. This will allow an administrator to easily drill into a specified time period for more details.

Health History and Data Retention

As shown in the previous images, the history of health findings is fully integrated throughout Skyline Health for vSAN. It can help answer the questions of when it occurred, for how long, and what other findings were triggered for that given period This is especially important for intermittent issues that are difficult to capture in real time.

vSAN Skyline Health data is retained for about 30 days, depending on the available capacity of the statsDB object where the data is stored. vSAN 8.0 U1 increases the capacity of the statsDB object, which may reduce conditions where health history retention is shorter due to the statsDB object capacity conditions. The health history views in vSAN will default to viewing a 24-hour time window but can be adjusted to a custom time window within the retention period of the data.

In-Product versus Online Health Findings

Many of the Health findings in Skyline Health for vSAN are built into the product. Meaning that if a new health finding is introduced or improved in a version of vSAN, one must be running that version of vSAN or newer to take advantage of those improvements.

Online health findings are checks built into the Skyline health framework with the same look and feel as other health findings, but they can be dynamically introduced or updated by VMware. This is extremely useful when new potential issues are identified by VMware and new VMware KB articles are released. Customers can be proactively informed about these new issues and resolutions before potentially encountering them on their own vSAN clusters. However, the authors would always recommend reviewing the Release Notes before attempting any vSAN or vSphere upgrade to that particular release.

When performing a manual retest of health findings, the display will provide an option for you to retest the environment with the online health findings as well as the in-product findings. Deselecting online health findings does not impact the execution of the in-product health findings.

Skyline Health and CEIP

In past editions, online health findings required activation of the Customer Experience Improvement Program (CEIP). Enabling the CEIP is no longer required as of vSAN 8.0, but VMware still highly encourages CEIP to be enabled, as it helps VMware improve its products and services, resolve issues, and advises customers on how best to deploy and use our products. To learn more about CEIP, check out the following online resource: https://vmwa.re/ceip. Enabling CEIP has other significant benefits.

Customers often ask what kind of data is sent back to VMware when CEIP is enabled. This is described in great detail in the link provided above, but the data collected is primarily to do with configuration information, such as which vSAN features are enabled, as well as some performance data and logs. No actual customer data is being captured, only metadata, or to put it another way, only information about data is captured (if that makes sense). The data that is captured is also obfuscated so that even when the configuration is reviewed, no information such as hostnames and VM names is available. There is a way for VMware support engineers to de-obfuscate the names, but this can only be done via customer consent as the customer needs to provide VMware support with a so-called obfuscation map. This map can be found in the vSphere Client under Monitor > vSAN > Support on the vSAN cluster object as demonstrated in the screenshot below.

Figure 102: Obfuscation map

We have seen great success for customers, both from a proactive and reactive perspective, when CEIP is enabled in an environment. CEIP is enabled by default in recent editions of vSAN but will honor the previous setting for any in-place upgrades. Please consider taking the step of ensuring that it is enabled for your environment.

Proactive Tests

While Skyline Health aims to continuously monitor the environment for known issues, vSAN also has a set of proactive tests that can be used as a part of a proof-of-concept (PoC) effort, or prior to introducing production workloads onto a newly formed vSAN cluster. These types of initial stress tests will help validate the operational consistency across the hosts that comprise a cluster, as well as serve as an early indicator of some issues that may not otherwise show up in a static test. For example, suppose a new vSAN cluster was built with servers received from your favorite server vendor. A proactive test may be able to detect if one of the hosts is unable to perform at the same rate as the other servers, due to an inconsistent firmware version of a Network Interface Card (NIC). Without performing this type of test, a cluster that is not operating optimally may be introduced into production.

The proactive tests have evolved over the many versions of vSAN and have been updated in vSAN 8.0 U1 to accommodate the architectural differences of the Express Storage Architecture. vSAN 8.0 U1 includes three tests:

- VM Creation Test
- Network Performance Test
- Storage Performance Test

Simply select the test that you wish to run and click the "Run Test" button to begin the test. A popup window is displayed giving you additional information about the test. The next screenshot shows the tests as they appear in the vSphere client. The Last Run Result field displays the time of the last test and whether the test was successful or not.

The actual tests that are run are well described in the vSphere Client. The "VM Creation Test" quickly verifies that virtual machines can be deployed on the vSAN datastore, and once that verification is complete, the sample VMs are removed. The VMs are created with whatever policy is the default policy for the vSAN datastore, and the test reports if the test was successful or not, along with any relevant error messages.

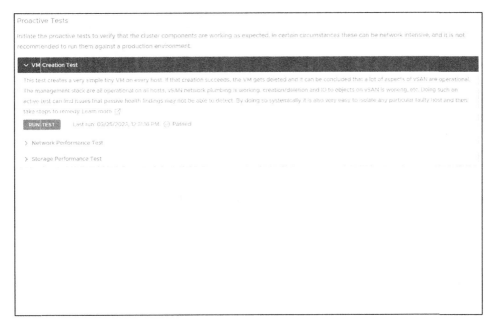

Figure 103: Proactive tests

The "Network Performance Test" performs a series of connectivity tests between hosts and measures effective throughput. Previous editions of this test used a target network speed to help the administrator know if they were meeting minimum throughput requirements. Since the Express Storage Architecture and Original Storage Architecture in vSAN have different requirements, vSAN 8.0 U1 adjusts this test to simply render the maximum effective throughput capable from each host.

Testing network performance is critically important for a distributed storage solution like vSAN. It is especially important when there might be complex network configurations that may involve several hops or routes when vSAN is deployed over L3.

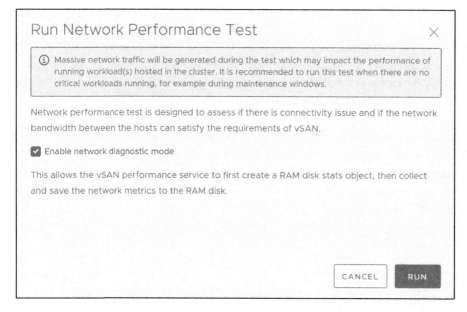

Figure 104: Enable network diagnostic mode

The "Network Performance Test" offers an additional option of including network diagnostics. These diagnostics can be useful in determining whether the bandwidth is sufficient for the type of vSAN cluster being deployed.

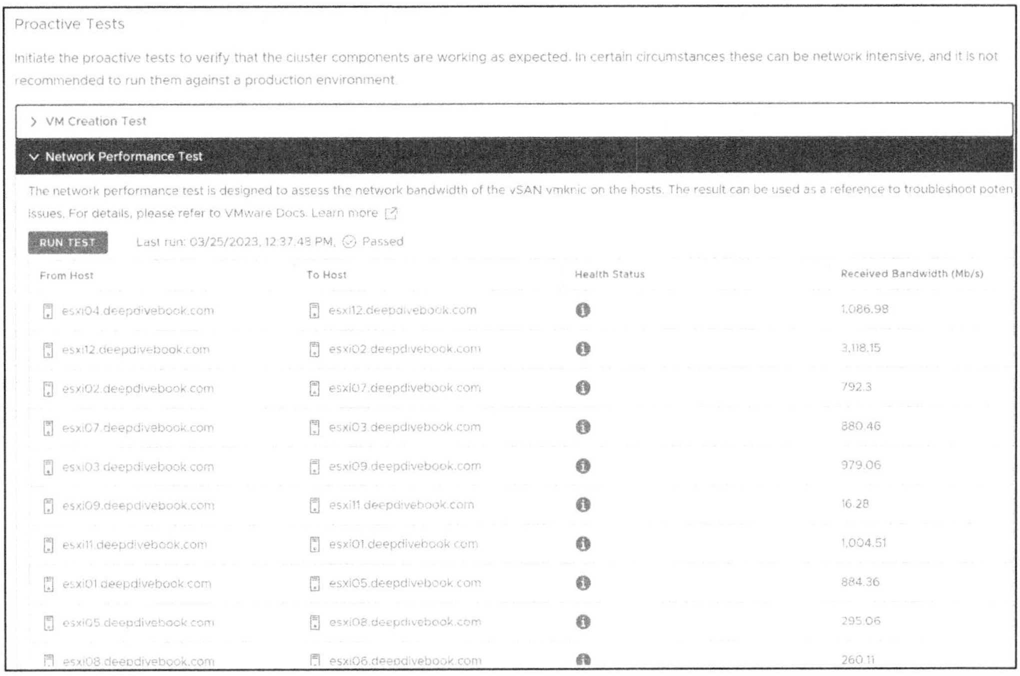

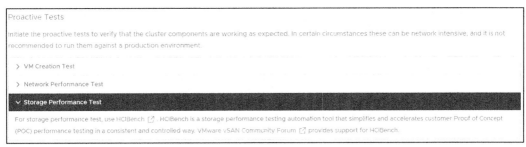

Figure 105: Proactive Tests Network Performance Test

The "Storage Performance Test" redirects the administrator to using HCIBench for all storage performance testing. HCIBench is a tool written by VMware for testing the aggregate storage performance of a distributed storage solution like vSAN. It uses common synthetic I/O generators including vdBench and FIO, and greatly simplifies the deployment and configuration of standardized testing. HCIBench is designed to be run as part of a PoC acceptance test and is tightly integrated with other management and operational aspects of vSAN. HCIBench is available from the VMware Fling site; http://flings.vmware.com. This location also includes documentation on how to quickly get started with the tool. Anyone involved in running storage benchmarks on vSAN is recommended to familiarize themselves with this tool.

Figure 106: Proactive Tests Storage Performance Test

The network performance test and storage performance tests using HCIBench can put tremendous stress on the network and servers in a vSAN cluster. It is recommended that these tools primarily play a part in a PoC process, or deployment validation step prior to introducing a cluster into production. Performing these tests with production workloads running could have an adverse effect on the performance of those workloads.

Performance Service

The Performance Service is responsible for capturing and storing the data that helps convey the behavior in the performance of the VMs that are consuming resources in a vSAN cluster. It serves to help administrators understand what type of resources the VMs are demanding from the cluster, and if they are performing to anticipated levels. Performance data collected by the vSAN performance service is mostly rendered as time-based graphs as commonly found with other performance metrics in the vSphere Client.

The performance service is automatically enabled in the most recent versions of vSAN, and as of vSAN 8.0 U1, it no longer provides an option in the UI to disable the service. The status of this service, and other vSAN services, are visible on the Cluster > Configure > vSAN > Services view in the vSphere client.

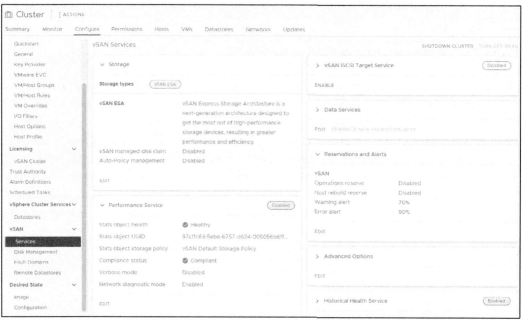

Figure 107: vSAN Performance Service status

The design used for the performance service ensures that data collection will not place any additional burden on the vCenter Server managing the cluster. While vSAN uses the vSphere Client to render vSAN-specific performance metrics, the vSAN performance services run in a distributed way. Performance data is collected by each host in the vSAN cluster and is stored in a special namespace object on the vSAN datastore. Known as the statistics database, or StatsDB object, it holds all of the performance metrics collected by the performance service. This object is automatically created when the performance service is started.

The metrics collected by the performance service may be available for up to 90 days, depending on the conditions of the cluster, such as host count and overall cluster capacity usage. vSAN renders most data to a time window of 1 hour, but it can be adjusted to as high as 24 hours.

A sampling interval (sometimes known as collection interval, time interval, or sampling rate) is a common method to collect and render performance metrics over a duration of time. Through the use of counters, it determines how much activity occurred during a period of time and presents that as a single value that represents the average for that time interval. This is the method used in vSAN, and in past versions, the time interval to collect and render the metrics was 5 minutes.

vSAN 8.0 U1 allows users to select a new time range option. The "Real-time" option will render some performance metrics at a 30-second sampling interval for the past hour and will be retained at this higher level for up to 7 days. This finer level of granularity will allow the performance graphs to be much more representative of the actual workload and system behavior.

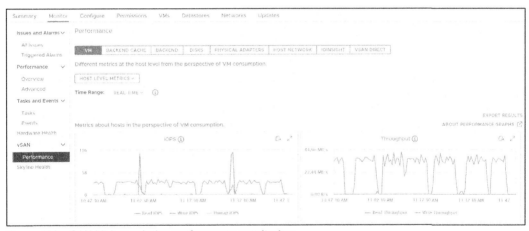

Figure 108: vSAN high-resolution performance monitoring

Since a much higher level of a sampling interval collects a significant amount of data and can begin to place a computational burden on the hosts, this "Real-time" option will be limited to a subset of metrics. vSAN 8.0 U1 accommodates the additional needs of this higher-resolution performance metrics by expanding the statsDB object to 512GB and running a *HighResolutionStatsCollector* service on each host.

Just as with other objects, the Performance Service statsDB object can be managed using a storage policy. The storage policy can be assigned by clicking on the Edit button associated with the Performance Service, as shown in the image below.

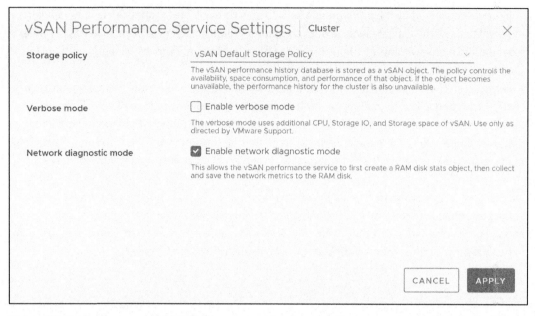

Figure 109: Performance service enabled

Note that the health finding also includes several tests to ensure that the performance service is functioning normally. A verbose mode is also available. This gathers additional CPU, storage I/O, and storage capacity information and should only be used if VMware Technical Support directs you to do so – this is stated in the UI. Finally, there is a new Network diagnostics mode option, which is disabled by default. If enabled, this allows the vSAN Performance Service to create a RAM disk stats object which can subsequently be used for the collection and storing of network metrics. Typically, this is also only done when a customer is directed to do so by VMware support. The advantage is that it provides more detailed performance data but be aware that it generates a lot more data.

The performance service in vSAN is convenient and powerful for day-to-day monitoring and will be an appropriate tool to use for the majority of performance monitoring cases. There are times when additional diagnostics capabilities are needed. vSAN offers another feature known as IOInsight that is able to provide capabilities not available in the performance service. IOInsight will be discussed later in this chapter.

Performance Diagnostics

The Performance Diagnostics feature is a capability intended for the proof of concept (PoC) and evaluation phases of a vSAN cluster deployment. It is found in Cluster > Monitor > vSAN > Performance Diagnostics, and when executed, will analyze benchmarks performed on a cluster to offer guidance on how a cluster could be adjusted to attain higher performance in that specific environment. At the time of this writing, this service is not available for a vSAN cluster running the vSAN Express Storage Architecture.

Network Monitoring

vSAN is a distributed storage system, placing data strategically across hosts to ensure resilience. As a result, it relies on the network for almost every aspect of its operation. vSAN's network diagnostics are an enhanced set of performance metrics and alerts that provide details of network communication that is commonly unavailable. By navigating to an ESXi host in a vSAN cluster, then selecting Monitor > vSAN > Performance > Physical Adapters, there are several new metrics and counters to look at such as Port Drop Rate, RX CRC Error, TX Carrier Errors, and so on. Some of these metrics even have customizable alert thresholds that can be adjusted to fit the needs of an environment. While the source of any identified issues from these metrics (such as a misconfigured switch, bad network cable, etc.) may be beyond the capabilities of vSphere to remediate the issue, these continuously captured metrics can still be very effective in isolating a potential cause of an issue in troubleshooting efforts.

Figure 110: Networking Diagnostics

vSAN IOInsight

The vSAN Performance Service provides the vast majority of storage-related metrics for a vSAN environment. These performance metrics are usually sufficient for the vast majority of day-to-day operations. There are times where more detailed information is needed on the characteristics of read and write operations from a guest VM. But gathering these types of metrics can be resource intensive and is usually only needed during troubleshooting efforts.

IOInsight is a feature of vSAN that allows a user to gather these unique storage metrics not captured by the vSAN performance service. Initially introduced as a VMware Fling and now fully incorporated into the product, it captures specific VM and VMDK-level metrics in a manner that makes it ideal for troubleshooting performance. Unlike traditional sampling interval techniques, IOInsight considers every I/O seen at the vSCSI layer of the VM. Aggregation occurs simply for the rendering of data as viewed in the vSphere Client. This level of detail cannot be achieved with other metrics collected by the performance service, which are limited to 5-minute or 30-second intervals.

vSAN IOInsight is ideally suited for scenarios where a problematic host or VM has been identified, and additional data is required to add clarity to findings that have already been observed using other performance metrics. It will not only capture IOPS through a higher level of granularity not possible with the performance service, but also captures I/O size distribution, I/O alignment, read/write ratios, sequential/random I/O ratios, and distribution of latency for I/O activity.

vSAN IOInsight may be run against individual VMs or hosts, or the entire vSAN cluster. It is run for a defined period to capture workload characteristics. The time duration ranges from 1 minute to 24 hours. The data collection operation may be interrupted by the administrator if necessary. Because of the consumption of resources that it uses, IOInsight is not intended for continual use.

IOInsight requires the vSAN performance service to be enabled in order to capture data. The data collected by IOInsight is stored in the performance service statsDB object. While vSAN 8.0 U1 increased the object size of the statsDB object, storing multiple data collections of IOInsight, running the performance service in verbose mode, or using network diagnostics mode can truncate the retention time of other performance metrics.

To gather an instance of vSAN IOInsight metrics, navigate to Cluster > Monitor > vSAN > Performance, and then select IOINSIGHT from the list of options. Unless an instance of IOInsight has been previously created, there will be none found initially. Click on the NEW INSTANCE option to create an I/O Insight run. A prompt to select the monitoring target appears; by default, all hosts in the cluster are selected. Alternatively, you can select individual hosts or VMs.

Figure 111: vSAN IOInsight targets

The next step is to provide a name and duration for the instance. Note the warning about monitoring overhead. This should be considered when running I/O Insight on a production system. By default, the duration is 10 minutes, but this can be reduced to 1 minute minimum or left to run for 24 hours maximum. I changed it to 5 minutes for the purpose of this demonstration.

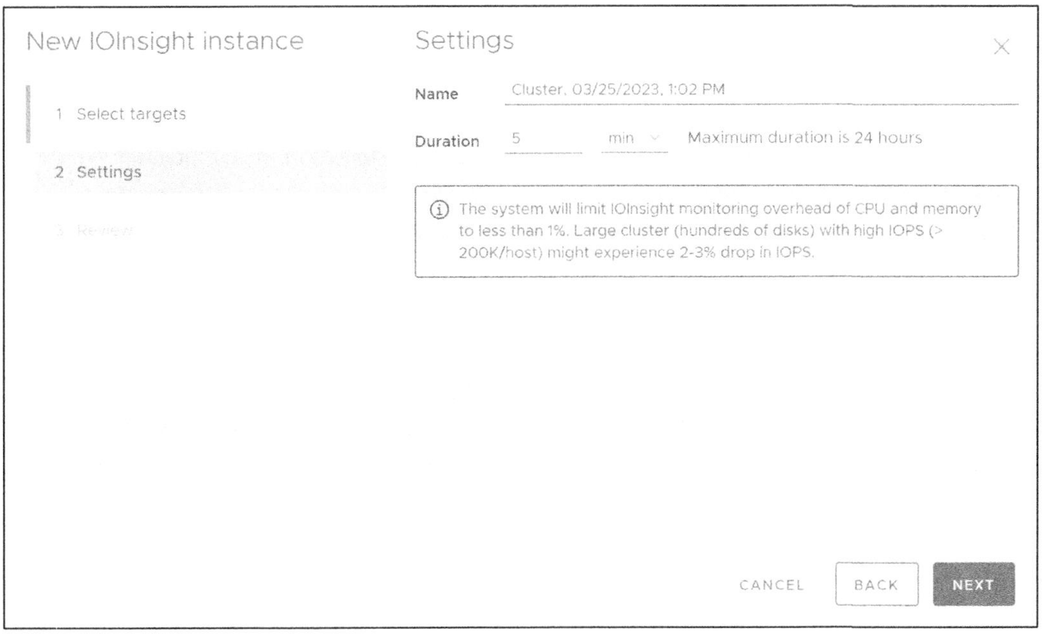

Figure 112: vSAN IOInsight name and duration

After initiating the instance, the new instance now appears in the IOINSIGHT view. It provides a status field that details how much time is remaining until the operation is complete. An administrator can view the metrics from the running instance or can choose to stop the run at any time as well. If an administrator chooses to view the metrics from a running instance, these are updated at 10-second intervals. **Figure 113: vSAN IOInsight results** show some of the storage metrics from a VM's hard disk (VMDK) which resides on a vSAN datastore, as gathered by IOInsight.

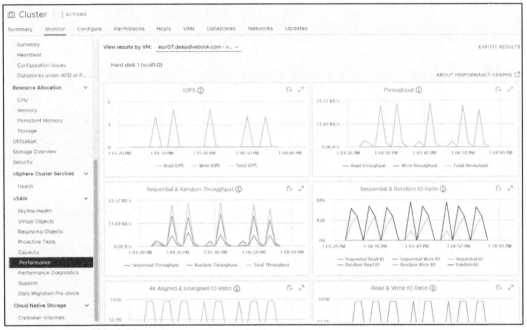

Figure 113: vSAN IOInsight results

Finally, vSAN IOInsight provides administrators with the ability to export the metrics from an instance run. By clicking on the EXPORT RESULT link as shown in the top left-hand corner of Figure 113, a zip file that includes both graph images and raw data in CSV file format is created.

I/O Trip Analyzer

While vSAN IOInsight provides unique, highly detailed performance metrics for VMs, the I/O Trip Analyzer in vSAN examines the path of a read or a write operation and provides information about the latency incurred at different stages in the I/O path. This tool complements vSAN IOInsight to provide administrators with additional information when performing troubleshooting, or even getting a better understanding of the I/O path.

I/O Trip Analyzer is a VM-centric tool. Thus, to enable I/O Trip Analyzer, navigate to any VM that you wish to query, select the Monitor tab, then vSAN, and then select I/O Trip Analyzer. This will drop you to the I/O Trip Analyzer page, which prompts administrators to click on the "RUN NEW TEST" button. Simply click on this button to launch it. A prompt for the duration of the I/O Trip

Analyzer test appears, which defaults to 5 minutes. This can be changed to a maximum of 60 minutes if so desired. Finally, click on the "RUN" button after the time has been chosen. Note that only a single I/O Trip Analyzer test can be run on the cluster at a time. Like vSAN IOInsight, the UI is updated with the amount of time left before the test is complete. Once the test completes, the "VIEW RESULT" button is highlighted, and the data path can be examined. Note how with the ESA, it will show data paths for the components that reside on the RAID-1 performance leg, and the RAID-6 capacity leg of the given virtual disk.

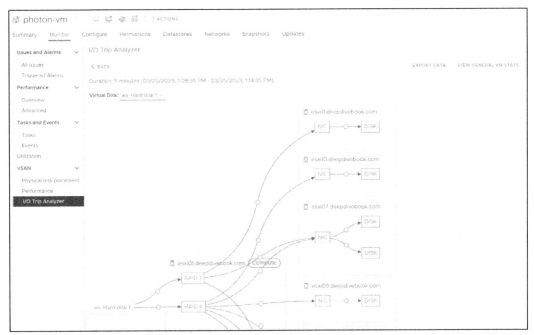

Figure 114: I/O Trip Analyzer results

To see the latency at any point in the I/O path, simply click on one of the dots. This displays the kind of latency introduced at that layer. I/O Trip Analyzer also provides a potential cause for the latency as well as some insights in terms of how you can potentially resolve a latency issue. If a significant amount of latency is introduced, the diagram will highlight it using colors for the respective layer where the latency is introduced.

The metrics provided also display the standard deviation for read and write latencies. This is a measurement of latency variability, where increased values represent a larger degree of variability in latency during the collection period. The map paired with the performance metrics can help indicate the primary source of the latency.

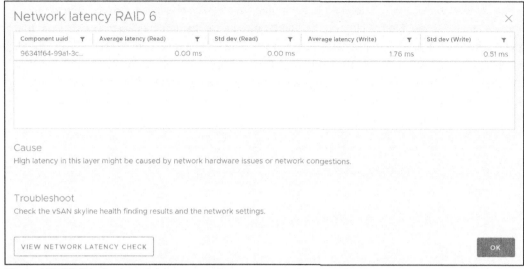

Figure 115: I/O Trip Analyzer latency

Note that there are some limitations to using both vSAN IOInsight, as well as I/O Trip Analyzer. At the time of writing, it is not possible to vMotion a VM that currently has metrics being gathered by vSAN IOInsight. The vMotion will succeed but data collection will stop and cannot be viewed. The advice from the authors is therefore to override any DRS automation for any VMs that are being traced so that DRS does not interfere with the data collection. The reason for this is that the tracing is happening at the ESXi host level. A user world is created on the host where the VM is running to trace the I/O. If the VM is moved to another ESXi host, the user world doesn't know what has happened to the VM and obviously cannot continue to monitor it.

There are also a few limitations regarding I/O Trip Analyzer. At the time of writing, it could not be used with vSAN Stretched Cluster, iSCSI, or Kubernetes Persistent Volumes created via CSI-CNS. These restrictions will most likely be lifted over time.

Now that we have provided an overview of Skyline Health and associated services, let's now turn our attention to some of the more common management tasks an administrator might be faced with when managing vSAN.

Host Management

VMware vSAN has a scale-up and scale-out storage architecture, which allows for seamless scaling no matter which approach is selected. Resources can be scaled up by adding storage devices to each host in the cluster, which will allow each host to contribute more capacity and potentially more performance capabilities. Resources can also be scaled out by adding more hosts to a cluster, which provides additional compute, network, and storage resources for the workloads to use.

Those who have been managing vSphere environments for a while will not be surprised that host management with vSAN is extremely simple; adding more resources (either a combination of compute and storage capacity or just storage capacity) can truly be as simple as adding a new storage device to a host or adding a new host to a cluster. Let's look at some of these tasks in more detail.

Adding Hosts to the Cluster

Adding hosts to the vSAN cluster is quite straightforward. Of course, you must ensure that the host meets vSAN requirements or recommendations such as a NIC port (25GbE is the minimum requirement for clusters running ESA) and storage devices such as NVMe-based triple-level cell (TLC) as defined in the VMware Compatibility Guide for vSAN.

When adding hosts to a cluster, we recommend that host specifications be as uniform as possible. While this has been a long-standing recommendation for vSphere clusters, it is especially important for vSAN clusters that provide storage resources for the cluster. As market conditions and hardware availability change, perfect uniformity of hosts is not always possible. VMware does support clusters with hosts that have these non-uniform host specifications, but reasonable levels of symmetry across hosts are preferred.

Also, pre-configuration steps such as a VMkernel port for vSAN communication should be considered, although these can be done after the host is added to the cluster. After the host has successfully joined the cluster, you should observe the size of the vSAN datastore grow according to the size of the additional storage devices claimed by vSAN in the new host. Just for completeness' sake, these are the steps required to add a host to a vSAN cluster using the vSphere Client:

1. Right-click the cluster object and click Add Hosts.
2. Fill in the IP address or host name of the server, as shown below.

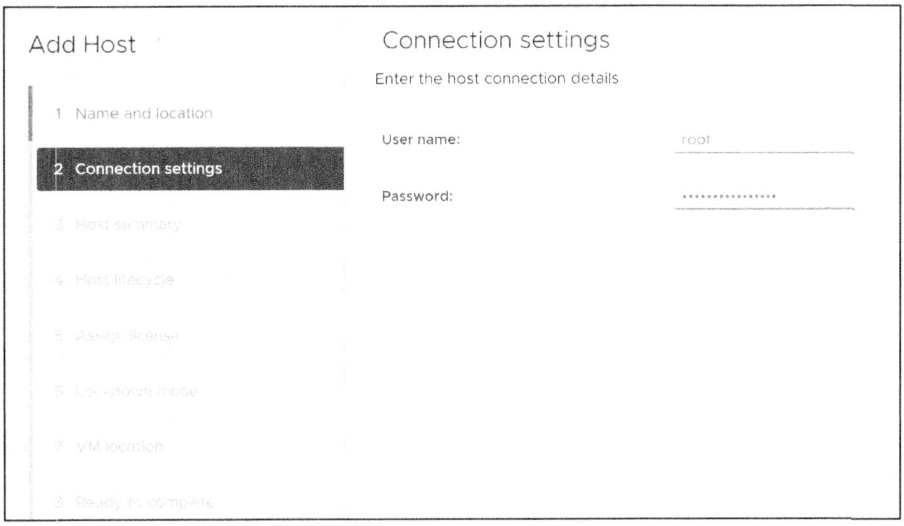

Figure 116: Adding a host to the cluster

3.   Fill in the user account (root typically) and the password.
4.   Accept the **SHA1 thumbprint** option.
5.   Click **Next** on the Host summary screen.
6.   Click **Next** on the Host lifecycle screen.
7.   Select the license to be used.
8.   Enable lockdown mode if needed and click **Next**.
9.   Click **Next** in the resource pool section.
10. Click **Finish** to add the host to the cluster.

And that is all that is needed. If the host is added to the cluster, and vSAN ESA's "managed disk claim" capability is enabled, vSAN will automatically claim the devices for use with vSAN. You will learn more about managing storage devices and the use of storage pools later in the storage device management section of this chapter.

Removing Hosts from the Cluster

Should you want to remove a host from a cluster, you must first ensure that the host is placed into maintenance mode. The various options will be discussed in further detail in the next section. After the host has been successfully placed into maintenance mode, you may safely remove it from the vSAN cluster. To remove a host from a cluster using the vSphere client, follow these steps:

1.   Right-click the host and click **Enter Maintenance Mode** and select the appropriate vSAN migration option from the screen below and then click **OK**. If the plan is to indeed remove this host from the cluster, then a full data migration is the recommended maintenance mode option. If it is a temporary maintenance operation that should last less than 60 minutes, and therefore no rebuild of vSAN objects will be initiated, "Ensure accessibility" (default option) may be chosen.

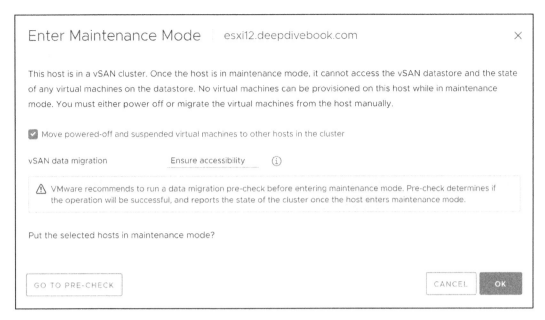

Figure 117: Enter maintenance mode

2. Now all the virtual machines will be migrated (vMotion) to other hosts. If DRS is enabled on the cluster, this will happen automatically. If DRS is not enabled on the cluster, the administrator will have to manually migrate VMs from the host entering maintenance mode for the operation to complete successfully.
3. When migrations are completed, depending on the selected vSAN migration option, vSAN components may also be rebuilt on other hosts in the cluster.
4. When maintenance mode has been completed, right-click the host again and select the move to option to move the host out of the cluster.
5. If you wish to remove the host from vCenter Server completely, right-click on the host once again, and select remove from inventory.
6. Read the text presented twice and click Yes when you understand the potential impact.

Maintenance Mode

The previous section briefly touched on maintenance mode when removing an ESXi host from a vSAN cluster. Since vSAN hosts contribute storage resources to a cluster, maintenance mode includes functionality unique to vSAN clusters that we will elaborate on here. When an ESXi host is placed in maintenance mode, the primary focus is on migrating VM compute resources from that ESXi host to other hosts in the cluster; however, with vSAN, maintenance mode provides you with the option to migrate storage resources as well as compute resources. The vSAN maintenance mode options related to data migration are as follows:

*   **Ensure Accessibility**: This option evacuates enough data from the host entering maintenance mode to ensure that all VM storage objects are accessible after the host is taken offline. This is not a full data evacuation. Instead, vSAN examines the storage

objects that could end up without quorum or data availability when the host is placed into maintenance mode. It then ensures that there are enough components belonging to the object available to achieve quorum and remain accessible. vSAN (or to be more precise the cluster level object manager) will have to successfully reconfigure all objects that would become inaccessible due to a host entering maintenance mode and no longer providing its storage to the vSAN datastore. One example where this could happen is when VMs are configured with "failures to tolerate" set to 0. Another example is when there is already a host with a failure in the cluster, or indeed another host is in maintenance mode. Ensure Accessibility is the default option of the maintenance mode workflow and the recommended option by VMware if the host is going to be in maintenance for a short period of time. If the maintenance time is expected to be reasonably long, administrators should decide if they want to fully evacuate the data from that host to avoid risk to their VMs and data availability. When a host is placed into maintenance mode, it no longer contributes storage to the vSAN datastore, and any components on the datastore are marked as ABSENT.

- **Full Data Migration**: This option is a full data evacuation and essentially creates replacement copies for every piece of data residing on storage devices on the host being placed into maintenance mode. vSAN does not necessarily copy the data from the host entering maintenance mode; however, it can and will also use the hosts holding replica or stripe with parity of the object to avoid creating a bottleneck on the host entering maintenance mode. In other words, in an eight-host cluster, when a host is placed in maintenance mode using full data migration, then potentially all eight hosts will contribute to the re-creation of the impacted components. The host does not successfully enter maintenance mode until all affected objects are reconfigured and compliance is ensured when all the component(s) have been placed on different hosts in the cluster. This is the option that VMware recommends when hosts are being removed from the cluster, or there is a longer-term maintenance operation planned.

- **No Data Migration**: This option does nothing with the storage objects. As the name implies, there is no data migration. It is important to understand that if you have objects that have *number of failures to tolerate* set to 0, you could impact the availability of those objects by choosing this option. There are some other risks associated with this option. For example, if there is some other "unknown" issue or failure in the cluster, or there is another maintenance mode operation in progress that the administrator is not aware of, this maintenance mode option can lead to VM or data unavailability. For this reason, VMware only recommends this option when there is a full cluster shutdown planned (or on the advice of VMware support staff).

Again, just to reiterate an important point made earlier, when a host is placed into maintenance mode, it no longer contributes storage to the vSAN datastore. Any components that reside on the physical storage of the host that is placed into maintenance mode are marked as ABSENT.

Maintenance Mode and Host Locality

Much like the original storage architecture of vSAN, the vSAN ESA supports shared-nothing architectures. These types of applications often have their own built-in data replication capabilities, making the use of data resilience in vSAN redundant. When data resilience is not provided by vSAN, special attention must be paid to ensure that the data and the application instances providing the solution remain available during maintenance events.

Some independent software vendors (ISV) such as Cloudian, Dell EMC, and Minio use the vSAN Data Persistence platform (DPp) to ensure their shared-nothing applications and data remain available during maintenance events. The DPp coordinates all of this activity for the administrator. DPp is discussed in more detail in chapter 9.

For other shared-nothing applications that do not use the DPp, vSAN can be configured to accommodate their unique traits through a feature known as *host locality*. This is essentially the deployment of virtual machines which use *failures to tolerate* value of 0 (thus, no protection) in its policy. It ensures that the compute and storage for a particular VM are co-located on the same host. Hadoop's HDFS is one such example, but this configuration may be applicable to other shared-nothing applications that use their own built-in replication capability, such as NoSQL databases like Cassandra.

Note that support for this *host locality* policy setting is only available on special request (RPQ) – it is not generally available. Customers wishing to use such a policy would need to raise a request via their local VMware contacts.

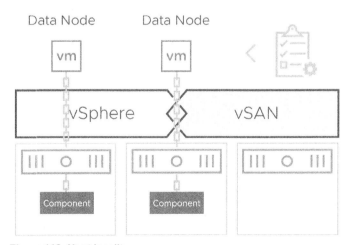

Figure 118: Host locality

There are a number of caveats around host locality that have yet to be ironed out before the feature can be generally available. One such restriction is the use of maintenance mode. Since the VM's compute and storage must reside on the same host, one cannot vMotion the VM or evacuate the data from this host during a maintenance mode operation. Users will have to rely on the built-in application protection mechanism if a host is required to be taken offline for maintenance, etc.

As mentioned in the Data Locality section of Chapter 4, using the ESA for shared nothing applications may simplify the operational model of supporting some shared-nothing applications. With its ability to store data with high levels of space efficiency and no compromise on performance, it may make sense for these shared-nothing applications to use a storage policy configured with RAID-5. This configuration would avoid the need to request approval from VMware and would be consistent with other application deployments.

Default Maintenance / Decommission Mode

One other important point is the default maintenance mode setting when a product like vSphere Lifecycle Manager is being used. Lifecycle management refers to the process of installing software, maintaining it through updates and upgrades, and decommissioning it. Certain lifecycle operations require placing hosts into maintenance mode, and even rebooting them depending on the update.

The default maintenance mode (decommission mode) option is set to `ensureAccessibility` but this can be controlled through an advanced setting. The advanced setting is called `vSAN.DefaultHostDecommissionMode` which is set on a per-host basis. It allows administrators to set the default maintenance mode to an option other than Ensure Accessibility, as listed in the next table.

Maintenance Mode Option	Description
ensureAccessibility	vSAN data reconfiguration should be performed to ensure storage object accessibility
evacuateAllData	vSAN data reconfiguration should be performed to ensure storage object accessibility
noAction	No special action should take place regarding vSAN data

Table 8: vSAN.DefaultHostDecommissionMode Options

Maintenance Mode for Updates and Patching

It is best to draw a comparison to a regular storage environment first when discussing options for updates and patches. When working on a traditional storage array, updates are typically done in a rolling fashion. If you have two controllers, one will be taken offline and upgraded while the other remains active and handles all the I/O. In this dual controller scenario, you are at risk while performing the upgrade because if the active controller hits a problem during the upgrade of the offline controller, no further I/O can flow and the whole array is offline.

The primary difference when working on vSAN as a virtualization administrator is that *you have a bit more flexibility*. Each node in the cluster can be thought of as a storage controller, and even with one node out of the cluster, a second node failure may not impact all VM workloads (depending on the size of the vSAN cluster and the *failures to tolerate* setting of course). Coupled with other vSphere features, such as HA, for instance, you can reduce your level of risk during maintenance operations. The question that a vSphere or vSAN administrator must ask themselves is what level of risk they are *willing* to take, and what level of risk they *can* take.

From a vSAN perspective, when it comes to placing a host into maintenance mode, you will need to ask yourself the following questions:

- **Why am I placing my host in maintenance mode?** Am I going to upgrade my hosts and expect them to be unavailable for just a brief period? Am I removing a host from the cluster altogether? This will play a big role in which maintenance mode data migration option you should use.
- **How many hosts do I have?** When using three hosts, the only option you have is Ensure Accessibility or No Data Evacuation because, by default, vSAN always needs three hosts to store objects, whether it be a RAID-1 mirror using two replicas, or a RAID-5 configuration where the data is striped with parity across three hosts. Therefore, with a three-node cluster, you will have to accept some risk by using maintenance mode. There is no way to do a Full Data Evacuation with just 3 nodes. Therefore, VMware recommends 4 hosts in a vSAN cluster when using RAID-1 or RAID-5. This allows vSAN to self-heal on failures and continue to provide full protection of VMs during maintenance.
- **How long will the move take?** The answer to this question depends on a number of factors, such as:
  - How much space has been consumed?
  - How capable is my network interconnect? Do I have 25GbE, teamed 25GbE, or 100GbE?
  - How large is my cluster?
- **Do I want to move data from one host to another to maintain availability levels?** Only stored components need to be moved, not the "raw capacity" of the host! That is, if 6 TB of capacity is used out of 12 TB, 6 TB will be moved.
- **Do I just want to ensure data accessibility and take the risk of potential downtime during maintenance?** Only components of those objects at risk will be moved. For example, if only 500 GB out of the 6 TB used capacity is at risk, that 500 GB will be moved.

All of the maintenance mode options have their own reasons for use, as well as trade-offs and other considerations. For example, when you select full data migration, to maintain availability levels, your "maintenance window" will be elongated, as you could be copying terabytes of data over the network from host to host. It could potentially take hours to complete depending on the capabilities of the hosts and your network. If your ESXi upgrade (including a host reboot) takes about 20 minutes, is it acceptable to wait hours for the data to be migrated? Or do you consider it a managed risk, where the level of resilience is below the level prescribed by the storage policy for only a short time, yet the operation is completed in a matter of minutes rather than hours?

If the maintenance mode takes longer than 1 hour, then you may have components begin to rebuild and resync on other nodes on the cluster, which will consume additional resources. Remember that 60 minutes is when the clomd repair delay timeout expires, and absent components are automatically rebuilt. This timer is tunable, so if you know maintenance is going to take longer than 60 minutes, you could change it to a higher value to avoid the rebuilds taking place.

However, the main risk is if another failure occurs in the cluster during the maintenance window. Then you risk the availability to your VMs and your data. Historically, we've had customers overcome this by using a *failures to tolerate* setting of 2, which means that maintenance can occur on one of the hosts storing the object data, and one can still tolerate another host storing that object data failing while maintaining availability. For some customers, this is not always possible because a *failures to tolerate* setting of 2 requires at least 6 hosts in a cluster.

In vSAN 8.0 U1, the ESA introduced support of durability components. Durability components increase the availability of the very latest written data to objects impacted by a degraded event, such as a host entered into maintenance mode. While it does not mimic the increase of resilience by changing the storage policy from FTT=1 to FTT=2, it does ensure that newly written data is always resilient should a subsequent failure occur during a maintenance mode event and is often a sufficient enough step to ensure proper resilience during a maintenance mode event using *ensure accessibility*. The use of durability components in the ESA is available only for objects using RAID-5 or RAID-6 erasure coding. For more information on durability components, see Chapter 4.

The authors cannot give you advice on what the best approach is for your organization. We do strongly feel that for normal software or hardware maintenance tasks that only take a short period of time (less than 1 hour), it will be acceptable to use the Ensure Accessibility maintenance mode data migration option. You should still, however, discuss *all* approaches with your storage team and look at their procedures. What is the agreed SLA with your business partners and what fits from an operational perspective?

One final point to note on maintenance modes; as was mentioned earlier, it is possible to change the clomd repair delay timeout to be something much larger if you are involved in a maintenance task that is going to take some hours, but you do not want to have any data rebuilding during this maintenance. Approach this with caution, however, since your VMs will be at risk for an extended period. And it is important to remember to put this setting back to the default after maintenance has finished. This is because certain failure scenarios will also use this timeout before rebuilding failed components, so you want this to kick off as soon as possible, and not be delayed. After all, you modified the timer value.

With the capabilities of recent versions of vSAN including durability components, the support of features like Quickboot's "Suspend to Memory" option, and architectural differences in ESA that eliminated some of the longer host restart times associated with the OSA, adjusting the clomd repair delay timeout value will generally not be needed. If you find that adjusting it is necessary, it can be found in the "Advanced Options" section, under the configuration of services. This has already been highlighted in the book; see Advanced Settings in chapter 4, **Figure 48**.

Maintenance Mode and vSphere Lifecycle Manager

VMware Lifecycle Manager (vLCM) uses maintenance mode operations to automatically place hosts in maintenance in a rolling fashion during upgrades. vLCM, by default, uses Ensure Accessibility as the data migration option. This is deemed acceptable as any required components to keep a VM available will still be evacuated from the host entering maintenance mode. Upgrade operations, along with reboot operations, are not expected to exceed the 60-minute timeout associated with the commencement of rebuild activity.

Multiple hosts in Maintenance Mode simultaneously

Placing multiple vSAN hosts into maintenance mode introduces challenges not always obvious to an administrator. Since vSAN is a distributed storage system, the more hosts in a cluster that are offline, the fewer storage and compute resources are available. This can not only create capacity-constrained conditions but also the potential inability to re-protect the VMs at levels prescribed by the storage policy, due to a lack of the minimum required hosts. The latter is most common on smaller clusters with relatively few hosts.

To address capacity-constrained conditions as a result of one or more hosts placed into maintenance mode (or removed), Skyline Heath for vSAN will report whether the vSAN cluster has sufficient capacity to re-protect all VMs per their prescribed storage policy. It checks to ensure there will be enough capacity on the datastore should it lose the contributing devices from a single host. This additional logic prevents scenarios that occurred with much earlier versions of vSAN, where multiple hosts could be placed into maintenance mode even if the reprotection of those VMs created a capacity-full condition.

vSAN also performs prechecks to help administrators determine if entering a host into maintenance mode will introduce issues, such as capacity-constrained conditions, or the inability to protect data using its prescribed storage policy. This is described in more detail below.

Maintenance Mode Pre-Check

In the section "Removing Hosts from the Cluster" earlier in this chapter, we saw an example of the popup window (**Figure 117**) which appears when you request a host to be placed into maintenance mode. In the lower left-hand corner of that popup window, the was a "Go to Pre-Check" button. This is the data migration precheck and it will determine if there are any issues, such as object compliance, availability, or capacity issues, if the administrator proceeds with the maintenance mode operation.

When the "Go to Pre-Check" button is clicked, the administrator is automatically brought to the Cluster > Monitor > vSAN > Data Migration Pre-Check section in the vSphere UI. From here the administrator can choose which host the pre-check for data migration should be run on (it should be set to the host that was selected for maintenance mode). The other configurable option is the vSAN data migration setting, which is one of "Full data migration", "Ensure accessibility" or "No data migration", all of which have been described earlier in this chapter. This should also be set to whatever was chosen as the data migration option in the maintenance mode window.

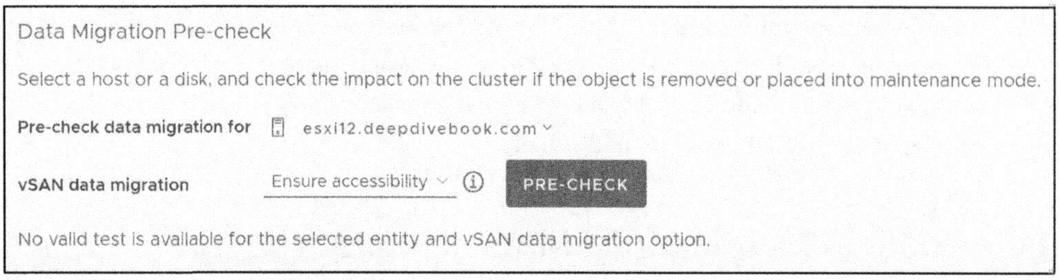

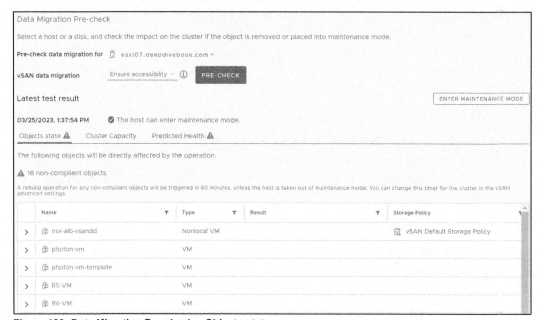

Figure 119: Data Migration Pre-check

Once the "Pre-Check" button is clicked, several tests to check the impact of placing this host into maintenance mode are run. Remember that placing a host into maintenance mode, effectively removes this host from providing any storage capacity to the vSAN cluster. Thus, in a 3-node cluster, every single RAID-1 object will be unprotected and thus displayed as non-compliant. The test result will inform the administrator if the host can be placed in maintenance mode or not and then report on the Objects state, as shown next.

Figure 120: Data Migration Pre-check – Objects state

The precheck also reports on cluster capacity, both before and after the maintenance mode operation. This is useful as on an overloaded cluster, it may not be possible to move all components from the storage on the host that is entering maintenance mode to the remaining hosts in the cluster. This check will highlight such a predicament.

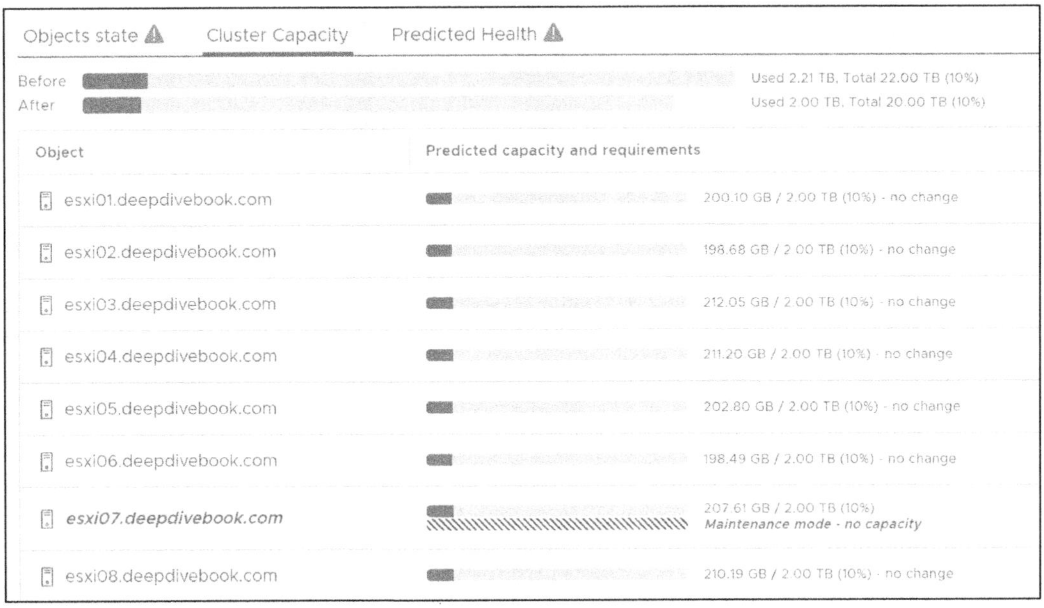

Figure 121: Data Migration Pre-check – Cluster Capacity

Finally, the Data Migration pre-check reports on the impact that the maintenance mode operations will have on the health of the vSAN cluster. Since this is a 3-node vSAN cluster, all RAID-1 objects will be impacted; there is no place to move the components that are currently on the host that is entering into maintenance mode, so all objects will be unprotected and thus non-compliant with their policy.

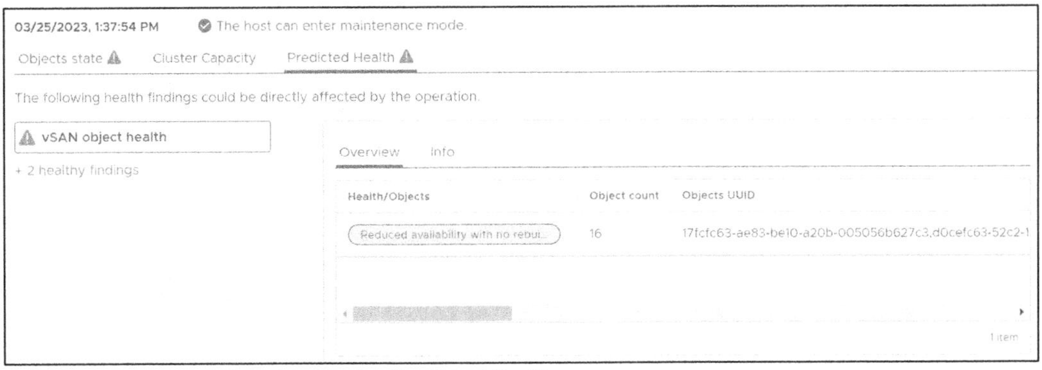

Figure 122: Data Migration Pre-check – Predicted Health

The Data Migration pre-check is an extremely useful feature to examine the impact of maintenance mode operations and should be used regularly by vSAN administrators to understand what impact taking a host out of the vSAN cluster has on the overall system from an availability, capacity, and health perspective.

Stretched Cluster Site Maintenance

In vSAN Stretched Cluster, there is no way to place a complete site or even a specific fault domain into maintenance mode. We will discuss the impact of this, and our guidance, in chapter 7.

Shutting down a cluster

A vSAN cluster provides all of its own storage resources for the cluster, so naturally, shutting down a cluster requires different operational practices than the shutdown of a vSphere cluster using external storage. Up until recently, vSAN administrators had to perform several manual steps to gracefully shut down the entire vSAN cluster. This typically involved a process of shutting down all VMs and placing each host into maintenance mode using the 'no data evacuation' option. Once each host was in maintenance mode, they could be safely powered off.

More recent editions of vSAN have introduced a cluster shutdown feature. Introduced in vSAN 7.0 U3 and enhanced in vSAN 8.0, this provides the administrator the ability to shut down a cluster in a single step.

To trigger a cluster shutdown, right click the cluster object, select vSAN in the drop-down menu, and then select "shutdown cluster". This will launch a window that initiates a shutdown pre-check as shown below. Note that there is a requirement for all VMs to be powered off before the cluster can be shut down. Some VMs, such as Agent VMs and the vCenter Server VM (if it exists) can be automatically managed. The remaining customer VMs are checked by the shutdown pre-check to make sure they are powered off. As per *VMware KB article 85594*, any VMs that are not powered off will be identified during the shutdown pre-check and will need to be powered off manually by the administrator. The figure below displays the set of shutdown pre-checks that are run before a cluster can be shut down and highlights the fact that some VMs are still powered on, preventing the shutdown from proceeding.

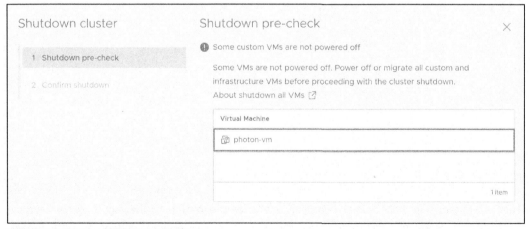

Figure 123: Cluster Shutdown pre-check

vSAN 8.0 U1 introduces support of the cluster shutdown feature via PowerCLI. New cmdlets included in PowerCLI 13.1 will allow an administrator to initiate these events programmatically. This can be especially important for those environments that have sustained on-battery conditions with no secondary source of power.

Upgrade Considerations

vSAN is integrated with vSphere Lifecycle Manager (vLCM). vLCM understands that it is upgrading a vSAN cluster. Therefore, it will automatically take care of selecting a host in the cluster to upgrade and place it into maintenance mode using the default setting of 'ensure accessibility'. It then does the upgrading, reboots the host if needed, and once the host has reconnected to vCenter Server and re-joins the cluster, vLCM takes the host out of maintenance mode and lets the 'out of date' components resynchronize. It then selects the next host and repeats the upgrade task in a rolling fashion until all nodes in the cluster are upgraded.

vLCM not only does hypervisor lifecycle management but also supports firmware lifecycle management as well. In the past, this was a manual process, with administrators needing to download third-party tools along with the appropriate firmware versions to carry out this task on a per-host basis. Today, this can be automated through vLCM. There are some prerequisites before administrators can use vLCM to apply firmware updates, such as ensuring that the vSAN cluster is lifecycle managed with a single image. Firmware updates require a special firmware and drivers add-on which is vendor-provided. The add-on contains the firmware packages. Note that VMware does not host these firmware packages in its own online depots. Instead, each vendor hosts their add-ons in their own proprietary depot. Access to the depot is provided through a vCenter Server plugin, called a "hardware support manager". The appropriate "hardware support manager" must be selected when converting from baseline to image-based lifecycle management, and selecting the appropriate Firmware and Drivers Addon, as shown below.

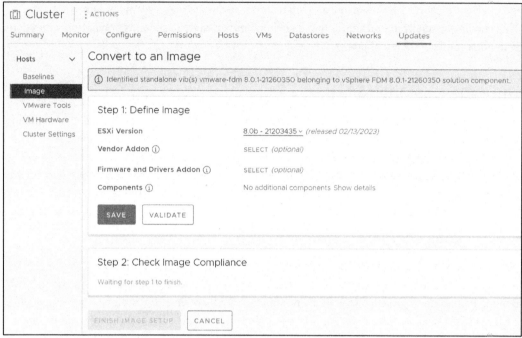

Figure 124: Firmware and Drivers Addon

At the time of writing, there are hardware support managers available for Cisco, DELL, Fujitsu, Hitachi, HPE and Lenovo.

vLCM is also aware of vSAN topologies. It will understand the host placement in vSAN stretched clusters, 2-node clusters, and fault domain configurations, and can orchestrate the upgrades of those different vSAN configurations.

An important consideration relates to the vSAN *on-disk format*. On-disk formats are discussed in Chapter 4. *VMware KB article 2145267* provides an excellent overview of the various on-disk formats that vSAN has had with its various releases. While most on-disk format changes have been minor and did not require a rolling upgrade, there is the potential for a rolling upgrade to be required.

The primary consideration with the on-disk format change (referred to as a DFC) is the evacuation of all data on the respective device to perform the underlying disk format change. In the ESA, the device is evacuated, placing the object data on other devices or hosts in the cluster. The device is removed from service, recreated with a new disk format, and reentered into service. This process is not as invasive in the ESA as it was in the OSA. The ESA performs these maintenance activities on a per-device basis, where the OSA would often have maintenance boundary of a disk group. This smaller maintenance domain of the ESA may reduce the amount of data movement during these activities.

You may well ask what happens when there are not enough resources in the cluster to accommodate a full device evacuation, especially on two-node or three-node vSAN clusters that may have very few storage devices, and very few locations to relocate the data. In this case, there is an option to do the DFC with 'Allow Reduced Redundancy' where only one copy of the data is available during the DFC.

Allowing reduced levels of redundancy can introduce risk, and it is another reason why VMware recommends an additional host be available in the cluster. Having an additional host in the cluster will mean VMs will be fully protected against a failure occurring in the cluster during this task. As mentioned, not every on-disk format change requires an evacuation to format the disks. The most recent on-disk formats that were made to vSAN did not require one.

Storage Device Management

One of the design goals for vSAN, as already mentioned, is the ability to scale up the storage capacity. This requires the ability to add new devices, replace existing devices with larger devices, and easily replace failed devices. This next section discusses the procedures involved in doing these tasks in a vSAN environment.

Adding Storage Devices for use by vSAN

The removal of the construct of a disk group in the ESA makes for a much simpler experience in managing storage devices that are used by vSAN. All storage devices claimed by a vSAN ESA host reside in a storage pool for that host. A storage pool is simply a way to identify the devices claimed for use by a vSAN host, and thus, there is only one storage pool per host. Unlike disk groups, devices in a storage pool remain fully independent from each other and can be added or removed as desired.

The following example shows how to manually claim a device for use by the vSAN ESA. This is a cluster-based task, so one can easily claim multiple devices across multiple hosts.

1. Click your vSAN cluster in the left pane.
2. Click the **Configure** tab on the right side.
3. Click **vSAN > Disk Management**.
4. As shown below, one gets a cluster overview of hosts, the number of devices in use, their health state, capacity, and network partition information. This is useful in determining if there is a network partition, and which host or hosts are in a different network partition group. For disk management tasks across the cluster, one can choose the options of "View Cluster Objects," "Claim Unused Disks" or "Change Disk Claim Mode." In this case, we will click on **Claim Unused Disks**.

Figure 125: vSAN disk management

5.   A list of unused disks will be presented for the purposes of claiming by vSAN, as shown below. Note here that if the cluster is configured for the ESA, it will check for device compatibility and warn against any detected device compatibility issues.

Figure 126: Claiming unused disks

Since all storage devices in an ESA cluster will contribute to both capacity and performance, it greatly simplifies assigning storage devices to be used by vSAN. As you may have noticed above, the ESA also allows for a "vSAN managed disk claim" mode to make this effort even easier. It reintroduces a capability initially provided with much earlier versions of vSAN but removed due to some of the management complexities with disk groups. The ESA makes this automatic claiming easier to implement.

By clicking on "Change Disk Claim Mode" one can instruct vSAN to automatically claim all compatible storage devices. The setting can be configured on a per-cluster basis to best suit the needs of the environment. One can enable it or disable this cluster-based setting, as shown below.

Figure 127: vSAN ESA Managed Disk Claim

When this process completes, the claimed devices show up in storage pool of the vSAN host and will contribute to the advertised resources of the vSAN cluster. We will talk about the other storage management options throughout the rest of this section.

Removing Storage Devices used by vSAN

Administrators can remove a storage device from vSAN once they have selected the "View Disks" as shown below.

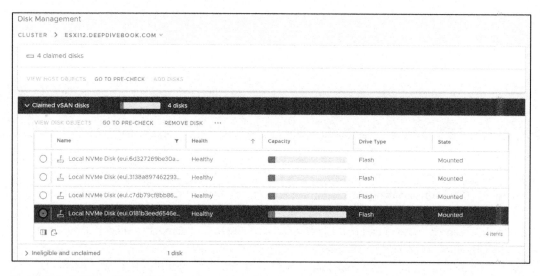

Figure 128: Remove Disk option

Before the Remove task starts, the administrator is prompted to evacuate the components that are currently on that storage device, as shown in the next figure. vSAN allows administrators to evacuate these storage devices without placing the host where the device resides into maintenance mode. Another useful feature like what was seen in the Host Maintenance Mode section is that the disk removal actions also include a "Pre-Check" option. As before, you can choose "Full data evacuation", Ensure accessibility" and "No data evacuation". An administrator can also go directly to the pre-check option from the drop-down menu list above.

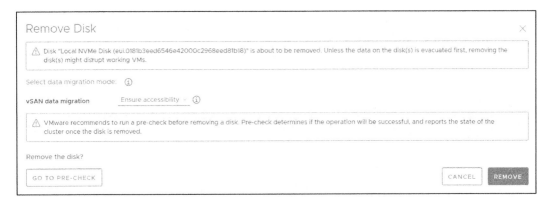

Figure 129: Migration mode when removing a claimed disk

Evacuating the VM components from storage device claimed by vSAN in a host's storage pool is not a required step for removing a storage device for use by vSAN, but the authors believe that most administrators would like to move the VM components currently on the storage device to other storage devices in the cluster before deleting it. If you don't do this step, and evacuate the data, you may be left with degraded components that are no longer highly available. vSAN will then need to reconfigure these components when the storage device is deleted. As highlighted many times now, if there is another failure while the objects are degraded, it may lead to the unavailability of data.

However, there may be valid reasons for wanting to delete a storage device without first evacuating all the data, and those options are also provided. Just like with ESXi hosts, administrators can choose simply to ensure accessibility, or indeed not to evacuate the data at all.

If you are planning on performing a full data evacuation of a storage device, vSAN will validate first whether sufficient space is available within the cluster to do so. Note that just as with the removal of a host, the removal of all of the storage devices in a host using a full data migration on a cluster with an insufficient number of hosts for the associated storage policy is simply not possible, as there is nowhere to move the resilient data to.

You will generally find that with the ESA, the step of adding and removing storage devices used by vSAN will be simpler, and far less invasive than when using the construct of disk groups, found in the OSA.

Erasing a Storage Device

In some cases, other features or operating systems may have used NVMe devices before vSAN is enabled. In those cases, vSAN will not be able to reuse the devices when the devices still contain partitions or even a file system. Note that this has been done intentionally to prevent the user from selecting the wrong devices. If you want to use a storage device that has been previously used, you can wipe the devices manually, either via the command line or from the vSphere Client.

The Erase Partitions option in the vSphere Client is found by selecting an ESXi host, the selecting Configure > Storage Devices, as shown below.

Storage Devices								
REFRESH ATTACH DETACH RENAME TURN ON LED TURN OFF LED ERASE PARTITIONS MARK AS FLASH DISK MARK AS REMOTE ...								
Name ▼	LUN ▼	Type ▼	Capacity ▼	Datastore ▼	Operational State ▼	Hardware Acceleration ▼
☐ Local NVMe Disk (eui.c7db79cf8bb86dfd000c2965366a2ab1)	2	disk	512.00 GB	🗐 vsanDatas...	Attached	Not support...
☐ Local NVMe Disk (eui.3138a897462293c3000c296128e8608c)	3	disk	512.00 GB	🗐 vsanDatas...	Attached	Not support...
☑ Local VMware Disk (mpx.vmhba0:C0:T0:L0)	0	disk	32.00 GB	Not Consumed	Attached	Not support...
☐ Local NVMe Disk (eui.6d327269be30a00d000c296330c71f5...	0	disk	512.00 GB	🗐 vsanDatas...	Attached	Not support...
☐ Local NVMe Disk (eui.0181b3eed6546e42000c2968eed81b18)	1	disk	512.00 GB	🗐 vsanDatas...	Attached	Not support...

Figure 130: Erase partition

It is possible to remove an NVMe device from a storage pool through the Command Line Interface (CLI). However, this should be done with absolute care and the authors strongly recommend going through the UI for such operations, as shown on the previous pages.

Similarly, if a storage device was previously used for another function and the wish is to now use it for vSAN, its partitions can be erased using the UI as already seen. Alternatively, another method is to use the CLI to wipe a disk. The disk can be erased from the commands line using the `esxcli vsan storage` utility.

The above options assume that you have an existing vSAN cluster. Some other less conventional ways are included here in case you do not have a vSAN cluster (i.e., vSAN has been disabled), and thus you do not have the above options available. In those cases, disks can be erased:

- Using the command `partedUtil`, a disk partition management utility that is included with ESXi.
- Booting the host with the `gparted` bootable ISO image.

The `gparted` procedure is straightforward. You can download the ISO image from **http://gparted.org/**, and create a boot CD from it. Then, boot the ESXi host from it. After that, it is simply a matter of deleting all partitions on the appropriate disk and clicking **Apply**.

> **Warning: The tasks involved with wiping a storage device are destructive, and it will be nearly impossible to retrieve any data after wiping the storage device.**

The `partedUtil` method is slightly more complex because it is a command-line utility. Administrators will need to SSH to the ESXi host that contains the storage devices that need its partitions erased. The `partedUtil` binary is available and preinstalled on the ESXi host. The following steps are required to wipe a storage device using `partedUtil`. If you are not certain which device to wipe, make sure to double-check the device ID using `esxcli storage core device list`:

Step 1: Display the partition table
```
~ # partedUtil get /vmfs/devices/disks/naa.500xxx
24321 255 63 390721968
1 2048 6143 0 0
2 6144 390721934 0 0
```

Step 2: Display partition types
```
~ # partedUtil getptbl /vmfs/devices/disks/naa.500xxx
gpt
24321 255 63 390721968
1 2048 6143 381CFCCC728811E092EE000C2911D0B2 vsan 0
2 6144 390721934 77719A0CA4A011E3A47E000C29745A24 virsto 0
~ #
```

Step 3: Delete the partitions
```
~ # partedUtil delete /vmfs/devices/disks/naa.500xxxxxx 1
~ # partedUtil delete /vmfs/devices/disks/naa.500xxxxxx 2
```

If you are looking for more guidance about the use of `partedUtil`, read the following VMware Knowledge Base (KB) article: 1036609.

Turn on the LED on an NVMe device

vSphere has historically provided a way to turn on and off a storage device, known as "blinking" the device. The ability to correctly identify a storage device becomes critically important for device removal or replacement activities.

You'll find the buttons for turning on and off LEDs when you select a storage device in the UI, under Host > Configure > Storage Devices, as seen earlier in **Figure 130** when we looked at the "Erase Partitions" option. As you can probably guess, clicking on the "Turn On Led" turns the LED on; clicking on the "Turn Off Led" icon turns the LED off again.

The ability to blink a device is highly dependent on the respective capabilities of the storage controllers. NVMe-based devices use their own dedicated storage controller embedded on each device and may or may not support device blinking. Since the vSAN ESA only allows the use of NVMe devices, you will want to check to ensure that device blinking is supported on the vSAN ReadyNode certified for ESA. One may need to install additional tools such as the HPE Smart Storage Admin (SSA) CLI to enable the capability.

vSAN Capacity Monitoring and Management

We've described how vSAN aggregates storage from devices across hosts in a vSAN cluster to provide capacity resources. The distributed architecture of vSAN requires a different way of reporting on capacity usage and consumption than commonly found with a traditional storage array. The total capacity advertised by a cluster is the aggregate total of all of the storage devices claimed for use by vSAN in the hosts that comprise a vSAN cluster. Different levels of resilience can be assigned per VM or per VMDK thanks to storage policies. As a result, the cluster capacity advertised as available does not reflect the capacity available for data in a resilient manner, as it will be dependent on the assigned policy.

To accommodate vSAN's distributed architecture, and the ability to granularly define levels of resilience for different data, vSAN provides a capacity dashboard to give detailed information about the space consumption of a cluster. Navigate to Cluster > Monitor > vSAN > Capacity to see this information.

There are two views available, Capacity Usage and Capacity History. The default view is Capacity Usage, which has several distinct sections, such as Capacity Overview, What If Analysis, and Usage breakdown, as shown next.

Figure 131: vSAN Capacity Overview

Capacity Overview

To help the administrator understand how much capacity is used, or remains, the Capacity Overview portion of the dashboard provides a simple way to visualize vSAN datastore capacity and is the best way to understand how much data is stored, and how much capacity remains free on a cluster.

This portion of the dashboard shows the total capacity advertised by a cluster from the devices claimed for use by vSAN. It presents a sum total of raw capacity available. Note the use of the term "Actually written" associated with a dark green color to convey the data written after factoring in levels of resilience applied to the objects, thin provisioning, and data compression. An additional lighter green color may be visible in the circumstance where the "Object Space

Reservation" (OSR) policy rule is used.

The Capacity Overview will provide visual indicators should capacity usage exceed desired thresholds. vSAN requires free capacity to carry out some of its internal operations. The colors on the capacity overview may change as these thresholds are exceeded and may also have additional threshold indicators if the operations reserve and host rebuild reserve are enabled for the cluster. All of these visual indicators provide boundaries to help guide the administrator to the best operational practices. Just as with other types of storage solutions, or even your smartphone, vSAN may not perform optimally if storage utilization is so high that there is insufficient free capacity to perform internal operations.

Operations reserve and Host rebuild reserve

Two optional reservation mechanisms are available when configuring a standard vSAN cluster. The operations reserve and host rebuild reserve do as the names imply, ensuring that sufficient capacity is reserved for operational activities and that sufficient free space is available if a host were to fail for a sustained period of time. They are configurable from the Cluster > Configure > vSAN > Service page under the Reservations and Alerts section, as shown below.

Figure 132: Reservations and Alerts

As per the description in the UI, which is displayed when the Edit button is clicked and the Reservation and Alerts wizard is launched, enabling operations reserve helps ensure that there will be enough space in the vSAN cluster for internal operations to complete successfully. Enabling host rebuild reserve allows vSAN to maintain enough free capacity to tolerate one host failure.

When the reservation is enabled and capacity usage reaches the limit, new workloads will not deploy on the vSAN cluster. This gives a vSAN administrator the ability to avoid situations where the vSAN datastore completely fills up. This has been problematic in the past and can be a difficult situation to recover from since vSAN is not able to carry out its own internal housekeeping operations, never mind handle virtual machine workloads.

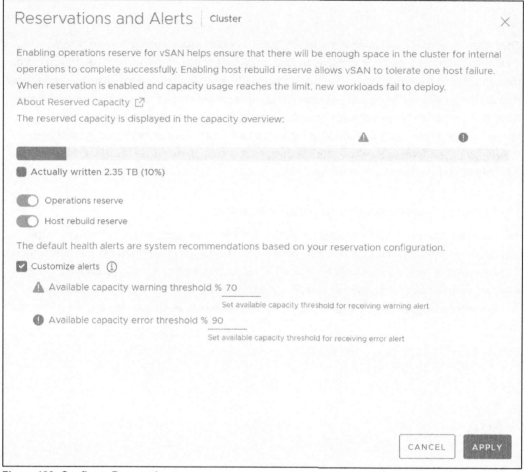

Figure 133: Configure Reservations

Once the operations reserve and host rebuild reserve are enabled, the Capacity Overview is now updated to reflect these new reservation settings. Note that Operation reserve can be enabled without needing to enable Host rebuild reserve. However, to enable Host rebuild Reserve, Operational reserve must first be enabled.

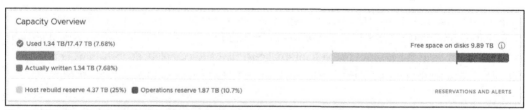

Figure 134: Reservations Enabled in Capacity Overview

Note that the reserved capacity feature is not supported on a vSAN stretched cluster, vSAN clusters with fault domains, or vSAN clusters with less than four hosts. You will see a message in the Reservations and Alerts wizard highlighting this limitation.

What If Analysis / Thin Provisioning Considerations

There are two very useful features in the What if analysis section of Capacity Usage. The first allows you to see how much effective free space is available if all workloads were provisioned with a particular policy. For example, RAID-1 deployments would require capacity set aside for another replica if the *failures to tolerate* was set to 1. Capacity would need to be set aside for 2 full replicas if *failures to tolerate* was set to 2. By selecting the appropriate policy to match these requirements, the What If analysis can provide guidance as to how many workloads can be provisioned with such policies on the vSAN datastore.

Below are two examples of using the What if analysis. The first uses the vSAN Default Storage Policy which uses RAID-1 with failures to tolerate set to 1. The second uses a RAID-5 policy. Note the effective free space for workloads that use those different policies.

Figure 135: What If Analysis – FTT=1, RAID-1 Policy

Figure 136: What If Analysis – FTT=1, RAID-5 Policy

One final item to highlight in the What If analysis is the oversubscription option. vSAN will provision all objects as thin provisioned, unless explicitly told to do otherwise via the Object Space Reservation parameter. The advantage to using thin-provisioned objects is that workloads are not consuming any more capacity than is completely necessary. It is not uncommon in data center environments to see 40% to 60% of unused capacity within the VM. You can imagine that if a VM were thick provisioned, it would drive up the cost, but it would also make vSAN less flexible in terms of the placement of components.

Of course, there is an operational aspect to thin provisioning. There is always a chance of filling up a vSAN datastore when you are severely overcommitted and many VMs are claiming new disk capacity. This is not different in an environment where NFS is used, or VMFS with thin provisioned VMs.

This oversubscription view informs the administrator about the amount of capacity that would be consumed should the thin provisioned objects grow to their maximum size. It is also expressed as a ratio, where "2x" would mean that a cluster would need 2 times the amount of physical capacity currently available should the thin provisioned objects grow to their maximum size. A ratio can be a good value to incorporate into monitoring and design. For example, a customer may find that perhaps a 5x oversubscription ratio provides a good balance of workload consolidation without a high risk of exhausting capacity resources.

When certain capacity usage thresholds are reached, vCenter Server will raise an alarm to ensure that the administrator is aware of the potential problem that may arise when not acted upon. By default, this alarm is triggered when the 75% full threshold is exceeded with an exclamation mark (severity warning), and another alarm is raised when 85% is reached (severity critical). (Note that this issue will also raise an alarm in the Skyline Health section).

Usage breakdown

In the lower part of the Capacity overview section, one can see a breakdown of which objects are consuming space. These are separated into VMs, User objects, and System usage. If the "expand all" text is selected, a breakdown of the different objects and services is displayed, as shown below.

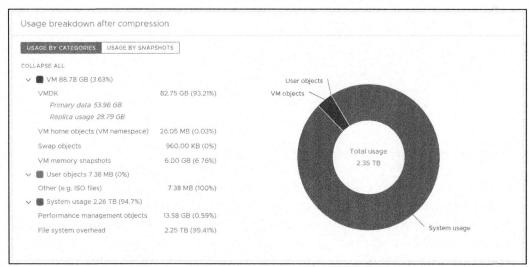

Figure 137: Usage breakdown by categories – Expand All

Under the VM usage breakdown, objects include:
- Virtual Machine Disk Files (includes VMDKs, linked clones, etc.)
  - o   The usage is shown as different types such as Primary data and its replica usage
- VM home objects (VM namespace)
- Swap objects
- VM memory snapshots

Also included as part of the breakdown are user objects. Depending on the data services enabled, this may display container block volumes, ISO file storage, and other types of data. Note that the usage 'donut' will only show percentages of data usage, and not free capacity on the cluster. For new clusters with very little data stored, this will give the visual impression of a large percentage of data used for "system usage." Once more data is stored on the vSAN cluster the percentage used for "system usage" will reduce dramatically.

Finally, the System usage section highlights various vSAN overheads. The vSAN ESA will consume additional capacity for administrative purposes, consisting of global metadata and filesystem overheads that are used to help process, store, and retrieve the data efficiently. Some overheads are related to the objects themselves, while other types of overheads are global and help vSAN store large amounts of data efficiently. In the Usage breakdown portion of the dashboard, they are displayed as the following.

- Filesystem overhead
- Performance management objects

With the new snapshot engine of the vSAN ESA, the Usage breakdown portion of the dashboard now includes a "Usage by Snapshots" view. This will display the total amount of data used by snapshots, and the relative percentage that the snapshots consume for the data written to the cluster.

Finally, there is also a Capacity History which enables administrators to go back in time and review capacity usage charts for a given period (default is 1 day, maximum is 30 days). From here, you can observe the total capacity, free capacity, and used capacity of the vSAN datastore from the last X number of days (where 30 >= X >=1) or indeed, add their own custom data range. This is a great tool for forecasting the future capacity requirements of the vSAN cluster, as well as observing changes in storage policies or space reclamation through UNMAP.

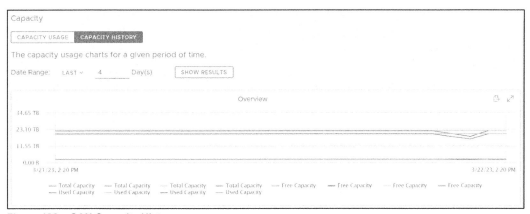

Figure 138: vSAN Capacity History

Storage Device Full Scenario

You might ask, "What happens when the vSAN datastore gets full?" To answer that question, you should first ask the question, "What happens when an individual storage device fills up?" because this will occur before the vSAN datastore fills up.

Before explaining how vSAN reacts to a scenario where a storage device is full, it is worth knowing that vSAN will try to prevent this scenario from happening. vSAN balances capacity across the cluster and can and will move components around, or even break up components when this can prevent a storage device full scenario. vSAN can relocate data to other hosts and storage devices so long as it has a sufficient amount of free space and does not violate the storage policy rules of the object, such as placing two of the object's components that help make it resilient onto a single host.

It should also be noted that the new reservation options (operations reserve, host rebuild reserve) discussed earlier can be used to mitigate the impact of this situation should it arise, by ensuring that there is enough space set aside to prevent the storage device from filling up. However, these reservations are not available to all vSAN configurations as mentioned. It is only available on vSAN clusters that are comprised of at least four hosts, and cannot be used with vSAN stretched clusters, or with vSAN clusters that use fault domains. So, it is still a possibility in some configurations.

In the event of a storage device reaching full capacity, vSAN pauses (technically called *stun*) the VMs that are trying to write data and require additional new disk space for these writes; those that do not need additional disk space continue to run as normal. Note that vSAN-based VMs are deployed thin by default and that this only applies when new blocks need to be allocated to this thin-provisioned disk.

This is identical to the behavior observed on VMFS when the datastore reaches capacity. When additional storage capacity is made available on the vSAN datastore, the stunned VMs may be resumed via the vSphere Web Client. Administrators should be able to see how much capacity is consumed on a per-device basis via the Configure > vSAN > Disk Management view and viewing the storage devices on a per host basis as shown in the next figure.

Figure 139: Monitoring physical disks

The usage of each device claimed by vSAN is there simply for visibility, and one of the reasons why this is not displayed in the "Monitor" portion of the user interface in the vSphere Client. vSAN is responsible for the placement and of object components and the balance of capacity utilization across storage devices.

UNMAP Support

UNMAP is a way for storage systems to reclaim space once consumed on a volume or datastore, but no longer used. Historically UNMAP was available on storage arrays serving VMFS datastores and used in one of two ways. The first use case was for files on a VMFS datastore that were deleted, the UNMAP commands associated with the SCSI protocol could reclaim the previously used storage capacity so it can be used elsewhere.

The second, and perhaps more common use case was for reclaiming capacity inside guest VMs, which could vary in the amount of data they store over time. Temporarily storing data in a thin-provisioned VMDK will inflate the virtual disk, but it will not shrink if some of those files are deleted. Using UNMAP commands inside the guest can help reclaim this no-longer-used capacity, effectively shrinking the VMDK to a size that reflects the data it is storing.

When we look at these scenarios in the context of vSAN, the first use case is not relevant, as vSAN has an acute understanding of object access. Thus, if a VM is moved from, or deleted from the vSAN datastore, vSAN can reclaim and use that space.

In the vSAN ESA, UNMAP support for guest VMs is not only supported but enabled in ESA clusters by default. The service can now be found in the Advanced Options of the Configure > vSAN > Services dashboard where one toggles the service on or off if needed. The UNMAP process is completely automated, so there is not very much to consider from an operational perspective. One caveat to be aware of is that this is not supported by all guest OSes. Typically, it is supported in the later versions of Microsoft Windows and various Linux distributions. Also, note that there could be some performance impact while the UNMAP operation is running.

There are several caveats and considerations when running UNMAP on vSAN. This includes a reliance on the version of VM Hardware used by the virtual machine. We would urge you to read the official VMware documentation (https://vmwa.re/vsanesaunmap) to obtain the full list of requirements when using this feature.

vCenter Server Management

vCenter Server is an important part of most vSphere deployments because it is the main tool used for managing and monitoring the virtual infrastructure. In the past, new features introduced to vSphere often had a dependency on vCenter Server to be available, like vSphere DRS for instance. If vCenter Server was unavailable, that service would also be temporarily unavailable; in the case of vSphere DRS, this meant that no load balancing would occur during this time.

Fortunately, vSAN does not rely on vCenter Server in any shape or form, not even to make configuration changes or to create a new vSAN cluster. Even if vCenter Server goes down, vSAN continues to function, and VMs are not impacted whatsoever when it comes to vSAN functionality. If needed, all management tasks can be done through esxcli or rvc, the Ruby vSphere Console that ships with vCenter Server.

You might wonder at this point why VMware decided to align the vSAN cluster construct with the vSphere HA and DRS construct, especially when there is no direct dependency on vCenter Server and no direct relationship. There are several reasons for this, so let's briefly explain those before looking at a vCenter Server failure scenario.

The main reason for aligning the vSAN cluster construct with the vSphere HA and DRS cluster construct is user experience. Today, when vSAN is configured/enabled, it takes just a handful of clicks in the cluster properties section of the vSphere Client. This is primarily achieved because a compute cluster already is a logical grouping of ESXi hosts.

This not only allows for ease of deployment but also simplifies upgrade workflows and other maintenance tasks that are typically done within the boundaries of a cluster. On top of that, capacity planning and sizing for compute is done at cluster granularity; by aligning these constructs, storage can be sized accordingly.

A final reason is of course availability. vSphere HA is performed at the cluster level, and it is only natural to deal with the new per-VM accessibility consideration within the cluster because vSphere HA at the time of writing does not allow you to fail over VMs between clusters; it can only failover a VM to another host within the same cluster. In other words, life is much easier when vSphere HA, DRS, and vSAN all share the same logical boundary and grouping.

Running vCenter Server on vSAN

A common support question relates to whether VMware supports the vCenter Server that is managing vSAN to run in the vSAN cluster. The concern would be a failure scenario where the access to the vSAN datastore is lost and thus VMs, including vCenter Server, can no longer run. The major concern here is that no vCenter Server (and thus no tools such as rvc) is available to troubleshoot any issues experienced in the vSAN environment. Fortunately, vSAN can be fully managed via esxcli commands on the ESXi hosts. So, to answer the initial question, yes, VMware will support customers hosting their vCenter Server on vSAN (as in it is supported), but in the rare event that the vCenter Server is not online and you need to manage or troubleshoot issues with vSAN, the user experience will not be as good. This is a decision that should be given some careful consideration.

vSAN Storage Services

As we have seen many times throughout this book, the vSAN datastore is typically consumed by VMs deployed on the same cluster where vSAN is enabled. However, a vSAN ESA datastore can also be consumed remotely through several different vSAN Storage Services, namely the iSCSI Target Service, and HCI Mesh. These services allow vSAN datastores to be consumed from remote clients. In this section, we will look at these storage services in further detail and highlight operations considerations where applicable.

vSAN iSCSI Target Service

This service enables an iSCSI Target on the vSAN Cluster, which then allows remote/external iSCSI initiators to consume storage on the vSAN datastore.

Enable vSAN iSCSI Target Service

Configurable options for the iSCSI Target Service include the default network (VMkernel) for the iSCSI traffic. A storage policy must also be associated with the target, which is then used to create a VM Home Namespace object to store iSCSI metadata. Authentication protocols include CHAP (Challenge Handshake Authentication Protocol), where the target authenticates the initiator, as well as mutual (bi-directional) CHAP, where both the initiator and the target authenticate one another. The final consideration is the TCP port on which the initiator and target communicate. By default, this is port 3260.

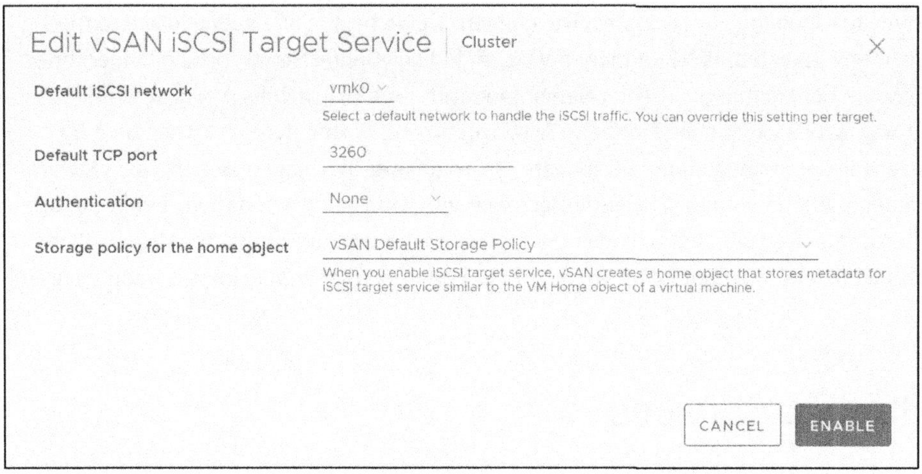

Figure 140: vSAN iSCSI Target Service Setup

Information about the service is now displayed on the Cluster > Configure > vSAN > Services page.

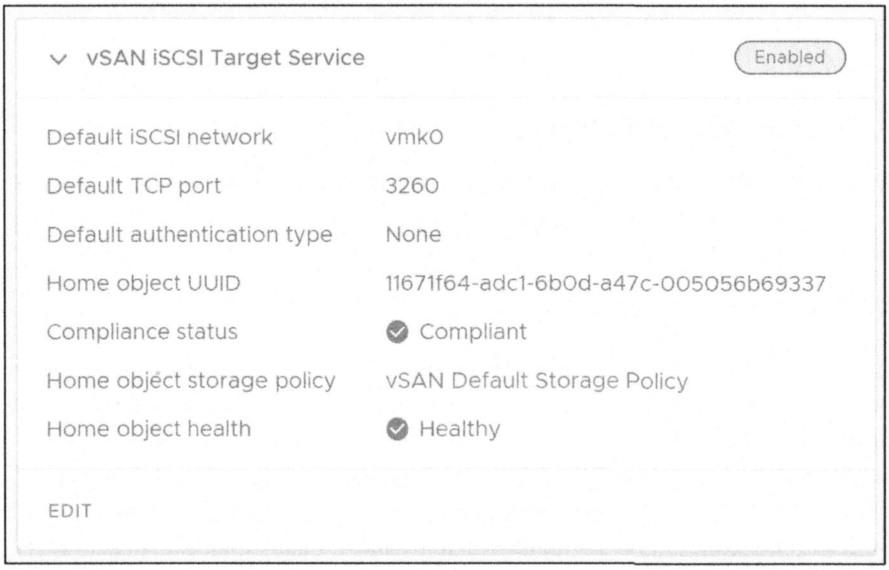

Figure 141: vSAN iSCSI Target Service Enabled

Create a vSAN iSCSI Target

Once the iSCSI Target Service is enabled, a new iSCSI Target Service menu entry appears in Cluster > Configure > vSAN.

iSCSI Targets and Initiator Groups can now be created. Administrators will need to create the target IQN (iSCSI Qualified Name), along with a target alias and a storage policy. If the IQN is left blank, the system will automatically generate one for you. However, a target alias must be supplied, once again, you may add the TCP port on which the initiator and target communicate. By default, this is port 3260. Other settings include Authentication (CHAP/Mutual CHAP) and the network to use for iSCSI. A network selection is presented since the iSCSI Targets can be configured to use different networks than that defined for the service. Note that during the creation of the iSCSI target a storage policy can be selected. If the Auto policy management feature is enabled, then by default the optimal policy is shown under storage policy during both the iSCSI target and iSCSI LUN creation.

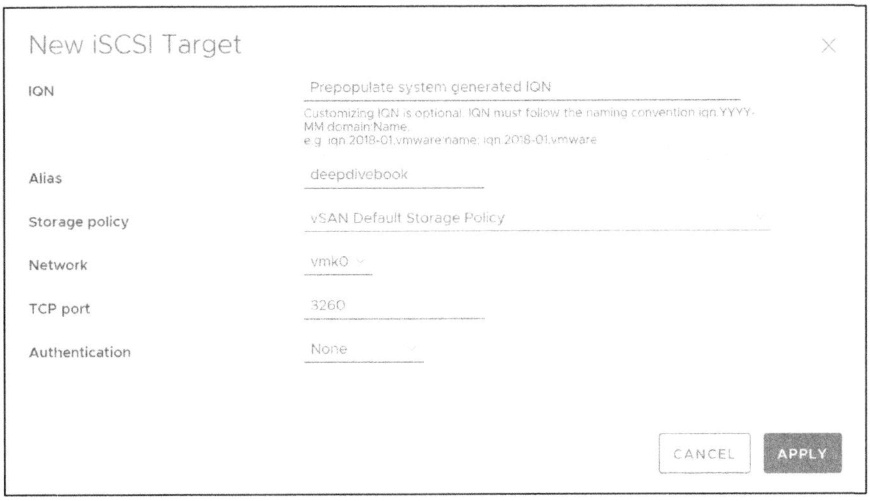

Figure 142: vSAN iSCSI Target Create

Create a vSAN iSCSI LUN

The vSAN iSCSI Target should now be visible in the vSphere client. From here, vSAN iSCSI LUNs can now be created. This is the step that defines among other things, the size of the volume. The main consideration here is to assign a LUN ID.

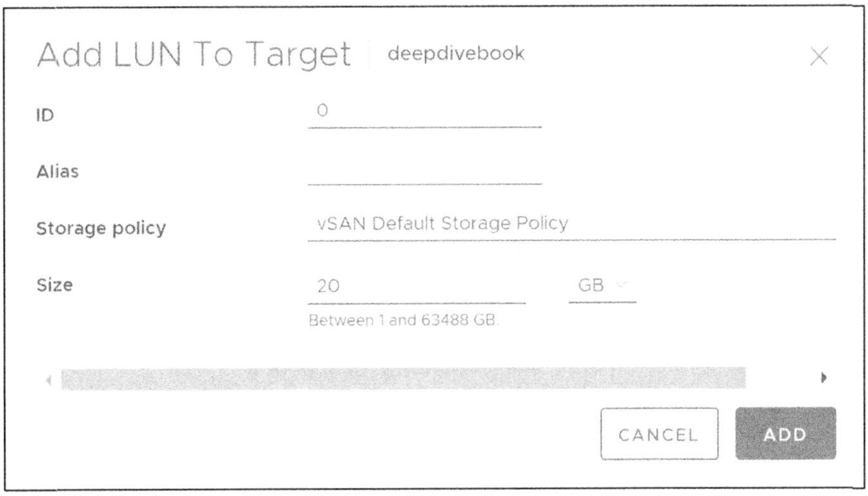

Figure 143: vSAN iSCSI LUN Create

Create a vSAN iSCSI Initiator Group

The final step is to grant access to the target (and any LUNs on the target) to the remote initiators. To do this, the initiators first need to be added to an initiator group. This can be done at various points in the UI. One way is via the iSCSI Target Service. From there, select the Initiator Groups view. Next, under the vSAN iSCSI Initiator Groups, click on Add. This opens a wizard which requests you to provide an initiator group name and add the initiator(s) IQN. The IQN is a specifically formatted identifier, which looks something like iqn.YYYY.MM.domain:name. Note that this IQN comes from the remote initiator; it is not the local vSAN target initiator.

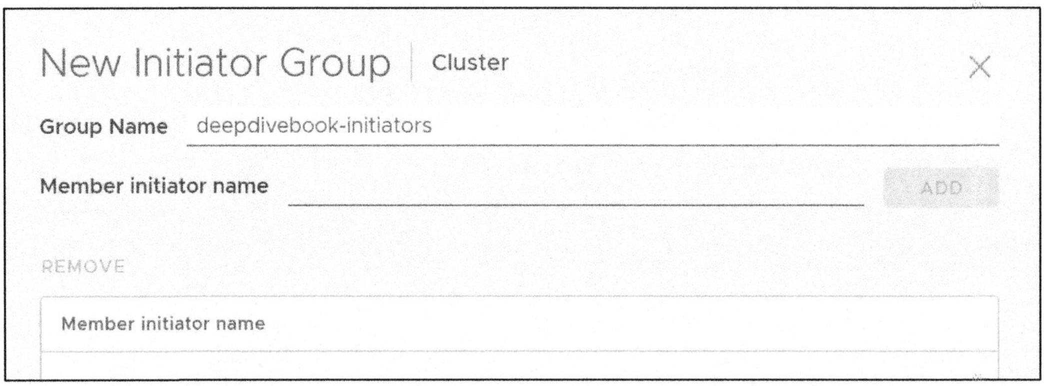

New Initiator Group | Cluster   X

Group Name   deepdivebook-initiators
_____

Member initiator name   ADD
_____

REMOVE

Member initiator name

Figure 144: vSAN iSCSI Initiator Create

The initiator group must now be given access to the target. In the Initiator Groups view, under Accessible Targets, click on Add, and add the vSAN iSCSI target created previously. This now completes the step of granting members of the initiator group "deepdivebook-initiators" access to target "deepdivebook", and thus access to LUN ID 0 which was created on that target.

The vSAN iSCSI Target Service is intended for a very specific set of use cases. This service is intended to provide a block-based volume for external physical servers running Windows or Linux. It can also provide a block-based volume for guest VMs. This helps administrators accommodate legacy workload configurations running on physical systems or virtual machines. The vSAN iSCSI service does not support presenting iSCSI targets and LUNs to other ESXi hosts, or any third-party hypervisor. Other operational considerations include the following:

- L3 Routing between initiators and targets (on the vSAN iSCSI network) is supported
- Jumbo Frames (on the vSAN iSCSI network) is supported
- IPv4 and IPv6 are both supported
- IPsec / IP Security supported (available on ESXi hosts using IPv6 only)
- NIC Teaming configurations (on the vSAN iSCSI network) supported
- iSCSI feature *Multiple Connections per Session* (MCS) not supported

vSAN iSCSI Target Service and vSAN Stretched Cluster

One final consideration is related to vSAN Stretched Clusters and iSCSI. Let's first describe a little about the iSCSI on vSAN architecture. With the iSCSI implementation on vSAN, there is the concept of a target I/O owner for vSAN iSCSI. The I/O owner is what the iSCSI initiator connects to. However, the I/O owner may be on a completely different vSAN node/host to the actual iSCSI LUN backed by a vSAN VMDK object. This is not a problem for vSAN deployments, as this can be considered akin to a VM's compute residing on one vSAN host and the VM's storage residing on a completely different vSAN host. This 'non-locality' feature of vSAN allows us to do operations like maintenance mode, vMotion, capacity balancing, and so on without impacting the performance of the VM. The same is true for the vSAN iSCSI Target Service implementation; an administrator should be able to move the I/O owner to a different host, and even migrate the iSCSI LUNs to different hosts while not impacting iSCSI performance. This enables the vSAN iSCSI implementation to be unaffected by operations such as maintenance mode, balancing tasks, and of course any failures in the cluster.

The key issue however is if the initiator is somewhere on-site A, and the target I/O owner is on site B. In this case, the iSCSI traffic (as well as any vSAN traffic) will need to traverse the inter-site link. In a nutshell, there could be an additional inter-site trip for iSCSI traffic, and this is why VMware did not support iSCSI on vSAN Stretched Clusters for some time. A mechanism to offer some sort of locality between the iSCSI initiator and the target I/O owner was needed. Fortunately, this has been accounted for in recent editions of vSAN, as described in chapter 4, and is available in the ESA.

Once the I/O owner has been placed correctly, and the iSCSI initiator does not have to traverse the interconnect to communicate, we can consider the behavior of iSCSI LUNs in a vSAN stretched cluster. A scenario could arise where the I/O owner is residing on one site in the stretched cluster, whilst the actual vSAN object backing the iSCSI LUN (VMDK) could be on the other site. This is not an issue. For write workloads, no matter if it is VM or iSCSI, all the traffic between the iSCSI initiator (which has established connectivity through the I/O owner) and the iSCSI target has to traverse the inter-site link since write data is written to both sites anyway (RAID-1). Thus, writes are not a concern. When it comes to read workloads, the ability to read data from the local site for both iSCSI and VM workloads is available, avoiding the need to traverse the inter-site link. This means that it doesn't matter which site the I/O owner resides. The real concern is to be able to place the initiator and the I/O owner on the same site, and this functionality is now available.

vSAN File Service

The native file services capability introduced in version 7.0 of vSAN is not supported in vSAN 8.0 or vSAN 8.0 U1 when using the ESA. If you are interested in using vSAN File Services immediately, you can continue to use this capability found in the vSAN OSA. Enhancements continue to be introduced with the vSAN file services, up to and including vSAN 8.0 U1.

vSAN HCI Mesh / Remote vSAN Datastores

vSAN HCI Mesh allows administrators to mount the datastore of another vSAN cluster. This allows VM instances to consume compute and memory resources on one cluster while consuming storage resources of another cluster. The VMs in the clusters consuming the storage resources of a vSAN cluster can be residing in a vSAN cluster or a vSphere cluster.

One of the most significant benefits of this is the ability to consume available datastore capacity found on another cluster, or to perhaps use cluster-specific services on another cluster, such as data-at-rest encryption. With HCI Mesh, a VM instance would be running on what is referred to as a *client cluster*, while the data for that VM is stored on what is referred to as a *server cluster*.

The hosts in a client cluster do not require any vSAN licenses to connect to a server cluster, but they need to reside in a vSphere cluster to allow a connection. A client cluster can be as small as a single host, but as with other topologies, single-host vSphere clusters give up some of the fundamental benefits of clustering, so a client cluster of greater than one is highly recommended. As of vSAN 8.0 U1, for the ESA, the client and server clusters must be managed by the same vCenter Server.

Mount a Remote vSAN Datastore

With the vSAN ESA in vSAN 8.0 U1, the ability to mount a remote datastore is dependent on the fact that the datastore resides in the same datacenter in the vCenter Server inventory. To mount the remote datastore, navigate to one of the clusters in the data center and select Configure > vSAN > Remote Datastores. This should automatically provide a view of the local vSAN datastore, as shown below if one exists.

Figure 145: HCI Mesh Remote Datastores (Local)

By clicking on the "Mount Remote Datastore" option, a list of vSAN datastores belonging to vSAN clusters within the same datacenter is displayed.

Figure 146: HCI-Mesh Mount Remote Datastore

When the remote datastore is selected as a mount candidate, several compatibility checks are run to ensure that the requirements are met, and that none of the limitations around HCI Mesh are exceeded. Figure 147 shows the list of compatibility checks.

Figure 147: HCI-Mesh Remote Datastore Compatibility Check

There are a significant number of compatibility checks. These ensure that neither the source nor the destinations cluster is a 2-node or vSAN stretched cluster, both of which are currently unsupported with HCI Mesh. It also checks licensing and ensures that none of the mounting limits are exceeded. Also important is ensuring there are low latency, and high bandwidth connections between the local and remote clusters.

Once the mount operation completes, the remotely connected datastores can be viewed in the same Remote Datastores view that we just completed the mounting of the datastore, shown in the image below. A Remote Datastores view is also available when highlighting the vCenter Server in the vSphere Client and clicking Configure > vSAN > Remote Datastores.

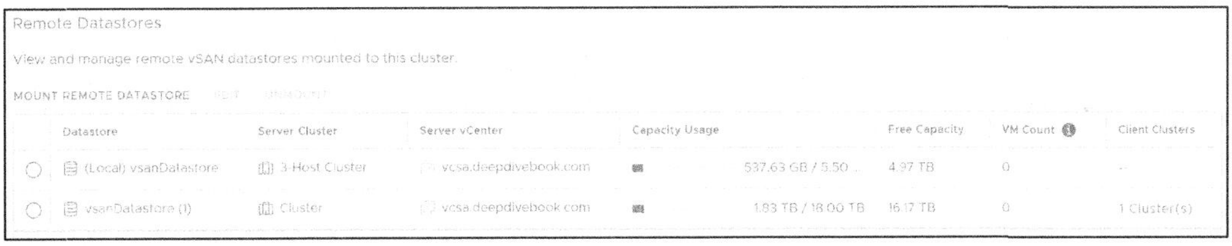

Datastore	Server Cluster	Server vCenter	Capacity Usage	Free Capacity	VM Count	Client Clusters
(Local) vsanDatastore	3-Host Cluster	vcsa.deepdivebook.com		537.63 GB / 5.50 ...	4.97 TB	0	-
vsanDatastore (1)	Cluster	vcsa.deepdivebook.com		1.83 TB / 18.00 TB	16.17 TB	0	1 Cluster(s)

Figure 148: HCI-Mesh Local and Remote datastore

Note the VM Count column. The VM Count is only referring to virtual machines owned by the local cluster on the remote vSAN datastore. There could be virtual machines deployed to this datastore by the vSAN cluster that "owns" the vSAN datastore, i.e., its local vSAN cluster, or indeed other remote clusters that are also mounting the datastore. They do not show up in the VM Count. Only VMs created by this cluster appear in this column.

VMs are provisioned on remote datastores in the same way as VMs are provisioned on local datastores. Customers select a storage policy when provisioning a VM, and both local and remote datastores which are compliant with the policy are shown as suitable datastores for the deployment. In the polices chapter earlier in this book, we saw how storage rules could be used to differentiate between multiple vSAN datastores, including those that are encrypted, have deduplication and compression capabilities as well as choosing between hybrid and all-flash vSAN datastores. See the Storage rules section in chapter 5 for further details.

HCI Mesh and vCLS

Some additional operational considerations need to be considered when working with HCI-Mesh. The first of these relates to the VMware vSphere Cluster Services (vCLS) virtual machines. vCLS is a mechanism that decouples both vSphere DRS and vSphere HA from vCenter Server. vCLS ensures the availability of critical services even when vCenter Server is impacted by a failure.

vCLS is a consideration if the remote vSAN datastore is the only datastore available to a compute cluster. In such a case, vCenter Server / ESX Agent Manager (EAM) will try to provision the vCLS VMs onto the remote vSAN datastore. The remote vSAN datastore may not be the most optimal datastore – perhaps it is only mounted to the cluster temporarily. In the past administrators had no control over the placement of the vCLS VMs, but recent editions of vSAN allow administrators to choose which datastore to use for vCLS and prevent it from using the remote vSAN datastore. Navigate to Cluster > Configure > vSphere Cluster Services > Datastore and click on the 'Add' button to choose which datastores to use for vCLS, as shown below.

Figure 149: Selecting a vCLS datastore

Similarly, if you are using an HCI Mesh with a single ESXi node in the vSphere cluster, then neither DRS nor HA is relevant. Thus, vCLS can be disabled. This is achieved by enabling a feature called 'Retreat Mode' for vCLS. Refer to VMware KB article 80472 for details on how to turn on 'Retreat Mode'.

One final consideration for administrators relates to maintenance mode. Administrators should now be cognizant of the fact that a vSAN datastore may be used by both the local cluster as well as remote clusters. Any maintenance mode operation could adversely impact the remote workloads on the shared vSAN datastore, not just the local ones. Actions that impact availability or performance, such as rebuilding and resynching of objects, will also affect objects belonging to remote workloads. It is something administrators, who so far have only needed to worry about local workloads, will need to consider when doing maintenance on clusters participating in HCI Mesh. This is especially true when doing operations such as taking a complete cluster offline for maintenance.

HCI Mesh Requirements and Limitations

This section attempts to highlight the main requirements and limitations of HCI Mesh as they relate to the vSAN ESA. Note that these are accurate at the time of writing, but many may change over time, as updated releases of vSAN appear. Once again, the authors recommend checking the vSAN Release Notes for future releases to see if any of these requirements/limitations have changed or been relaxed.

- HCI Mesh for vSAN ESA requires vSAN 8.0 U1 or later running on the server cluster
- Client clusters must be running vSphere or vSAN 8.0 U1 or later
- Stretched Clusters and 2-node configurations are not supported when using HCI Mesh with vSAN ESA
- A vSAN Datastore can be mounted by a maximum of 10 vSAN client clusters
- A vSAN cluster can mount a maximum of 5 remote vSAN datastores
- A vSAN Datastore can be mounted by up to 128 hosts. This includes the "local hosts" for that vSAN Datastore
- For vSAN ESA, both the mounting host/cluster and remote cluster need to be managed by the same vCenter Server and appear in the same Datacenter
- 25Gbps connectivity is required with 100Gbps preferred
- L2 and L3 connectivity are both supported
- RDMA is not supported
- IPv6 needs to be enabled on the hosts
- Network Load Balancing: LACP, Load-based teaming, and active/standby are all supported.
- Network Load Balancing: Dual VMkernel configuration / air-gapped configurations are explicitly not supported
- Data-in-transit encryption is not supported, data-at-rest encryption is supported
- VMs cannot span datastores, in other words, you cannot store the first VMDK on the local vSAN datastore and the second VMDK of the same VM on a remote vSAN datastore
- Remote provisioning (on a mounted remote vSAN datastore) of vSAN File Shares, iSCSI volumes, and/or CNS persistent volumes is not supported
- vSphere client clusters can mount a remote datastore powered by vSAN ESA, or vSAN OSA, but the client cluster can only mount one type. The client clusters cannot mount a mixture of remote vSAN ESA and vSAN OSA clusters.

Failure Scenarios

We have already discussed some of the failure scenarios in Chapter 4, "Architectural Details," and in Chapter 5, "VM Storage Policy and VM Provisioning". In those chapters, we explained the difference between *absent* components and *degraded* components. From an operational perspective, though, it is good to understand how a storage device failure, network problem, or host failure impacts your vSAN cluster. Before we discuss them, let's first shortly recap the two different failure states, because they are fundamental to these operational considerations:

- **Absent**: vSAN does not know what has happened to the component that is missing. A typical example of this is when a host has failed; vSAN cannot tell if it is a real failure or simply a reboot. When this happens, vSAN waits for 60 minutes by default before new replica components are created. This is called the CLOM delay timeout, CLOM being shorthand for Cluster Level Object Manager.

- **Degraded**: vSAN knows what has happened to the component that is missing. A typical example of when this can occur is when a storage device has failed, and it is generating sense codes for the NVMe devices that allow vSAN to understand that this device has failed and is never recovering. When this happens, vSAN instantly spawns new components to make all impacted objects compliant again with their selected policy.

One other feature that should be mentioned here is the concept of durability components or delta components, which are part of the OSA, and introduced with limitations for the ESA in vSAN 8.0 U1. Durability components provide a mechanism to maintain the required level of resilience for vSAN objects (e.g., virtual machines) when components go absent. If a host is placed into maintenance mode, a durability component is created on behalf of the components stored on that host, ensuring all recently written data remains resilient. An ancillary benefit to durability components is that once a host exits out of maintenance mode, the updated data can be merged quickly into the primary components that comprise an object.

For the ESA, the support of durability components is limited to objects using RAID-5 or RAID-6 erasure coding and is used on during planned maintenance activities, such as entering a host into maintenance mode.

Now that you know what the different states are, and understand the concept of durability components, let's look again at the different types of failures, or at least the "most" common, and what the impact is. Note that in all the scenarios below, durability components are used to improve both the resync times and provide a higher level of availability to vSAN

Storage Device Failure

A storage device failure is probably the most common failure that can happen in any storage environment, and vSAN is no different. The question, of course, is this: How does vSAN handle a storage device failure? What if it is doing a write or read to or from that device after it has failed?

The vSAN ESA has simplified the considerations of storage devices claimed by the cluster. Since the ESA does not use the concept of disk groups, nor discrete caching devices, we no longer need to contemplate the failure scenarios around disk groups and the behavior of a failure of a discrete capacity device versus a caching device. The vSAN ESA treats all claimed devices as individual contributors of storage. Thus, if a storage device fails, it only impacts the data on that device.

If a read error is returned from a storage component in a RAID-1 configuration, vSAN checks to see whether a replica component exists and reads from that instead. Every RAID-1 object is created, by default, with *failures to tolerate* set to 1, which means that there are always two identical copies of your object available.

There are two separate scenarios when it comes to reading data. The first one is where the problem is recoverable, and the second one is an irrecoverable situation. When the issue is recoverable, the I/O error is reported to the *Distributed Object Manager* (DOM) object owner. A component re-creation takes place to replace the failed one. This new component is synchronized with the help of the functioning/working component or components, and when that is completed, the errored component is deleted. However, if for whatever reason, no replica component exists, vSAN will report an I/O error to the VM. This is an unlikely scenario and something an administrator would have had to create a policy with *failures to tolerate* of 0 specifically set, or there have been multiple failures or maintenance mode operations on the cluster.

Like read errors, write failures are also propagated up to the DOM object owner. The components are marked as degraded, and a component re-creation is initiated. When the component re-creation is completed, the cluster directory (*cluster monitoring, membership, and directory service* [CMMDS]) is updated.

As mentioned previously, the vSphere Client provides the ability to monitor how much data is being resynced in the event of a failure. Selecting the vSAN cluster object in the vCenter Server inventory, then selecting Monitor, vSAN, and then "Resyncing Objects" will show this information. It will report on the number of resyncing objects, the bytes left to resync, and the estimated time for the resyncing to complete, as shown below.

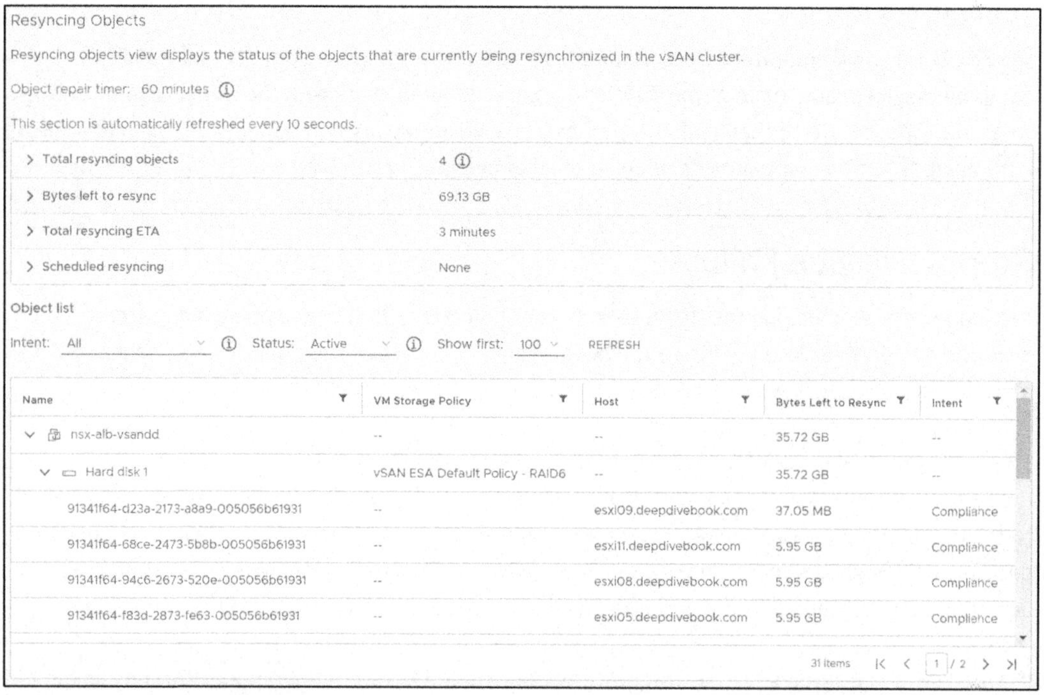

Figure 150: Resyncing Objects

Storage Device Failure with Erasure Coding

As you have read in chapter 5, "VM Storage Policies and VM Provisioning", the vSAN ESA supports different data placement schemes. In addition to RAID-1, vSAN supports both RAID-5 and RAID-6 erasure coding, which allows data to be stored resiliently, with higher levels of space efficiency than RAID-1 mirroring, and with the ESA, no compromises in performance.

For the vSAN ESA, RAID-5 uses one of two erasure coding schemes depending on the size of the cluster. For cluster sizes smaller than 6 hosts, it will use a 2+1 scheme, spreading the data and parity fragments across a minimum of 3 hosts. For cluster sizes that are 6 or more hosts, it uses a 4+1 schema, spreading the data and parity fragments across a minimum of 5 hosts. Both of these RAID-5 erasure codes can tolerate one host failure while maintaining data availability. To tolerate two failures, one can use a RAID-6 erasure code. It will use a 4+2 scheme, which spreads the data and parity fragments across a minimum of 6 hosts.

To understand how failures are handled with erasure coding, it is important to understand that it uses Exclusive OR (XOR) operations on the data to calculate the parity. With RAID-5, let's take the example of a single disk failure. If it is simply the parity fragment of a VM that is impacted, then obviously reads and writes can continue to flow, but there is no protection for the VM until parity is rebuilt elsewhere in the cluster. If it is one of the data fragments that is impacted, then the missing data blocks are calculated for reads by using the remaining data components and the XOR parity results. With these pieces of information, the missing data blocks can be re-calculated if an I/O request is issued prior to the data being rebuilt. This is known as an inline functional repair.

With RAID-6, there is a double parity calculation to allow any VM with this policy setting to tolerate a double failure. If the double failure impacts both parity segments, then that is ok since we still have a full copy of the data. If it impacts 2 data segments, then that is ok since the data can be rebuilt using the remaining data and the parity. If the double failure impacts both a data segment and a parity segment, then this is ok as well as we simply rebuild the missing data blocks using the remaining data blocks and the remaining parity segment, similar to the approach described with RAID-5 erasure coding.

The advantage of erasure coding versus RAID-1 mirroring is guaranteed levels of space savings when storing data resiliently. Since the vSAN ESA uses a log-structured file system in a way that always stores the data as a fully aligned, full stripe writes, it does not have the performance penalties that were commonly associated with erasure coding when using the OSA.

Host Failure

Assuming vSAN VM storage policies have been created with *failures to tolerate* set to at least 1, a host failure in a vSAN cluster is like a host failure in a cluster where the storage device has failed. The main difference is that the vSAN host that has failed will have outdated object components when the host returns.

In the case of a host failure, after 60 minutes vSAN will start re-creating components because vSAN assumes the likelihood of the host returning online is now slim. Most likely this is not a transient failure. When the reconstruction of the storage objects is completed, the cluster directory (CMMDS) is once again updated with new information about the object. In fact, it is updated at each step of the process, from failure detection to the start of resync, resync progress, and when the rebuild is complete.

The ESA uses much of the same detection and repair logic found in recent versions of the OSA. For example, if a failed host comes back online sometime after the CLOMD repair delay timeout has expired, vSAN will look at the amount of the data remaining for the new component to complete rebuilding and compare it to how long it would take to repair the component on the host that was previously offline. It will then choose the option that will be quickest to complete and discard the unused component after the resynchronization completes. vSAN maintains a bitmap of changed blocks in the event of components of an object being unable to synchronize due to a failure on a host, network, or storage device. This allows updates to vSAN objects composed of two or more components to be reconciled after a failure. Let's use a RAID-1 example to explain this. If a host with replica A of object X has been partitioned from the rest of the cluster, the surviving components of X have a quorum and data availability, so they continue functioning and serving writes and reads. These surviving components of X are the other capacity leg replica/mirror and possibly one or more of the performance leg replicas/mirrors. While A is "absent," all writes performed to X are persistently tracked in a bitmap by vSAN, that is, the bitmap is tracking the regions that are still out of sync. If the partitioned host with replica A comes back and vSAN decides to reintegrate it with the remaining components of object X, the bitmap is used to resynchronize component A.

vSAN will also be able to resume resynchronization should there be any interruption in the repair process, possibly caused by a transient network interruption. This type of safeguard allows vSAN to recognize data already resynchronized prior to the interruption and prevents unnecessary reprocessing of already resynchronized data.

While the vSAN ESA uses much of the same detection and repair logic found in recent versions of the OSA, the one exception at the time of this writing is the use of durability components. The use of durability components in the ESA is limited to vSAN 8.0 U1 and will only be used during planned maintenance events such as entering a host into maintenance mode. Whereas the OSA will use durability components for unplanned host failures in addition to planned maintenance events.

We've covered how vSAN handles data failures, but what happens to a VM? When a host has failed, all VMs that were running on the host at the time of the failure will be restarted by vSphere HA. vSphere HA can restart the VM on any available host in the cluster whether or not it is hosting vSAN components, as demonstrated in the next diagram.

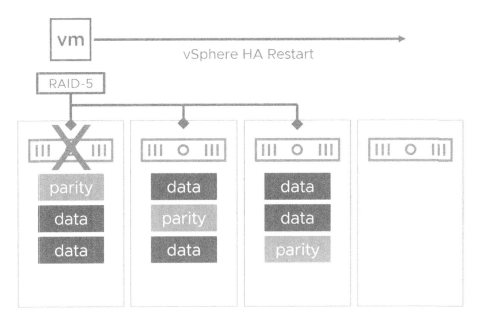

Figure 151: vSAN 1 host failed, HA restart

In the event of an isolation of a host, vSphere HA can and will also restart the impacted VMs. As this is a slightly more complex scenario, let's look at it in more depth.

Network Partition

A vSAN network partition could occur when there is a vSAN network failure. In other words, some hosts can end up on one side of the vSAN cluster, and the remaining hosts on another side. vSAN health findings will surface warnings related to network issues in the event of a partition. There has also been a significant enhancement to Network in the recent version to assist with troubleshooting network issues.

After explaining the host and disk failure scenarios in the previous sections, it is now time to describe how isolations and partitions are handled in a vSAN cluster. Let's look at a typical scenario first and explain what happens during a network partition based on this scenario.

In the scenario depicted in the next diagram, vSAN is running a single VM on ESXi-01. This VM has been provisioned using a VM storage policy that has the *number of failures to tolerate* set to 1 using RAID-5. We will use RAID-5 erasure coding in these examples since RAID-5 and RAID-6 will be the dominant data placement scheme used for most clusters using the ESA.

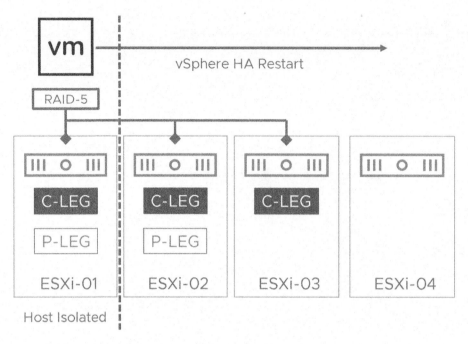

Figure 152: vSAN I/O flow: Failures to tolerate = 1

Because vSAN has the capability to run VMs on hosts that are not holding any active storage components of that VM, this question arises: What happens in the case where the network is isolated? As you can imagine, the vSAN network plays a big role here, made even bigger when you realize that it is also used by vSphere HA for network heart beating. For that reason, as mentioned before, vSAN must be configured before vSphere HA is enabled, so that the vSAN network is used. The following steps describe how vSphere HA and vSAN will react to an isolation event:

- HA will detect there are no network heartbeats received from esxi-01 on the vSAN network.
- HA primary will try to ping the secondary esxi-01.
- HA will declare the secondary esxi-01 is unavailable.
- VMs on esxi-01 will be restarted on one of the other hosts, as shown in the next diagram.
- The vSphere administrator, through the vSphere HA isolation response setting, decides what happens to the original VM on the isolated host. Options are to power off, leave powered on, or disable. We recommend using power off.

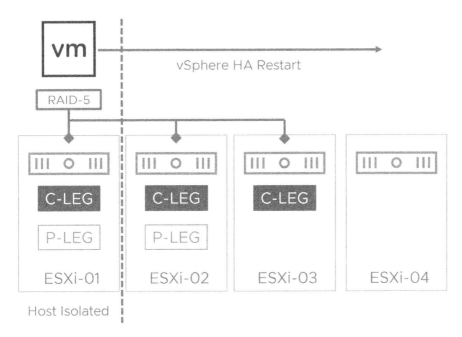

Figure 153: vSAN partition with one host isolated: HA restart

What if something has gone terribly wrong in my network and esxi-01 and esxi-04 end up as part of the same partition? What happens to the VMs then? Well, that is where quorum voting helps to make decisions on what actions to take. The next diagram should make it a bit easier to understand the behavior.

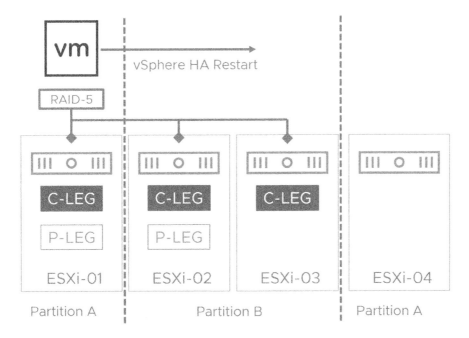

Figure 154: vSAN partition with multiple hosts in a partition

Now this scenario is indeed slightly more complex. There are two partitions. One partition is running the VM and has a portion of the capacity leg erasure coded stripe with parity and a performance leg component. Another partition has the other portion of the capacity leg erasure coded stripe with parity and a performance leg component. Guess what happens? For RAID-5, vSAN uses the vote count of the capacity and performance leg components in a partition to determine if any partition has quorum, which partition that should be. In this case, partition B has more than 50% of the components/votes of this object and therefore is the winner. This means that the VM will be restarted on either esxi-02 or esxi-03 by vSphere HA. Note, however that as this is a partition scenario and not an isolation. The isolation response will not be triggered, and as such the VM running on esxi-01 will not be powered off! The VM running on esxi-01 will not be able to access the vSAN datastore however, as it has lost quorum!

> **We would like to stress that it is highly recommended to set the isolation response to power off, even though it does not help in the above scenario.**

But what if esxi-01 and esxi-04 were isolated, what would happen then? The next diagram will show this, but as expected the result would be very similar to the partition above.

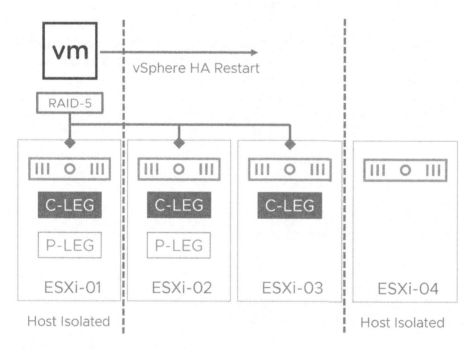

Figure 155: vSAN 2 hosts isolated: HA restart

Remember the rule we discussed earlier?

> *"The winner is declared based on the percentage of components available or percentage of votes available within that partition."*

If the partition has access to more than 50% of the components or votes (of an object), it has won. For each object, there can be at most one winning partition. This means that when esxi-01 and esxi-04 are isolated, either esxi-02 or esxi-03 can restart the VM because 60% of the components of the RAID-5 object reside within this part of the cluster.

To prevent these scenarios from occurring, it is most definitely recommended to ensure the vSAN network is made highly available through NIC teaming and redundant network switches, as discussed in Chapter 3, "vSAN Installation and Configuration." Note that in the above situation, as these hosts are isolated from the rest of the network, the isolation response will be triggered and the VM running on esxi-01 will be powered off by vSphere HA.

vCenter Server Failure Scenario

What if you would lose the vCenter Server? What will happen to vSAN, and how do you rebuild this environment? Even though vSAN is not dependent on vCenter Server, other components are. If, for instance, vCenter Server fails and a new instance needs to be created from scratch, what is the impact on your vSAN environment?

After you rebuild a new vCenter Server, you simply recreate a new vSAN-enabled cluster and add the hosts back to the cluster. vCenter Server is responsible for tracking the membership of hosts in a vSAN cluster. It uses a configuration generation identification number to continuously track the member state of the vCenter Server and the vSAN-enabled ESXi hosts. If vCenter Server is unavailable for a certain length of time, once it reestablishes communication with the vSAN cluster, it compares this generation ID number with the ESXi hosts. If they are not the same, vCenter Server realizes that changes have taken place since it was last online, so it requests an update from all of the hosts in the cluster to make sure its configuration is synchronized. There is no need for any administrative action here; this is all taken care of automatically. The latest configuration Generation number can be viewed on the ESXi hosts via the command `esxcli vsan cluster get`.

```
[root@esxi-dell-i:~] esxcli vsan cluster get
Cluster Information
   Enabled: true
   Current Local Time: 2018-10-10T14:09:26Z
   Local Node UUID: 5b8d18eb-4fb4-670a-94b7-246e962f4ab0
   Local Node Type: NORMAL
   Local Node State: AGENT
   Local Node Health State: HEALTHY
   Sub-Cluster Master UUID: 5b8d1919-8d9e-2806-dfb3-246e962f4978
   Sub-Cluster Backup UUID: 5b8d190c-5f7c-50d8-bbb8-246e962c23f0
   Sub-Cluster UUID: 52e934f3-5507-d5d8-30fa-9a9b392acc72
   Sub-Cluster Membership Entry Revision: 7
   Sub-Cluster Member Count: 4
   Sub-Cluster Member UUIDs: 5b8d1919-8d9e-2806-dfb3-246e962f4978, 5b8d190c-5f7c-50d8-
bbb8-246e962c23f0, 5b8d18f9-941f-f045-7457-246e962f48f8, 5b8d18eb-4fb4-670a-94b7-
246e962f4ab0
   Sub-Cluster Member HostNames: esxi-dell-l.rainpole.com, esxi-dell-k.rainpole.com, esxi-
dell-j.rainpole.com, esxi-dell-i.rainpole.com
   Sub-Cluster Membership UUID: 2a8f965b-671a-921c-0c8b-246e962f4978
   Unicast Mode Enabled: true
   Maintenance Mode State: OFF
   Config Generation: e4e74378-49e1-4229-bfe9-b14f675d23e6 10 2018-10-10T12:57:50.947
[root@esxi-dell-i:~]
```

One additional consideration, however, is that the loss of the vCenter Server will also mean the loss of the VM storage policies that the administrator has created. SPBM will not know about the previous VM storage policies and the VMs to which they were attached. vSAN, however, will still know exactly what the administrator had asked for, policy-wise, and keep enforcing it. Today, there is no way in the UI to export existing policies, but there is an application programming interface (API) for VM storage policies has been exposed. Using PowerCLI, administrators can export, import, and restore policies very quickly and easily. Refer to the official PowerCLI documentation (https://vmwa.re/powercli) for more detail on SPBM cmdlets.

Summary

vSAN has always provided the ability to easily accommodate change. The ability to scale up and scale out clusters as needed and connect to resources in other clusters all through the same UI makes many day-2 related tasks easy. With the introduction of the ESA, the vSAN team was able to take many of these common operational tasks, such as disk management, even easier and more intuitive in the UI. For those who prefer the command line, esxcli is a great alternative to the vSphere Client. For those who prefer PowerShell, VMware has a wide variety of PowerCLI to help automate your management tasks.

07

Stretched Cluster Use Case

This chapter was developed to provide insights and additional information on a very specific type of vSAN configuration, namely stretched clusters. In this chapter, we will describe some of the design considerations, operational procedures, and failure scenarios that relate to a stretched cluster configuration specifically. But first, why would anyone want a stretched cluster?

Stretched cluster configurations offer the ability to balance VMs between datacenters. The reason for doing so could be anything, be it disaster avoidance or, for instance, site maintenance. All of this can be achieved with no downtime from a VM perspective since compute, storage, and network are available across both sites. On top of that, a stretched cluster also provides the ability to actively load balance resources between locations without any constraints when desired.

What is a Stretched Cluster?

Before we get into it, let's first discuss what defines a vSAN stretched cluster. When we talk about a vSAN stretched cluster, we refer to the configuration that is deployed when the stretched cluster workflow is completed in the vSphere Client. This workflow explicitly leverages a witness host, which can be physical or virtual, and needs to be deployed in a third site. During the workflow, the vSAN cluster is set up across two sites, with preferably an identical number of ESXi hosts distributed evenly between the two sites and as stated, a witness host residing at a third site. The data sites are connected via a high bandwidth/low latency network link. The third site hosting the vSAN witness host is connected over a network to both active/active "data" sites. The connectivity between the data sites and the witness site can be via lower bandwidth/higher latency network links. The diagram below shows what this looks like from a logical point of view.

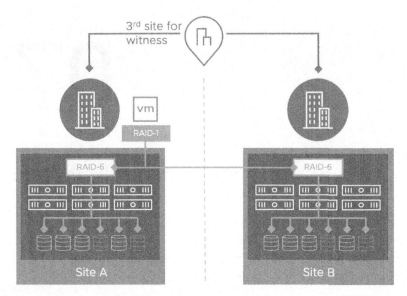

Figure 156: Stretched cluster scenario

Each site is configured as a vSAN fault domain. A maximum of three sites (two data, one witness) is supported in a stretched cluster configuration.

The nomenclature used to describe a vSAN Stretched Cluster configuration is X+Y+Z, where X is the number of ESXi hosts at data site A, Y is the number of ESXi hosts at data site B, and Z is the number of witness hosts at site C. Data sites are where VMs are deployed. The minimum supported configuration is 1+1+1 (3 nodes). Starting with vSAN 7.0 U2 the maximum configuration is 20+20+1 (41 nodes).

In vSAN stretched clusters, there is one witness host in a third location. For deployments that manage multiple stretched clusters, each cluster must have its own unique witness host, the shared witness deployment described in chapter 8 is not supported for a stretched cluster configuration at the time of writing. As mentioned before however, this witness host can be a virtual appliance, which does not even require a vSphere or vSAN license and is our preferred method of deployment for the witness.

By default, when a VM is deployed on a vSAN stretched cluster, it is deployed with a RAID-1 configuration. In previous versions of vSAN this was referred to as primary failures to tolerate. Thus, it will have one copy of its data on site A, the second copy of its data on site B, and a witness component placed on the witness host in site C. This configuration is achieved through fault domains. In the event of a complete site failure, there will be a full copy of the VM data as well as greater than 50% of the components available in the remaining two locations. This will allow the VM to remain available on the vSAN datastore. If the site which fails is the site where the VM is running, then the VM needs to be restarted on the other data site, vSphere HA will handle this task.

Note, however, that vSAN also provides the ability to specify what the level of protection within a site location should be. In previous versions of vSAN, this was referred to as secondary failures to tolerate. But before we dive further into all policy options, let's look at the configuration process first.

Requirements and Constraints

vSAN ESA stretched cluster configurations require vSphere 8.0.0 at a minimum. This implies both vCenter Server 8.0 and ESXi 8.0. This is the minimum version required for vSAN ESA stretched cluster support. However, we strongly recommend implementing the latest available version of vSAN, which at the time of writing is vSAN 8.0 Update 1. We have mentioned ESA a few times already, and at this point you may wonder why? Well, when it comes to vSAN OSA and vSAN ESA there are some differences, and even reasons why it may make more sense to go with vSAN ESA over vSAN OSA when deploying a stretched cluster configuration, we will explain that later in this chapter in a bit more detail.

From a licensing point of view, vSAN Enterprise is required to create stretched cluster configurations larger than 1+1+1. Yes, that is right, you could theoretically create a 1+1+1 stretched cluster configuration with the vSAN Standard or vSAN Advanced license and not breach the license agreement. However, in order to create a vSAN ESA cluster, at minimum the vSAN Advanced license is required. This means that it is possible to create a vSAN ESA 1+1+1 stretched cluster configuration with the vSAN Advanced license. Any cluster larger than 1+1+1 requires the vSAN Enterprise license.

There are no limitations placed on the edition of vSphere used for vSAN. However, for vSAN Stretched Cluster functionality, vSphere DRS is very desirable. DRS will provide initial placement of the workload and can also help with migrating VMs to their correct site when a site recovers after a failure. Otherwise, the administrator will have to manually carry out these tasks. Note that DRS is only available in the Enterprise Plus edition of vSphere.

As mentioned, both physical ESXi hosts and virtual appliances (nested ESXi host in a VM) are supported for the witness host. VMware is providing a pre-configured witness appliance for those customers who wish to use it. A witness host/VM cannot be shared between multiple vSAN stretched clusters. Also, note that VMware does not support cross hosting of Witness Appliances in a scenario where there are multiple stretched cluster configurations across two locations. That means that you can't run the witness of Stretched Cluster A on Stretched Cluster B when these two clusters are stretched across the same two geographical locations. At all times 3 locations are required to avoid any circular dependency during failure scenarios.

One thing we would like to point out is that SMP-FT, the enhanced Fault Tolerant VM mechanism introduced in vSphere 6.0, is supported on standard vSAN deployments, but at the time of writing is not supported on stretched cluster deployment. This support statement is true for both vSAN and *vSphere Metro Storage Cluster* (vMSC) based deployments unless you contain and pin all the SMP-FT VMs to a single location. How to do this is explained later in this chapter. The reason for this is the bandwidth and latency requirements associated with SMP-FT. vSAN iSCSI is fully supported in a vSAN ESA stretched cluster configuration.

Lastly, although vSAN ESA was not supported with HCI Mesh in vSAN 8.0, it is now supported with HCI-Mesh in 8.0 U1. However, we also want to point out that starting with vSAN Original Storage Architecture (OSA) version 8.0 U1, HCI Mesh and Stretched Clusters are a supported combination. Again, at the time of writing, this applies to vSAN OSA only, and such a configuration is not supported with vSAN ESA stretched clusters.

Now that we have discussed some of the constraints, let's look at the vSAN stretched cluster bandwidth and latency requirements.

Networking and Latency Requirements

When vSAN is deployed in a stretched cluster across multiple sites, certain networking requirements must be adhered to.

- Between data sites both Layer 2 and Layer 3 are supported
    - Layer-2 is recommended for simplicity
- Between the data sites and the witness site Layer 3 is required
    - This is to prevent I/O from being routed through a potentially low bandwidth witness site
- Maximum round trip latency between data sites is 5ms
- Maximum round trip latency between data sites and the witness site is 200ms
- A bandwidth of 25 Gbps between data sites is required for vSAN ESA
- A bandwidth of 100 Mbps between data sites and the witness site is recommended

Networking in any stretched vSphere deployment is always a hot topic. We expect this to be the same for vSAN stretched deployments. VMware has published two documents that hold a lot of detail about network bandwidth calculations and network topology considerations. The above bandwidth recommendations are exactly that, recommendations. Requirements for your environment can be determined by calculating the exact needs as explained in the following two documents.

- vSAN stretched cluster bandwidth sizing guidance - https://vmwa.re/bandwidth
- vSAN stretched cluster guide - https://vmwa.re/stretched

Witness Traffic Separation and Mixed MTU

By default, when using vSAN Stretched Clusters, the Witness VMkernel interface tagged for vSAN traffic must have connectivity with each vSAN data node's VMkernel interface tagged with vSAN traffic. It is also supported to have a dedicated VMkernel interface for witness traffic separation on stretched cluster configurations. This allows for more flexible configurations, but also lowers the risk of having data traffic traverse the witness network. Configuration of the Witness VMkernel interface at the time of writing can be achieved through the command line interface utility esxcli. Below is an example of the command used in our lab to designate the VMkernel interface vmk1 to witness traffic.

```
esxcli vsan network ip add -i vmk1 -T=witness
```

> **Note that the vSAN Witness Host will only have a VMkernel interface tagged for "vSAN Traffic". It will not have traffic tagged as "Witness".**

One thing to note is that even in the case of witness traffic separation it is still required to have different networks for vSAN traffic and witness traffic. Not doing so may lead to multi-homing issues and various warnings in vSAN Skyline Health.

vSAN ESA Efficiency

To ensure data resilience across sites, a vSAN stretched cluster must send writes across an inter-site link (ISL). It must do so as efficiently as possible as the ISL is limited by bandwidth and latency. To address this, vSAN (both OSA and ESA) uses a "proxy owner" to minimize the use of the ISL. It lives on the opposite site of the object owner and will receive a cloned write from the object owner so that it can process subsequent I/O within the site. In other words, in the situation we sketched in the next diagram, a write from the VM located on the preferred site is sent to the proxy on secondary location before RAID-1 is applied within the secondary location.

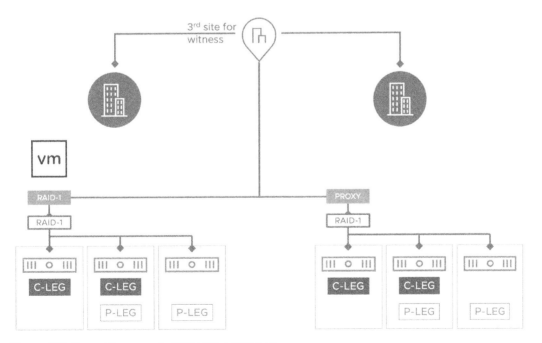

Figure 157: Proxy Owner and vSAN ESA efficiency

In the vSAN ESA, the method described above remains the same, but with a twist. The vSAN ESA compresses the data once before cloning that write across the ISL, when compression is enabled. Ultimately, this reduces the data sent across the ISL between the two sites for the same workloads when using vSAN ESA. This new approach will also provide a higher effective write throughput across the ISL, as reducing the amount of data to transmit results in a lower amount of consumed bandwidth. This ultimately enables you to run more VMs on the same stretched cluster.

vSAN ESA also prepares the data differently than vSAN OSA. As explained in previous chapters, it will coalesce many small writes in memory before persisting the data to disk. Fewer I/Os that are larger will reduce the number of write operations, and provide a more uniform method of data delivery across the ISL. This more efficient approach reduces resource utilization and can improve the performance consistency of VMs in a stretched cluster.

When using the vSAN OSA, VM performance could be affected if the VM used a storage policy that applied a secondary level of resilience to the VM - especially RAID-5/6 erasure coding. This was primarily due to the read-modify-write step that occurred when committing that RAID-5/6 stripe with parity at each site before it could send the write acknowledgment back to the guest VM.

The ESA in vSAN 8.0 writes data using fewer resources. It eliminates the read-modify-write step when writing data resiliently using erasure coding. Incoming write I/Os from the guest will be coalesced and briefly written as a 2-way or 3-way mirror (depending on the storage policy) before sending the write acknowledgment to the VM. This approach is also used in a vSAN ESA stretched cluster, where the write operation is cloned to the proxy owner, and the 2-way or 3-way mirror occurs on each site before it writes it as an efficient, fully aligned, full stripe write. Avoiding the read-modify-write sequence found in the OSA can lower the write latency for your VMs while freeing up additional host resources.

Another benefit of vSAN ESA over vSAN OSA is how RAID-5 has been implemented. With vSAN OSA when the number of hosts within each location is limited and you want to have local protection within a location you unfortunately are limited to RAID-1. With vSAN ESA you have the option to go for RAID-5. Depending on the size of the cluster, you can deploy a 2+1 configuration or a 4+1 configuration in each location as specified within the storage policy. Where a RAID-1 configuration has a 100% capacity overhead, RAID-5 in a 2+1 configuration only has a 50% overhead, yet both can be used on a vSAN ESA 3+3+1 Stretched Cluster configuration. Before we go to deep, let's look at some other new concepts that are introduced when configuring a stretched cluster first.

New Concepts in vSAN Stretched Cluster

A common question is how a stretched cluster differs from regular fault domains. Fault domains enable what might be termed "rack awareness" where the components of VMs could be distributed amongst multiple hosts in multiple racks. Should a rack failure event occur, the VM (from a storage point of view) would continue to be available. These racks would typically be hosted in the same datacenter, and if there were a datacenter-wide event, fault domains would not be able to assist with VM availability.

A stretched cluster essentially builds on the foundation of fault domains, and now provides what might be termed "datacenter awareness." A vSAN stretched cluster can now provide availability for VMs even if a datacenter, or site, suffers a catastrophic outage. This is achieved primarily through intelligent component placement of VM objects across sites, alongside features such as site preference, read locality, and the witness host.

The witness host must have a connection to both the master vSAN node and the backup vSAN node to join the cluster (the master and backup were discussed previously in Chapter 4, "Architectural Details"). In steady-state operations, the master node resides in the "preferred site"; the backup node resides in the "secondary site."

Note that the witness appliance ships with its own license, so it does not consume any of your vSphere or vSAN licenses. Hence it is our recommendation to always use the appliance over a physical witness host. The Witness Appliance also has a different icon in the vSphere Client than a regular ESXi host, allowing you to easily identify the witness appliance as shown below. This is only the case for the witness appliance, however. A physical appliance will show up in the client as a regular host and also requires a vSphere license!

Figure 158: Witness appliance icon

Another added benefit of the witness appliance is the operational aspect of the witness. If for whatever reason maintenance is needed on the physical host, the witness appliance will enable you to do maintenance without disruption when the appliance runs on a vSphere cluster as vSphere provides the ability to migrate the appliance while running. On top of that, in case the witness appliance fails, you also can simply replace the current witness by deploying a new one and initiating the "Change Witness Host" wizard in the Fault Domains section of the UI as shown in the next screenshot. Now, of course, this is also possible when you have a spare physical host, but in our experience, customers do not have unused hardware available for a quick replacement.

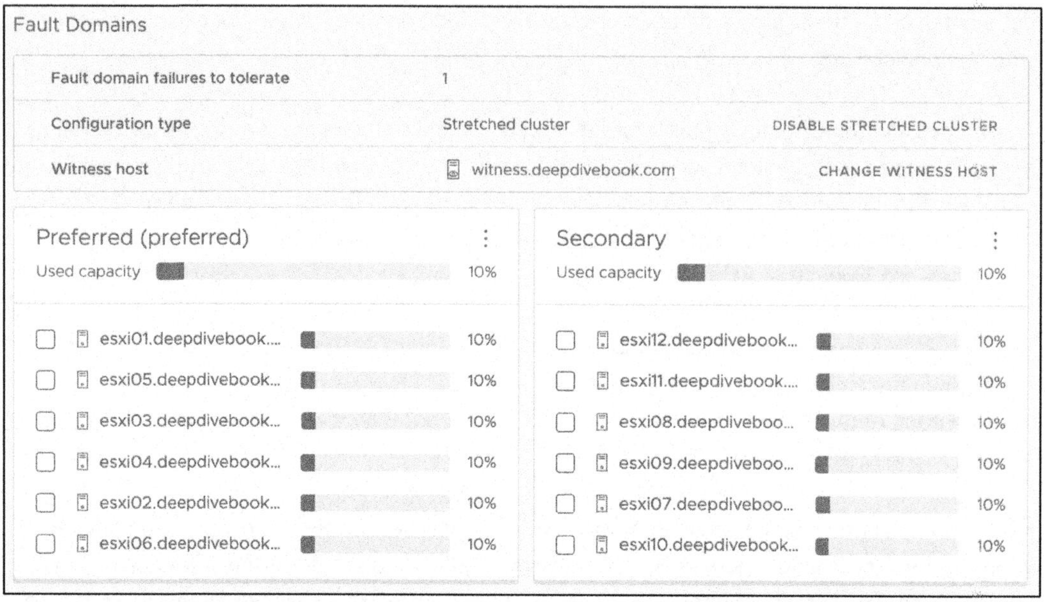

Figure 159: Change witness host

Another new term that will show up during the configuration of a stretched cluster, and was just mentioned, is "preferred site" and "secondary site." The "preferred" site is the site that vSAN wishes to remain running when there is a network partition between the sites and the data sites can no longer communicate. One might say that the "preferred site" is the site expected to have the most reliability.

Since VMs can run on any of the two sites, if network connectivity is lost between site 1 and site 2, but both still have connectivity to the witness, the "preferred site" binds itself to the witness and gains ownership over all components. The vSAN components on the preferred site remain active, while the vSAN components on the secondary site are marked instantly as absent as quorum is lost. This also means that, in this situation, any VMs running in the secondary site will need to be restarted in the preferred site to be usable and useful again. vSphere HA, when enabled on the stretched cluster, will take care of this automatically for you.

In non-stretched vSAN clusters, a VM's read operations are distributed across all replica copies of the data in the cluster. In the case of a policy setting of *Failures to tolerate* =1 using RAID-1, which results in two copies of the data, 50% of the reads will come from replica 1, and 50% will come from replica 2. In the case of a policy setting of *Failures to tolerate* =1 using RAID-5, which results in either a 2+1 configuration or a 4+1 configuration, the reads will be distributed across the cluster.

However, we wish to avoid this situation with a vSAN stretched cluster, as we do not wish to read data over the inter-site link, which could add unnecessary latency to the I/O and waste precious inter-site link bandwidth. Since vSAN stretched cluster supports a maximum of (primary) *Failures to tolerate* = 1, there will be two copies of the data (replica 1 and replica 2). Rather than doing 50% reads from site 1 and 50% reads from site 2 across the site link, the goal is to do 100% of the read

IO for any given VM from the local site, wherever possible. In previous versions of vSAN, this was a per host setting. Starting with vSAN 6.7U1, this setting, called Site Read Locality, has been placed into the Advanced options under vSAN > Configure > Services. This makes it extremely simple to set cluster wide, as shown below:

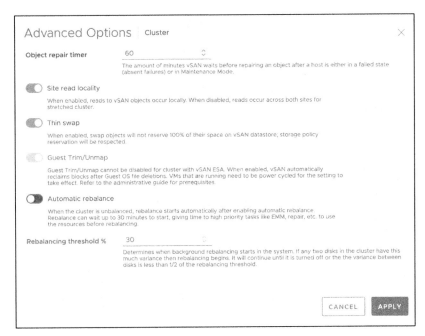

Figure 160: Site Read Locality

The distributed object manager (DOM) in vSAN, is responsible for dealing with read locality. DOM is not only responsible for the creation of storage objects in the vSAN cluster, but it is also responsible for providing distributed data access paths to these objects. There is a single DOM owner per object. There are three roles within DOM: client, owner, and component manager. The DOM owner coordinates access to the object, including reads, locking, and object configuration and reconfiguration. All object changes and writes also go through the owner. In vSAN stretched cluster, an enhancement to the DOM owner of an object means that it will now consider the "fault domain" where the owner runs and will read 100% from the replica that is in the same "fault domain."

Witness Failure Resilience

Every installation of a vSAN stretched cluster has a witness host of some sort. As mentioned, this can be a virtual appliance or a physical host. The question that always arises is what about the availability of the witness host, as it plays a crucial role during failure scenarios?

Over the years we have had customers asking if it was supported to enable vSphere Fault Tolerance (FT) on a witness appliance. Common questions pertained to whether or not they could clone the witness appliance, leave it on standby, and power it on when the "active" witness appliance had failed? Similarly, they asked if they should back up the witness appliance? The answer to all these questions is **no**. It is not supported to enable FT on the appliance, it is not supported to backup and recover the appliance, and it is not recommended to clone the appliance either.

Starting with vSAN 7.0 U3 a new feature was introduced around Witness failure resilience. What is this feature exactly? Let's look at the diagram of the stretched cluster again.

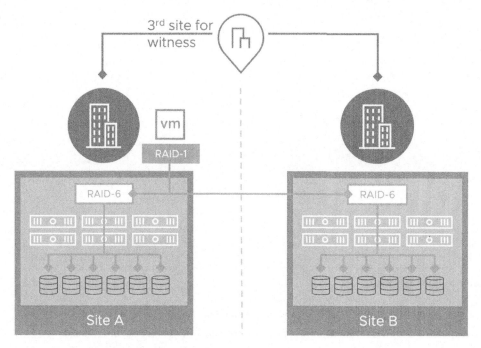

Figure 161: Stretched cluster scenario

In the diagram, we have 3 locations. In the case where Site A fails, all VMs will be restarted in Site B. If, however, at a later stage the witness is impacted by a failure, all VMs running would be inaccessible. Why? Well, 2 out of 3 sites have failed and as a result, so we have lost quorum. This is where the new witness failure resilience feature comes into play. Starting with vSAN 7.0 U3, when a site has failed, vSAN will recalculate the votes for all objects. This is because it is assuming that the witness may also be impacted by a failure over time. This recalculation of votes can take up to five minutes, depending on the number of objects/VMs. If the witness now fails, after the recalculation has been completed, the VMs (running in Site B) will remain running. As votes have been recalculated quorum will not be lost.

In the "full site failure" scenario we will demonstrate what that looks like from a votes perspective by inspecting the objects through rvc, the Ruby vSphere Console command line tool, in the failure scenario section of this chapter.

Configuration of a Stretched Cluster

The installation of a vSAN stretched cluster is almost identical to how fault domains are implemented, with a couple of additional steps. This part of the chapter will walk the reader through a stretched cluster configuration.

Before we get started with the actual configuration of a stretched cluster, we will need to ensure the witness host is installed, configured, and accessible from both data sites. This will most likely involve the addition of static routes to the ESXi hosts and witness appliance, which will be covered shortly. When configuring your vSAN stretched cluster, only data hosts must be in the (vSAN) cluster object in vCenter Server. The witness host must remain outside of the cluster and must not be added to the vSAN cluster.

The deployment of the witness host is pretty much straightforward and like the deployment of most virtual appliances as shown below. One thing to point out however is that there are different virtual appliances on vmware.com/download available, one for the OSA and one for the ESA. Make sure to download the correct one before you get started. Also, in our example below we have used a version pre 8.0 U1, so the build number and version you will deploy will be different. However, the process remains the same.

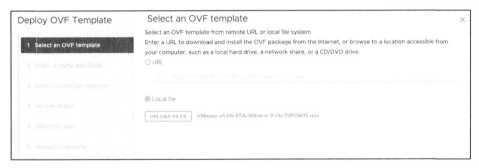

Figure 162: Witness appliance deployment

The only real decisions that need to be made is regarding the expected size of the stretched cluster configuration, and of course where the Witness Appliance is hosted. Note, that the witness appliance should always be hosted in a third location, and it cannot run on any of the ESXi hosts which are part of the stretched cluster configuration. This to ensure that in the case of a site isolation vSAN can properly determine who has ownership of the data. We have seen customers hosting the witness appliance in one of the two locations where their vSAN stretched cluster is also running. If the location which holds the witness, and a portion of the vSAN stretched cluster hosts, goes down, then the full stretched cluster will be unavailable as quorum is lost.

There are two options offered in terms of size for vSAN ESA. As shown in the below screenshot, a "large" deployment can hold up to 21,000 witness components. This means that if a VM consists of four objects, the cluster can host up to 5250 VMs, as each object requires a witness component to be stored on the witness host. The "Extra Large" configuration can store up to 64,000 witness components. So, depending on the number of objects per VM, and the number of VMs per cluster, you will have to determine which Witness Appliance size to deploy, in general Large should suffice.

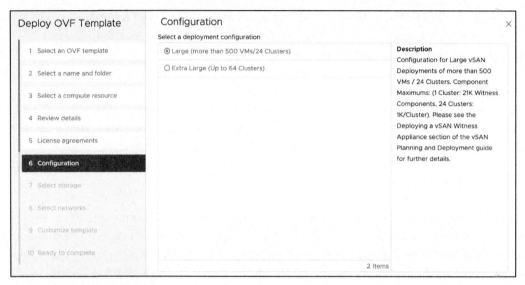

Figure 163: Configuration size

Next, the datastore where the witness appliance will need to be stored and the network that will be used for the witness appliance will need to be selected. Note that you will need to specify the destination network for both witness traffic (secondary network) and management traffic.

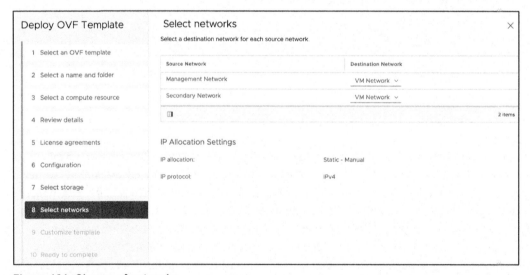

Figure 164: Change of networks

Next, you will have the option to customize the OVF Template by providing networking information, such as IP address and DNS, for the management network. On top of that, the root password for the virtual ESXi host will need to be entered on this screen as shown in the screenshot below.

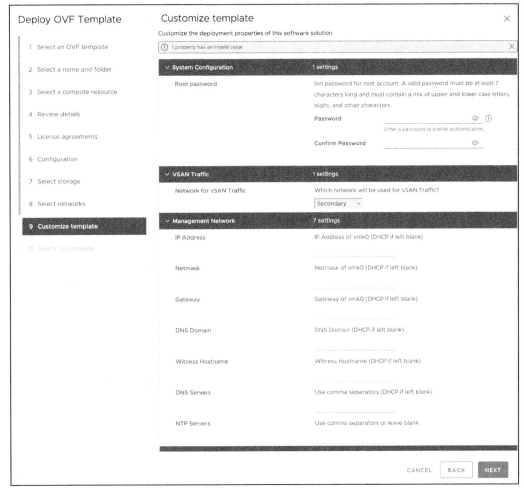

Figure 165: Change of networks

After this has been done and the witness has been deployed it can be added to the vCenter Server inventory where the stretched cluster configuration is deployed as a host. But remember not to add it to any type of vSphere or vSAN cluster; it must remain outside the cluster as a stand-alone host. One thing to stress, when you add it to vCenter Server, make sure the "Virtual SAN Witness" license is selected as demonstrated in the next screenshot.

Figure 166: Witness License

Once the witness appliance/nested ESXi host has been added to vCenter Server, the next step is to configure the vSAN network correctly on the witness. When the witness is selected in the vCenter Server inventory, navigate to Manage > Networking > Virtual Switches. The witness has two port groups predefined called Management Network and *secondaryPG. Do not remove these port groups, as it has a special modification to make the MAC addresses on the network adapters match the nested ESXi MAC addresses.*

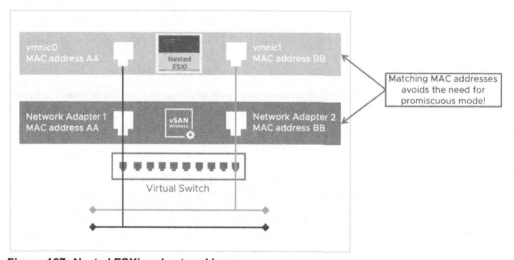

Figure 167: Nested ESXi and networking

Finally, before we can configure the vSAN stretched cluster, we need to ensure that the vSAN network on the hosts residing in the data sites can reach the witness host's vSAN network, and vice-versa. To address this, there are two options:

1. Define a static route
2. Override the default gateway for the vSAN VMkernel adapter

Static routes tell the TCP/IP stack to use a different route to reach a particular network rather than using the default gateway. We can instruct the TCP/IP stack on the data hosts to use a different network route to reach the vSAN network on the witness host rather than via the default gateway, and similarly, we can tell the witness host to use an alternate route to reach the vSAN network on the data hosts rather than via the default gateway.

Note once again that in most situations, the vSAN network is most likely a stretched L2 broadcast domain between the data sites, but L3 is required to reach the vSAN network of the witness appliance. Therefore, static routes are needed between the data hosts and the witness host for the vSAN network but may not be required for the data hosts on different sites to communicate with each other over the vSAN network.

The esxcli commands used to add a static route is:
```
esxcli network ip route ipv4 add -n <remote network> -g <gateway>
```

As mentioned, the second option is to override the default gateway and specify a specific gateway for your vSAN environment. This gateway will need to have a route to your witness network. Using this method avoids the need to manually enter routes using the CLI and is preferred for most customers. The screenshot below shows how to override the default gateway.

Figure 168: Override default gateway

Lastly, before we create the cluster, we will need to test the network configuration. To do so, we use the vmkping -I <vmk> <ipaddress> command to check that the witness and physical hosts can communicate over the vSAN network. Now that the witness is up and accessible, forming a vSAN stretched cluster takes less than a couple of minutes. The following are the steps that should be followed to install vSAN stretched cluster.

Configure Step 1a: Create a vSAN Stretched Cluster

In this example, there are thirteen hosts available. Six hosts reside in each site of this stretched cluster. The thirteenth host is the witness host, it is in the same virtual datacenter and is not added to the cluster, but it has been added as an ESXi host to this vCenter Server. Note, that physically this witness host is located in a third location. This example is a 6+6+1 deployment, meaning six ESXi hosts at the preferred site, six ESXi hosts at the secondary site, and one witness host in a third location.

Depending on how you are configuring your cluster you can decide to either create the stretched cluster during the creation of the vSAN cluster itself or do this after the fact in the fault domain view. Both workflows are similar and so is the result. We are going to demonstrate how to create a vSAN stretched cluster out of an existing cluster, simply because we have already shown the configuration of a normal cluster using the Quickstart workflow in chapter 3.

Configure Step 1b: Create Stretch Cluster

If your vSAN cluster has already been formed, it is easy to create a stretched cluster configuration separately. To configure stretched cluster and fault domains when a vSAN cluster already exists, navigate to the cluster object followed by Configure > vSAN > Fault Domains view as shown below, and click on the button "configure" in the stretched cluster section, which begins the stretched cluster configuration.

Figure 169: Start of stretched cluster creation

Depending on whether you create the vSAN cluster as part of the workflow you may need to claim disks as well when the vSAN cluster is set up.

Configure Step 2: Assign Hosts to Sites

At this point, hosts can now be assigned to stretch cluster sites as shown in the figure below. Note that the names have been preassigned. As described earlier, the preferred site is the one that will run VMs if there is a split-brain scenario in the cluster. In this example, hosts esxi01 - esxi06 will remain in the preferred site, and hosts esxi07 - esxi12 will be assigned to the secondary site.

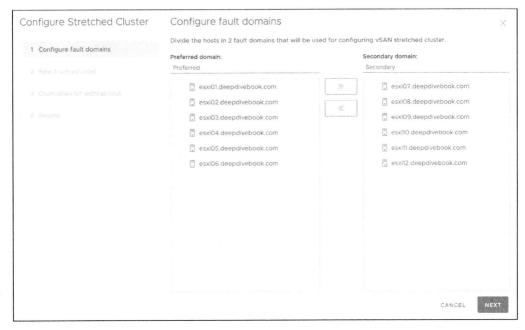

Figure 170: Host selection and site placement

Configure Step 3: Select a Witness Host and Claim Disks

The next step is to select the witness host. At this point, host "witness.deepdivebook.com" is chosen. Note once again that this host does not reside in the cluster. It is outside of the vSAN ESA cluster.

Figure 171: Witness host selection

When the witness is selected, NVMe devices need to be chosen to create a storage pool. This section, however, is only displayed when not using the preconfigured Witness Appliance. We are including it in the book for completeness sake. In our lab we used a virtual witness but did not have the ability to test with the appliance yet, as it was not available at the time of writing. The Witness Appliance is available however at the time of the release of vSAN 8.0 U1.

Figure 172: Witness disk claim

Configure Step 4: Verify the Configuration

Verify that the preferred fault domain and the secondary fault domains have the desired hosts, and that the witness host is the desired witness host as shown below and click **Finish** to complete the configuration.

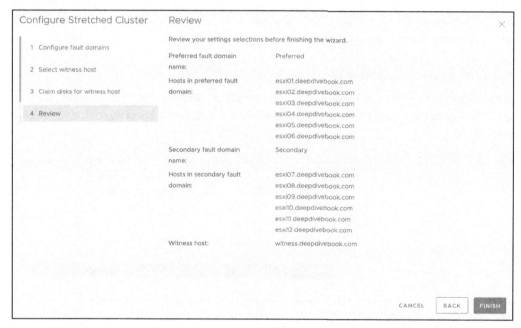

Figure 173: Summary of a stretched cluster configuration

When the stretched cluster has completed configuration, which can take several seconds, verify that the fault domain view is as expected, as shown in the next screenshot.

Fault Domains

Fault domain failures to tolerate	1	
Configuration type	Stretched cluster	DISABLE STRETCHED CLUSTER
Witness host	witness.deepdivebook.com	CHANGE WITNESS HOST

Preferred (preferred) :

Used capacity 10%

	esxi01.deepdivebook....	10%
	esxi05.deepdivebook...	10%
	esxi03.deepdivebook...	10%
	esxi04.deepdivebook...	10%
	esxi02.deepdivebook...	10%
	esxi06.deepdivebook...	10%

Secondary :

Used capacity 10%

	esxi12.deepdivebook...	10%
	esxi11.deepdivebook....	10%
	esxi08.deepdiveboo...	10%
	esxi09.deepdiveboo...	10%
	esxi07.deepdiveboo...	10%
	esxi10.deepdivebook...	10%

Figure 174: Stretched Cluster view

Configure Step 5: Skyline Health Stretched Cluster

Before doing anything else, use vSAN Skyline Health to ensure that all the stretched cluster health findings have passed. Depending on how the cluster is configured, you will potentially see various failed health findings. This is probably because of the fact that we have just stretched the cluster and various objects which reside on the cluster are now stretched across the cluster incorrectly and are not adhering to their associated policy.

Figure 175: Stretched cluster health

If we look at the "vSAN optimal datastore default policy configuration" check first, then we immediately notice that vSAN has recognized that the cluster is now a stretched cluster and that the default policy is not stretched. The next screenshot demonstrates this.

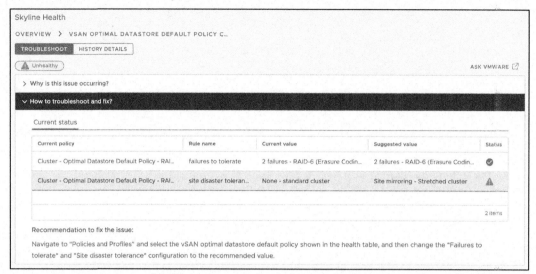

Figure 176: vSAN optimal datastore default policy configuration failed

What we will do next is change the configuration of the default policy as suggested by the Skyline Health findings.

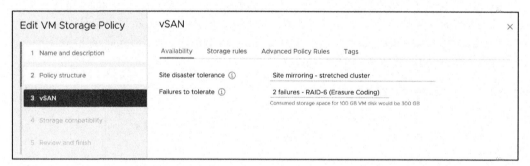

Figure 177: Default policy changes

After the changes are made, vSAN will inform you that the policy (most likely) is being used by multiple objects and if you want to apply the policy to those objects manually or now. We select now and save the changes by clicking "Yes". This will then automatically result in a resync of those objects to ensure they are compliant again.

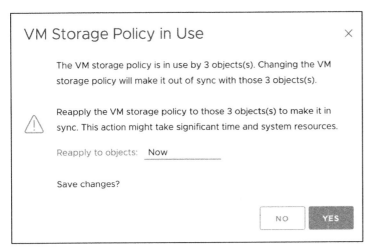

Figure 178: VM Storage Policy in Use

You can check the progress of the resync in the "Resyncing Objects" view on your cluster object under Monitors - vSAN.

If we now click "Retest" on Skyline Health, some of our problems should be resolved. Unfortunately, as can be seen in the next screenshot, not all problems have been solved.

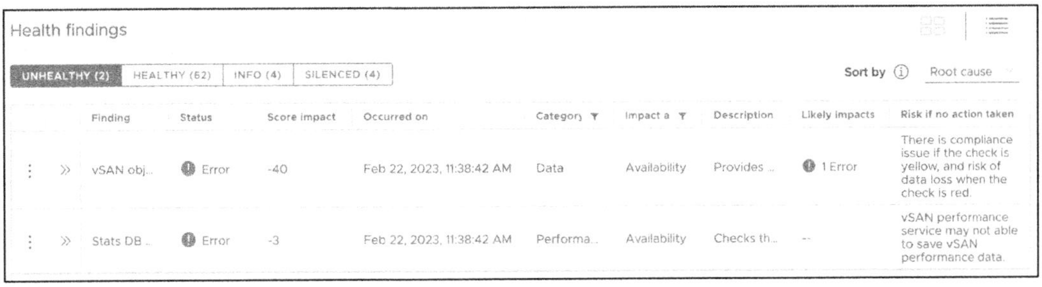

Health findings									
UNHEALTHY (2)	HEALTHY (62)	INFO (4)	SILENCED (4)				Sort by ⓘ	Root cause	
	Finding	Status	Score impact	Occurred on	Category ▼	Impact a ▼	Description	Likely impacts	Risk if no action taken
⋮ ≫	vSAN obj..	⊘ Error	-40	Feb 22, 2023, 11:38:42 AM	Data	Availability	Provides ..	⚠ 1 Error	There is compliance issue if the check is yellow, and risk of data loss when the check is red.
⋮ ≫	Stats DB ..	⊘ Error	-3	Feb 22, 2023, 11:38:42 AM	Performa..	Availability	Checks th..	--	vSAN performance service may not able to save vSAN performance data.

Figure 179: Skyline health findings

We still have these problems listed with various objects. Let us inspect which objects these are in the "Virtual Objects" view under "Monitor – vSAN". As shown in the next screenshot, the only object which is in a state of "reduced availability with no rebuild" is the "Performance management object".

Figure 180: Object issues

The "Performance management object" is created automatically when the vSAN cluster is formed. In order to correct this situation, we will delete and recreate the performance management object using rvc, the Ruby vSphere Console command line tool available on the vCenter Server. How to use rvc is described in more depth at a later stage, for now it is good to know that the following two commands are available to solve this issue.

```
vsan.perf.stats_object_delete <cluster>
vsan.perf.stats_object_create <cluster>
```

Another option is to place all hosts of the "secondary" site in maintenance mode with full data evacuation before creating the cluster, and then click "repair object immediately" after the stretched cluster has been created and hosts have been taken out of maintenance mode again.

Figure 181: Repair immediately

The last step we would recommend customers to take is to validate the latency between the hosts within the different location, and of course we have a Skyline Health findings for that as well. We also recommend enabling "health history" so that you have a history of issues triggered in the past. This could potentially help with troubleshooting or understanding certain failure scenarios and responses better.

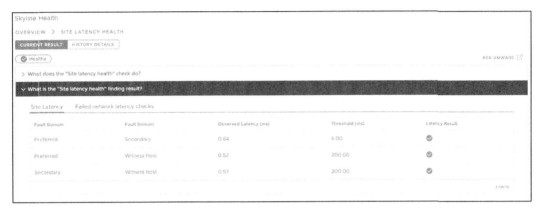

Figure 182: Skyline Health Stretched Cluster Latency

That is all it takes to create a stretched cluster from an existing cluster. Note, these last couple of steps we have conducted, changing the default policy, and repairing the object, would not have been needed if we would have created the stretched cluster immediately when we created the cluster itself. That may seem very easy from a vSAN perspective, but there are some considerations from a vSphere perspective to consider.

These are not required, but in most cases recommended to optimize for performance and availability. The vSAN stretched cluster guide (https://vmwa.re/stretched) outlines all vSphere recommendations in-depth. Since our focus in this book is vSAN, we will not go into that level of detail. Instead, you should refer to the stretched cluster guide mentioned previously in this chapter.

We will however list some of the key recommendations for each of the specific areas:

vSphere DRS:
- Create a Host group per data site, containing each of the hosts of a particular site.
- Create VM groups per site, containing the VMs that should reside in a particular site.
- Create a VM/Host rule to create affinity between the VM and host groups.
- Create a "should" rule for these affinity groups to ensure that during "normal" operations, VMs reside in the correct site, but do have the ability to failover when needed.

This will ensure that VMs will not freely roam around the stretched cluster, it will help from an operational perspective to provide insights around the impact of a full site failure, and it will allow you to distribute VMs running scale-out services such as Active Directory and DNS across both sites.

Lastly, we want to point out that starting with vSAN 7.0 U2 DRS is **tightly integrated** with vSAN. In previous versions when a failure occurred it could happen that when hosts recovered from the failure that DRS would automatically migrate VMs back to their original location. If a VM is moved, by DRS, to its original location before the resync of its object had completed, vSAN would be unable to read from the local site. Both the vMotion process, as well as the traversing of read I/O could lead to a degradation of performance and a prolonged resynchronization process. Starting with vSAN 7.0 U2, DRS will not migrate VMs of which objects are to be resynced.

Pre-vSAN 7.0 U2 customers would configure DRS to "manual" or "partially automated" during these failure scenarios to avoid the above situation. As a result of the integration between DRS and vSAN, this is no longer needed as DRS knows which objects belong to which VMs and which objects are being replicated!

vSphere HA:
- Enable vSphere HA admission control and set it to use the percentage-based admission control policy and to 50% for both CPU and memory. This means that if there is a full site failure, the remaining site has enough unreserved capacity to power-on all of the VMs.
- Make sure to specify additional isolation addresses, one in each site using the advanced setting `das.isolationAddress0` and `das.isolationAddress1`. The IP address needs to be on the vSAN network. This means that in the event of a site failure, a host in the remaining site can still ping an isolation response IP address when needed on the vSAN network and isolation can be validated, and when needed action can be taken.
- Configure the Isolation Response to "Power off and restart VMs".
- Disable the default isolation address if it can't be used to validate the state of the environment during a partition. Setting the advanced setting `das.usedefaultisolationaddress` to false does this.
- Disable the insufficient heartbeat datastore warnings, as without traditional external storage you will not have any datastores to use as vSAN datastores cannot be used for datastore heart beating. Setting the advanced setting `das.ignoreInsufficientHbDatastore` to true does this.

These settings will ensure that when a failure occurs, sufficient unreserved resources are available to coordinate the failover and power-on the VMs (admission control). These VMs will be restarted within their respective sites as defined in the VM/host rules. In the case of an isolation event, all necessary precautions have been taken to ensure all the hosts can reach their respective host isolation response IP address(es).

That is not of course where it stops, there is one important aspect of availability in a stretched cluster that we will need to discuss first, and this is policy settings.

Failures To Tolerate Policies

The vSphere Client uses the terminology "Site disaster tolerance" and "Failures to tolerate" to explain the different levels of available for a stretched cluster shown in the screenshot below.

Figure 183: vSphere Client VM storage policy for a stretched cluster

Let's list all the different options which are available within the vSphere Client for a stretched cluster configuration when defining a policy:

- Site Disaster Tolerance – None – standard cluster
- Site Disaster Tolerance – Host mirroring – 2 node cluster
- Site Disaster Tolerance – Site mirroring – stretched cluster
- Site Disaster Tolerance – None – keep data on preferred (stretched cluster)
- Site Disaster Tolerance – None – keep data on secondary (stretched cluster)
- Site Disaster Tolerance – None – stretched cluster
- Failures to tolerate – No data redundancy
- Failures to tolerate – No data redundancy with host affinity
- Failures to tolerate – 1 Failure – RAID-1
- Failures to tolerate – 1 Failure – RAID-5
- Failures to tolerate – 2 Failure – RAID-1
- Failures to tolerate – 2 Failure – RAID-6
- Failures to tolerate – 3 Failure – RAID-1

The first decision that needs to be made is the *Site Disaster Tolerance*. This is the "*Primary Level of Failures To Tolerate*" and specifies whether objects should be mirrored across locations. Note that this is essentially a RAID-1 mirror. Administrators also have the ability to specify that an object should not be replicated and should only be made available in a specific location i.e., site. You can imagine that this is useful in a scenario where the application is already replicating its data to the other location natively. A good example would be Oracle RAC or Microsoft SQL Always On, or even Microsoft Active Directory for that matter. In this scenario, "preferred" and "secondary" refers to the location where the data is going to be stored. It is up to the administrator to ensure that the VM itself runs in the same location.

Failures to tolerate then specifies how the object within each location then needs to be protected.

You could specify that you would like to mirror objects across locations via *Site Disaster Tolerance* (RAID-1) and have a RAID-5 or RAID-6 configuration within each location. This RAID-5 or RAID-6 configuration would then allow you to survive one (or multiple) host failures in the remaining site after a full site failure has occurred, without losing access to the object. The diagram below shows what this looks like logically, note that for simplicity reasons we have only depicted the capacity leg, the performance leg will remain a RAID-1 configuration within each location.

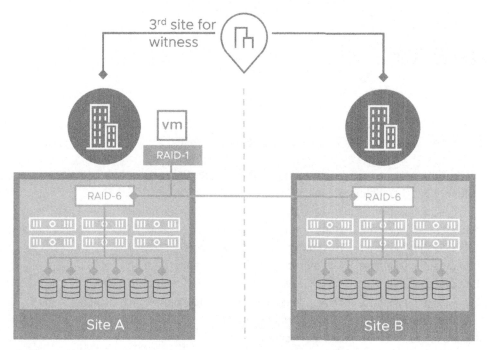

Figure 184: RAID-1 across locations, RAID-6 within locations

The added benefit of local protection within each location is that when a device, or host has failed, data can now be resynced or rebuilt locally. If only the top-level RAID-1 configuration exists, components impacted by a failure would need to be resynced across the network between the two locations. This lengthens the time it would take to protect the component, and as such during that time your data is at risk. Hence, we typically recommend customers to take advantage of this secondary level of protection within a site.

One thing we do want to point out however is that a failure of the witness host is considered a full site failure, meaning that it could take out a full one-third of the available votes for all objects. Any further failures that occur after the witness site has failed could place data at risk if quorum is lost, depending on the number of hosts in the cluster and the selected policy for the object of course. We realize that this can be difficult to grasp, so let's look at the various failure scenarios.

Site Disaster Tolerance Failure Scenarios

There are many different failures that can occur in a datacenter. It is not our goal to describe every single one of them, as that would be a book by itself. In this section, we want to describe some of the failures, and recovery of these failures, which are particular to the stretched cluster configuration. Hopefully, these will give you a better insight into how a stretched cluster works.

In this example, there is a 6+6+1 stretched vSAN deployment. This means that there are six data hosts at site 1, six data hosts at site 2, and a witness host at a third site.

A single VM has been deployed, we selected a policy that dictates that the data needs to be stretched across locations and be protected within each location with RAID-1. When the physical disk placement is examined, we can see that the replicas are placed on the preferred and secondary data site respectively as shown in the Fault Domain column, and the witness component is placed on the witness. This ensures that we have a quorum mechanism used for full site failures. Note, that in a stretched cluster implementation you will have a performance leg and a capacity leg in each of the locations.

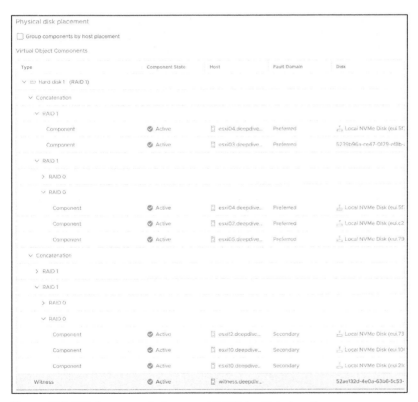

Figure 185: VM Component placement RAID-1 within locations

When we deploy a VM that is stretched across locations and protected within each location with RAID-5, the physical disk placement will look as demonstrated in the next screenshot.

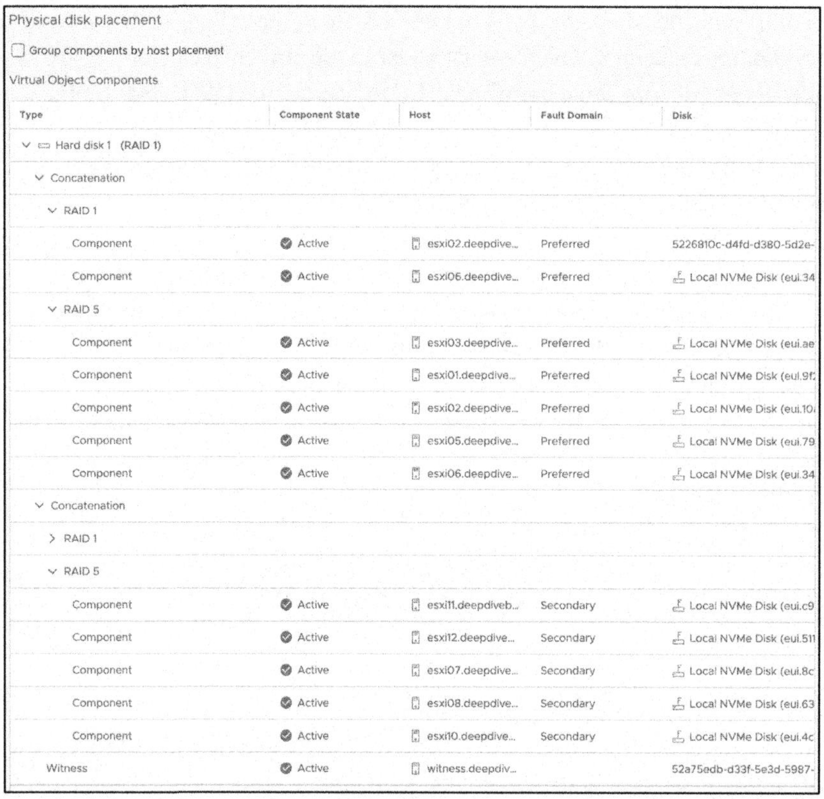

Physical disk placement

Group components by host placement

Virtual Object Components

Type	Component State	Host	Fault Domain	Disk
Hard disk 1 (RAID 1)				
Concatenation				
RAID 1				
Component	Active	esxi02.deepdive...	Preferred	5226810c-d4fd-d380-5d2e-
Component	Active	esxi06.deepdive...	Preferred	Local NVMe Disk (eui.34
RAID 5				
Component	Active	esxi03.deepdive...	Preferred	Local NVMe Disk (eui.ae
Component	Active	esxi01.deepdive...	Preferred	Local NVMe Disk (eui.9f
Component	Active	esxi02.deepdive...	Preferred	Local NVMe Disk (eui.10
Component	Active	esxi05.deepdive...	Preferred	Local NVMe Disk (eui.79
Component	Active	esxi06.deepdive...	Preferred	Local NVMe Disk (eui.34
Concatenation				
RAID 1				
RAID 5				
Component	Active	esxi11.deepdiveb...	Secondary	Local NVMe Disk (eui.c9
Component	Active	esxi12.deepdive...	Secondary	Local NVMe Disk (eui.511
Component	Active	esxi07.deepdive...	Secondary	Local NVMe Disk (eui.8c
Component	Active	esxi08.deepdive...	Secondary	Local NVMe Disk (eui.63
Component	Active	esxi10.deepdive...	Secondary	Local NVMe Disk (eui.4c
Witness	Active	witness.deepdiv...		52a75edb-d33f-5e3d-5987-

Figure 186: VM Component placement RAID-5 within locations

The next step is to introduce some failures and examine how vSAN handles such events. Before beginning these tests, please ensure that vSAN Skyline Health is working correctly, and that all vSAN health findings have passed. This will make troubleshooting much easier.

Skyline Health should be referred to regularly during failure scenario testing. Note that alarms are now raised for any health finding that fails. Alarms may also be referenced at the cluster level throughout this testing, depending on the type of failure being triggered.

Finally, when the term site is used in the failure scenarios, it implies a full fault domain.

Single data host failure—Secondary site

The first test is to introduce a failure of a host in one of the data sites, either the "preferred" or the "secondary" site. The sample virtual machine deployed for test purposes currently resides on the preferred site and the failure occurs on the secondary site and impacts a component as shown in the next diagram.

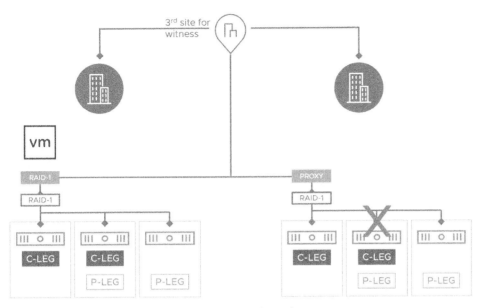

Figure 187: Failure scenario – host failed secondary site

In the first part of this test, the host which holds a component in the secondary site has been powered off, simulating a temporary outage and loss of a component.

There will be several power events, and potentially HA events, related to the host visible in the vSphere Client. When you change to the physical disk placement view of the impacted virtual machine in the UI, the components that were on the secondary host will go "absent" after a few moments, as shown in the next screenshot. The other thing we should point out is that the VM remains accessible. One final thing to point here is that during unplanned downtime, with vSAN ESA, durability components are not created. At the time of writing these are only created during planned downtime, and specifically only for RAID-5 and RAID-6.

Type	Component State	Host	Fault Domain	Disk
∨ ▭ Hard disk 1 (RAID 1)				
∨ Concatenation				
> RAID 1				
> RAID 1				
∨ Concatenation				
∨ RAID 1				
Component	⚠ Absent	▯ Object not found		52064afe-5a33-0e6a-c90d-28ab1d
Component	✅ Active	▯ esxi12.deepdive...	Secondary	⌁ Local NVMe Disk (eui.73e02203
∨ RAID 1				
∨ RAID 0				
Component	✅ Active	▯ esxi07.deepdive...	Secondary	⌁ Local NVMe Disk (eui.137290ff8
Component	⚠ Absent	▯ Object not found		52079f38-3845-d466-c8e7-95ee2f
Component	✅ Active	▯ esxi07.deepdive...	Secondary	⌁ Local NVMe Disk (eui.8c1d5fb9C
∨ RAID 0				
Component	✅ Active	▯ esxi12.deepdive...	Secondary	⌁ Local NVMe Disk (eui.73e02203
Component	✅ Active	▯ esxi10.deepdive...	Secondary	⌁ Local NVMe Disk (eui.100c619d9
Component	✅ Active	▯ esxi10.deepdive...	Secondary	⌁ Local NVMe Disk (eui.21db2ab3I
Witness	✅ Active	▯ witness.deepdiv...		52ae132d-4e0a-63b6-5c53-b62ead
∨ Virtual machine swap object (RAID 1)				
∨ Concatenation				
▯			51 vSAN components on 13 hosts |< < 1 / 4 > >|	

Figure 188: VM Component absent

As mentioned, the virtual machine continues to be accessible. This is because there is a full copy of the data available on the hosts on the preferred site, and there are more than 50% of the votes available. Opening a console to the virtual machine verifies that it is still very much active and functioning. Since the ESXi host which holds the compute of the virtual machine is unaffected by this failure, there is no reason for vSphere HA to act, meaning that the VM is not restarted.

At this point, vSAN Skyline Health can be examined. There will be several failures, as shown in the next figure, since a host in the secondary site is no longer available, as one might expect.

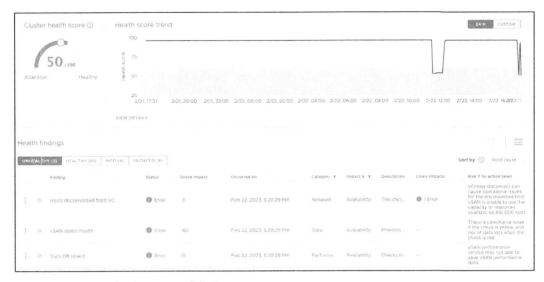

Figure 189: Health findings tests failed

When examining these tests in your environment, please note that before starting a new test, it is strongly recommended to wait until the failed host has successfully rejoined the cluster and the resync has been completed. All "failed" health finding tests should show OK before another test is started. Also, confirm that there are no "absent" components on the VMs objects and that all components are once again active. Failure to do this could introduce more than one failure in the cluster, and result in the VM being unavailable.

Single data host failure—Preferred site

This next test will not only check vSAN but will also verify vSphere HA functionality. If each site has multiple hosts and host affinity rules are defined, then a host failure on the preferred site will allow vSphere HA to restart the virtual machine on another host on the same site. In this test, the configuration is 6+6+1, but we have not defined any rules, so the virtual machine will be restarted on a random host in the cluster, in either of the two locations.

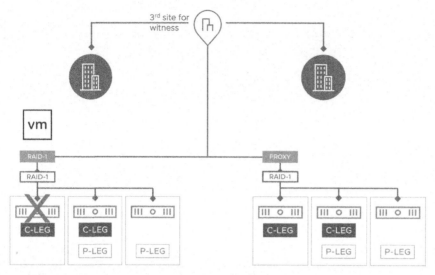

Figure 190: Failure scenario – host failed preferred site

After the failure has occurred in the preferred site there will be a few vSphere HA related events. Like the previous scenario, if there were any components on the host, these will show up as "absent." In this case the host on which a VM was running was failed. The VM has a RAID-5 policy associated with it, as we can see below.

Type	Component State	Host	Fault Domain	Disk	Disk UUID
∨ ⌱ Hard disk 1 (RAID 1)					
∨ Concatenation					
∨ RAID 1					
Component	✅ Active	esxi02.deepdive...	Preferred	5226810c-d4fd-d380-5d2e-167e8e8d588f	5226810c-d4fd-d380-5d2e-167e8e8d588f
Component	✅ Active	esxi06.deepdive...	Preferred	Local NVMe Disk (eui.3404c2f2bc7ec8ac0...	52bb6e68-37b7-4cf6-eecf-aaf67604c243
∨ RAID 5					
Component	✅ Active	esxi03.deepdive...	Preferred	Local NVMe Disk (eui.aecae4d6b4a86d41...	529bc122-d0e7-dc34-f0cd-cebe0cd978dd
Component	⚠ Absent	Object not found		5276a526-4f97-75f4-9171-2647e84ac91d	5276a526-4f97-75f4-9171-2647e84ac91d
Component	✅ Active	esxi02.deepdive...	Preferred	Local NVMe Disk (eui.10a4ddfcaba2b4f40...	526c259d-ce6d-24ca-a3f4-614fe9825012
Component	✅ Active	esxi05.deepdive...	Preferred	Local NVMe Disk (eui.7921d4845de220210...	52d86cba-306a-2d89-e6ab-9f217805d5e8
Component	✅ Active	esxi06.deepdive...	Preferred	Local NVMe Disk (eui.3404c2f2bc7ec8ac0...	52bb6e68-37b7-4cf6-eecf-aaf67604c243
∨ Concatenation					
∨ RAID 1					
Component	✅ Active	esxi10.deepdive...	Secondary	Local NVMe Disk (eui.3a36e5c3656521b0...	5248df1e-c3bd-37eb-4ec1-6cf03668f5c91
Component	✅ Active	esxi07.deepdive...	Secondary	52d5d195-15bf-9efa-977a-a0d52dbf4448	52d5d195-15bf-9efa-977a-a0d52dbf4448
∨ RAID 5					
Component	✅ Active	esxi11.deepdive...	Secondary	Local NVMe Disk (eui.c9edb858d7878a3d...	52d111ac-ba75-9504-3673-fd0f623dc9c8
Component	✅ Active	esxi12.deepdive...	Secondary	Local NVMe Disk (eui.511bd573294ec320...	526e9f52-f970-db3a-539e-ac319d59a5be
Component	✅ Active	esxi07.deepdive...	Secondary	Local NVMe Disk (eui.8c1d5fb90264fa6d0...	52d139f4-8d36-cfba-f358-6bfc0919af8z
Component	✅ Active	esxi08.deepdive...	Secondary	Local NVMe Disk (eui.630bf7d20b1ca0a3...	526eff5d-ae2d-8fec-7c53-39ea6c43e1d7

Figure 191: Absent components with RAID-5

Note that these components will be rebuilt fully after 60 minutes automatically by vSAN leveraging the remaining component within the location. However, when desired, you can manually trigger the rebuild of these components by clicking "Repair objects immediately" in the vSAN Skyline Health under vSAN Object Health.

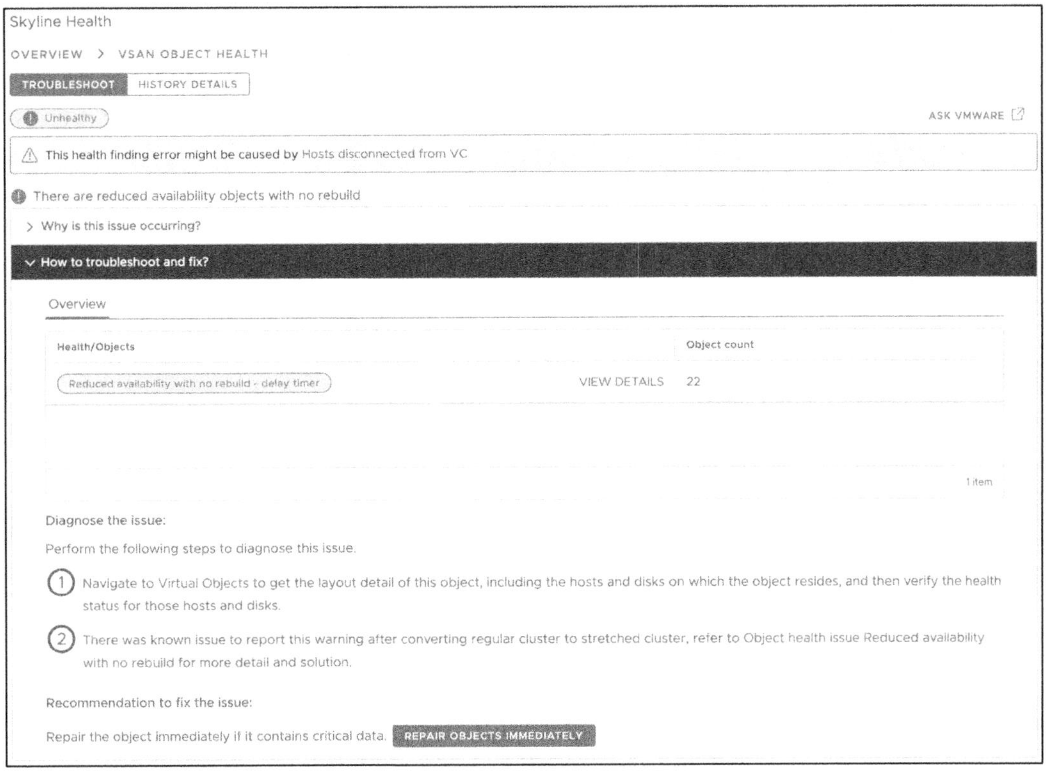

Figure 192: Repair objects immediately

Since the host on which the virtual machine's compute resides is no longer available, vSphere HA will restart the virtual machine. If VM/Host affinity rules are configured, then HA will restart the VM on another host in the same site. It is important to validate this has happened as it shows that the VM/host affinity rules are correctly configured, and vSphere HA acts accordingly.

It should also be noted that these rules should be configured as "should" rules and not as "must" rules in most scenarios. If "must" rules are configured, then vSphere HA will only be able to restart the virtual machine on hosts that are in the same host group on the same site/fault domain and will not be able to restart the virtual machine on hosts that reside on the other site. "Should" rules will allow vSphere HA to restart the virtual machine on hosts that are not in the same VM/host affinity group, i.e., in the event of a complete site failure.

Information about the restart of the virtual machine can be found in the vSphere Client and in the log file `/var/log/fdm.log` on the ESXi host which is the vSphere HA primary. Note that it usually takes between 30-60 seconds before a failover has occurred. If trying to monitor these HA events via the vSphere Client, ensure that you regularly refresh the vSphere client, or you may not see it.

		Description		Type		Date Time		Task		Target		Us
☐	>	Alarm 'Virtual machine memor...	ⓘ Information			02/23/2023, 9:02:10...				🖥 Stretched - RAID-5		
☐	>	Alarm 'Virtual machine CPU u...	ⓘ Information			02/23/2023, 9:02:10...				🖥 Stretched - RAID-5		
☐	>	Message from esxi07.deepdiv...	ⓘ Information			02/23/2023, 9:01:01 ...				🖥 Stretched - RAID-5		vp
☐	⌄	Alarm 'vSphere HA virtual ma...	ⓘ Information			02/23/2023, 9:01:02...				🖥 Stretched - RAID-5		

> **Date Time:** 🕐 02/23/2023, 9:01:02 AM
> **Type:** ⓘ Information
> **Target:** 🖥 Stretched - RAID-5
> **Description:**
> Alarm 'vSphere HA virtual machine failover failed' on Stretched - RAID-5 changed from Gray to Green
> **Related events:**
> There are no related events.

☐	⌄	vSphere HA restarted this virt...	⚠ Warning			02/23/2023, 9:01:01 ...				🖥 Stretched - RAID-5		

> **Date Time:** 🕐 02/23/2023, 9:01:01 AM
> **Type:** ⚠ Warning
> **Target:** 🖥 Stretched - RAID-5
> **Description:**
> vSphere HA restarted virtual machine Stretched - RAID-5 on host esxi07.deepdivebook.com in cluster Cluster
> **Event Type Description:**
> The virtual machine was restarted automatically by vSphere HA on this host. This response may be triggered by a failure of the host the virtual machine
> power-off of the virtual machine (eg. if the vmx process was killed).
> **Related events:**
> There are no related events.

Figure 193: Failure scenario – HA events in vSphere Client

Full Site Failure – Data Site

This next test in essence is very similar to a single host failure. The big difference of course is that in a full site scenario, typically 50% of your cluster resources are now missing. When a full site failure occurs, it will not be possible to rebuild your components. This is because the second fault domain is missing completely as demonstrated in the diagram below.

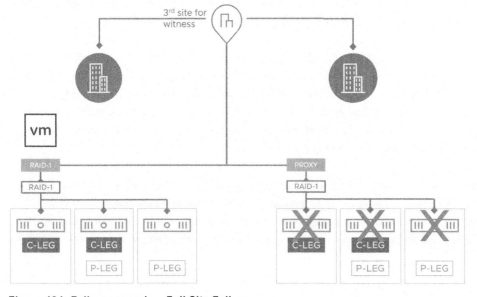

Figure 194: Failure scenario – Full Site Failure

After the failure has occurred in the secondary site, all VMs will automatically be restarted in the preferred location. Do however note that this will only be the case when VM-Host rules were configured as "**should rules**", as already highlighted. When "must rules" have been configured vSphere HA will not violate these. For more details on vSphere HA and VM/Host rules please refer to the vSphere 6.7 Clustering Deep Dive book by Frank Denneman, Duncan Epping, and Niels Hagoort.

Starting with vSAN 7.0 Update 2, DRS understands the state of objects on vSAN. DRS will verify with vSAN the state of the environment, and it will not migrate VMs back according to the defined rules until the resync has completed. When the VMs are healthy and the resync has fully completed, DRS will automatically migrate the VMs back to comply with the specified VM/Host rules (when DRS is configured to Fully Automated that is).

> **vSAN and DRS are tightly integrated starting with vSAN 7.0 U2. As a result, it is no longer needed to change the automation mode of DRS after a failure has occurred.**

The last thing we would like to discuss as part of this failure scenario is the witness failure resilience. We have already briefly discussed it in a previous section, but we now want to show what the immediate impact is of this feature using rvc. As stated, the secondary site has failed completely. We will examine the impact of this failure through rvc, the Ruby vSphere Console on the vCenter Server. This should provide us with a better understanding of the situation and how the witness failure resilience mechanism works. Let's look at the output of rvc for our VM directly before the failure first.

```
RAID_1
  Concatenation
    RAID_1
      Component: 2103f663-2a32-588e-9f88-005056b600ad (state: ACTIVE (5), host: esxi06.deepdivebook.com, capacity: 52fe9834-baf1-28a9-81d6-b927dda59f58, cache: ,
                                                       votes: 2, usage: 0.0 GB, proxy component: true)
      Component: 2103f663-4cd9-5a8e-3d80-005056b600ad (state: ACTIVE (5), host: esxi04.deepdivebook.com, capacity: 5233350e-4c8b-d61b-7c53-c2c8cbf551ce, cache: ,
                                                       votes: 1, usage: 0.0 GB, proxy component: true)
    RAID_5
      Component: 2103f663-dc24-5c8e-a848-005056b600ad (state: ACTIVE (5), host: esxi04.deepdivebook.com, capacity: 525bbc8d-5698-886c-b31e-1fd82a61794e, cache: ,
                                                       votes: 1, usage: 0.0 GB, proxy component: true)
      Component: 2103f663-6640-5d8e-4608-005056b600ad (state: ACTIVE (5), host: esxi05.deepdivebook.com, capacity: 52456125-85e4-193f-5995-d3eeb8fec714, cache: ,
                                                       votes: 2, usage: 0.0 GB, proxy component: true)
      Component: 2103f663-6a3d-5e8e-794f-005056b600ad (state: ACTIVE (5), host: esxi01.deepdivebook.com, capacity: 5276a526-4f97-75f4-9171-2647e84ac91d, cache: ,
                                                       votes: 2, usage: 0.0 GB, proxy component: true)
      Component: 2103f663-a838-5f8e-8ea0-005056b600ad (state: ACTIVE (5), host: esxi06.deepdivebook.com, capacity: 52bb6e68-37b7-4cf6-eecf-aaf67604c243, cache: ,
                                                       votes: 1, usage: 0.0 GB, proxy component: true)
      Component: 2103f663-622a-608e-ab00-005056b600ad (state: ACTIVE (5), host: esxi03.deepdivebook.com, capacity: 522f3385-d5c7-bfb6-70de-66a799b95d22, cache: ,
                                                       votes: 2, usage: 0.0 GB, proxy component: true)
  Concatenation
    RAID_1
      Component: 2103f663-9244-618e-741b-005056b600ad (state: ACTIVE (5), host: esxi09.deepdivebook.com, capacity: 52079f38-3845-d466-c8e7-95ee2f17d165, cache: ,
                                                       votes: 1, usage: 0.0 GB, proxy component: false)
      Component: 2103f663-4651-628e-0e68-005056b600ad (state: ACTIVE (5), host: esxi11.deepdivebook.com, capacity: 52d9f834-d542-2239-eced-fbd562c802a7, cache: ,
                                                       votes: 1, usage: 0.0 GB, proxy component: false)
    RAID_5
      Component: 2103f663-0858-638e-a089-005056b600ad (state: ACTIVE (5), host: esxi07.deepdivebook.com, capacity: 52d139f4-8d36-cfba-f358-6bfc0919a18c, cache: ,
                                                       votes: 2, usage: 0.0 GB, proxy component: false)
      Component: 2103f663-5c65-648e-87a3-005056b600ad (state: ACTIVE (5), host: esxi10.deepdivebook.com, capacity: 5248df1e-c3bd-37eb-4ec1-6cf0366f5c91, cache: ,
                                                       votes: 2, usage: 0.0 GB, proxy component: false)
      Component: 2103f663-8077-658e-6f0a-005056b600ad (state: ACTIVE (5), host: esxi09.deepdivebook.com, capacity: 52064afe-5a33-0e6a-c90d-28ab1d011345, cache: ,
                                                       votes: 1, usage: 0.0 GB, proxy component: false)
      Component: 2103f663-e863-668e-7e1a-005056b600ad (state: ACTIVE (5), host: esxi11.deepdivebook.com, capacity: 52d9f834-d542-2239-eced-fbd562c802a6, cache: ,
                                                       votes: 1, usage: 0.0 GB, proxy component: false)
      Component: 2103f663-4847-678e-ea60-005056b600ad (state: ACTIVE (5), host: esxi12.deepdivebook.com, capacity: 529940bd-e3c1-1698-3154-cc5353e11d48, cache: ,
                                                       votes: 2, usage: 0.0 GB, proxy component: false)
Witness: 2103f663-b042-688e-e3d1-005056b600ad (state: ACTIVE (5), host: witness.deepdivebook.com, capacity: 5234ea77-7b1e-4e8d-faf6-e0de587c86dc, cache: ,
                                               votes: 10, usage: 0.0 GB, proxy component: false)
```

Figure 195: rvc output votes before failure

As can be seen, the witness component holds 10 votes, and each RAID-5 configuration holds 8 votes. The RAID-1 configurations hold 3 and 2 votes respectively After the full site failure has been detected, the votes are recalculated to ensure that a witness host failure does not impact the availability of the VMs. Below shows the output of rvc once again.

```
RAID_1
  Concatenation
    RAID_1
      Component: ef13f663-263d-5d65-4ee7-005056b600ad (state: ACTIVE (5), host: esxi04.deepdivebook.com, capacity: 528e7c0a-090c-747a-f5d9-74c81cc463c3, cache: ,
                                                       votes: 3, usage: 0.0 GB, proxy component: false)
      Component: ef13f663-ceb6-5f65-f6de-005056b600ad (state: ACTIVE (5), host: esxi02.deepdivebook.com, capacity: 5226810c-d4fd-d380-5d2e-167e8e8d588f, cache: ,
                                                       votes: 3, usage: 0.0 GB, proxy component: false)
    RAID_5
      Component: ef13f663-ecfa-6065-d702-005056b600ad (state: ACTIVE (5), host: esxi01.deepdivebook.com, capacity: 5276a526-4f97-75f4-9171-2647e84ac91d, cache: ,
                                                       votes: 6, usage: 0.0 GB, proxy component: false)
      Component: ef13f663-72b1-6165-1c85-005056b600ad (state: ACTIVE (5), host: esxi04.deepdivebook.com, capacity: 528e7c0a-090c-747a-f5d9-74c81cc463c2, cache: ,
                                                       votes: 3, usage: 0.0 GB, proxy component: false)
      Component: ef13f663-6ef0-6265-3a30-005056b600ad (state: ACTIVE (5), host: esxi06.deepdivebook.com, capacity: 52fe9834-baf1-28a9-81d6-b927dda59f57, cache: ,
                                                       votes: 6, usage: 0.0 GB, proxy component: false)
      Component: ef13f663-c4a9-6365-bd6d-005056b600ad (state: ACTIVE (5), host: esxi02.deepdivebook.com, capacity: 526c259d-ce6d-24ca-a3f4-614fe9825012, cache: ,
                                                       votes: 3, usage: 0.0 GB, proxy component: false)
      Component: ef13f663-04dd-6465-71b0-005056b600ad (state: ACTIVE (5), host: esxi03.deepdivebook.com, capacity: 521ba88f-8e5f-30c7-a29e-683976ef631b, cache: ,
                                                       votes: 6, usage: 0.0 GB, proxy component: false)
  Concatenation
    RAID_1
      Component: ef13f663-6ca8-6565-a3ed-005056b600ad (state: ABSENT (6), csn: STALE (16!=23), host: Unknown, capacity: 5249c5f0-d39b-4437-432c-e5fe7a38ba18, cache:
                                                       votes: 1, proxy component: false)
      Component: ef13f663-5492-6665-65a1-005056b600ad (state: ABSENT (6), csn: STALE (16!=23), host: Unknown, capacity: 52079f38-3845-d466-c8e7-95ee2f17d165, cache:
                                                       votes: 1, proxy component: false)
    RAID_5
      Component: ef13f663-c647-6765-eff5-005056b600ad (state: ABSENT (6), csn: STALE (16!=23), host: Unknown, capacity: 5249c5f0-d39b-4437-432c-e5fe7a38ba17, cache:
                                                       votes: 1, proxy component: false)
      Component: ef13f663-2691-6865-754a-005056b600ad (state: ABSENT (6), csn: STALE (16!=23), host: Unknown, capacity: 521d489d-434a-3765-1b7e-789681b4761a, cache:
                                                       votes: 1, proxy component: false)
      Component: ef13f663-3446-6965-ce68-005056b600ad (state: ABSENT (6), csn: STALE (16!=23), host: Unknown, capacity: 529f8ef9-bcb6-6ee9-6835-3718303b7715, cache:
                                                       votes: 1, proxy component: false)
      Component: ef13f663-ea2b-6a65-5fe6-005056b600ad (state: ABSENT (6), csn: STALE (16!=23), host: Unknown, capacity: 52079f38-3845-d466-c8e7-95ee2f17d164, cache:
                                                       votes: 1, proxy component: false)
      Component: ef13f663-884d-6b65-879e-005056b600ad (state: ABSENT (6), csn: STALE (16!=23), host: Unknown, capacity: 526bfb7e-1974-e5d3-779b-acbe21b67c80, cache:
                                                       votes: 1, proxy component: false)
Witness: ef13f663-6a9d-6c65-5ccb-005056b600ad (state: ACTIVE (5), host: witness.deepdivebook.com, capacity: 52ae132d-4e0a-63b6-5c53-b62ead400846, cache: ,
                                                       votes: 1, usage: 0.0 GB, proxy component: false)
```

Figure 196: rvc output votes after failure

As can be seen, the votes for the various components have changed, the surviving data site has an increase in votes, the witness on the witness host went from 10 votes to 1, and on top of that, the votes for the failed location have been decreased. Resulting in a situation where quorum would not be lost even if the witness component on the witness host is impacted by a failure. Do note, that the redistribution process of the votes can take up to 5 minutes to complete, depending on the size of the cluster. Nevertheless, a very useful feature for stretched cluster configurations.

Witness host failure—Witness site

A common question that is asked is what happens when the witness host has failed. This should have no impact on the run state of the virtual machine since there is still a full copy of the data available and greater than 50% of the votes are also available, but the witness components residing on the witness host should show up as "absent."

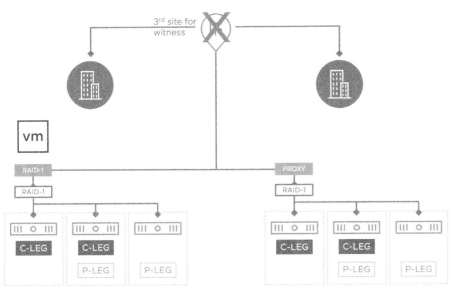

Figure 197: Failure scenario – Witness host failed

In our environment, we've simply powered off the witness host to demonstrate the impact of a failure. After a short period of time, the witness component of the virtual machine appears as "absent" as shown next.

Physical disk placement

☐ Group components by host placement

Virtual Object Components

Type	Component State	Host	Fault Domain	Disk
∨ ⊏⊐ Hard disk 1 (RAID 1)				
〉 Concatenation				
∨ Concatenation				
∨ RAID 1				
Component	✅ Active	🖥 esxi08.deepdive…	Secondary	🗄 Local NVMe Disk (eui.630bf7
Component	✅ Active	🖥 esxi12.deepdive…	Secondary	🗄 Local NVMe Disk (eui.9bc91c
Component	✅ Active	🖥 esxi11.deepdiveb…	Secondary	🗄 Local NVMe Disk (eui.26938c
∨ RAID 6				
Component	✅ Active	🖥 esxi08.deepdive…	Secondary	🗄 Local NVMe Disk (eui.630bf7
Component	✅ Active	🖥 esxi12.deepdive…	Secondary	🗄 Local NVMe Disk (eui.9bc91c
Component	✅ Active	🖥 esxi10.deepdive…	Secondary	🗄 Local NVMe Disk (eui.100c61
Component	✅ Active	🖥 esxi11.deepdiveb…	Secondary	🗄 Local NVMe Disk (eui.c9edbi
Component	✅ Active	🖥 esxi09.deepdive…	Secondary	🗄 Local NVMe Disk (eui.5c83b9
Component	✅ Active	🖥 esxi07.deepdive…	Secondary	🗄 Local NVMe Disk (eui.8c1d5fi
Witness	⚠ Absent	🖥 Object not found		52ae132d-4e0a-63b6-5c53-b62€

Figure 198: Failure scenario – Witness component absent

However, the virtual machine is unaffected and continues to be available and accessible. The rule for vSAN object accessibility is, as we have discussed multiple times now, at least one full copy of the data must be available, and more than 50% of the components that go to make up the object are available. In this scenario both RAID configurations of the data are available, leaving access to the VM intact.

Network failure—Data Site to Data Site

The next failure scenario we want to describe is a site partition. If you are planning on testing this scenario, then we highly recommend ensuring that the host isolation response and host isolation addresses are configured correctly before conducting the tests. At least one of the isolation addresses should be pingable over the vSAN network by each host in the cluster. The environment shown below depicts our configuration and the failure scenario.

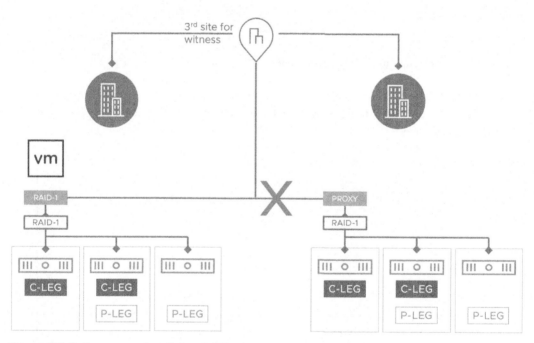

Figure 199: Failure scenario – Network failure

This scenario is special because when the inter-site link has failed, the "preferred" site forms a cluster with the witness, and most components (data components and witness) will be available to this part of the cluster. The secondary site will also form its own cluster, but it will only have a single copy of the data and will not have access to the witness. This results in the components of the virtual machine object getting marked as absent on the secondary site since the host can no longer communicate to the other data site where the other copy of the data resides, nor can it communicate to the witness. This means that the VMs can only run on the preferred site, where most of the components are accessible.

From a vSphere HA perspective, since the host isolation response IP address is on the vSAN network, both data sites should be able to reach the isolation response IP address on their respective sites, and even more importantly, the HA agents (FDM) within each location can still communicate with each other. Meaning that each site will elect its own primary host, and each site will form a sub-cluster. Therefore, vSphere HA does not trigger a host isolation response! This means that the VMs that are running in the secondary site, which has lost access to the vSAN datastore, cannot write to disk but are still running from a compute perspective. It should be noted that during the recovery, the host(s) that has lost access to the disk components will instantly kill the impacted VM instances. This does however mean that until the host has recovered, potentially two instances of the same VM can be accessed over the network, of which only one is capable of writing to disk and the other is not.

vSAN 6.2 introduced a mechanism to avoid this situation. This feature will automatically kill the VMs on the secondary site has have lost access to the components on the secondary site. This is to ensure they can be safely restarted on the preferred site, and when the link recovers there will not be two instances of the same VM running, not even for a brief second. If you want to disable this behavior, you can set the advanced host setting called *vSAN.AutoTerminateGhostVm* to 0. We, however, recommend leaving this setting configured to the default.

On the preferred site, the impacted VMs that were running on the secondary site, will be almost instantly restarted. On average this restart takes around 30-60 seconds. After the virtual machine has been restarted on the hosts on the preferred site, use the vSphere client to navigate to Cluster > Monitor > vSAN > Virtual Objects, select the VM you are interested in, and click on View placement details. This should show you that two out of the three components are available, and since there is a full copy of the data and more than 50% of the components are available, the VM is accessible. This is demonstrated in the screenshot below. Note that it is the secondary fault domain that is listed as absent in this case. We have collapsed some of the RAID configurations so that we can show both the preferred and secondary fault domain of a single RAID-1 configuration, but the same logic would apply to the other objects as well.

Type	Component State	Host	Fault Domain	Disk
∨ 💾 Hard disk 1 (RAID 1)				
∨ Concatenation				
> RAID 1				
∨ RAID 1				
> RAID 0				
∨ RAID 0				
Component	✅ Active	🖥 esxi04.deepdive...	Preferred	💾 Local NVMe Disk (eui.5f794c
Component	✅ Active	🖥 esxi02.deepdive...	Preferred	💾 Local NVMe Disk (eui.c2a24c
Component	✅ Active	🖥 esxi05.deepdive...	Preferred	💾 Local NVMe Disk (eui.7921d4
∨ Concatenation				
> RAID 1				
∨ RAID 1				
> RAID 0				
∨ RAID 0				
Component	⚠ Absent	🖥 Object not found		52a9b7bc-f318-0ee9-1939-6bed
Component	⚠ Absent	🖥 Object not found		520b26d9-cf7e-c2d1-cfc8-8ada6
Component	⚠ Absent	🖥 Object not found		521d489d-434a-3765-1b7e-7896
Witness	✅ Active	🖥 witness.deepdiv...		52ae132d-4e0a-63b6-5c53-b62e

Figure 200: Preferred Site components available

Impact of multiple failures

As discussed in the policy section, vSAN had two layers of protection in a stretched cluster. The first layer is across sites, the second layer is within sites. One thing however that not many people realize is that to not lose access to an object in a vSAN stretched cluster, more than 50% of the total combined votes for that object **across all locations** need to be available. What does this mean?

Let's look at a scenario where we have a stretched cluster and a virtual machine that is protected with RAID-1 across sites, and RAID-1 within the site.

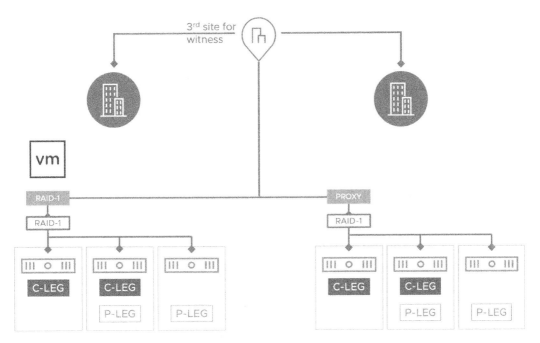

Figure 201: Scenario with dual-layer protection

In the above scenario, we have VM which is running in Site A. This VM is protected across locations and within the locations with both RAID-1. What is important in this case is to understand how the voting mechanism works. Although it is not explicitly shown, both data sites will have a number of votes, so will the witness component for this particular object in the witness location. This can be examined through rvc, the Ruby vSphere Console on the vCenter Server, as shown in other examples. For simplicity reason we will list the votes for each location for a single object, in this case the VMs virtual disk.

- o Witness Site – 24 votes
  - Witness component – 24 votes
- o Data Site 1 – 23 votes in total
  - Perf Leg – 3 votes
  - Perf Leg – 2 votes
  - Cap Leg - RAID-1 – RAID-0 – 4 votes
  - Cap Leg - RAID-1 – RAID-0 – 2 votes
  - Cap Leg - RAID-1 – RAID-0 – 4 votes
  - Cap Leg - RAID-1 – RAID-0 – 4 votes
  - Cap Leg - RAID-1 – RAID-0 – 4 votes
  - Cap Leg - RAID-1 – RAID-0 – 2 votes
- o Data Site 2 – 24 votes in total
  - Perf Leg – 3 votes
  - Perf Leg – 3 votes
  - Cap Leg - RAID-1 – RAID-0 – 3 votes
  - Cap Leg - RAID-1 – RAID-0 – 3 votes
  - Cap Leg - RAID-1 – RAID-0 – 3 votes
  - Cap Leg - RAID-1 – RAID-0 – 3 votes
  - Cap Leg - RAID-1 – RAID-0 – 3 votes
  - Cap Leg - RAID-1 – RAID-0 – 3 votes

This results in a total combined number of votes of 71. For the Witness site that is 24 votes, for Site 1 that is 24 and for Site 2 that is 23. Now if you have the Witness location fail you lose 24 votes. If now Site 1 – Replica A fails, you will end up losing access to the object as 47 out of 71 votes would be missing. Even though the full RAID-1 configuration of Site 2 is still available, the full object becomes unavailable. The same of course applies to RAID-5, and RAID-6.

In a previous example failure scenario, we already discussed the witness failure resilience mechanism. This ensures that in the case of a double failure, where first a full site fails and then the witness host fails, the VM and its components are still available. Again, we would like to point out that this mechanism, at the time of writing, only works for scenarios where all components in a single location are impacted by a failure and after the recalculation of the votes has completed the witness fails. If the witness fails first then, unfortunately, there's no recalculation happening at this stage. If simultaneous failures occur, unfortunately no recalculation would have occurred, which means that objects will be inaccessible.

Hopefully, the above explanation makes it clear how the voting mechanism works in vSAN stretched clusters and why in certain failure scenarios a restart of the virtual machine may or may not occur.

Operating a Stretched Cluster

We have discussed how to configure a stretched cluster, and how a stretched cluster acts during certain failure scenarios. We have, however, not discussed yet if there are any specific things to consider when it comes to the operational aspects of a stretched cluster. Operating vSAN is discussed in chapter 6, there are however a few exceptions and things to know when it comes to a stretched cluster configuration.

The first concept we want to discuss is **Maintenance Mode** and Upgrades or Updates. Hopefully, everyone uses vSphere Lifecycle Manager (vLCM) for lifecycle management of their vSphere (and vSAN) hosts. One common question we have received over the years is what customers should do with the witness appliance. Although we have not discussed it yet, this also applies to witness hosts which are part of a 2-node cluster. 2-node clusters will be discussed in the next chapter though! Do you upgrade the witness, or do you simply deploy a new version of the appliance and click on "Change Witness Host" under Fault Domains, displayed in the next screenshot?

Fault Domains			
Fault domain failures to tolerate	1		
Configuration type	Stretched cluster		DISABLE STRETCHED CLUSTER
Witness host	witness.deepdivebook.com		CHANGE WITNESS HOST

Preferred (preferred)		Secondary	
Used capacity	10%	Used capacity	10%
☐ esxi01.deepdivebook.com	10%	☐ esxi12.deepdivebook.com	10%
☐ esxi05.deepdivebook.com	10%	☐ esxi11.deepdivebook.com	10%
☐ esxi03.deepdivebook.com	10%	☐ esxi08.deepdivebook.com	10%
☐ esxi04.deepdivebook.com	10%	☐ esxi09.deepdivebook.com	10%
☐ esxi02.deepdivebook.com	10%	☐ esxi07.deepdivebook.com	10%
☐ esxi06.deepdivebook.com	10%	☐ esxi10.deepdivebook.com	10%

Figure 202: Changing witness for a stretched cluster

Before you decide on a strategy, it is good to know that starting with vSAN 7.0 U3 it is now also supported to upgrade the Witness Appliance using vLCM. This greatly simplifies the update, or upgrade process. We do not have a preference when it comes to lifecycle management of the appliance, we have seen customers successfully using either the update as well as the replacement approach. It boils down to what you feel most comfortable with. There are, however, a few things to take into consideration.

First of all, the witness host must be a dedicated witness host, shared witness hosts are not supported at the time of writing. Note that shared witness hosts are also only supported for 2-node clusters. Secondly, vLCM can only support virtual witness hosts. At the time of writing upgrading and updating of **physical** witness hosts is not supported using vLCM either.

When it comes to updating the entire cluster, we recommend using vLCM for all hosts, and preferably integrated with your OEM's firmware management solution. This way both vSphere, as well as the firmware of all components, are at the correct version. Especially for a vSAN cluster, this is extremely important. Hence vSAN Skyline Health validates your environment against the most current VMware Compatibility Guide whenever it runs. Note that when vLCM is used, the virtual witness host is always updated (or upgraded) first, after which the hosts in the preferred and secondary site are remediated.

As mentioned, simply replacing the witness host is also a possibility using the UI. Although we do not have a recommendation in terms of which strategy to use, we would recommend getting familiar with both the vLCM strategy as well as the "Change Witness Host" procedure, in case the witness host ever needs to be replaced in a failure scenario.

The last thing we want to mention is that, at the time of writing, there is no option to place a full site into maintenance at once. Maintenance happens on the host level. Administrators must work at the host granularity, placing each host in a site into maintenance mode individually. Additional manual steps may be required, such as modifying the DRS affinity to ensure that all workloads are failed over to the site that is to remain online and available. Once the workloads have been migrated, administrators can begin placing hosts into maintenance mode with the 'ensure accessibility' option. This option should be used if there is a possibility of VMs using the *failures to tolerate* set to 0. If all VMs protected by the stretched cluster are using *failures to tolerate* > 0, then the 'no data evacuation' option may be used when placing hosts into maintenance mode. Documenting the existing host groups, VM groups, and VM/Host rules in DRS prior to any modifications will help return the state of the cluster back to its condition prior to maintenance efforts.

Another thing that is important to realize is that monitoring for disk capacity is slightly different. Although all regular screens still provide useful information, there is one additional section in the UI we would recommend to regular monitor. The previous screenshot shows vSAN capacity per fault domain, as well as per host within each fault domain. In an environment where all VMs are replicated between locations, the capacity consumption is typically equal between both locations. However, we have many customers that have workloads that do not need to be replicated between locations, and they leverage VM Storage Policies to specify where the VM needs to be located. In other words, using policies they specify in which fault domain all components of the VM (or file share, etc.) need to be stored. This can then lead to a situation where one fault domain has less free capacity than the other, which is of course useful to know when provisioning decisions are made.

Another aspect of managing a stretched cluster that we want to stress is that the use of standardized **VM Storage Policy names** is key. We also recommend customers to regularly validate if VMs are associated with the correct policy. Unfortunately, we have witnessed situations where VMs were supposed to be mirrored across locations, but because of an incorrectly assigned policy, were not mirrored. In normal situations this is not a problem. However, it is during an unexpected site failure that you typically find out that some business-critical VM was not replicated. vSAN offers a feature which can help preventing this scenario to a certain extent, which is Auto-Policy Management. As described in previous chapters, Auto-Policy Management can create a default policy for your datastore based on the number of hosts and features enabled (including Stretched Clustering). When verifying the currently associated policies, make sure to also verify the policy associated with the vCLS VMs. The vCLS VMs are vSphere HA and DRS related management VMs that are automatically deployed during the creation of a cluster, and are typically deployed with the default storage policy associated with the datastore. For those who want to automate the reporting process, you can, for instance, use PowerCLI to create a report of all VMs and their associated policies.

Another important aspect is **VM/Host rules**. This is a hot topic in every stretched cluster architectural or operational discussion. Should you create rules and specify in which location a VM should run? We believe that this is desired. It provides you the ability to control where a particular VM runs, and as a result, it will give you a better understanding of what the impact is on IT services and Applications when a (site) failure has occurred. However, it also subsequently means that there's another aspect to manage. You will regularly need to validate if the rules associated to the groups are still accurate, and if the VMs belong to the correct VM to Host group. Of course, it is possible to automate this process with a tool like PowerCLI.

Lastly, **Skyline Health**. We have already shown a few Skyline Health findings (often referred to as health checks) in the various sections in this chapter, but we want to stress some of them as they are extremely valuable when troubleshooting or just for assessing the general health of your vSAN ESA stretched cluster configuration.

The first thing we would recommend doing is to get familiar with the various checks. Skyline Health has a long list of all the checks, but all stretched cluster related checks fortunately are categorized accordingly. You can simply filter on "stretched" in the column "Category" to limit the current view to stretched cluster related checks only, as demonstrated in the next screenshot.

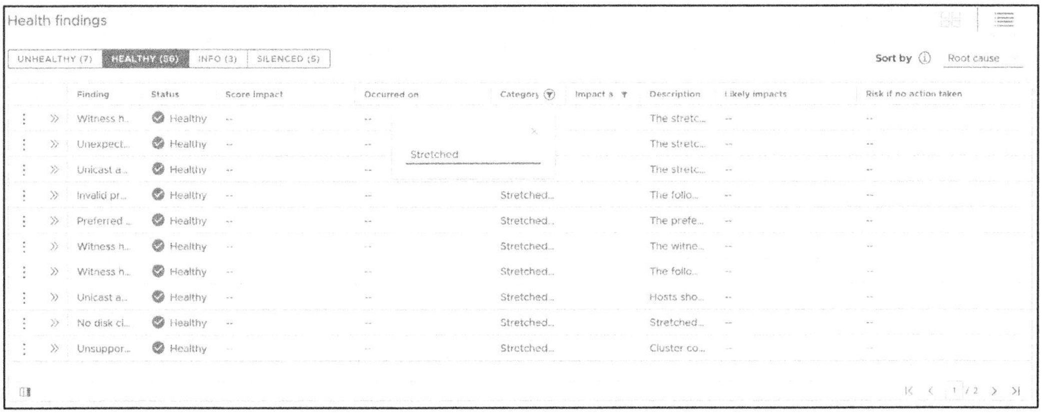

Figure 203: Filtering Skyline Health

There are two pages worth of checks. We have already shown the Site Latency Health finding. This check verifies the latency between the two locations and will be triggered when thresholds are triggered. Between the data sites this threshold is 5ms roundtrip latency, and between the witness location and the data site it is 200ms. Note that occasionally exceeding these thresholds will most likely not result in a poor experience, we do recommend however to keep latency as low as possible and bandwidth as high as possible. Relatively high latency and low bandwidth will definitely impact the user experience.

There are also several checks available for issues with the Witness Host. As the witness host plays a critical role in the availability of your workloads it is highly recommended to investigate failed checks as soon as possible. We have seen customers running environments with a failed witness host for a prolonged time, without realizing that a second failure could immediately impact a large portion of their workloads. Replacing a Witness Appliance is a simple process, and we would highly recommend testing this before taking the stretched cluster into production.

Summary

A vSAN stretched cluster architecture will allow you to deploy and migrate workloads across two locations without the need for complex storage configurations and operational processes. On top of that, it comes at a relatively low cost that enables most VMware users to deploy this configuration when there are dual datacenter requirements. As with any explicit architecture, there are various design and operational considerations. We would like to refer you to the official VMware documentation and https://core.vmware.com/ as the source of the most updated and accurate information.

08

Two Host vSAN Cluster Use Case

Two host configurations were introduced in vSAN 6.1 and are often used by customers looking to deploy workloads into remote office or branch office locations. Unfortunately, this configuration is often confused with the VMware Remote Office / Branch Office license, which is nothing more than a license key that allows you to run 25 virtual machines across several locations on as many ESXi hosts as needed. In no shape or form is this license key associated with the two-host configuration. It is important to make that distinction before we begin, as it is a question that comes up time and again.

When configuring a two host vSAN cluster it quickly becomes obvious that it is very similar to a stretched cluster configuration. The main difference is that normally a two-host cluster would have both hosts located in the same location, whereas in a stretched cluster configuration, hosts would be located in different locations. Another difference is that it is not uncommon to see a single vCenter Server instance managing numerous two host vSAN clusters. It is quite common to see hundreds of two host vSAN clusters registered in the same vCenter Server. The below diagram displays what this could look like from a logical point of view.

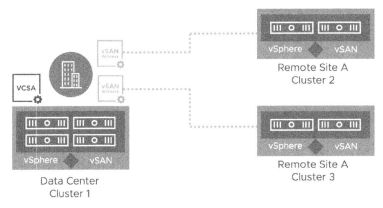

Figure 204: Multiple two host clusters

As mentioned earlier, a two-host configuration closely resembles a stretched cluster configuration when it comes to the setup and implementation. There are however some differences in functionality, and there are some design considerations as well. Before we investigate those, let us first look at how to configure a two host vSAN cluster.

Configuration of a two-host cluster

Configuring a two-host cluster can simply be done through the interface we have seen many times by now at this point in the book. We can use the Quickstart wizard, or simply go to your cluster object and configure vSAN there. As we have seen the Quickstart wizard multiple times already in the book, on this occasion we will show you how to configure vSAN using the Configure option on your cluster object. Then select *Two node vSAN cluster* as depicted below.

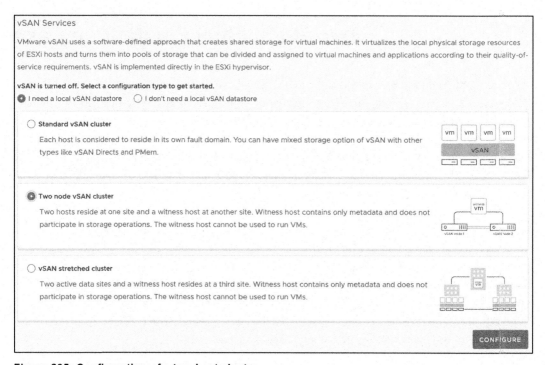

Figure 205: Configuration of a two-host cluster

Next, enable vSAN ESA for this cluster and verify that it has passed (or not) all the compatibility checks. As shown, in the next screenshot, we have some failed tests. This is the result of running our lab virtually, but fortunately it does not stop us from completing the wizard.

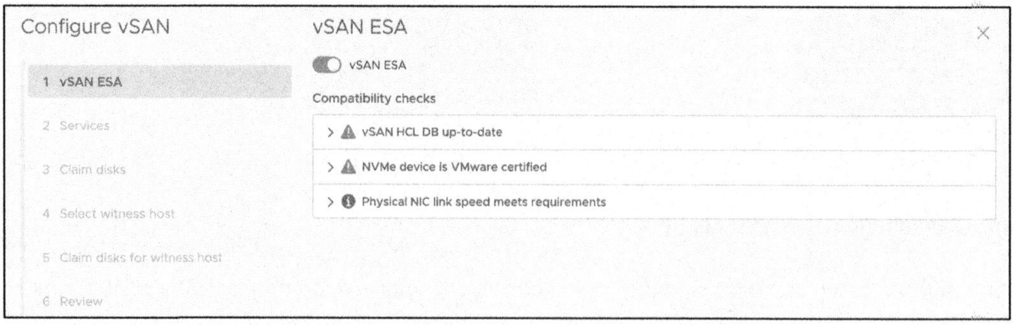

Figure 206: Configuration of a two-host cluster

You will of course make sure that all compatibility checks have passed in your production environment before proceeding. Once the checks have passed, select all the services which you require. Note that all services are available even though it is a two host vSAN cluster. From a product or feature standpoint, there is no limitation. However, with only two hosts, you will not be able to set *failures to tolerate* value greater than 1, nor will you be able to select RAID-5 or RAID-6 for availability. This is because these erasure coding features require 3 (2+1) or 6 hosts (3+1 for RAID-5 and 4+2 for RAID-6) respectively. What may however limit you is, of course, the vSAN and vSphere license you have procured. In our case, we have an ESA cluster, but we will not use any of the additional services at this point.

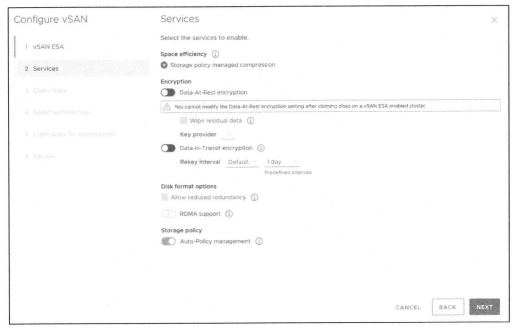

Figure 207: Data services

Next, we will need to claim the devices that will form the vSAN shared datastore. This step is the same as during the creation of a normal vSAN cluster as can be seen in the next screenshot.

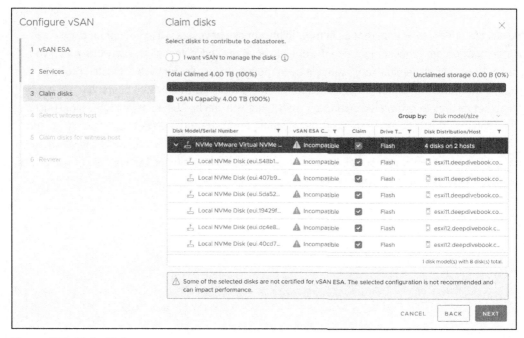

Figure 208: Claim Disks

In the next step, we are going to select the host that will act as the witness host. In our case, this is the virtual witness appliance. After that, we will need to claim the disks for this witness host as this witness host will store the witness components for the virtual machines running on the two-host cluster. This again is very similar to the configuration of a stretched cluster. The step missing however is the creation of fault domains (preferred and secondary) and the selection of the host that belongs to these locations. This is because the fault domains are automatically implied; each physical host and the witness are in their own respective fault domain, as we shall see next.

Figure 209: Selecting the witness host

Now we can review the two-node configuration and complete the creation by clicking finish. After we have clicked finish, we can simply examine the configuration in the vSphere Client. One thing that immediately stands out is that even though we did not create fault domains and we did not specify which hosts belong to which fault domain, faults domains have been configured and each of the two hosts is assigned to their own unique fault domain.

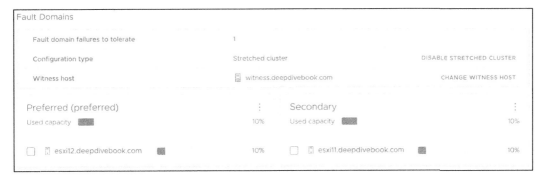

Figure 210: Fault domains in a two-host configuration

That completes the configuration of a two-host cluster. In this case, we have shown a regular two host configuration.

What is interesting to know is that when another 2-host cluster is created, the same vSAN Witness Appliance can be selected. This capability, shared witness host, was introduced in vSAN 7.0 U1 and designed for customers with multiple 2-host clusters who want to limit the number of Witness Appliances deployed.

There are some limitations and considerations for a shared witness deployment. First and foremost, the size of the vSAN Witness Appliance determines how many 2-host clusters the witness can be shared. The largest vSAN Witness Appliance can support up to 64 2-host clusters and a maximum of 64.000 components. Typically, the component limit should not be a concern, as this means you can store a 1000 witness components per cluster. This means you can run easily over a hundred VMs per 2-host cluster before you hit this limit. We have not seen any customers reaching those numbers in a 2-host cluster yet. Having said that, you could be that one customer that does deploy a large number of VMs. Therefore, it is important to make sure you select the correct witness appliance size and monitor the number of components as, potentially, you could reach the maximum limits.

It is possible to monitor the currently assigned number of configurations to your shared witness host. Simply right click the host, click on "vSAN" and click "assign as shared witness host". You will now be presented with a window that shows the currently assigned two-host clusters.

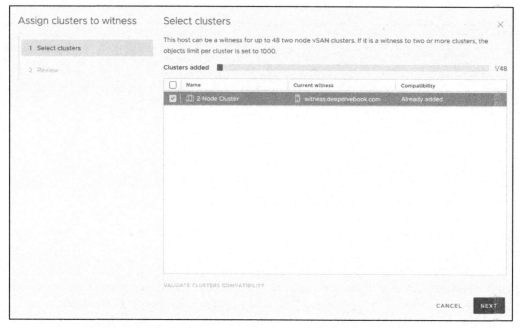

Figure 211: Assign as shared witness host

You can look at the same information by clicking on the witness appliance and then go to "Monitor", Two Node Clusters". As demonstrated in the next screenshot, you will be presented with a list of clusters, the witness component count, and information like the limits.

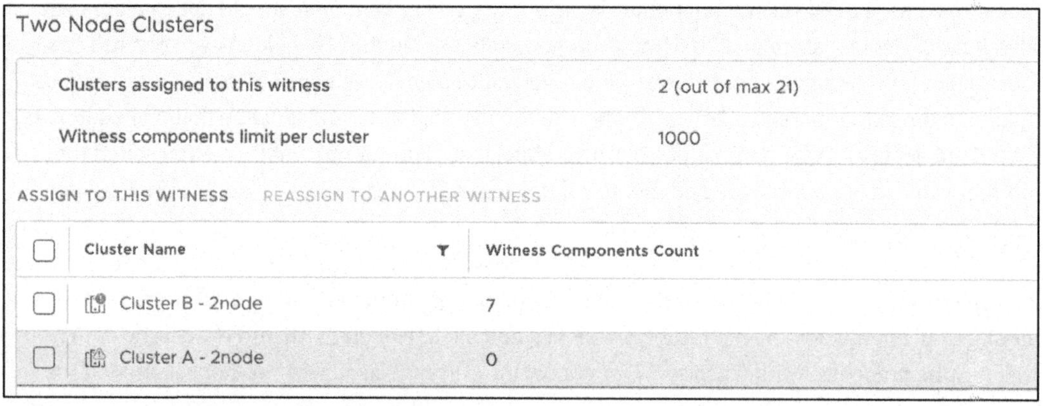

Two Node Clusters	
Clusters assigned to this witness	2 (out of max 21)
Witness components limit per cluster	1000

ASSIGN TO THIS WITNESS   REASSIGN TO ANOTHER WITNESS

	Cluster Name	▼	Witness Components Count
☐	Cluster B - 2node		7
☐	Cluster A - 2node		0

Figure 212: Two-host Clusters information

In the above screenshot, you can also see the option "Assign to this witness". This option allows you to assign this shared witness to an existing 2-host configuration. This 2-host configuration will already have a witness assigned, but this witness is typically a non-shared witness. Using the "Assign To This Witness" option you can migrate from non-shared to shared, but you can also use this option to replace a currently shared witness appliance with a new shared witness appliance.

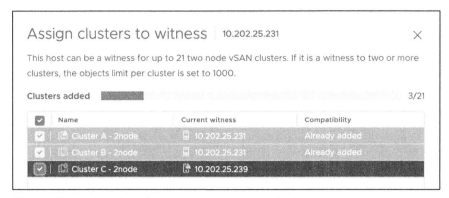

Figure 213: Assign shared witness to an existing cluster

There is another rather unique configuration possible as well. This is a configuration that has started to become more and more popular amongst customers as it lowers the cost of the deployment significantly.

vSAN Direct Connect

When VMware first introduced the two-host cluster option, the immediate request that we heard from customers was to cross-connect the hosts. This is something that customers have done for vMotion for the longest time and doing the same for vSAN with 25 GbE NICs (or higher) without the need for a 25 GbE switch (or higher) would provide the ability to deliver great performance at a relatively low cost. Starting with vSAN 6.5, cross-connecting two-host configurations became fully supported. Please note that this only works with, and only is supported for, two-host clusters.

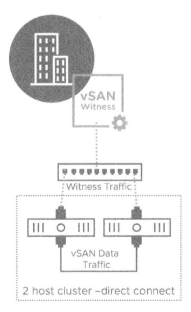

Figure 214: vSAN Direct Connect

As demonstrated in the diagram above, this will require Witness Traffic Separation to be configured for vSAN. We have already described how to do this in the stretched cluster chapter as the same functionality can be leveraged to separate witness traffic from vSAN data traffic in a 2 host vSAN cluster configuration. If you are considering deploying a two-host configuration with direct connect, please make sure you are familiar with the required *esxcli* command.

Now that we have seen the configuration, and the two-host direct connection option, let's look at requirements, constraints, and two host cluster specific support statements.

Support statements, requirements, and constraints

In a vSAN two host configuration support, requirements and constraints are slightly different than in a stretched cluster configuration. Let's start by listing all requirements and constraints, followed by support statements that are different for two host configurations versus a stretched cluster configuration.

- 500ms maximum latency is tolerated between the two-host cluster and the witness host
- Between data sites both Layer 2 and Layer 3 are supported
    - Layer-2 is recommended for simplicity
- Between the data sites and the witness site Layer 3 is required
    - Prevents I/O from being routed through a potentially low bandwidth witness site
- In the case of multiple locations, multiple witness VMs running in a central location may share the same VLAN
- When only a single VLAN is available per 2-host location, it is supported to tag the Management Network for Witness traffic
- VM Storage Policies can only be configured with *Number of Failures To Tolerate* = 1 and RAID-1 (Mirroring) due to the fact that there are only 2 hosts in the cluster
- Bandwidth between vSAN Hosts hosting VM objects and the Witness Host is dependent on the number of objects residing on vSAN. A standard rule of thumb is 2Mbps for every 1000 components on vSAN. Because vSAN hosts have a maximum number of 27000 components per host, the maximum bandwidth requirement from a 2 Host cluster to the Witness Host supporting it, is 54Mbps
- SMP-FT is supported when using 2 Host configurations in the same physical location. SMP-FT requires appropriate vSphere licensing. The vSAN Witness Appliance managing a 2 Host cluster may not reside on the cluster it is providing quorum for. SMP-FT is not a feature that removes this restriction
- By default, in a two-host configuration and a stretched configuration vSAN only reads from the fault domain in which the VM resides. This is very valuable as it lowers bandwidth requirements. For a two-host cluster, which is located in the same datacenter, this reading from a single host adds no value. The vSAN *"DOMOwnerForceWarmCache"* setting can be configured to force reads across hosts in a 2-host configuration. This can be configured in the UI via "Advanced Options", simply disable "Site read locality".

One major difference when comparing two host clusters with a stretched cluster however is that, with a two-host configuration, it is supported to cross host the witness appliance when you only have 2 locations via a special support request (RPQ). What does this exactly mean, and what would be the use case for this? Well, the use case for this would be when there are two locations within 500ms RTT latency and both need some form of compute and storage for local services. As shown in the diagram below, each remote location hosts the witness for the other location. This way only two locations are required, instead of 3 normally.

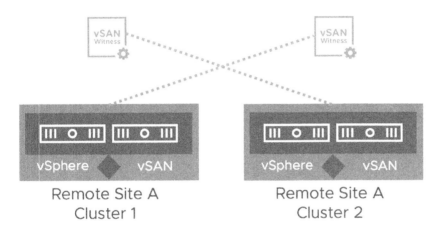

Figure 215: Cross host witness

Although briefly mentioned in the requirements above, we do want to explicitly show two common network architectures for connecting remote locations to a centralized datacenter. In our experience, in almost all cases L3 networking is configured between the central datacenter and the remote location. In some of the cases we have seen multiple networks being available per remote location, and in most cases, we see a single network available. The following diagrams depict these two scenarios.

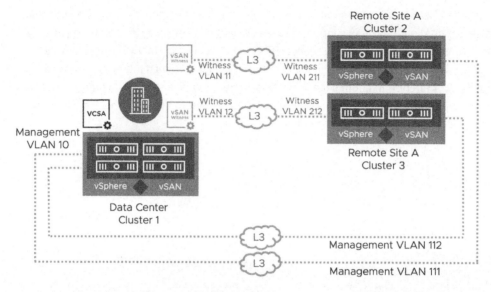

Figure 216: Multiple VLANs per remote location

In the above scenario, per location also two static routes will be required to be defined. One for Management VLAN 10 to the remote location Management VLAN, and one for the witness VLAN to the Witness VLAN. Note that in the case where you have many remote locations, the above scenario does not scale extremely well, and will add a layer of complexity as a result.

Of course, as mentioned, this can be simplified by having a single network for each location that shares both Management as well as Witness traffic. The following diagram depicts this scenario.

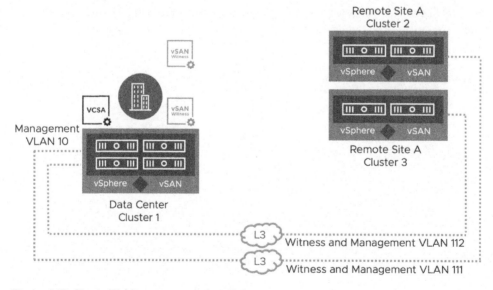

Figure 217: Single VLANs per remote location

Please note that in the case of the above scenario a static route from the management network to the remote location is still required, and the witness appliance will need to be modified so that the management VMkernel interface is also tagged for Witness traffic. Although in the above examples we have shown multiple witness appliances, of course, these architectures are also supported with a shared witness configuration!

Nested Fault Domains in a 2-node Cluster

One thing we have not discussed yet are Nested Fault Domains in a 2-node cluster. This functionality was added in vSAN 7.0 U3 and significantly increases the availability of workloads running on a 2-node vSAN cluster. How does this work? Well simply said, similar to what you can do in a stretched cluster, you can do in a 2-node cluster. In other words, you can specify that a VM needs to be replicated across hosts, and you can specify how the VM needs to be protected within a host. The following screenshot demonstrates the policy configuration required to mirror across hosts, and protect the workload within a host with RAID-1

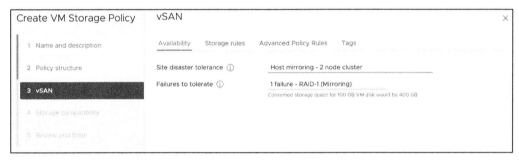

Figure 218: Host mirroring and RAID-1

If you then deploy a VM using this policy and inspect the objects of the VM by going to the Monitor section of the VM and clicking on Physical Disk Placement under vSAN then you will notice that you will have a RAID-1 configuration for the performance leg and a RAID-1 configuration for the capacity leg in each host. Note, that a RAID-1 configuration within a host does mean that you will need to have 3 devices within each host.

At this point you may wonder if other policy configurations are also possible. Indeed, they are. You could, for instance, also create policy for a RAID-6 configuration, or a RAID-5 configuration. One thing we do need to point out is that Adaptive RAID-5 is not available within a host. Meaning that regardless of the number of devices, you will always get a 2+1 configuration when you use a RAID-5 policy in combination with "Host mirroring".

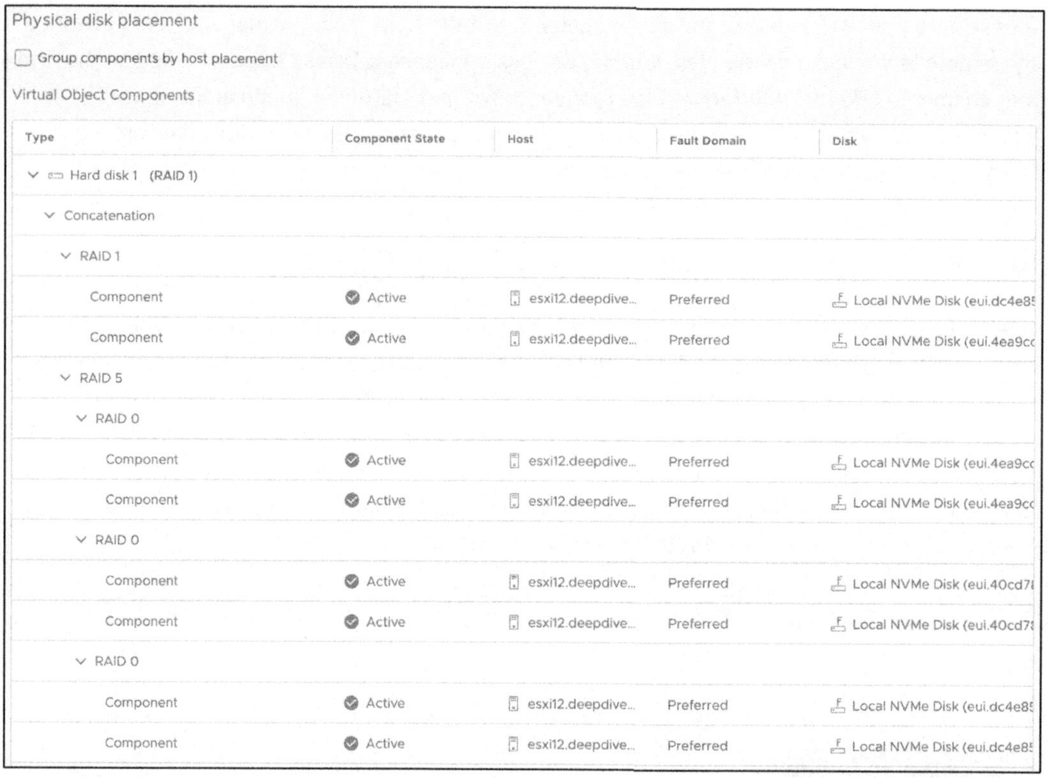

Physical disk placement				
☐ Group components by host placement				
Virtual Object Components				
Type	**Component State**	**Host**	**Fault Domain**	**Disk**
∨ ⊏ Hard disk 1 (RAID 1)				
∨ Concatenation				
∨ RAID 1				
Component	✅ Active	🗄 esxi12.deepdive...	Preferred	📇 Local NVMe Disk (eui.dc4e85
Component	✅ Active	🗄 esxi12.deepdive...	Preferred	📇 Local NVMe Disk (eui.4ea9cc
∨ RAID 5				
∨ RAID 0				
Component	✅ Active	🗄 esxi12.deepdive...	Preferred	📇 Local NVMe Disk (eui.4ea9cc
Component	✅ Active	🗄 esxi12.deepdive...	Preferred	📇 Local NVMe Disk (eui.4ea9cc
∨ RAID 0				
Component	✅ Active	🗄 esxi12.deepdive...	Preferred	📇 Local NVMe Disk (eui.40cd7
Component	✅ Active	🗄 esxi12.deepdive...	Preferred	📇 Local NVMe Disk (eui.40cd7
∨ RAID 0				
Component	✅ Active	🗄 esxi12.deepdive...	Preferred	📇 Local NVMe Disk (eui.dc4e85
Component	✅ Active	🗄 esxi12.deepdive...	Preferred	📇 Local NVMe Disk (eui.dc4e85

Figure 219: Host mirroring and RAID-5

We realize the above screenshot only shows one of the hosts of the host mirror, of course on the second page of the Virtual Object Components view you would see the RAID-5 configuration of "esxi11", the other ESXi host in this two host vSAN cluster.

Summary

A vSAN two host configuration will allow you to deploy a limited number of VMs in (potentially) remote locations without the need for complex storage configurations and operational processes. On top of that, these locations can be managed through a centralized vCenter Server instance, lowering operational cost and overhead.

09

Cloud-Native Applications Use Case

Kubernetes is now the de-facto platform for cloud native applications. However, Kubernetes continues to rely on an external provider for two resources – production ready load balancers and persistent storage. In this chapter, we will explore how vSAN can provide a platform not just for virtual machine workloads, but also for the newer container-based, cloud-native applications. We will show vSAN integration with upstream Kubernetes distributions through the vSphere Container Storage Interface (CSI), as well as vSAN integrations with VMware's own Tanzu branded Kubernetes distributions. This will not be a deep dive into all elements of Kubernetes. Instead, we will focus on those objects in Kubernetes that are relevant to storage, particularly vSAN.

The initial release of the vSAN ESA in vSAN 8.0 was missing the support of Cloud Native Storage. vSAN 8.0 U1 closes the gap by now offering CNS support with vSAN ESA.

What is a container?

It is not possible to talk about Kubernetes without first describing what a container is. In its simplest form, a container can be considered a very special sort of process that runs in an operating system. This special process represents an application. These processes are special only because they leverage operating system features such as control groups (cgroups) and namespaces for limiting and isolating system resources used by the container. In the early days of containers, they were often compared to virtual machines, and some very simplistic viewpoints described them as virtual machines "without the need for an operating system". In some respects, this is correct, but since a container is a process running in an operating system, it does still require an OS. Admittedly, many containers run in the same operating system, since again the container is just a process.

One additional item to mention in the context of containers is the requirement to have a container runtime installed in the operating system. This is sometimes called a container engine. A **container runtime** knows how to run containers on the host operating system and takes care of cgroup and namespace creation for containers. A container runtime could be said to do operating system virtualization rather than hypervisor hardware virtualization. It takes operating system components like the process tree, the file system and the network stack and carves them up into secure isolated constructs called containers.

The really neat thing about containers is portability. Developers could create their container-based application on their laptop, and then deploy it to an on-premises based Kubernetes distribution such as Tanzu Kubernetes, or to a cloud-based Kubernetes distribution, such as Google Kubernetes Engine. While container technology had existed for many years, it was not until Docker (the company) came along and made it very easy for developers to package their containers using Docker (the product) and make them portable, that containers began to gain popularity.

Why Kubernetes?

Now you might be wondering why we need Kubernetes if containers are so great. In a nutshell, Kubernetes allows us to manage containers at scale, or indeed the applications running in containers. The term container "orchestration" is used a lot, but in essence, Kubernetes is a platform that allows us to provision, scale in and out, update and upgrade, and generally life cycle manage container-based applications. Of course, there is much more to Kubernetes than just containers. Microservices, which is the splitting up of an application into its constituent parts, is another major aspect of Kubernetes. This separation of monolithic application functionality into microservices brings in the concept of Service Mesh, which deals with the partitioning or segmentation of applications at a network and security level. However, Microservices and Service Mesh are beyond the scope of what we wish to discuss in this chapter. Instead, our focus will be on how applications that run in Kubernetes, and which require persistent storage, can leverage vSAN to meet those requirements.

Kubernetes Storage Constructs

Since this book is all about storage, the focus in this section is to highlight just those Kubernetes objects that have some relationship to the underlying storage. We will expand this somewhat to bring in some other Kubernetes objects that are involved in consuming storage, e.g., pods, but suffice to say the scope will not cover every Kubernetes object.

Before delving into the different objects, it is interesting to note that in the early days of containerization, not much thought was given to persistent storage. The feeling was that you would spin up your container, get it to do some units of work, capture the result and then discard the container before starting the whole process over once more. The terminology to describe this scenario is "stateless" and for some time, containers were positioned for stateless workloads. Any writes to disk that were needed during this work was done to ephemeral storage. Once the container was discarded, so was the data. However, while there was a lot of value in being able to run stateless workloads, people soon realized the value of being able to run "stateful" containerized workloads as well. A pressing concern was the need to persist data in case a container crashed. Thus, a mechanism to provide persistent storage for containers was desired.

Let's now look at the Kubernetes storage objects in some more detail.

Storage Class

As the name implies, this is a way for a Kubernetes cluster administrator to define different "classes" of storage to a developer. When Kubernetes is running on vSphere, these Storage Classes allow different sorts of vSphere datastores to be chosen through integration with Storage Policy Based Management (SPBM). Let's look at how this is achieved, as well as some of the other attributes of a Storage Class.

One of the entries that is placed in a Storage Class manifest is "provisioner". This is probably a good place to expand on the purpose of a Container Storage Interface (CSI) driver or plugin. Essentially a CSI driver is what enables Kubernetes to provision persistent volumes on top of different underlying infrastructures, such as vSphere, AWS, Google Cloud, etc., and consume available infrastructure storages. For Kubernetes clusters that are running as a set of virtual machines on vSphere, this cluster will be consuming vSphere datastores for persistent volumes. In this case, the provisioner is the vSphere CSI driver, "csi.vsphere.vmware.com". This driver is also referred to as the vSphere Container Storage Plug-in, and its purpose is to provision Kubernetes persistent volumes on vSphere storage.

Note: There are many, many CSI drivers in the marketplace. Many of the storage array vendors provide their own CSI driver to interact directly with their own storage array. However, for vSAN, the only supported CSI driver is the vSphere CSI driver.

When the provisioner in the Storage Class is set to vSphere CSI driver, a parameter called "storagepolicyname" may also be defined. This parameter is used to map a Kubernetes Storage Class to a vSphere storage policy. Since vSAN is very much integrated with the Storage Policy-Based Management (SPBM) feature of vSphere, different Kubernetes Storage Classes can be created to reflect different aspects of vSAN storage. This means that any persistent volumes that are created using a particular storage class will be instantiated on the vSAN datastore with the storage policy referenced by "storagepolicyname". If "storagepolicyname" is not defined, vSphere datastores have a default policy associated with them, and that is what is chosen in those cases.

Another configurable option is "allowVolumeExpansion", which enables the online growth of Persistent Volumes. Note that at the time of going to print, the vSphere CSI driver only supports expansion on block-based persistent volumes. Volume expansion is not supported on file-based persistent volumes. The use-cases for block and file-based persistent volumes will be discussed shortly.

One can also specify a "reclaimPolicy" in the StorageClass. This tells Kubernetes what to do with a Persistent Volume (PV) that is bound to a Persistent Volume Claim (PVC) when the Persistent Volume Claim is deleted. You can think of a PVC as an ownership claim on a set of raw disk resources that are encompassed by the PV. But as is shown here, having a PVC distinct from a PV gives administrators more control over the lifecycle of the storage. By default, the bound Persistent Volume is also "Deleted" with the Persistent Volume Claim, but the reclaim policy can be set to be "Retained" or "Recycled". In this case, the PV can continue to exist without the PVC, meaning it could be reused should the need arise.

Finally, another optional parameter that one might find in the Storage Class manifest is the filesystem type "parameters.csi.storage.k8s.io/fstype". This defines how a persistent volume is formatted. Options for block volumes are "ext4", and "xfs". The only format option available for file volumes is "nfs4".

Here is an example of a simple Storage Class containing a vSAN policy for block volumes. This is referred to as a YAML manifest, YAML short for Yet Another Markup Language. This is how users interact with Kubernetes. The YAML manifests are sent to the Kubernetes API Server through a command called kubectl. The Kubernetes API Server then validates and configures the objects that are requested in the manifest.

```
kind: StorageClass
apiVersion: storage.k8s.io/v1
metadata:
  name: vsan-sc
provisioner: csi.vsphere.vmware.com
allowVolumeExpansion: true
parameters:
  storagepolicyname: "vSAN Default Storage Policy"
  csi.storage.k8s.io/fstype: "ext4"
```

Compare this to the next example of a simple Storage Class containing a vSAN policy for file volumes. Note the only difference is "parameters.csi.storage.k8s.io/fstype" set to "nfs4" instead of "ext4" used above. Note also that the "allowVolumeExpansion" parameter has been omitted from this StorageClass since this is a feature that is only available on block volumes at the time of writing.

```
kind: StorageClass
apiVersion: storage.k8s.io/v1
metadata:
  name: vsan-file-sc
provisioner: csi.vsphere.vmware.com
parameters:
  storagepolicyname: "vSAN Default Storage Policy"
  csi.storage.k8s.io/fstype: nfs4
```

Persistent Volumes

A Persistent Volume, or PV for short, is an allocation of storage resources that can be used by a containerized application to store data. In the case of Kubernetes running on vSphere and using vSAN as a storage platform, persistent volumes map to VMDKs on the vSAN datastore. The VMDK that are instantiated on the vSAN datastore to create a PV are a special virtual disk known as a First Class Disk (FCD) or Improved Virtual Disks (IVD). These special disks enable disk-centric operations outside of the lifecycle of the virtual machine, e.g., the disk can have a snapshot, can be restored from a snapshot, can be cloned, etc. Historically, these were always virtual machine centric operations. FCDs allow these operations to occur at the granularity of a virtual disk.

It is important to note that PVs are not tied to the lifecycle of the containerized application which uses them. In Kubernetes, the containerized application is called a pod. PVs can exist independent of any pod that uses them. Indeed, a pod can be deleted and can be recreated to use the PV without any loss of data from the PV. The concept of a pod will be covered in more detail shortly.

Persistent Volumes can also be provisioned statically by the way, i.e., a virtual disk could be created manually outside of Kubernetes and then mapped to a Persistent Volume construct. However, a much more elegant approach to creating Persistent Volumes is to provision them dynamically through a Persistent Volume Claim (PVC).

Persistent Volume Claim

As we have just learned, the way to dynamically create a Persistent Volume (PV) in Kubernetes is through a Persistent Volume Claim (PVC). Let's take a look at some of the attributes that one might find in a PVC manifest when dynamically creating PVs on vSphere storage, notably vSAN.

One of the first attributes is the "spec.accessMode". vSAN supports a number of different access modes for volumes, but the two most common access modes for Kubernetes PVs are read write once (RWO) and read-write-many (RWX). RWO access mode implies that a persistent volume can only be accessed from a single pod. RWX access mode implies that a persistent volume can be accessed from multiple pods. The vSphere CSI driver does not support multi-attach RWX block volumes at the time of writing. It only supports multi-attach RWX file volumes via vSAN File Services. RWO block volumes are fully supported on the vSAN datastore.

Caution: At the time of writing, there is no support for file based (RWX) persistent volumes on vSAN ESA, as vSAN File Service is not supported yet in vSAN ESA. Only block based (RWO) volumes are supported on vSAN ESA at this time. However, considering that support for vSAN File Service should be available on vSAN ESA at some point in the near future, the authors decided to include a discussion on RWX volumes in the book. vSAN File Service continues to be supported on vSAN OSA, and by extension, RWX volumes are also support on vSAN OSA. In fact, the same vSAN OSA datastore with vSAN File Service enabled can be used to provision both RWO block volume and RWX file volumes.

With the above caveat in mind, let's continue to look at PVCs. Another attribute of a Persistent Volume Claim manifest is "spec.resources.requests.storage" where the size of the Persistent Volume is specified. Other than that, the only important entry in the PVC YAML manifest is a reference to the Storage Class, which has been described earlier. This maps a request for a volume to a particular storage policy on vSphere, and this in turn guides vSphere to create the volume on the appropriate vSphere datastore.

Here is an example of a simple PVC manifest for a 2GB RWO block volume.

```
apiVersion: v1
kind: PersistentVolumeClaim
```

```
metadata:
  name: vsan-claim
spec:
  storageClassName: vsan-sc
  accessModes:
    - ReadWriteOnce
  resources:
    requests:
      storage: 2Gi
```

Here is an example of a simple PVC for a 2GB RWX file volume. Notice that the only difference between the block and file PVC is the different "spec.storageClassName" setting which requests that the volume is formatted with a different filesystem type, and of course the "spec.accessModes" setting.

```
apiVersion: v1
kind: PersistentVolumeClaim
metadata:
  name: vsan-file-claim
spec:
  storageClassName: vsan-file-sc
  accessModes:
    - ReadWriteMany
  resources:
    requests:
      storage: 2Gi
```

Pod

Now that we have successfully learned how to build Kubernetes Persistent Volumes on vSphere datastores such as vSAN, let's look at how an application can consume those volumes. In its simplest form, a pod is a Kubernetes construct comprising of one or more containers. All containers within the pod share storage and network resources. For the purposes of this book, the only aspect of a pod that we are interested in is how it can consume external storage. Thus, the parts of a pod manifest that should be configured are "spec.volumes" which references a Persistent Volume Claim (PVC), and "spec.containers.volumeMounts" which mounts the volume into the pods. The "spec.containers.volumeMounts.name" mounts the volume which matches "spec.volumes.name" from the same pod manifest.

Here is an example of a pod with a single *busybox* container image that is claiming a Persistent Volume from the PVC "vsan-claim". This *busybox* container provides a number of Unix utilities in a single executable. Referencing the PVC via "claimName" (which was created previously), this creates a request for a 2GB read write once (RWO) block volume matching the Storage Class "vsan-sc". Within Kubernetes, this volume create request is sent to the vSphere CSI driver components since this is the provisioner that is specified in the StorageClass. This in turn talks to another component called CNS, short for Cloud Native Storage, in the vCenter Server. After applying the various YAML manifest (Storage Class, PVC, and pod), this should result in a 2GB volume being instantiated on a vSAN datastore. It is created with a configuration that matches the default vSAN storage policy as this is what was placed in the Storage Class. If successful, the volume is attached to the Kubernetes worker node where the pod resides. From there, it will be formatted as an "ext4" filesystem and mounted onto the folder "/demo" in the *busybox* pod by a Kubernetes component called the kubelet, which runs on each Kubernetes worker nodes.

```
apiVersion: v1
kind: Pod
metadata:
  name: vsan-block-pod
spec:
  containers:
  - name: busybox
    image: busybox
    volumeMounts:
    - name: block-vol
      mountPath: "/demo"
    command: [ "sleep", "1000000" ]
  volumes:
    - name: block-vol
      persistentVolumeClaim:
        claimName: vsan-claim
```

The following YAML manifest is another example of a pod deployment. However, in this case, we are deploying 2 pods. Both pods will attempt to mount the same read write many (RWX) file volume. The PVC is as described in the "volume.persistentVolumeClaim.claimName" attribute. This should request the vSphere CSI driver to create the volume on the vSAN datastore, as well as export it as a vSAN File Share via vSAN File Service. If this is successful, the same volume should be mounted onto both pods and accessible in the *busybox* containers on the "/nfsvol" folder. Referencing the PVC manifest above, this should be a 2GB file share.

Note that the following manifest creates 2 pods. Multiple manifests can reside in the same YAML file if they are separated with "---" to indicate a different manifest.

```
apiVersion: v1
kind: Pod
metadata:
  name: file-pod-a
spec:
  containers:
  - name: busybox
    image: busybox
    volumeMounts:
    - name: file-vol
      mountPath: "/nfsvol"
    command: [ "sleep", "1000000" ]
  volumes:
    - name: file-vol
      persistentVolumeClaim:
        claimName: vsan-file-claim

---

apiVersion: v1
kind: Pod
metadata:
  name: file-pod-b
spec:
  containers:
  - name: busybox
```

```
    image: busybox
    volumeMounts:
    - name: file-vol
      mountPath: "/nfsvol"
    command: [ "sleep", "1000000" ]
  volumes:
    - name: file-vol
      persistentVolumeClaim:
        claimName: vsan-file-claim
```

vSphere CSI in action – block volume

To demonstrate the creation of a block PV through a PVC, and then accessing the resulting volume from a pod, I will use a small Kubernetes cluster made up of 1 control plane node and 2 worker nodes. Suffice to say that this Kubernetes cluster is deployed on vSphere infrastructure, and already has the vSphere CSI driver installed.

Let's check the nodes in the cluster. One of the nodes is the control-plane, master, as per the role. The others are the workers. The Kubernetes version that has been deployed to this cluster is v1.23.3. We will use the "kubectl" command to interact with the Kubernetes cluster API server to query the state of the cluster, as well as to make requests of the cluster to create new objects.

```
% kubectl get nodes
NAME          STATUS    ROLES                  AGE    VERSION
csisnap-cp0   Ready     control-plane,master   20d    v1.23.3
csisnap-wk0   Ready     <none>                 20d    v1.23.3
csisnap-wk1   Ready     <none>                 20d    v1.23.3
```

Next, we will show the vSphere CSI driver components. There is a single vSphere CSI controller pod, and one vSphere CSI node pod for each of the three nodes in the Kubernetes cluster. We will go into further detail regarding the different CSI components that make up the controller pod shortly. In this version of Kubernetes, which is an upstream, vanilla, Kubernetes, the CSI driver components are placed in the "vmware-system-csi" namespace. A Kubernetes namespace can be thought of as simply a way of organizing resources with a Kubernetes cluster. Therefore, we need to specify the namespace when querying for pods. Note that vSphere CSI driver version 2.5.x, shown here, has a total of 7 containers in the controller pod, as shown in the READY column. Other, older versions of the vSphere CSI driver may show fewer containers in the controller pod. Newer versions may show more containers as new features are continually added.

```
% kubectl get pods -n vmware-system-csi
NAME                                      READY   STATUS    RESTARTS       AGE
vsphere-csi-controller-5b6dfc6799-lmphc   7/7     Running   7 (11d ago)    19d
vsphere-csi-node-ggkng                    3/3     Running   0              19d
vsphere-csi-node-r6pfh                    3/3     Running   5 (11d ago)    19d
vsphere-csi-node-tsd4r                    3/3     Running   3 (11d ago)    19d
```

To create a sample application, we are going to work in the default namespace. Thus, it is not necessary to specify this namespace when we create, query, or delete the objects. Some objects, such as Storage Class and PV, are not namespace scoped, but PVCs and pods are. At present, there are no Storage Classes, PVCs, PVs, or pods in the default namespace on this cluster.

```
% kubectl get pods,pvc,pv,sc
No resources found
```

Next, apply a manifest that contains a Storage Class, a RWO block PVC, and a pod that we examined previously. As mentioned, these can all be added to the same manifest file so long as they are separated with "---" on its own line in the file. Thus, a single file can create multiple Kubernetes objects.

```
% kubectl apply -f demo-sc-pvc-pod-rwo.yaml
storageclass.storage.k8s.io/vsan-sc created
persistentvolumeclaim/vsan-claim created
pod/vsan-block-pod created
```

Check if the objects were created successfully. Let's check the Storage Class, the PVC, the PV that should have been created with the PVC, and finally the pod.

```
% kubectl get sc
NAME    PROVISIONER               RECLAIMPOLICY VOLUMEBINDINGMODE ALLOWVOLUMEEXPANSION AGE
vsan-sc csi.vsphere.vmware.com Delete         Immediate        true                 12s


% kubectl get pvc
NAME        STATUS VOLUME      CAPACITY ACCESS MODES STORAGECLASS AGE
vsan-claim  Bound  pvc-e086a59e….  2Gi   RWO          vsan-sc      15s


% kubectl get pv
NAME          CAPACITY ACCESS MODES RECLAIM STATUS CLAIM      STORAGECLASS REASON AGE
pvc-e086a59e… 2Gi      RWO          Delete  Bound  vsan-claim vsan-sc             16s


% kubectl get pod
NAME           READY STATUS  RESTARTS AGE
vsan-block-pod 1/1   Running 0        20s
```

It would appear that all objects have been created successfully. One final check is to open a shell to the pod and check to see if a 2GB RWO block volume has been formatted and mounted to the *busybox* container within the pod. This is done using the "kubectl exec" command. Since the pod only contains a single container, we do not need to explicitly specify the container within the pod, but if the pod held more than one container, the container name would also need to be specified on the command line.

```
% kubectl exec -it vsan-block-pod -- sh
/ # df -h
Filesystem               Size    Used Available Use% Mounted on
overlay                  77.7G   12.1G    61.6G  16% /
tmpfs                    64.0M       0    64.0M   0% /dev
/dev/sdb                  1.9G    6.0M     1.8G   0% /demo
/dev/sda3                77.7G   12.1G    61.6G  16% /dev/termination-log
/dev/sda3                77.7G   12.1G    61.6G  16% /etc/resolv.conf
/dev/sda3                77.7G   12.1G    61.6G  16% /etc/hostname
/dev/sda3                77.7G   12.1G    61.6G  16% /etc/hosts
shm                      64.0M       0    64.0M   0% /dev/shm
tmpfs                    15.5G   12.0K    15.5G   0%
/var/run/secrets/kubernetes.io/serviceaccount
```

```
tmpfs                    7.8G        0     7.8G   0% /proc/acpi
tmpfs                   64.0M        0    64.0M   0% /proc/kcore
tmpfs                   64.0M        0    64.0M   0% /proc/keys
tmpfs                   64.0M        0    64.0M   0% /proc/timer_list
tmpfs                    7.8G        0     7.8G   0% /proc/scsi
tmpfs                    7.8G        0     7.8G   0% /sys/firmware
/ # cd /demo
/demo # ls
lost+found
/demo # mount | grep "/dev/sdb"
/dev/sdb on /demo type ext4 (rw,relatime)
```

A 2GB block volume has now been successfully attached (/dev/sdb) as requested by the PVC manifest, formatted as ext4 as requested in the Storage Class manifest, and mounted to /demo as requested in the Pod manifest.

Cloud-Native Storage (CNS) for vSphere Administrators – block volume

One of the primary goals of VMware when running Kubernetes on vSphere is to provide as much information as possible to the vSphere Administrator. This is to help with monitoring, capacity planning, troubleshooting, etc. To that end, VMware added a Cloud-Native Storage (CNS) section to the vSphere UI to provide this visibility. Since a persistent volume has now been created in a Kubernetes cluster running on vSphere and consuming vSAN storage, CNS now displays information about the PV in the vSphere UI. Below is what is visible in the UI for the volume created in the previous steps. The information displayed includes the name of the PV, whether it is a block or file type, any labels associated with the volume, which datastore it is provisioned on, the storage policy used for the volume, whether the storage policy is compliant or not, a volume ID, volume health, which Kubernetes cluster the PV is on (since there can be many Kubernetes clusters running on the same vSphere infrastructure), and then the Capacity Quota of the volume.

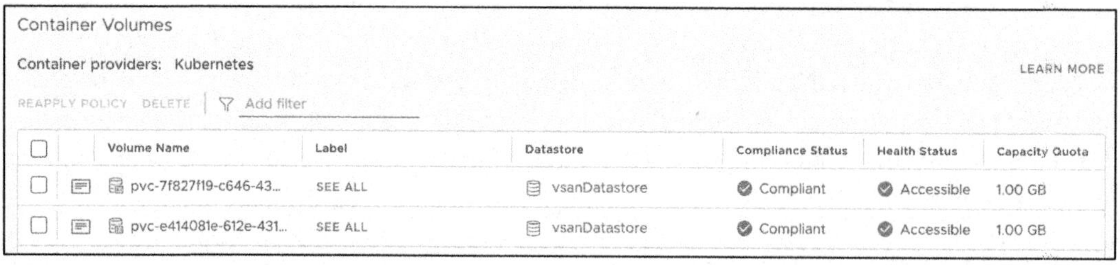

Figure 220: Cloud-Native Storage

The second column in the output above contains a "Details" icon. Clicking this icon reveals even more information about the persistent volume, with several different views. The first view is the Basics view, which provides a lot of vSphere specific information about the volume, but of particular interest is the VM which has the volume attached. This VM in this example is one of the Kubernetes worker nodes. This view also provides the full path to the VMDK object on the vSAN datastore. This is the First Class Disk (FCD) that is backing this Persistent Volume.

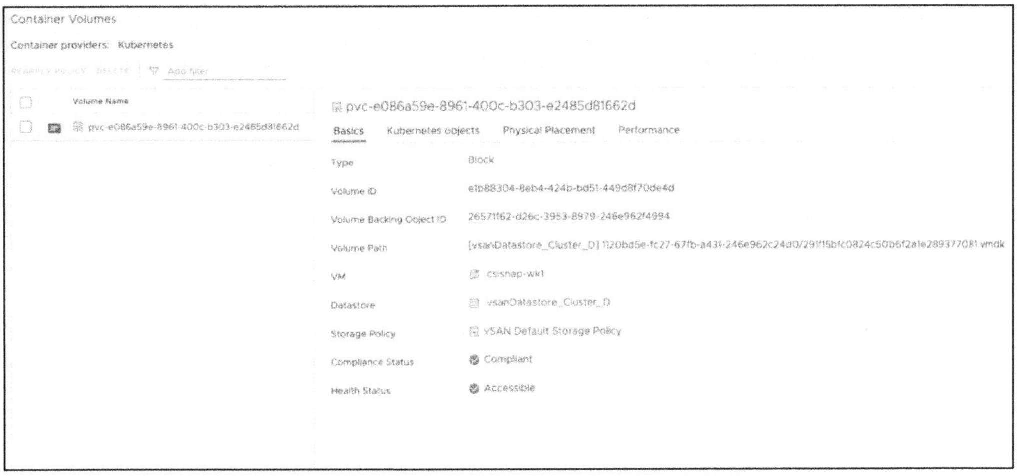

Figure 221: Cloud-Native Storage Basic View

The next view gives additional information about the Kubernetes objects, including the name of the persistent volume claim, the namespace where the PVC was created, and any pods that are currently using the volume. Since we did not specify any labels in the YAML manifests of the PVC, these fields are not populated. This view is also a great way to determine which applications are using which volumes in Kubernetes without having to do manual mappings of Kubernetes objects to vSphere datastore objects.

Figure 222: Cloud-Native Storage Kubernetes Objects View

The next view is of particular interest to vSphere administrators who are also responsible for vSAN storage. It displays the physical placement of the volume. If you recall, we placed a storage policy as a parameter in the Storage Class. The policy chosen at the time was the default storage policy for vSAN. Since this example uses vSAN OSA, the default policy is a RAID-1 configuration, mirroring the data and using a witness component for quorum. We can now see that the volume has been built using this policy. The three vSAN components are visible below; 2 data components (replicas) and 1 witness component. As mentioned, this volume is deployed on vSAN OSA. Obviously, the Physical Placement from a volume deployed on vSAN ESA will be different, as it will show both Performance Leg and Capacity Leg components.

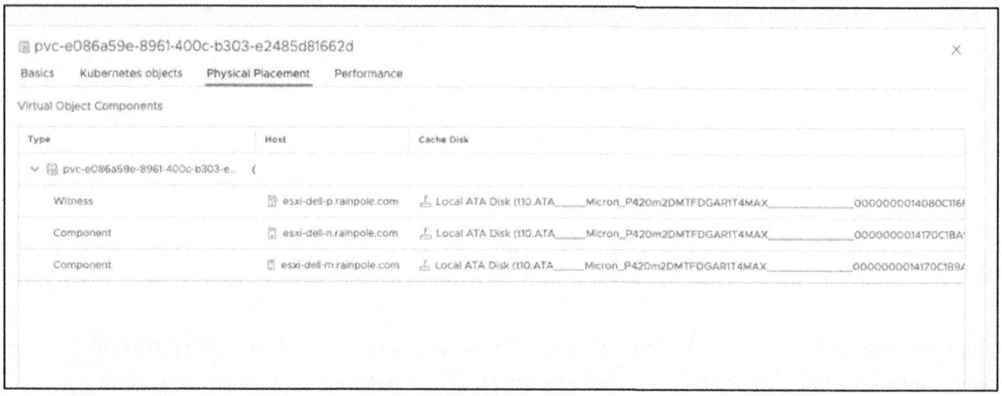

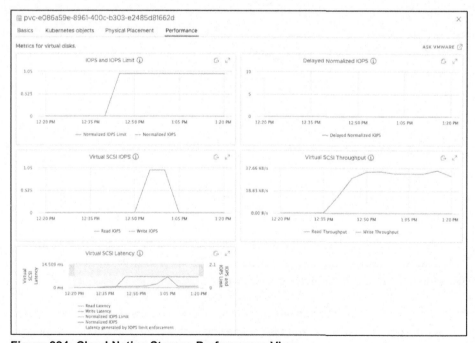

Figure 223: Cloud-Native Storage Physical Placement View

The very last view is a performance view, which means you can get visibility into the performance of individual persistent volumes. This is invaluable for a vSphere administrator when developers begin to complain about poorly performing applications and allows vSphere administrators to quickly assess if the poor performance is storage related.

Figure 224: Cloud-Native Storage Performance View

vSphere CSI in action – file volume

In this section, we turn our attention to dynamically creating a read-write-many (RWX) file volume. As mentioned, the vSphere CSI driver has been developed to include the ability to dynamically provision NFS file volumes on vSAN OSA. As was also previously highlighted, at the time of going to print, there was no support for vSAN File Service on vSAN ESA. Focusing on the vSAN OSA then, there is a requirement to have vSAN File Service enabled, however, and the details on how to do this are covered elsewhere in this book. Using standard Kubernetes manifests, requests to create a RWX persistent volume are sent to the vSphere CSI provider. This results in a dynamically provisioned file share that can be automatically mounted to multiple pods simultaneously.

When creating this file volume, the previously created block volume is left in place. Thus, when we query Kubernetes objects for this new file volume, the block volume objects will also be displayed.

Once more, we begin by deploying a manifest that contains the Storage Class, the PVC and the pods that will share the volume, as defined earlier in this chapter. Again, all objects can be defined in a single manifest and separated using the "---" divider. The difference this time is that two pods are created that share access to the same volume.

```
% kubectl apply -f demo-sc-pvc-pod-rwx.yaml
storageclass.storage.k8s.io/vsan-file-sc created
persistentvolumeclaim/vsan-file-claim created
pod/file-pod-a created
pod/file-pod-b created
```

The Storage Class, PVC, PV and pods can be queried as before, but now the outputs report Kubernetes objects for both block and file. Note that the access mode for the new PVC and PV is RWX, read write many.

```
% kubectl get sc
NAME            PROVISIONER     RECLAIMPOLICY   VOLUMEBINDINGMODE ALLOWVOLUMEEXPANSION  AGE
vsan-file-sc    csi.vsphere…    Delete          Immediate         false                13s
vsan-sc         csi.vsphere…    Delete          Immediate         true                 74m


% kubectl get pvc
NAME             STATUS   VOLUME          CAPACITY   ACCESS MODES   STORAGECLASS     AGE
vsan-claim       Bound    pvc-e086a59e…   2Gi        RWO            vsan-sc          74m
vsan-file-claim  Bound    pvc-13d1015d…   2Gi        RWX            vsan-file-sc     22s


% kubectl get pv
NAME            CAPACITY   ACCESS RECLAIM STATUS  CLAIM           STORAGECLASS      REASON  AGE
pvc-13d1015d…   2Gi        RWX    Delete  Bound   vsan-file-claim vsan-filesc               24s
pvc-e086a59e…   2Gi        RWO    Delete  Bound   vsan-claim      vsan-sc                   75m


% kubectl get pods
NAME            READY   STATUS    RESTARTS  AGE
file-pod-a      1/1     Running   0         36s
file-pod-b      1/1     Running   0         36s
vsan-block-pod  1/1     Running   0         75m
```

On this occasion, the same volume is mounted to both pods. The following steps will verify that the same volume is mounted on both pods, and that both pods can read and write to the volume. First, kubectl is used to exec into pod-a, and create a directory and file on the file volume that is mounted on "/demonfs". Then repeat the operation via pod-b.

```
% kubectl exec -it file-pod-a -- sh
/ # df -h
Filesystem                Size    Used Available Use% Mounted on
overlay                   77.7G   12.1G   61.6G  16% /
tmpfs                     64.0M      0   64.0M   0% /dev
vsan-fs1-b.rainpole.com:/52290524-f5a9-9415-2175-4bfa51e0a6fa
                          2.0G       0    1.9G   0% /demonfs
/dev/sda3                 77.7G   12.1G   61.6G  16% /dev/termination-log
/dev/sda3                 77.7G   12.1G   61.6G  16% /etc/resolv.conf
/dev/sda3                 77.7G   12.1G   61.6G  16% /etc/hostname
/dev/sda3                 77.7G   12.1G   61.6G  16% /etc/hosts
shm                       64.0M      0   64.0M   0% /dev/shm
tmpfs                     15.5G   12.0K   15.5G   0%
/var/run/secrets/kubernetes.io/serviceaccount
tmpfs                      7.8G      0    7.8G   0% /proc/acpi
tmpfs                     64.0M      0   64.0M   0% /proc/kcore
tmpfs                     64.0M      0   64.0M   0% /proc/keys
tmpfs                     64.0M      0   64.0M   0% /proc/timer_list
tmpfs                      7.8G      0    7.8G   0% /proc/scsi
tmpfs                      7.8G      0    7.8G   0% /sys/firmware

/ # cd /demonfs
/demonfs #
/demonfs # mkdir POD1
/demonfs # cd POD1
/demonfs/POD1 # echo "Pod1 was here" >> sharedfile
/demonfs/POD1 # cat sharedfile
Pod1 was here
/demonfs/POD1 # exit

% kubectl exec -it file-pod-b -- sh
/ # df -h
Filesystem                Size    Used Available Use% Mounted on
overlay                   77.7G   12.1G   61.6G  16% /
tmpfs                     64.0M      0   64.0M   0% /dev
vsan-fs1-b.rainpole.com:/52290524-f5a9-9415-2175-4bfa51e0a6fa
                          2.0G       0    1.9G   0% /demonfs
/dev/sda3                 77.7G   12.1G   61.6G  16% /dev/termination-log
/dev/sda3                 77.7G   12.1G   61.6G  16% /etc/resolv.conf
/dev/sda3                 77.7G   12.1G   61.6G  16% /etc/hostname
/dev/sda3                 77.7G   12.1G   61.6G  16% /etc/hosts
shm                       64.0M      0   64.0M   0% /dev/shm
tmpfs                     15.5G   12.0K   15.5G   0%
/var/run/secrets/kubernetes.io/serviceaccount
tmpfs                      7.8G      0    7.8G   0% /proc/acpi
tmpfs                     64.0M      0   64.0M   0% /proc/kcore
tmpfs                     64.0M      0   64.0M   0% /proc/keys
tmpfs                     64.0M      0   64.0M   0% /proc/timer_list
tmpfs                      7.8G      0    7.8G   0% /proc/scsi
tmpfs                      7.8G      0    7.8G   0% /sys/firmware
/ # cd /demonfs
/demonfs # ls
POD1
/demonfs # cd POD1
/demonfs/POD1 # ls
```

```
sharedfile
/demonfs/POD1 # cat sharedfile
Pod1 was here
/demonfs/POD1 # echo "Pod2 was also here" >> sharedfile
/demonfs/POD1 # cat sharedfile
Pod1 was here
Pod2 was also here
/demonfs/POD1 #
```

As viewed above, the files and directories created via pod-a are visible on the same volume from pod-b, and both pods are able to write to the volume. It seems that the read-write-many file share volume is working as expected.

Cloud-Native Storage (CNS) for vSphere Administrators – file volume

File volumes are also visible in the vSphere UI, providing some detailed information about how a vSAN file share is being used by Kubernetes. Much the same information is displayed as seen previously, with the Basics and Physical Placement views providing very similar information. One interesting view is the Kubernetes Objects view. Two pods are now shown sharing the same volume.

Figure 225: Cloud-Native Storage Kubernetes Object View (RWX)

There is also a Performance view as seen with RWO block volumes. The focus of the file volume performance charts is IOPS, Latency, and Throughput.

Before leaving RWX volumes, the Cluster > Configure > vSAN > File Shares view can be visited in the vSphere client UI to check that a vSAN File Share was indeed dynamically created to provide the backing for this Kubernetes volume.

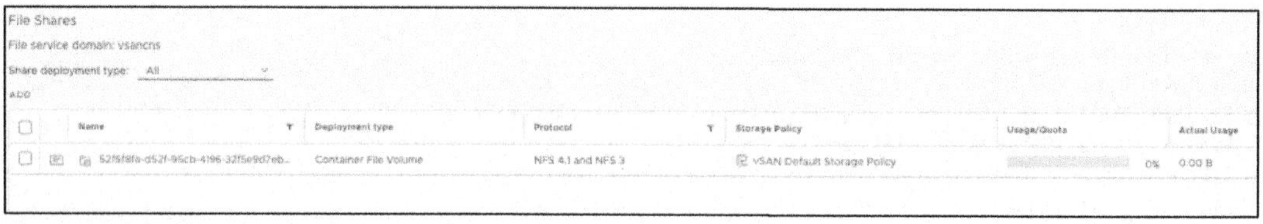

Figure 226: vSAN File Shares – Container File Volume

If the "Details" view is opened by clicking on the icon in the second column, much of the same information observed in the Container Volumes view is also available in this vSAN File Shares view. One thing to note is that there are two types of file shares; one is vSAN File Shares and the other is Container File Volumes. If the view is left at vSAN File Shares, dynamically created file shares that back Kubernetes RWX persistent volumes will not be visible. That is why the type is set to ALL in the previous screenshot, as this will show both vSAN File Shares and Container File Volumes.

vSphere CNS CSI architecture

In this section, the major components of how Kubernetes volumes can be backed by vSphere storage are examined. The vSphere CSI driver has been mentioned a few times, and the CNS component that resides on the vCenter Server has also been discussed. We also briefly mentioned first class disks (FCDs) also known as independent virtual disks (IVDs). It was mentioned that these are special vSphere storage volumes that are used to back Kubernetes PVs. We can think of the CNS component in vCenter Server as the storage control plane, handling the lifecycle operations of container volumes, e.g., create, delete, grow, etc., as well as other functions around metadata retrieval. It is this volume metadata that enables the vSphere client UI to display such detailed information regarding Kubernetes volumes. With the release of vSphere CSI v2.5 (March 2022), support for CSI snapshots was added to the vSphere CSI driver. This added an additional sidecar container to the controller pod. The purpose of this container is to watch for snapshot requests. This brought the total number of containers in the vSphere CSI controller to 7. At the time of writing, version 3.0 (April 2023) is the latest version of the vSphere CSI driver.

To put it simply, in the Kubernetes cluster, the vSphere CSI driver is the component that communicates to vSphere and handles the volume create and delete requests, as well as the attach and detach of a volume to a Kubernetes node. When Kubernetes is deployed on vSphere, this Kubernetes node is a virtual machine. The vSphere CSI driver communicates with the *kubelet* (Kubernetes agent on the worker nodes) for the formatting of the volume, as well as the mounting and unmounting of the volume to a pod running on the worker node. Another major component of the vSphere CSI driver is the CSI syncer. This component is what pushes the Kubernetes metadata regarding the volume to CNS on vCenter Server. This allows Kubernetes persistent volume information to be displayed in the vSphere client UI, as seen previously.

Next, let's look at the pods that are deployed in a vanilla, upstream Kubernetes cluster by the vSphere CSI driver. The pods that we see deployed are the vsphere-csi-controller pod and several vsphere-csi-node pods.

```
% kubectl get pods -n vmware-system-csi
NAME                                       READY   STATUS    RESTARTS      AGE
vsphere-csi-controller-7b87c8b9bc-fg8c4    7/7     Running   0             87m
vsphere-csi-node-ggkng                     3/3     Running   0             20d
vsphere-csi-node-r6pfh                     3/3     Running   5 (12d ago)   20d
vsphere-csi-node-tsd4r                     3/3     Running   3 (12d ago)   20d
```

vsphere-csi-controller pod

The vSphere CSI controller pod handles multiple activities when it comes to volume lifecycle management within Kubernetes. First and foremost, it provides the communication from the Kubernetes Cluster API server to the CNS component on vCenter Server for volume lifecycle operations and metadata syncing. It listens for Kubernetes events related to volume lifecycle, such as create, delete, attach, detach. This functionality is implemented by several distinct containers within the pod. Let's take a closer look at the containers which make up the vSphere CSI driver in Kubernetes.

```
% kubectl get pod vsphere-csi-controller-7b87c8b9bc-fg8c4 \
-n vmware-system-csi -o jsonpath='{.spec.containers[*].name}'
csi-snapshotter csi-attacher csi-resizer vsphere-csi-controller liveness-probe vsphere-
syncer csi-provisioner
```

As you can see, there are 7 containers (often referred to as container sidecars) in the pod. The aim of separating distinct features of the CSI driver into separate sidecar containers means that it simplifies the development and deployment of CSI drivers in general. What follows is a brief description of each container within the vSphere CSI controller pod.

csi-snapshotter

This container enables the vSphere CSI driver to support CSI snapshots. This container watches the Kubernetes API server for VolumeSnapshot objects. It works hand-in-hand with the snapshot controller which watches for Kubernetes VolumeSnapshotContent objects.

csi-attacher

This container monitors the Kubernetes API server for VolumeAttachment objects. If any are observed, it informs the vsphere-csi-controller that a new volume should be attached to a specified node. Similarly, if it observes that the object is removed, then informs the vsphere-csi-controller that a volume should be detached from a specified node.

csi-resizer

This container watches for online volume extend operations. Note that volume extend operations only work for block volumes at the time of writing. It does not provide volume extend operations for file-based volumes.

vsphere-csi-controller

This provides the communication from the Kubernetes Cluster API server to the CNS component on vCenter Server for persistent volume lifecycle operations.

liveness-probe

Monitors the overall health of the vSphere CSI controller pod. The kubelet (agent) that runs on the Kubernetes nodes uses this liveness-probe to determine if a container needs to be restarted. This helps to improve the availability of the vSphere CSI controller pod.

vsphere-syncer

Send metadata information back to the CNS component on vCenter Server so that it can be displayed in the vSphere client UI in the Container Volumes view.

csi-provisioner

Watches the Kubernetes API server for PersistentVolumeClaim objects. If any are observed, it informs the vsphere-csi-controller that a new volume should be created. Similarly, if it observes that the PVC is removed, then it informs the vsphere-csi-controller that the volume should be deleted (depending on the reclaimPolicy in the Storage Class).

vsphere-csi-node pod

Each node gets its own vsphere-csi-node pod. Within each pod are 3 containers.

```
% kubectl get pod vsphere-csi-node-ggkng -n vmware-system-csi -o
jsonpath='{.spec.containers[*].name}'
node-driver-registrar vsphere-csi-node liveness-probe
```

node-driver-registrar

This container establishes communication with the worker node's kubelet (which can be thought of as the Kubernetes agent that runs on the worker node). Once established, the kubelet can make volume operation requests, such as mount, unmount, format, etc.

vsphere-csi-node

This container performs volume operations associated with pod access, e.g., operations such as format, mount, unmount.

liveness-probe

Monitors the overall health of the vSphere CSI node pod. The kubelet (agent) that runs on the Kubernetes nodes used this liveness-probe to determine if a container needs to be restarted. This helps to improve the availability of the vSphere CSI node pod.

Tanzu Kubernetes Considerations

So far in this chapter, we have been discussing the upstream vSphere CSI driver. This is the vSphere Container storage plug-in that runs in a native, vanilla, Kubernetes cluster, deployed on vSphere infrastructure. For the most part, we can also think of VMware's Kubernetes offering, Tanzu Kubernetes Grid (TKG), as an upstream Kubernetes cluster. When referring to TKG here, I am referring to the standalone / multi-cloud version of Kubernetes from VMware which is deployed via the Tanzu command line or UI. This distribution is often referred to TKGm (m for multi-cloud), and while not an official name, we can use it here to differentiate it from other Tanzu offerings. The difference between TKGm and upstream Kubernetes is that our Tanzu team selects components from the plethora of open-source products that are available for Kubernetes. The team tests this Kubernetes stack, validates it, then offers VMware support for customers who purchase it. In other words, the team chooses the vSphere CSI drivers for storage, the various CNI drivers for networking, various Load Balancers, IAM components for identity management, and so on. Once deployed into production, VMware can now support this Kubernetes platform and your vSphere platform end-to-end. Thus, what we have read so far about the upstream vSphere CSI driver applies to TKGm. Note however that there may be a gap between the feature being made available in upstream Kubernetes, and the feature appearing in TKGm. This is because the Tanzu team have to complete their testing processes before releasing it with a TKGm build/version.

But VMware offers more than just TKGm. VMware also offers a product called vSphere with Tanzu. vSphere with Tanzu has the concept of a Supervisor cluster which is deployed when vSphere with Tanzu is enabled on a vSphere cluster. While workloads can be deployed directly onto the Supervisor cluster using Native Pods (also known as PodVMs), the Supervisor cluster is not considered a general-purpose Kubernetes cluster. General purpose Kubernetes clusters are provisioned using a TKG Service, one of many services available in vSphere with Tanzu. The TKG Service, or TKGS for short, can provision fully formed Kubernetes "guest" or "workload" clusters on vSphere through some simple YAML manifest files which describe the cluster configuration. Using Supervisor Namespaces, a vSphere administrator can allocate a certain amount of vSphere resources to a particular development team. Within these namespaces, development teams can provision their own TKG clusters, but never use more resources than the vSphere administrator has allocated. Teams can then develop and test their own applications, and indeed bring applications to production, in a controlled manner from a resource management perspective. The idea is that multiple different development teams can operate in an isolated manner on the same vSphere infrastructure using Supervisor Namespaces via vSphere with Tanzu.

This is important as this flavor of Tanzu Kubernetes does not use the upstream vSphere CSI driver. Let's try to explain the reason why this is the case. TKG clusters created by the TKG Service are placed on their own virtual workload networks which are not designed to have access to the management network where vCenter Server resides. This means that if the upstream vSphere CSI driver is deployed on a TKGS workload cluster in vSphere with Tanzu, it would be unable to reach the vCenter Server, nor would it be able to communicate to its associated CNS component for persistent volume lifecycle management. So how are persistent volumes created in TKGS provisioned clusters you might ask?

The creation of persistent volumes is achieved through a paravirtual CSI (pvCSI) running in the workload clusters that have been provisioned by the TKG Service. This is a modified version of the upstream CSI driver. The reason it is called pvCSI is that it "proxies" requests from the Tanzu Kubernetes workload cluster to the Supervisor cluster which in turn communicates to vCenter Server and CNS to create persistent volumes on the appropriate vSphere storage. The Supervisor cluster control plane nodes are multi-homed with one network interface on the vSphere management network and the other network interface on the workload network (the one used by the TKG workload clusters). In this way, PV operations from TKG workload clusters are sent to the Supervisor cluster, which in turn sends it to CNS in vCenter Server.

Note that the CNS views of the persistent volumes in vSphere with Tanzu reveal this proxying of volumes. For a PV created in a TKGS guest cluster, a vSphere administrator will be able to see the relationship between it and the volume that is created on the Supervisor cluster on its behalf, as well as information about which TKGS guest cluster it was created for.

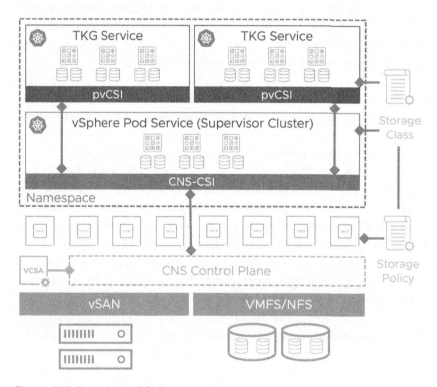

Figure 227: Paravirtual CSI Driver in vSphere with Tanzu

The reason why the pvCSI driver is called out as a consideration is that new CSI features typically get developed for the upstream CSI driver for vanilla Kubernetes distributions before filtering down to vSphere with Tanzu. Examples of this would be the support for CSI snapshots which has been in the upstream version of the vSphere CSI driver for some time but is still not available in vSphere with Tanzu pvCSI driver at the time of this book going to press.

Thus, it is extremely important to check whether a particular CSI driver capability is specifically available in the Kubernetes distribution that you are planning to use. This is not only true for TKG or vSphere with Tanzu, but also for other Kubernetes distributions that use the vSphere CSI driver, such as Rancher, OpenShift and Google Anthos. When you see that a feature is supported in the upstream vSphere CSI driver, do not assume that it is automatically available in all other Kubernetes distributions.

Supervisor Services & Data Persistence platform (DPp)

VMware continuously enhances vSAN. A primary goal is to build a platform for both container workloads and virtual machine workloads. Data Persistence platform (DPp) is another step on the journey towards enabling "cloud-native" applications to be deployed successfully on vSAN.

Many cloud-native applications implement what is known as a "shared nothing" architecture. These applications do not require shared storage as they are designed with built-in replication/protection features. Thus, we need vSAN to be able to cater for this. At the same time, these applications need to be vSAN and vSphere aware. Applications deployed to DPp have the built-in smarts to understand what action needs to be taken when there is an event on the underlying vSphere infrastructure, e.g., maintenance mode, upgrade, patching, etc.

Since these applications have built-in protection, it implies that vSAN does not need to provide protection at the underlying layer. Therefore, the storage objects for the cloud-native application may be provisioned with no protection. vSAN can hand off storage services to the application if the application already has those capabilities built-in (replication, encryption, erasure-coding, etc.). This means that vSAN does not duplicate these features at the infrastructure layer and avoids consuming more storage capacity than necessary. However, if these features are not available in the application, vSAN may still be leveraged to provide these capabilities.

There is also another deployment option from a storage perspective. To facilitate a high-performance data path for these cloud-native applications, the Data Persistence platform also introduces a new construct for storage called vSAN-Direct. vSAN-Direct allows applications to consume the local storage devices on a vSAN host directly. However, these local storage devices are still under the control of HCI management, so that health, usage, and other pertinent information about the device is bubbled up to the vSphere client. The primary goal here is to allow cloud-native applications to be seamlessly deployed onto vSAN whilst leveraging the native device speed with minimum overhead, but at the same time have those applications understand infrastructure operations such as maintenance mode, upgrades, and indeed host failures. Note that at the time of writing, if a decision is reached to use vSAN-Direct for DPp, then the whole of the vSAN cluster must be dedicated to vSAN-Direct. It is not supported to run traditional vSAN workloads and vSAN-Direct workloads side-by-side. As per the official documentation from VMware, "Use vSAN Direct if you are creating a dedicated hardware cluster for the shared nothing cloud-native services".

This is another option if considering the vSAN Data Protection platform for cloud-native applications. You may opt to use DPp without vSAN-Direct and implement vSAN objects with *failures to tolerate* set to 0 since the application is handling the replication. This option is also fully supported but may not deliver on the performance and speed that can be achieved with vSAN-Direct.

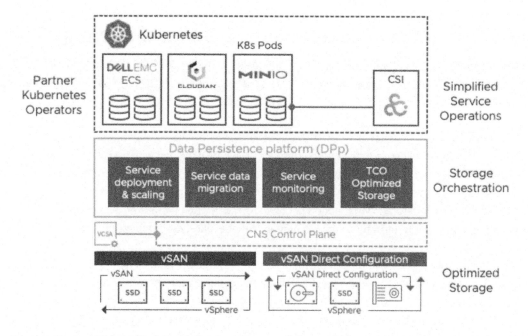

Figure 228: Data Persistence Platform

As mentioned, we have partnered with several cloud-native application vendors who have created bespoke Kubernetes operators that will work with the Data Persistence platform. Partners can define how their application should behave (e.g., re-shard, evacuate, delete and reschedule Pods, etc.) when a vSphere operation is detected. Partners can also create their own vCenter Server UI plugins so that operations (e.g., resize, scale in and out) that are specific to their particular Supervisor Service can be added to vCenter.

DPp Requirements

vSAN Data Persistence platform was first introduced in VMware Cloud Foundation (VCF) 4.2 in early 2021. The reason for requiring VCF was that there were a number of requirements to enable

DPp. Obviously, vSAN is a requirement, with or without the vSAN-Direct configuration. vSphere with Tanzu is also needed. And since Supervisor Services are deployed as a set of PodVMs on vSphere with Tanzu, NSX was also necessary. This is because PodVMs required network overlays for secure Pod-to-Pod communication, and the only product that could achieve this was NSX. Thus, while VCF was not a hard and fast requirement for DPp, it did have all the necessary components to enable it.

With the release of vSphere 8.0 U1, a significant enhancement was made to DPp requirements. DPp and Supervisor Services are now available without NSX and can be implemented using a vSphere Distributed Switch (VDS). An environment no longer needs to use VMware NSX to support the network connectivity requirements by applications that use the DPp. This enhancement applies to both the vSAN OSA and vSAN ESA.

PodVM network traffic will now use the user-configured VDS. A significant change to PodVMs is that they will no longer be exposed to the supervisor cluster internal network. Thus, PodVMs that back Supervisor Services and which wish to use the VDS will need to use either the "Load Balancer" or "Headless" service types. They cannot continue to use "ClusterIP" service type which may have been used previously.

Partners who already offer a certified Supervisor Service solution may need to update their partner/service operator and service instances to avoid using the ClusterIP service type. As we will see next, vSAN 7 U3 introduced the ability for partners using the DPp to decouple their offering from the vCenter Server version. This should make it relatively easy for partners to update their operators.

DPp deployment changes

When DPp first released, several services were embedded directly in vSphere. With the release of vSphere 7.0U3, the way in which vSphere administrators install, upgrade, and manage DPp services has changed. Now vSphere administrators need to retrieve the YAML manifests for the partner product and register the service with vCenter Server. After this step is complete, the service can be installed into vCenter, making them available to developers who wish to use the service in Kubernetes workloads.

The partner manifests are available in the following JFROG repository: https://vmwaresaas.jfrog.io/. Simply navigate to the appropriate partner folder under `Artifactory > Artifacts > vDPP-Partner-YAML` and select a YAML file to download. The path to the Velero Service is shown below:

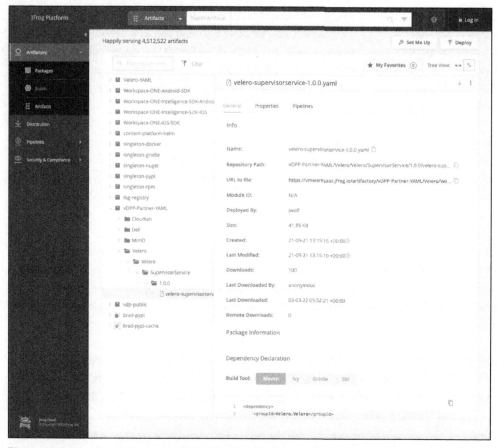

Figure 229: Data Persistence Platform Service Manifests

vSAN Stretched Cluster support

A frequently requested topology on which to deploy a Kubernetes cluster is a vSAN Stretched Cluster. This requires some careful consideration since a vSAN Stretched Cluster has only two availability zones/data sites and Kubernetes always has an odd number of control plane nodes, either 1, 3, 5, or 7. Thus you will always have a situation where one of the vSAN Stretched Cluster sites has more control plane nodes than the other. If the site with the most control plane nodes fails, then the control plane will not be available until vSphere HA has had time to restart the failed nodes on the remaining site and the control plane components such as the Kubernetes key-value store (etcd) has recovered. Thus, vSAN Stretched Cluster may provide highly available Kubernetes clusters, but not continuously available Kubernetes clusters. This is a major consideration if you plan to deploy a Kubernetes cluster on vSAN Stretched Cluster.

The official VMware documentation provides additional guidance on vSAN Stretch Clusters, such as enabling vSphere HA, DRS, Host and VM Affinity Groups, etc. However, when it comes to PV provisioning, the advice given in the official documentation is that the same storage policy should be used for all node VMs, including the control plane and worker, as well as all Persistent Volumes

(PVs). This single, standardized storage policy in vSphere equates to the Kubernetes administrator creating a single, standard Storage Class for all storage objects in the Kubernetes cluster.

Readers should also pay attention to the fact that while it might be possible to deploy native, upstream Kubernetes clusters on vSAN Stretched Clusters, there is still no support for vSphere with Tanzu and the TKG Service to use vSAN stretched clusters at the time of writing. In the VMware Tanzu for Kubernetes Operations documentation, the following reason is given for this lack of support:

> *Deployment on a stretched cluster is not supported by VMware, as the vSphere with Tanzu layer does not distinguish between stretched and non-stretched vSphere clusters and provisions VMs randomly across the two sites. As a result, vSphere with Tanzu may provision VMs in a way that does not allow enough resources to your applications, resulting in downtime. There is also a known issue in upstream ETCd which VMware has found can cause corruption of one or more ETCd replica. This can result in a cluster being unable to schedule pods, requiring significant time and effort to recover.*

It is the authors understanding that much of the ETCd brittleness referenced above should be addressed in Kubernetes version 1.25. However, this was not available with Tanzu Kubernetes at the time of writing. Once this version is released, we may see some new support statements around Kubernetes and vSAN Stretched Clusters.

The other major limitation at the time of writing is that currently only block based read-write-once (RWO) volumes are supported on vSAN Stretched Cluster. There is no support for dynamic read-write-many (RWX) vSAN File Service based file volumes in vSAN Stretched Cluster, either for vSAN OSA or vSAN ESA. Although, since there is currently no support for vSAN File Service on vSAN ESA at this time, this point is a little moot.

Other CSI driver features

Throughout this chapter, several different features of the vSphere CSI driver have been mentioned. Listing every CSI feature is beyond the scope of this book, but a feature that is supported at the time of writing in the vSphere CSI driver is the ability to hot extend block volumes while the pods remain online. Note however that this feature is currently not available for file volumes. CSI snapshots are also supported using the vSphere CSI driver, which should allow partner backup vendors to be able to take backups of applications that use persistent volumes on Kubernetes running on the vSphere platform. There are also several different topologies that are being investigated for support, such as a single Kubernetes cluster deployed across multiple vSphere clusters, often referred to as a multi-AZ deployment.

This GitHub page, maintained by the vSphere CSI engineering team, is a good starting point for details about vSphere CSI driver versions and supported features: https://github.com/kubernetes-sigs/vsphere-csi-driver

Summary

vSAN lends itself very nicely as a platform for both traditional virtual machine workloads and newer cloud-native workloads. Through the upstream vSphere CSI driver and the pvCSI driver for vSphere with Tanzu, vSAN can be used for block based read-write-once volumes. With upstream Kubernetes, vSAN OSA can also be used for file based read-write-many volumes, but this functionality will not be available in the vSAN ESA until vSAN File Service is first supported. We have also seen that VMware also have a number of different Kubernetes offerings. This does highlight a consideration that many vSphere CSI driver features are first developed for upstream and later implemented in pvCSI. Care must be taken when validating whether or not the Kubernetes distribution you are using does indeed have the vSphere CSI driver features you are looking for.

One other significant development in this space is the vSAN Data Persistence platform, or vSAN DPp for short. It allows our partners to create Supervisor Services for the vSphere with Tanzu platform. Traditionally, as mentioned, there were a considerable number of requirements around using previous versions of DPp which had to be considered. With the release of vSAN 8.0 U1 and vSphere 8.0 U1, these have been relaxed considerably, especially the requirement to use NSX. These less restrictive requirements for Supervisor Service and vSAN DPp should allow for easier adoption.

10

Command Line Tools

This chapter will look at some of the *command line interface* (CLI) tools that are available outside the vSphere client for examining various parts of the vSAN cluster. Some tools are available on the ESXi host, others are available via the vCenter Server command line. The vCenter Server command line tool is called the Ruby vSphere Console, or rvc for short. Administrators should familiarize themselves with both the esxcli toolset, as well as exploring various capabilities of rvc. Both will be discussed in this chapter.

CLI vSAN Cluster Commands

There is a namespace in esxcli for vSAN. Here, administrators will find several commands for managing and displaying the status of a vSAN cluster. An effort will be made to describe each of the sub-namespaces, but for the most part what the command does is self-explanatory. In places, where it makes sense to do so, sample command outputs will be provided.

esxcli vsan cluster

Using the esxcli vsan cluster commands, you can enable the host on which the command is run to join or leave a cluster, as well as display the current cluster status and members. This can be very helpful in a scenario where vCenter Server is unavailable and a particular host needs to be removed from the vSAN cluster. The restore functionality is not intended for customer invocation and is used by ESXi during the boot process to restore the active cluster configuration from configuration file.

```
Usage : esxcli vsan cluster {cmd} [cmd options]
Available Namespaces:
    • preferredfaultdomain - Commands for configuring a preferred fault domain for vSAN.
    • unicastagent - Commands for configuring unicast agents for vSAN.
Available Commands:
    • get - Get information about the vSAN cluster that this host is joined to.
    • join - Join the host to a vSAN cluster.
    • leave - Leave the vSAN cluster the host is currently joined to.
    • new - Create a vSAN cluster with current host joined. A random sub-cluster UUID
      will be generated.
    • restore - Restore the persisted vSAN cluster configuration.
```

One command we have frequently used during the development of this book is "leave". This command can be used to remove the vSAN configuration on a host which has been removed from the cluster but somehow still considers itself part of the cluster. Very helpful when recreating your vSAN configuration numerous times over the course of weeks.

In the below example of the "get" command, we can tell that this node has an AGENT role (as discussed in chapter 4, Architectural Details). It is also a NORMAL node (not a witness host), and it is HEALTHY. The vSAN cluster is a 12-node cluster, as we can see from the member count field, and if you count up the number of members' UUIDs or HostNames. Finally, it is not in maintenance mode, and vSAN ESA is enabled on this cluster.

```
[/:~] esxcli vsan cluster get
Cluster Information
   Enabled: true
   Current Local Time: 2023-02-24T07:32:33Z
   Local Node UUID: 63eb4c7e-051c-dfd9-34b3-005056b601a9
   Local Node Type: NORMAL
   Local Node State: AGENT
   Local Node Health State: HEALTHY
   Sub-Cluster Master UUID: 63eb4c85-4032-de05-d6e3-005056b61931
   Sub-Cluster Backup UUID: 63eb4c7b-6253-a587-92d2-005056b6e2f7
   Sub-Cluster UUID: 525f3ea1-2e9e-3925-0426-b493ec933d2b
   Sub-Cluster Membership Entry Revision: 11
   Sub-Cluster Member Count: 12
   Sub-Cluster Member UUIDs: 63eb4c85-4032-de05-d6e3-005056b61931, 63eb4c7b-6253-a587-
92d2-005056b6e2f7, 63eb4c80-46b6-1bda-ad52-005056b6ffaa, 63eb4c8a-3d92-de8e-6deb-
005056b6d069, 63eb4c7e-0e72-1cb4-63ed-005056b62a0b, 63eb4c7f-aa9b-e4ec-dff5-005056b6dbe9,
63eb4c83-256a-52df-89db-005056b66aa6, 63eb4c78-2ad2-bd6b-346c-005056b600ad, 63eb4c7e-051c-
dfd9-34b3-005056b601a9, 63eb4c7f-5d4d-d6e8-372f-005056b69337, 63eb4c7f-c921-d16e-ffac-
005056b627c3, 63eb4c8c-40ec-d3a5-1466-005056b6b98e
   Sub-Cluster Member HostNames: esxi08.deepdivebook.com, esxi07.deepdivebook.com, esxi10.
deepdivebook.com, esxi05.deepdivebook.com, esxi01. deepdivebook.com, esxi04.
deepdivebook.com, esxi06. deepdivebook.com, esxi03. deepdivebook.com, esxi02.
deepdivebook.com, esxi09. deepdivebook.com, esxi12. deepdivebook.com, esxi11.
deepdivebook.com
   Sub-Cluster Membership UUID: 6d8ef763-a475-9349-09d9-005056b61931
   Unicast Mode Enabled: true
   Maintenance Mode State: OFF
   Config Generation: 3dec555c-62c8-4986-99fa-c36160f8d9ec 7 2023-02-24T06:14:12.206
   Mode: REGULAR
   vSAN ESA Enabled: true
```

esxcli vsan datastore

This command allows administrators to do certain operations on the vSAN datastore. Note the guidance that many of these commands are not expected to be run at the host level, but rather at the cluster level. By default, the vSAN datastore name is vsanDatastore. If you do plan on changing the vsanDatastore name, do this at the cluster level via the vSphere client. It is highly recommended that if you are managing multiple vSAN clusters from the same vCenter Server that the vSAN datastores are given unique, easily identifiable names.

```
Usage : esxcli vsan datastore {cmd} [cmd options]

Available Namespaces:
```

- **name** - Commands for configuring vSAN datastore name.

Available Commands:
- **add** - Add a new datastore to the vSAN cluster. This operation is only allowed if vSAN is enabled on the host. In general, add should be done at cluster level. Across a vSAN cluster vSAN datastores should be in sync.
- **clear** - Remove all but the default datastore from the vSAN cluster. This operation is only allowed if vSAN is enabled on the host. In general, add should be done at cluster level. Across a vSAN cluster vSAN datastores should be in sync.
- **list** - List datastores in the vSAN cluster.
- **remove** - Remove a datastore from the vSAN cluster. This operation is only allowed if vSAN is enabled on the host. In general, remove should be done at cluster level. Across a vSAN cluster vSAN datastores should be in sync.

esxcli vsan debug

This command provides a lot of the functionality that administrators would historically have found only in rvc, especially the ability to query the status of objects. However, the command also has options to look at physical disks, and controllers, as well as displaying resync status, storage device information, evacuations of hosts/disk groups/storage pools, and individual virtual machine disk status.

Usage : **esxcli vsan debug** {cmd} [cmd options]

Available Namespaces:
- **disk** - Debug commands for vSAN physical **disks**
- **object** - Debug commands for vSAN objects
- **resync** - Debug commands for vSAN resyncing objects
- **advcfg** - Debug commands for vSAN advanced configuration options.
- **controller** - Debug commands for vSAN disk controllers
- **evacuation** - Debug commands for simulating host, disk or disk group evacuation in various modes and their impact on objects in vSAN cluster
- **limit** - Debug commands for vSAN limits
- **mob** - Debug commands for vSAN Managed Object Browser Service.
- **vmdk** - Debug commands for vSAN VMDKs

Most of these namespaces only provided a single command, either **list** or **get**. The only namespace that differs is mob, which allows administrators to start and stop the vSAN Managed Object Browser Service.

Again, the output is quite self-explanatory, but what is good to see from this output is the congestion values, and where they might occur. All other aspects as green as well, including operational and space, so quite a useful troubleshooting command to have available for physical disks. Also note that with vSAN 8.0 ESA the storage devices are now listed as being part of a "singleTier" Disk Tier.

```
[/:~] esxcli vsan debug disk list
UUID: 5226810c-d4fd-d380-5d2e-167e8e8d588e
   Name: eui.c2a24d01311f670e000c2961a56603aa
   Owner: esxi02.deepdivebook.com
   Version: 18
```

```
Disk Group: N/A
Disk Tier: singleTier
SSD: true
In Cmmds: true
In Vsi: true
Fault Domain: N/A
Model: VMware Virtual NVMe Disk
Encryption: false
Compression: false
Deduplication: false
Dedup Ratio: N/A
Overall Health: green
Metadata Health: green
Operational Health: green
Congestion Health:
      State: green
      Congestion Value: 0
      Congestion Area: none
      All Congestion Fields:
Space Health:
      State: green
      Capacity: 511.93 GB
      Used: 48.77 GB
      Reserved: 0.00 GB
```

We shall provide one additional example from the debug namespace, and that is looking specifically at an object. In this case, the last field is the object ID. This might be gleaned from the vSphere UI, either in the task view or in an event or log message. You can use the CLI to get further detail on a particular object, as shown here. You can see the health of the object, which policy it is using, the state of its components, and which object on the vSAN datastore the UUID corresponds to. Quite a useful command.

```
[/:~] esxcli vsan debug object list -u 3577f463-7621-e35a-15ca-005056b69337
Object UUID: 3577f463-7621-e35a-15ca-005056b69337
   Version: 18
   Health: healthy
   Owner: esxi05.deepdivebook.com
   Size: 16.00 GB
   Used: 0.62 GB
   Used 4K Blocks: 0.00 GB
   Policy:
      stripeWidth: 1
      cacheReservation: 0
      proportionalCapacity: 0
      hostFailuresToTolerate: 1
      forceProvisioning: 0
      spbmProfileId: 4b97756b-3c50-481a-a105-d6a7b1507f9a
      spbmProfileGenerationNumber: 0
      storageType: Allflash
      replicaPreference: Capacity
      CSN: 220
      SCSN: 210
      spbmProfileName: vSAN ESA Default Policy - RAID5
```

Configuration:

    Concatenation
        RAID_1
            Component: 3577f463-b0ae-0e5c-9bd8-005056b69337
                Component State: ACTIVE, Address Space(B): 273804165120 (255.00GB), Disk
UUID: 5276a526-4f97-75f4-9171-2647e84ac91e, Disk Name:
eui.9f2c32169be2e136000c296bb7e964c7:2
                Votes: 1, Capacity Used(B): 13770752 (0.01GB), Physical Capacity Used(B):
13770752 (0.01GB), Total 4K Blocks Used(B): 0 (0.00GB), Host Name: esxi01
            Component: 1678f463-da69-931f-dce7-005056b69337
                Component State: ACTIVE, Address Space(B): 273804165120 (255.00GB), Disk
UUID: 52c96bff-07de-13f0-6316-e0e963f8918f, Disk Name:
eui.4c10459df34aa914000c296cf3023648:2
                Votes: 1, Capacity Used(B): 13729792 (0.01GB), Physical Capacity Used(B):
13729792 (0.01GB), Total 4K Blocks Used(B): 0 (0.00GB), Host Name: esxi10
        RAID_5
            Component: 0054f763-ae32-e46d-199b-005056b6d069
                Component State: ACTIVE, Address Space(B): 205353123840 (191.25GB), Disk
UUID: 52d5d195-15bf-9efa-977a-a0d52dbf4447, Disk Name:
eui.d0792d30ff2120c3000c296a2062ffd3:2
                Votes: 1, Capacity Used(B): 119092480 (0.11GB), Physical Capacity Used(B):
129105920 (0.12GB), Total 4K Blocks Used(B): 0 (0.00GB), Host Name: esxi07
            Component: 0054f763-f4db-e76d-c3a0-005056b6d069
                Component State: ACTIVE, Address Space(B): 205353123840 (191.25GB), Disk
UUID: 52bc11ad-287b-f72b-6b39-ce7c35c83640, Disk Name:
eui.0272ca25e762674d000c296045a17ba9:2
                Votes: 1, Capacity Used(B): 119092480 (0.11GB), Physical Capacity Used(B):
125304832 (0.12GB), Total 4K Blocks Used(B): 0 (0.00GB), Host Name: esxi06
            Component: 0054f763-d045-e96d-7372-005056b6d069
                Component State: ACTIVE, Address Space(B): 205353123840 (191.25GB), Disk
UUID: 5239b96a-ce47-0179-ef8b-a4bf518075fe, Disk Name:
eui.84daaf35c42714b0000c296c6a68eb95:2
                Votes: 1, Capacity Used(B): 119092480 (0.11GB), Physical Capacity Used(B):
128712704 (0.12GB), Total 4K Blocks Used(B): 0 (0.00GB), Host Name: esxi03
            Component: 0054f763-1a28-eb6d-31fb-005056b6d069
                Component State: ACTIVE, Address Space(B): 205353123840 (191.25GB), Disk
UUID: 526c259d-ce6d-24ca-a3f4-614fe9825012, Disk Name:
eui.10a4ddfcaba2b4f4000c29693066aa9b:2
                Votes: 1, Capacity Used(B): 119092480 (0.11GB), Physical Capacity Used(B):
128712704 (0.12GB), Total 4K Blocks Used(B): 0 (0.00GB), Host Name: esxi02
            Component: 0054f763-a0bf-ed6d-0174-005056b6d069
                Component State: ACTIVE, Address Space(B): 205353123840 (191.25GB), Disk
UUID: 52456125-85e4-193f-5995-d3eeb8fec714, Disk Name:
eui.c1c779599e9d8147000c296ad9b852ee:2
                Votes: 1, Capacity Used(B): 119092480 (0.11GB), Physical Capacity Used(B):
129105920 (0.12GB), Total 4K Blocks Used(B): 0 (0.00GB), Host Name: esxi05

    Type: vdisk
    Path: /vmfs/volumes/vsan:525f3ea12e9e3925-0426b493ec933d2b/3477f463-881b-f9e9-741c-
005056b69337/photon-VM.vmdk (Exists)
    Group UUID: 3477f463-881b-f9e9-741c-005056b69337
    Directory Name: N/A

esxcli vsan faultdomain

Fault domains were introduced to allow vSAN to be rack, room, or site aware. What this means is that components belonging to objects that are part of the same virtual machine can be placed not just in different hosts, but in different racks. This means that should an entire rack fail (e.g., power failure), there is still a full set of virtual machine components available, so the VM remains accessible.

Probably not a useful command for generic vSAN deployments but could be useful when Rack Awareness or Stretched Cluster has been implemented since both of those require the use of Fault Domains to group multiple hosts into a single fault domain. If you are using any of those features, then you could use this command to determine which hosts are in which fault domain.

For standard vSAN deployments, each host is in its own fault domain, so the command will return a unique fault domain for every host.

```
Usage : esxcli vsan faultdomain {cmd} [cmd options]

Available Commands:
    •   get - Get the fault domain name for this host.
    •   reset - Reset Host fault domain to default value
    •   set - Set the fault domain for this host
```

esxcli vsan health

This is a very useful command to see the overall health of the system.

```
Usage: esxcli vsan health {cmd} [cmd options]

Available Namespaces:
    •   cluster - Commands for vSAN Cluster Health
```

As you can see, there is only a single available namespace, cluster.

```
Usage: esxcli vsan health cluster {cmd} [cmd options]

Available Commands:
    •   get - Get a specific health check status and its details
    •   list - List a cluster wide health check across all types of health checks
```

However, it is also useful as administrators can use it to run individual health checks. For example, if an administrator ran the following command:

```
esxcli vsan health cluster list -w
```

As well as displaying the status of the vSAN health, this command would return the short name of all of the health checks. This short name could now be used to get a specific health check and its details.

In this example, we will look at the status of a single test called vSAN Storage Space, or in shorthand, diskspace.

```
[/:~] esxcli vsan health cluster get -t diskspace
Storage space          green

Checks for free capacity tier disk space across the entire cluster
Ask VMware:
http://www.vmware.com/esx/support/askvmware/index.php?eventtype=com.vmware.vsan.health.tes
t.diskspace

Cluster level
Utilization                        Health   Warning threshold (GB)   Error threshold (GB)
------------------------------------------------------------------------------------
9.72% (1989.51GB of 20477.30GB) green      14334.11                 18429.57
```

esxcli vsan iscsi

This command allows us to query the configuration and status of iSCSI home namespaces, iSCSI targets and LUNs on vSAN.

```
Usage : esxcli vsan iscsi {cmd} [cmd options]

Available Namespaces:
    •   initiatorgroup - Commands to manipulate vSAN iSCSI target initiator group
    •   target - Commands for vSAN iSCSI target configuration
    •   defaultconfig - Operation for default configuration for vSAN iSCSI Target
    •   homeobject - Commands for the vSAN iSCSI target home object
    •   status - Enable or disable iSCSI target support, query status.
```

In the commands that follow, we will first query whether or not the iSCSI service is enabled?

```
[/:~] esxcli vsan iscsi statusget
   Enabled: true
```

Next, we list the initiator groups. This will display the name of the initiator group, what the IQN of the initiator is, and then the IQNs of any targets that have been added to the initiator groups.

```
[/:~] esxcli vsan iscsi initiatorgroup list
Initiator group
   Name: sqlserver-ig
   Initiator list: iqn.1991-05.com.microsoft:sqlserver2016.rainpole.com, iqn.1991-
05.com.microsoft.sqlsrv2.rainpole.com
   Accessible targets:
         Alias: vsan-iscsi-target
         IQN: iqn.1998-01.com.vmware.52f91d3fbdf294d4-805fec05d214a05d
Initiator group
   Name: filserver-ig
   Initiator list: iqn.1991-05.com.microsoft:cor-win-2012.rainpole.com, iqn.1991-
05.com.microsoft:win2012-dc-b.rainpole.com
   Accessible targets:
         Alias: vsan-iscsi-target
```

```
     IQN: iqn.1998-01.com.vmware.52f91d3fbdf294d4-805fec05d214a05d
```

Now that we have seen things from the initiator side, let us turn our attention to the target side. Here we can list the target information, and correlate these to any that have been added to the initiator group shown above. Unfortunately, due to the length of the command output, it is not easy to display, but hopefully, you can see the relevant detail.

```
[/:~] esxcli vsan iscsi target list
Alias
-----------------
vsan-iscsi-target
tgt-for-sql

iSCSI Qualified Name (IQN)
-------------------------------------------------------
iqn.1998-01.com.vmware.52f91d3fbdf294d4-805fec05d214a05d
iqn.1998-01.com.vmware.5261586411b1be81-3b5333f32fec6960

Interface  Port  Authentication type   LUNs
---------  ----  -------------------   ----
vmk3       3260  No-Authentication      2
vmk3       3260  No-Authentication      2

Is Compliant  UUID
------------  ------------------------
true          c52a675a-49f4-ca24-c6be-246e962c2408
true          2a9e695a-c2af-a8a6-5a68-246e962f5270

I/O Owner UUID
5982f466-c59d-0e07-aa4e-246e962f4850
5982f466-c59d-0e07-aa4e-246e962f4850
```

The last example we have for iSCSI is to display which LUNs have been mapped to which target. From the output above, we have seen several targets listed. Here we can list the LUN information and correlate any LUNs that have been mapped to a particular target shown above. Again, the way the command is displayed doesn't easily lend it to being reproduced in an easily readable format for the book, but hopefully, you can see that this target has 2 LUNs mapped.

```
[/:~] esxcli vsan iscsi target lun list -t tgt-for-sql
ID  Alias        Size
--  -----------  ----------
 0  sqldb-lun    153600 MiB
 1  witness-sql    5120 MiB

UUID
------------------------------------
21a0695a-ff8e-676f-9db6-246e962f5270
f5a2695a-c010-9e5c-3fc2-246e962c2408

Is Compliant  Status
------------  ------
true          online
true          online
```

esxcli vsan maintenancemode

`maintenancemode` is an interesting command option. You might think this would allow you to enter and exit maintenance, but it doesn't. All this option allows you to do is to cancel an in-progress vSAN maintenance mode operation. This could still prove very useful, though, especially when you have decided to place a host in maintenance mode and selected the Full Data Migration option and want to stop this data migration process (which can take a very long time) and instead use the Ensure Access option.

```
Usage : esxcli vsan maintenancemode {cmd} [cmd options]

Available Commands:
    • cancel - Cancel an in-progress vSAN maintenance mode operation.
```

This command does not allow you to enter or exit maintenance mode. Note that you can place a node in maintenance mode leveraging `esxcli system maintenanceMode set -e true -m noAction` where "-m" specifies the data evacuation option, and if components need to be moved from the host entering maintenance mode or not.

esxcli vsan network

This command will display details about the VMkernel interface used for the vSAN network by this host.

```
Usage : esxcli vsan network {cmd} [cmd options]

Available Namespaces:
    • ip - Commands for configuring IP network for vSAN.
    • ipv4 - Compatibility alias for "ip"
    • security - Commands for configuring vSAN network security settings

Available Commands:
    • clear - Clear the vSAN network configuration.
    • list - List the network configuration currently in use by vSAN.
    • remove - Remove an interface from the vSAN network configuration.
    • restore - Restore the persisted vSAN network configuration.
```

In this example, it can clearly be seen that vSAN is using vmk2. Note also that there is a considerable amount of multicast information included here. This is historic information, and if you are using a version of vSAN that is later than 6.6, most likely this information is unused. However, there is a corner case scenario where a cluster may revert from multicast to unicast, and therefore the information is still displayed.

```
[/:~] esxcli vsan network list
Interface
   VmkNic Name: vmk2
   IP Protocol: IP
   Interface UUID: f9d6025a-0177-fcd1-3c38-246e962f4910
   Agent Group Multicast Address: 224.2.3.4
```

```
Agent Group IPv6 Multicast Address: ff19::2:3:4
Agent Group Multicast Port: 23451
Master Group Multicast Address: 224.1.2.3
Master Group IPv6 Multicast Address: ff19::1:2:3
Master Group Multicast Port: 12345
Host Unicast Channel Bound Port: 12321
Data-in-Transit Encryption Key Exchange Port: 0
Multicast TTL: 5
Traffic Type: vsan
```

The first IP address, 224.2.3.4 is used for the master/backup communication, whereas the second address, 224.1.2.3, is used for the agents. `esxcli vsan network list` is a useful command to view the network configuration and status should a network partition occur.

esxcli vsan policy

This command allows you to query, clear and set the default policy of the vSAN datastore. However, as has been mentioned a few times already in this book, we would strongly recommend not changing the default policy, but instead creating a new policy, and setting that as the default on the vSAN datastore.

```
Usage : esxcli vsan policy {cmd} [cmd options]

Available Commands:
    • cleardefault - Clear default vSAN storage policy values.
    • getdefault - Get default vSAN storage policy values.
    • setdefault - Set default vSAN storage policy values.
```

Here is the output querying the default policy which has not been modified in any way.

```
[/:~] esxcli vsan policy getdefault
Policy Class  Policy Value
------------  --------------------------------------------------------
cluster     (("hostFailuresToTolerate" i1))
vdisk       (("hostFailuresToTolerate" i1))
vmnamespace (("hostFailuresToTolerate" i1))
vmswap      (("hostFailuresToTolerate" i1) ("forceProvisioning" i1))
vmem        (("hostFailuresToTolerate" i1) ("forceProvisioning" i1))
```

Here we can see the different VM storage objects that make up a VM deployed on a vSAN datastore, and we can also see the default policy values. Although the policy value is called host failures to tolerate, it actually is the equivalent to the failures to tolerate in the vSphere client. All the objects will tolerate at least one failure in the cluster and remain persistent. The class vdisk refers to VM disk objects (VMDKs). The class vmnamespace is the VM home namespace where the configuration files, metadata files, and log files belonging to the VM are stored. The vmswap policy class is, of course, the VM swap. One final note for vmswap is that it also has a forceProvisioning value. This means that even if there are not enough resources in the vSAN cluster to meet the requirement to provision both VM swap replicas to meet the failures to tolerate requirement, vSAN will still provision the VM with a single VM swap instance. The final entry is vmem. This is the snapshot memory object when a snapshot is taken of a VM, and there is a request to also snapshot memory.

These policy settings, and the reasons for using them, are explained in detail in chapter 5, VM Storage Policies and VM Provisioning.

If you do want to change the default policy to something other than these settings, there is a considerable amount of information in the help file about each of the policies. The command to set a default policy is as follows:

```
# esxcli vsan policy setdefault <-p|--policy> <-c|--policy-class>
```

However, as stated earlier, VMware recommends avoiding configuring policies from the ESXi host. This is because you would have to repeat all of the steps on each of the hosts in the cluster. This is time-consuming, tedious, and prone to user error. The preferred method to modify policies is via the vSphere web client, or if that is not possible, via rvc, the Ruby vSphere Console.

esxcli vsan resync

The bandwidth and throttle commands can be used to get to first examine whether the resync bandwidth is too large for the cluster, and is possibly impacting workloads, and if it is, to throttle the bandwidth.

```
Usage : esxcli vsan resync {cmd} [cmd options]

Available Namespaces:
    •   bandwidth - Commands for vSAN resync bandwidth
    •   throttle - Commands for vSAN resync throttling
```

Outputs are displayed in Megabits per second (Mbps). However, considering the number of changes that have been made to the Quality of Service around VM traffic and resync traffic, modifying these parameters should hopefully be a last resort in the current versions of vSAN.

esxcli vsan storage

This command looks at all aspects of vSAN storage, from disk group configurations, to adding and removing storage devices to/from disk groups. Which also means that for vSAN ESA this command does not provide a lot of insights.

```
Usage : esxcli vsan storage {cmd} [cmd options]

Available Namespaces:
    •   automode - Commands for configuring vSAN storage auto claim mode.
    •   diskgroup - Commands for configuring vSAN diskgroups
    •   tag - Commands to add/remove tags for vSAN storage

Available Commands:
    •   add - Add physical disk for vSAN usage.
```

- **list** - List vSAN storage configuration.
- **remove** - Remove physical disks from vSAN disk groups.

esxcli vsan storagepool

This command looks at all aspects of vSAN ESA storage, from individual devices to the pool of storage itself. This command enables you to add devices to a pool, but also to mount and unmount devices from a pool.

```
Usage: esxcli vsan storagepool {cmd} [cmd options]

Available Commands:
  add                 Add physical disk for vSAN usage.
  list                List vSAN storage pool configuration.
  mount               Mount vSAN disk from storage pool.
  rebuild             Rebuild vSAN storage pool disks.
  remove              Remove physical disk from storage pool usage.
                      Exactly one of --disk or --uuid param is required.
  unmount             Unmount vSAN disk from storage pool.
```

To see which devices are currently part of the storagepool on the option "list" can be used. As shown in the output below, it provides information about the state of the devices, whether it is encrypted, the disk type (singleTier refers to vSAN ESA) and when the device was added to the storagepool.

```
[:~] esxcli vsan storagepool list
eui.c2a24d01311f670e000c2961a56603aa
   Device: eui.c2a24d01311f670e000c2961a56603aa
   Display Name: eui.c2a24d01311f670e000c2961a56603aa
   vSAN UUID: 5226810c-d4fd-d380-5d2e-167e8e8d588e
   Used by this host: true
   In CMMDS: true
   On-disk format version: 18
   Checksum: 7329727139373076158
   Checksum Ok: true
   Is Mounted: true
   Is Encrypted: false
   Disk Type: singleTier
   Creation Time: Wed Feb 15 12:15:59 2023

eui.10a4ddfcaba2b4f4000c29693066aa9b
   Device: eui.10a4ddfcaba2b4f4000c29693066aa9b
   Display Name: eui.10a4ddfcaba2b4f4000c29693066aa9b
   vSAN UUID: 526c259d-ce6d-24ca-a3f4-614fe9825012
   Used by this host: true
   In CMMDS: true
   On-disk format version: 18
   Checksum: 18183413059938831412
   Checksum Ok: true
   Is Mounted: true
   Is Encrypted: false
   Disk Type: singleTier
```

```
    Creation Time: Wed Feb 15 12:15:59 2023

eui.9500d68cb453e39a000c2966beada3f8
    Device: eui.9500d68cb453e39a000c2966beada3f8
    Display Name: eui.9500d68cb453e39a000c2966beada3f8
    vSAN UUID: 526f8b7c-ffe9-ede3-c611-dbb854eb2d2c
    Used by this host: true
    In CMMDS: true
    On-disk format version: 18
    Checksum: 6905207063754415749
    Checksum Ok: true
    Is Mounted: true
    Is Encrypted: false
    Disk Type: singleTier
    Creation Time: Wed Feb 15 12:15:59 2023

eui.b9939136f34e5126000c29628b9141da
    Device: eui.b9939136f34e5126000c29628b9141da
    Display Name: eui.b9939136f34e5126000c29628b9141da
    vSAN UUID: 52a399df-a404-4662-820e-72292fd0c2a4
    Used by this host: true
    In CMMDS: true
    On-disk format version: 18
    Checksum: 6533754714626300358
    Checksum Ok: true
    Is Mounted: true
    Is Encrypted: false
    Disk Type: singleTier
    Creation Time: Wed Feb 15 12:15:59 2023
```

esxcli vsan trace

This command allows you to configure where vSAN trace files are stored, how much trace log to retain, when to rotate them and if they should also be redirected to syslog.

```
Usage : esxcli vsan trace {cmd} [cmd options]

Available Commands:
    •   get - Get the vSAN tracing configuration.
    •   set - Configure vSAN trace. Please note: This command is not thread safe.

Usage: esxcli vsan trace set [cmd options]

Description:
    •   set - Configure vSAN trace. Please note: This command is not thread safe.

Cmd options:
    •   -l|--logtosyslog=<bool> - Boolean value to enable or disable logging urgent
        traces to syslog.
    •   -f|--numfiles=<long> - Log file rotation for vSAN trace files.
    •   -p|--path=<str> - Path to store vSAN trace files.
    •   -r|--reset=<bool> - When set to true, reset defaults for vSAN trace files.
    •   -s|--size=<long> - Maximum size of vSAN trace files in MB.
```

To see what the current trace settings are, you can use the **get** option.

```
[/:~] esxcli vsan trace get
   VSAN Traces Directory:/vsantraces
   Number Of Files To Rotate: 8
   Maximum Trace File Size: 45 MB
   Log Urgent Traces To Syslog: true
```

Additional Non-esxcli Commands for vSAN

In addition to the esxcli vsan namespace commands, there are a few additional CLI commands found on an ESXi host that may prove useful for monitoring and troubleshooting.

vsantop

vsantop is a relative new command. Most of you are probably familiar with esxtop, and as expected vsantop provides performance details of vSAN on a host level. The tool works very similar to esxtop. You can use the the "?" character for help, add and remove fields using "fF", change the order using "oO" and select entities via "E". When you run vsantop you get presented with the following.

```
[root@localhost:~] vsantop
 8:49:26am | entity type: host-domclient
     nodeId   iops throughput latyAvg latStd   ioCount congestion   oio   iopsRead
throughput
622b0a3e-d      1      8128      176     129        8          0     1      18128
```

As mentioned, "E" can be used to look at various entities, and there is a significant amount of detail provided by vsantop, below you find the list of entities that can be inspected.

```
Current Entity type: host-domclient

      1: cache-disk              2: capacity-disk           3: clom-disk-fullness-
stats
      4: clom-disk-stats         5: clom-host-stats          6: clom-slack-space-stats
      7: cluster                 8: cluster-domclient        9: cluster-domcompmgr
     10: cluster-domowner       11: cluster-remotedomclient 12: cluster-resync
     13: cmmds                  14: cmmds-net               15: cmmds-update-latency
     16: cmmds-workloadstats    17: cmmds-world-cpu         18: ddh-disk-stats
     19: disk-group             20: dom-per-proxy-owner     21: dom-proxy-owner
     22: dom-world-cpu          23: host                    24: host-cpu
*    25: host-domclient         26: host-domcompmgr         27: host-domowner
     28: host-memory-heap       29: host-memory-slab        30: host-vsansparse
     31: lsom-world-cpu         32: nfs-client-vol          33: nic-world-cpu
     34: object                 35: psa-completion-world-cpu 36: psa-split-stats
     37: rdma-net               38: rdma-world-cpu          39: rdt-net
     40: rdt-world-cpu          41: statsdb                 42: system-mem
     43: virtual-disk           44: virtual-machine         45: vmdk-vsansparse
     46: vsan-cpu               47: vsan-direct-cluster      48: vsan-direct-disk
     49: vsan-direct-host       50: vsan-distribution        51: vsan-file-service
     52: vsan-file-service-vdfs 53: vsan-host-net            54: vsan-iscsi-host
     55: vsan-iscsi-lun         56: vsan-iscsi-target        57: vsan-memory
     58: vsan-pnic-net          59: vsan-vnic-net            60: vscsi
```

```
61: clom-workitem-stats        62: kvstore              63: splinter-overall-stats
64: splinter-operation-stats   65: splinter-lookup-stats 66: splinter-task-stats
67: splinter-trunk-page-stats  68: splinter-branch-page-stats
69: splinter-memtable-page-stats
70: splinter-filter-page-stats
71: splinter-range-page-stats  72: splinter-misc-page-stats  73: splinter-snowplough-
stats
74: splinter-range-delete-stats
75: splinter-checkpoint-stats  76: splinter-meta-page-stats  77: splinter-premini-stats
78: vsan-esa-cluster-resync    79: vsan-esa-disk-iolayer-handle-stats
80: vsan-esa-disk-iolayer-stats
81: vsan-esa-disk-layer        82: vsan-esa-disk-layer-allocator-stats
83: vsan-esa-disk-layer-block-engine-stats
84: vsan-esa-disk-layer-congestion-stats
85: vsan-esa-distribution      86: vsan-esa-disk-layer-mdr-handle-stats
87: vsan-esa-disk-layer-partition-stats
88: vsan-esa-disk-layer-transaction-stats
89: vsan-esa-disk-layer-world-cpu
90: vsan-esa-disk-scsifw       91: vsan-esa-dom-scheduler   92: vsan-zdom-gsc
93: zdom-io                    94: zdom-llp                 95: zdom-overview
96: zdom-seg-cleaning          97: zdom-snapshot            98: zdom-vtx
99: zdom-world-cpu
```

The question arises, what should you be monitoring with vsantop, and the answer is simple, nothing. This tool is not intended for day-to-day operations. It should only be used during performance troubleshooting, and only in the situation where the required data can't be found via the vSphere Client. To completely honest, we (the authors) have not encountered a situation ourselves where we need vsan-top to troubleshoot a particular situation.

osfs-ls

osfs-ls is more of a troubleshooting command than anything else. It is useful for displaying the contents of the vSAN datastore. The command is not in your search path but can be found in the location shown in the example output below. In this command, we are listing the contents of a VM folder on the vSAN datastore. This can prove useful if the datastore file view is not working correctly from the vSphere client, or it is reporting inaccurate information for some reason or other:

```
[/:~] cd /vmfs/volumes/vsanDatastore/
[/:~] /usr/lib/vmware/osfs/bin/osfs-ls photon-VM/
.fbb.sf
.fdc.sf
.pbc.sf
.sbc.sf
.vh.sf
.pb2.sf
.sdd.sf
.jbc.sf
photon-VM-61981811.hlog
photon-VM.vmx
.3577f463-7621-e35a-15ca-005056b69337.lck
photon-VM.vmdk
photon-VM.vmsd
vmx-photon-VM-ae25ef4523b1d6fcffd0f7eb47bf025e950978696edbe4198da8e22175a2e744-2.vswp
photon-VM-3.scoreboard
vmware-1.log
```

```
photon-VM-1.scoreboard
vmware-2.log
vmware-3.log
photon-VM.nvram
photon-VM-aux.xml
photon-VM-2.scoreboard
photon-VM.scoreboard
photon-VM-72f1aed1.vswp.lck
photon-VM-72f1aed1.vswp
vmware.log
photon-VM.vmx.lck
photon-VM.vmx~
```

cmmds-tool

`cmmds-tool` is another useful troubleshooting command from the ESXi host and can be used to display lots of vSAN information. It can be used to display information such as configuration, metadata, and state about the cluster, hosts in the cluster, and VM storage objects. Many other high-level diagnostic tools leverage information obtained via `cmmds-tool`. As you can imagine, it has a number of options, which you can see by just running the command.

The `find` option may be the most useful, especially when you want to discover information about the actual storage objects backing a VM. You can, for instance, see what the health is of a specific object. In the below example, we want to find additional information about a DOM object represented by UUID **3577f463-7621-e35a-15ca-005056b69337**. As you can see, the output below is not the most human-friendly, as is possibly only useful when you need to work on vSAN from an ESXi host. Otherwise, esxcli or rvc is the recommended CLI tool of choice as the command outputs are far more readable.

```
[root@esxi-dell-e:~] cmmds-tool find -u 3577f463-7621-e35a-15ca-005056b69337

owner=63eb4c7e-051c-dfd9-34b3-005056b601a9(Health: Healthy) uuid=3577f463-7621-e35a-15ca-
005056b69337 type=DOM_OBJECT rev=19 minHostVer=3  [content = ("Configuration" (("CSN"
1222) ("SCSN" 1210) ("addressSpace" 171179869184) ("scrubStartTime" 1+1677126672654124)
("objectVersion" i18) ("highestDiskVersion" i18) ("muxGroup" 1748774772592640)
("groupUuid" 3477f463-881b-f9e9-741c-005056b69337) ("raidFact" i143) ("subClusterUUID"
525f3ea1-2e9e-3925-0426-b493ec933d2b) ("zDomMetaAddressSpace" 1273804165120)
("zDomDataAddressSpace" 1821412495360) ("scrubEta" i357960) ("compositeUuid" 3577f463-
7621-e35a-15ca-005056b69337) ("objCapabilities" i4)) ("Concatenation" (("scope" i1))
("RAID_1" (("scope" i3)) ("Component" (("capacity" (l0 1343597383)) ("addressSpace"
1273804165120) ("componentState" 15) ("componentStateTS" 11677139608) ("faultDomainId"
63eb4c7e-0e72-1cb4-63ed-005056b62a0b) ("flags" i128) ("nVotes" i1) ("lastScrubbedOffset"
12415923200) ("subFaultDomainId" 63eb4c7e-0e72-1cb4-63ed-005056b62a0b)
("resyncTputSoFarKB" i1025) ("expectedFullProvisionedBytes" 1343597383)) 3577f463-b0ae-
0e5c-9bd8-005056b69337 5276a526-4f97-75f4-9171-2647e84ac91e) ("Component" (("capacity" (l0
1343597383)) ("addressSpace" 1273804165120) ("componentState" 15) ("componentStateTS"
11677146688) ("faultDomainId" 63eb4c80-46b6-1bda-ad52-005056b6ffaa) ("flags" i128)
("nVotes" i1) ("lastScrubbedOffset" 12415923200) ("subFaultDomainId" 63eb4c80-46b6-1bda-
ad52-005056b6ffaa) ("resyncTputSoFarKB" i1939) ("expectedFullProvisionedBytes"
1343597383)) 1678f463-da69-931f-dce7-005056b69337 52c96bff-07de-13f0-6316-e0e963f8918f))
("RAID_5" (("stripeBlockSize" 1131072) ("scope" i3)) ("Component" (("capacity" (l0
14380819456)) ("addressSpace" 1205353123840) ("componentState" 15) ("componentStateTS"
11677153285) ("faultDomainId" 63eb4c7b-6253-a587-92d2-005056b6e2f7) ("flags" i536870912)
("nVotes" i1) ("lastScrubbedOffset" 1100532224) ("subFaultDomainId" 63eb4c7b-6253-a587-
92d2-005056b6e2f7) ("resyncTputSoFarKB" i27482) ("expectedFullProvisionedBytes"
14380819456)) 0054f763-ae32-e46d-199b-005056b6d069 52d5d195-15bf-9efa-977a-a0d52dbf4447)
("Component" (("capacity" (l0 14380950528)) ("addressSpace" 1205353123840)
("componentState" 15) ("componentStateTS" 11677153286) ("faultDomainId" 63eb4c83-256a-
```

52df-89db-005056b66aa6) ("flags" i536870912) ("nVotes" i1) ("lastScrubbedOffset"
1100532224) ("subFaultDomainId" 63eb4c83-256a-52df-89db-005056b66aa6) ("resyncTputSoFarKB"
i23348) ("expectedFullProvisionedBytes" 14380950528)) 0054f763-f4db-e76d-c3a0-005056b6d069
52bc11ad-287b-f72b-6b39-ce7c35c83640) ("Component" (("capacity" (10 14380950528))
("addressSpace" 1205353123840) ("componentState" 15) ("componentStateTS" 11677153286)
("faultDomainId" 63eb4c78-2ad2-bd6b-346c-005056b600ad) ("flags" i536870912) ("nVotes" i1)
("lastScrubbedOffset" 1100532224) ("subFaultDomainId" 63eb4c78-2ad2-bd6b-346c-
005056b600ad) ("resyncTputSoFarKB" i23072) ("expectedFullProvisionedBytes" 14380950528))
0054f763-d045-e96d-7372-005056b6d069 5239b96a-ce47-0179-ef8b-a4bf518075fe) ("Component"
(("capacity" (10 14380877127)) ("addressSpace" 1205353123840) ("componentState" 15)
("componentStateTS" 11677168358) ("faultDomainId" 63eb4c7e-051c-dfd9-34b3-005056b601a9)
("flags" i536871040) ("nVotes" i1) ("lastScrubbedOffset" 1100401152) ("subFaultDomainId"
63eb4c7e-051c-dfd9-34b3-005056b601a9) ("resyncTputSoFarKB" i1924)
("expectedFullProvisionedBytes" 14380877127)) 0054f763-1a28-eb6d-31fb-005056b6d069
526c259d-ce6d-24ca-a3f4-614fe9825012) ("Component" (("capacity" (10 14380819456))
("addressSpace" 1205353123840) ("componentState" 15) ("componentStateTS" 11677153285)
("faultDomainId" 63eb4c8a-3d92-de8e-6deb-005056b6d069) ("flags" i536870912) ("nVotes" i1)
("lastScrubbedOffset" 1100401152) ("subFaultDomainId" 63eb4c8a-3d92-de8e-6deb-
005056b6d069) ("resyncTputSoFarKB" i24673) ("expectedFullProvisionedBytes" 14380819456))
0054f763-a0bf-ed6d-0174-005056b6d069 52456125-85e4-193f-5995-d3eeb8fec714))))],
errorStr=(null)

owner=63eb4c7e-051c-dfd9-34b3-005056b601a9(Health: Healthy) uuid=3577f463-7621-e35a-15ca-
005056b69337 type=POLICY rev=19 minHostVer=3 [content = (("stripeWidth" i1)
("cacheReservation" i0) ("proportionalCapacity" i0) ("hostFailuresToTolerate" i1)
("forceProvisioning" i0) ("spbmProfileId" "4b97756b-3c50-481a-a105-d6a7b1507f9a")
("spbmProfileGenerationNumber" l+0) ("storageType" "Allflash") ("replicaPreference"
"Capacity") ("CSN" 1222) ("SCSN" 1210) ("spbmProfileName" "vSAN ESA Default Policy -
RAID5"))], errorStr=(null)

owner=63eb4c7e-051c-dfd9-34b3-005056b601a9(Health: Healthy) uuid=3577f463-7621-e35a-15ca-
005056b69337 type=CONFIG_STATUS rev=15 minHostVer=3 [content = (("state" i519) ("CSN"
1222) ("SCSN" 1210) ("highestDiskVersion" i18) ("objectVersion" i18) ("muxGroup"
1748774772592640) ("addressSpace" 117179869184) ("zdomObject" i1))], errorStr=(null)

owner=63eb4c7e-051c-dfd9-34b3-005056b601a9(Health: Healthy) uuid=3577f463-7621-e35a-15ca-
005056b69337 type=OBJECT_STATS rev=0 minHostVer=3 [content = (1858476544 1475761152
11824768 16071808 10 i0 i195887384 i0 l0)], errorStr=(null)

Looking at the output we realize that most of the information for administrators may not be very useful, which is not strange as this tool is mainly intended for troubleshooting purposes and is most often used by VMware Global Support Services. There is however one setting we want to emphasize as it could be useful for administrators as well. In Chapter 5 we described how to disable compression on a per VM/VMDK basis with vSAN ESA. In the vSphere Client it is, however, not very apparent if compression has been disabled or not. Well, except when you verify the capabilities configured through the associated policy of course. Using CMMDS you can also identify the objects which have compression disabled. The next output has this highlighted, "'compressionState". Do note, that this will only be shown when compression is disabled explicitly.

```
cmmds-tool find -t DOM_OBJECT -u acc02864-1867-b894-8aed-00f663db4264
```

```
owner=63d1b6d4-50c4-82e0-1b1c-00f663db4264(Health: Healthy) uuid=acc02864-1867-b894-8aed-
00f663db4264 type=DOM_OBJECT rev=3 minHostVer=3 [content = ("Configuration" (("CSN" 11)
("addressSpace" 1273804165120) ("scrubStartTime" 1+1680392364070291) ("objectVersion" i17)
("checksumPolicy" i256) ("compressionState" i1) ("highestDiskVersion" i17) ("muxGroup"
1435270552306054656) ("groupUuid" acc02864-1867-b894-8aed-00f663db4264) ("raidFact" i143)
```

There are, of course, many other options available to this command that can run. For example, a -o <owner> will display information about all objects of which <owner> is the owner. This can be a considerable amount of output.

Type is another option and can be specified with a -t option. From the preceding output, types such as DISK, HEALTH_STATUS, DISK_USAGE, and DISK_STATUS can be displayed. Other types include DOM_OBJECT, DOM_NAME, POLICY, CONFIG_STATUS, HA_METADATA, HOSTNAME, and so on.

As you can see, this very powerful command enables you to do a lot of investigation and troubleshooting from an ESXi host. Again, exercise caution when using this command. Alternatively, use only under the guidance of VMware support staff if you have concerns.

vdq

The vdq command serves a few purposes and is really a great troubleshooting tool to have on the ESXi host. The first option to this command tells you whether disks on your ESXi host are eligible for vSAN, and if not, what the reason is for the disk being ineligible.

The second option to this command is that once vSAN has been enabled, you can use the command to display disk mapping information, which is essentially which devices are grouped together in a storage pool. The third option of this command which we want to highlight is that you can use it to verify the diskFormatVersion of the devices.

Let's first run the option to query all disks for eligibility for vSAN use. The next example is from a host that already has vSAN enabled:

```
[/:~] vdq -q
[
   {
       "Name"       : "eui.10a4ddfcaba2b4f4000c29693066aa9b",
       "VSANUUID" : "526c259d-ce6d-24ca-a3f4-614fe9825012",
       "State"      : "Ineligible for use by VSAN",
       "Reason"     : "Disk in use by storage pool",
"StoragePoolState": "In-use for Storage Pool",
"StoragePoolReason": "None",
       "IsSSD"      : "1",
"IsCapacityFlash": "N/A",
       "IsPDL"      : "0",
       "Size(MB)" : "524288",
    "FormatType" : "512e",
    "IsVsanDirectDisk" : "0"
    },
```

```
    {
        "Name"      : "eui.c2a24d01311f670e000c2961a56603aa",
        "VSANUUID" : "5226810c-d4fd-d380-5d2e-167e8e8d588e",
        "State"     : "Ineligible for use by VSAN",
        "Reason"    : "Disk in use by storage pool",
   "StoragePoolState": "In-use for Storage Pool",
   "StoragePoolReason": "None",
        "IsSSD"     : "1",
   "IsCapacityFlash": "N/A",
        "IsPDL"     : "0",
        "Size(MB)"  : "524288",
      "FormatType" : "512e",
     "IsVsanDirectDisk" : "0"
     },

    {
        "Name"      : "eui.b9939136f34e5126000c29628b9141da",
        "VSANUUID" : "52a399df-a404-4662-820e-72292fd0c2a4",
        "State"     : "Ineligible for use by VSAN",
        "Reason"    : "Disk in use by storage pool",
   "StoragePoolState": "In-use for Storage Pool",
   "StoragePoolReason": "None",
        "IsSSD"     : "1",
   "IsCapacityFlash": "N/A",
        "IsPDL"     : "0",
        "Size(MB)"  : "524288",
      "FormatType" : "512e",
     "IsVsanDirectDisk" : "0"
     },

    {
        "Name"      : "mpx.vmhba0:C0:T0:L0",
        "VSANUUID" : "",
        "State"     : "Ineligible for use by VSAN",
        "Reason"    : "Has partitions",
   "StoragePoolState": "Ineligible for use by Storage Pool",
   "StoragePoolReason": "Has partitions",
        "IsSSD"     : "0",
   "IsCapacityFlash": "0",
        "IsPDL"     : "0",
        "Size(MB)"  : "32768",
      "FormatType" : "512n",
     "IsVsanDirectDisk" : "0"
     },

    {
        "Name"      : "eui.9500d68cb453e39a000c2966beada3f8",
        "VSANUUID" : "526f8b7c-ffe9-ede3-c611-dbb854eb2d2c",
        "State"     : "Ineligible for use by VSAN",
        "Reason"    : "Disk in use by storage pool",
   "StoragePoolState": "In-use for Storage Pool",
   "StoragePoolReason": "None",
        "IsSSD"     : "1",
   "IsCapacityFlash": "N/A",
```

```
    "IsPDL"     : "0",
    "Size(MB)" : "524288",
 "FormatType" : "512e",
"IsVsanDirectDisk" : "0"
  }

]
```

The second useful option to the command is to dump out the vSAN disk mappings; in other words, which flash devices and/or which magnetic disks are in a disk group. The next example shows a sample output:

```
[/:~] vdq -i
[
  {
    "singleTier" : [
                    "eui.10a4ddfcaba2b4f4000c29693066aa9b",
                    "eui.c2a24d01311f670e000c2961a56603aa",
                    "eui.b9939136f34e5126000c29628b9141da",
                    "eui.9500d68cb453e39a000c2966beada3f8"
                    ]
  },
]
```

Lastly, you can also display information about each individual device from a metadata perspective. One useful aspect here is that you can verify the on-disk format version of each individual device.

```
[/:~] vdq -sH -d <device id>_  vdq -sH -d naa.55cd2e4150afff35
StoragePool_Metadata:
               checksum:   0x8a44b05a8cfbc1a6
                version:   0xb
            diskState:3:   0
            encrypted:1:   0
        diskFormatVersion: 18
               diskUUID:   522ec9c4-b835-18fc-fe34-4ecc9f197b40
        perfPartitionUUID: 522ec9c4-b835-18fc-fe34-4ecc9f197b41
               hostUUID:   642473a3-40eb-89a2-e187-e4434b7adb34
            clusterUUID:   52e38929-a315-07c2-eb78-3244bbcf4ae8
                dekUuid:   00000000-0000-0000-0000-000000000000
             diskType:3:   0
           creationTime:   1680736968
         dmekEnabled:1:    0
```

Although some of the commands shown in this section may prove useful to examine and monitor vSAN on an ESXi host basis, administrators ideally need something whereby they can examine the whole cluster. VMware recognized this very early on in the development of vSAN, and so introduced extensions to the rvc to allow a cluster-wide view of vSAN. The next topic delves into rvc.

Ruby vSphere Console (rvc) Commands

The previous section looked at ESXi host-centric commands for vSAN. These might be of some use when troubleshooting vSAN, but with large clusters, administrators may find themselves having to run the same set of commands repeatedly on the different hosts in the cluster. In this next section, we cover a tool that enables you to take a cluster-centric view of vSAN called the Ruby vSphere Console (rvc). It is also included in the VMware vCenter Server Appliance (VCSA). As mentioned in the introduction, rvc is a programmable interface that allows administrators to query the status of vCenter Server, clusters, hosts, storage, and networking. For vSAN, there are quite a number of programmable extensions to display a considerable amount of information that you need to know about a vSAN cluster. This section covers those vSAN extensions in rvc.

It provides a significant set of very useful commands that enable the monitoring, management, and troubleshooting of vSAN from the CLI.

You can connect rvc to any vCenter Server. On the vCenter Server, you log in via Secure Shell (SSH) and run `rvc <user>@<vc-ip>`. In our lab we leverage root to login to SSH and then use administrator@vsphere.local to login to rvc. This looks as follows:

```
root@localhost [ ~ ]# rvc administrator@vsphere.local@localhost
[DEPRECATION] This gem has been renamed to optimist and will no longer be supported.
Please switch to optimist as soon as possible.
Install the "ffi" gem for better tab completion.
password:
0 /
1 localhost/
>
```

After you log in, you will see a virtual file system, with the vCenter Server instance at the root. You can now begin to use navigation commands such as **cd** and **ls**, as well as tab-completion to navigate the file system. The structure of the file system mimics the inventory items tree views that you find in the vSphere client. Therefore, you can run `cd <vCenter Server>`, followed by `cd <datacenter>`. You can use ~ to refer to your current datacenter, and all clusters are in the "`computers`" folder under your datacenter. Note that when you navigate to a `folder/directory`, the contents are listed with numeric values. These numeric values may also be used as shortcuts. For example, in the vCenter Server shown in the output below there is only one datacenter, and it has a numeric value of 0 associated with it. We can then `cd` to 0, instead of typing out the full name of the datacenter. It also provides tab completion of commands.

```
> ls
0 /
1 localhost/
> cd 1

/localhost> ls
0 vSAN-ESA-DC (datacenter)

/localhost> cd 0

/localhost/ vSAN-ESA-DC> ls
0 storage/
1 computers [host]/
2 networks [network]/
3 datastores [datastore]/
```

```
4 vms [vm]/

/localhost/ vSAN-ESA-DC> cd 1

/localhost/ vSAN-ESA-DC /computers> ls
0 Cluster (cluster): cpu 65 GHz, memory 965 GB
1 witness.deepdivebook.com (standalone): cpu 5 GHz, memory 101 GB

/localhost/ vSAN-ESA-DC /computers> cd 0
/localhost/ vSAN-ESA-DC /computers/Cluster>
```

The full list of commands, at the time of writing, is shown here. However, this list of commands, as well as their functionality, is subject to change in future releases. You can use the <tab> key to do command completion in rvc, as shown below.

The names of the commands describe pretty well what the command is used for. However, a few examples from some of the more popular commands are shown later for your information.

```
/localhost/vSAN-ESA-DC/computers/Cluster> vsan.<tab-key>
vsan.apply_license_to_cluster
vsan.disable_vsan_on_cluster
vsan.host_exit_evacuation
vsan.observer_process_statsfile
vsan.support_information
vsan.bmc_info_get
vsan.disk_object_info
vsan.host_info
vsan.ondisk_upgrade
vsan.unmap_support
vsan.bmc_info_set
vsan.disks_info
vsan.host_wipe_non_vsan_disk
vsan.perf.
vsan.upgrade_status
vsan.check_limits
vsan.disks_stats
vsan.host_wipe_vsan_disks
vsan.proactive_rebalance
vsan.v2_ondisk_upgrade
vsan.check_state
vsan.enable_vsan_on_cluster
vsan.iscsi_target.
vsan.proactive_rebalance_info
vsan.vm_object_info
vsan.clear_disks_cache
vsan.enter_maintenance_mode
vsan.lldpnetmap
vsan.purge_inaccessible_vswp_objects
vsan.vm_perf_stats
vsan.cluster_change_autoclaim
vsan.fix_renamed_vms
vsan.login_iso_depot
vsan.reapply_vsan_vmknic_config
vsan.vmdk_stats
vsan.cluster_info
vsan.health.
vsan.obj_status_report
vsan.recover_spbm
vsan.whatif_host_failures
vsan.cluster_set_default_policy
```

```
vsan.host_claim_disks_differently
vsan.object_info
vsan.resync_dashboard
vsan.cmmds_find
vsan.host_consume_disks
vsan.object_reconfigure
vsan.scrubber_info
vsan.debug.
vsan.host_evacuate_data
vsan.observer
vsan.stretchedcluster.
```

To make this output easier to display, for certain commands we have separated out each of the columns and displayed them individually.

Deleting the Performance Statistics Database

When configuring our stretched cluster configuration, one of the issues we encountered was the fact that the new optimal vSAN storage policy wasn't properly applied to the vSAN Performance Statistics Database. Now, unfortunately, it is impossible to disable and enable the performance service from the UI to solve this problem. However, it is possible to simply use rvc to delete the database and recreate it. We used the following two command to achieve this, and to solve the issues we encountered with our performance statistics database.

```
vsan.perf.stats_object_delete /localhost/vSAN-ESA-DC/computers/Cluster
vsan.perf.stats_object_create /localhost/vSAN-ESA-DC/computers/Cluster
```

The output of vsan.check_limits

This command takes a cluster as an argument. It displays the limits on the cluster, on a per host as-is. These limits include network limits as well as disk limits, not just from a capacity perspective but also from a component perspective.

```
> vsan.check_limits /vcsa-06/CH-Datacenter/computers/CH-Cluster
+-------------------------+---------------+----------------------+
| Host                    | RDT           | Disks                |
+-------------------------+---------------+----------------------+
| esxi01.deepdivebook.com | Assocs: 58/   | Components: 0/27000  |
|                         | Sockets: 51/  |                      |
|                         | Clients: 1    |                      |
|                         | Owners: 2     |                      |
| esxi02.deepdivebook.com | Assocs: 79/   | Components: 0/27000  |
|                         | Sockets: 56/  |                      |
|                         | Clients: 7    |                      |
|                         | Owners: 6     |                      |
| esxi03.deepdivebook.com | Assocs: 50/   | Components: 0/27000  |
|                         | Sockets: 43/  |                      |
|                         | Clients: 4    |                      |
|                         | Owners: 3     |                      |
| esxi04.deepdivebook.com | Assocs: 20/   | Components: 0/27000  |
|                         | Sockets: 23/  |                      |
|                         | Clients: 1    |                      |
|                         | Owners: 0     |                      |
| esxi05.deepdivebook.com | Assocs: 30/   | Components: 0/27000  |
|                         | Sockets: 28/  |                      |
|                         | Clients: 2    |                      |
|                         | Owners: 1     |                      |
| esxi06.deepdivebook.com | Assocs: 51/   | Components: 0/27000  |
|                         | Sockets: 42/  |                      |
|                         | Clients: 4    |                      |
|                         | Owners: 3     |                      |
| esxi07.deepdivebook.com | Assocs: 24/   | Components: 0/27000  |
|                         | Sockets: 25/  |                      |
|                         | Clients: 1    |                      |
|                         | Owners: 1     |                      |
| esxi08.deepdivebook.com | Assocs: 36/   | Components: 0/27000  |
|                         | Sockets: 37/  |                      |
|                         | Clients: 1    |                      |
|                         | Owners: 1     |                      |
| esxi09.deepdivebook.com | Assocs: 16/   | Components: 0/27000  |
|                         | Sockets: 19/  |                      |
|                         | Clients: 1    |                      |
|                         | Owners: 0     |                      |
| esxi11.deepdivebook.com | Assocs: 2/    | Components: 0/27000  |
|                         | Sockets: 5/   |                      |
|                         | Clients: 1    |                      |
|                         | Owners: 0     |                      |
| esxi12.deepdivebook.com | Assocs: 2/    | Components: 0/27000  |
|                         | Sockets: 5/   |                      |
|                         | Clients: 1    |                      |
|                         | Owners: 0     |                      |
| esxi10.deepdivebook.com | Assocs: 18/   | Components: 0/27000  |
|                         | Sockets: 21/  |                      |
|                         | Clients: 1    |                      |
|                         | Owners: 0     |                      |
+-------------------------+---------------+----------------------+
```

The output of vsan.host_info

This command can be used to display specific host information. It provides information about what the role of the host is (master, backup, agent), what its UUID is, and what the other member UUIDs are (so you can see how many hosts are in the cluster) and of course information about networking and storage. It displays the adapter and IP address that the host is using to join the vSAN network, and which devices have been claimed for both the cache tier and capacity tier.

```
> vsan.host_info /localhost/vSAN-ESA-DC/computers/Cluster/hosts/esxi01.deepdivebook.com
Product: VMware ESXi 8.0.1 build-21260349
vSAN enabled: yes
Cluster info:
  Cluster role: agent
  Cluster UUID: 525f3ea1-2e9e-3925-0426-b493ec933d2b
  Node UUID: 63eb4c7e-0e72-1cb4-63ed-005056b62a0b
  Member UUIDs: ["63eb4c85-4032-de05-d6e3-005056b61931", "63eb4c7b-6253-a587-92d2-
005056b6e2f7", "63eb4c80-46b6-1bda-ad52-005056b6ffaa", "63eb4c8a-3d92-de8e-6deb-
005056b6d069", "63eb4c7e-0e72-1cb4-63ed-005056b62a0b", "63eb4c7f-aa9b-e4ec-dff5-
005056b6dbe9", "63eb4c83-256a-52df-89db-005056b66aa6", "63eb4c78-2ad2-bd6b-346c-
005056b600ad", "63eb4c7e-051c-dfd9-34b3-005056b601a9", "63eb4c7f-5d4d-d6e8-372f-
005056b69337", "63eb4c7f-c921-d16e-ffac-005056b627c3", "63eb4c8c-40ec-d3a5-1466-
005056b6b98e"] (12)
Node evacuated: no
Storage info:
  Auto claim: no
  Disk Mappings:
    None
FaultDomainInfo:
  Not configured
NetworkInfo:
  Adapter: vmk2 (10.202.25.61)
Data efficiency enabled: no
Encryption enabled: no
```

Summary

As you can see, an extensive suite of tools is available for managing and monitoring a vSAN deployment. With this extensive suite of CLI tools, administrators can drill down into the lowest levels of vSAN behavior.

The End

You have made it to the end of the book. Hopefully, you now have a good idea of how vSAN works and what vSAN can provide for your workloads in a VMware-based infrastructure.

We have tried to simplify some of the concepts to make them easier to understand. However, we acknowledge that some concepts can still be difficult to grasp. We hope that after reading this book everyone is confident enough to design, install, configure, manage, monitor, and even troubleshoot vSAN based hyperconverged infrastructures.

If there are any questions, please do not hesitate to reach out to either of the authors via Twitter or LinkedIn. We will do our best to answer your questions. Another option we would like to recommend for vSAN related questions is the VMware VMTN Community Forum. It is monitored by dozens of vSAN experts, and answers to questions are typically provided within hours. (https://vmwa.re/vsanvmtn)

Thanks for reading,

Cormac, Duncan, and Pete

Printed in Great Britain
by Amazon